Motivation Research and Marketing Management

Motivation Research
and Marketing Management

JOSEPH W. NEWMAN

Assistant Professor of Business Administration

HARVARD UNIVERSITY
GRADUATE SCHOOL OF BUSINESS ADMINISTRATION
DIVISION OF RESEARCH
Boston · 1957

Library of Congress Card No. 57–14787

PRINTED AT

THE PLIMPTON PRESS

NORWOOD, MASSACHUSETTS, U.S.A.

Foreword

IN the autumn of 1954, when Professor Newman began his study of motivation research, this young but fast-growing field of research was a subject of violent controversy. Motivation researchers employing different concepts and research techniques were pitted against each other, motivation researchers were challenged by those employing the more traditional research methods of market research, and the value and practicality of the results of motivation research were being challenged by marketing executives.

Professor Newman believed strongly that motivation research had a real potential for significant contributions to marketing management and hoped that his study would shed light on such questions as: Exactly what is motivation research in terms of case examples of what is being done? What are the concepts and approaches of the different researchers? What techniques are commonly used for what kind of problems? To what marketing problems has this kind of research been applied? What, if anything, is being learned from motivation research studies? Are they adding something to marketing knowledge? What problems are encountered in the use of this research and how can they be met effectively? Have results of this research actually been translated into action? If not, why not? What is the future of this development? On the basis of what has been done, does this type of research appear to offer promise of assistance in still other marketing problems?

As the broad research program of the School has developed, one part of our effort has been to explore the employment of the concepts and analytical methods of the social and behavioral sciences to appropriate business problems. One such area of business problems is the study of consumer behavior, which underlies marketing strategy and product planning. Motivation research represents an attempt to apply systematically the accumulated knowledge of human behavior and the analytical concepts and research methods of such behavioral sciences as psychology, sociology, and social anthropology to the buying behavior of individuals and groups.

This study makes no attempt to contribute to the methodology or techniques of motivation research; it seeks instead to help marketing executives understand what it is, how it can be employed, and some of the problems involved in its use. The author presents examples of motivation research in the context of the situation in which it was used, and discusses the concepts and the thinking behind the research, the use to which the results were put, and the role which such research can play in marketing management.

During the course of this study Professor Newman participated with five other members of our Faculty in a seminar on consumer behavior conducted by Professor Samuel A. Stouffer, Visiting Research Professor at the School from Harvard's Department of Social Relations. The seminar explored systematically the concepts and research methods and techniques of the behavioral sciences which might be employed in the study of consumer behavior. The seminar, as well as this study, was to provide a foundation for continuing research by our Faculty in the study of consumer behavior and the techniques of marketing research.

We are indebted to the Ford Foundation for the financial support and encouragement for this and other research in this area.

Bertrand Fox
Director of Research

Soldiers Field
Boston, Massachusetts
September 1957

Preface

SEVERAL ideas are of basic importance in this book. One is the conviction that products and services, and the activities attendant to their innovation and distribution, have one paramount purpose — the satisfaction of the wants of the people who buy and use them. The acceptance of this premise, however, leaves us with a disturbing situation. It is that our knowledge of what these wants are and how they are, or can be, met is woefully inadequate. This perplexing state of affairs has plagued both the practice and the teaching of marketing. Mounting dissatisfaction with it gave rise to the project on which the book is based.

A second core idea is that progress consists of evolving better conceptual schemes, i.e., more meaningful ways of looking at our world. Important voids in the understanding of buying behavior, then, can be expected to reflect the fact that we have been wearing conceptual blinders. This book is very much concerned, therefore, with ways of thinking about the people and the things with which marketing deals.

Another central idea is the recognition that buying and consumption are, after all, human acts serving human purposes. To understand their meaning, it makes good sense to start with people and their wants. While this approach is not completely strange to marketing, it nevertheless has been sadly neglected. Both economists and marketers have occupied themselves largely with abstractions such as prices, sales, shares of the market, and the like. While these data are of obvious importance, they are at the other end of the line from the human wants which give rise to them.

In view of what has just been said, it would appear advisable for marketing to get better acquainted with the behavioral disciplines which are devoted to learning more about what man is and how he lives. In this connection, the motivation research development, which came into the spotlight in the 1950's, provides a useful focal point for study because it represents the newer uses of behavioral science concepts and methods in marketing.

This book is based on a study of specific business applications of motivation research. It would not have been possible without the generous cooperation of a rather large number of people engaged in the conduct of research and the use of research findings. I spent many days with selected groups in the course of my field work and am grateful for the friendly receptions given me. The patient assistance of these people made it possible for me to become reasonably well acquainted with their ways of thinking and operating and to learn much about the behavioral sciences. I had access to a large number of private studies from which the case examples which appear in this book were selected.

In the course of my work, I also benefited greatly from the counsel of members of the Harvard Business School Faculty. In particular, I am indebted to Professor Bertrand Fox, Director of Research, and Professor Malcolm P. McNair for their support and guidance. I also wish to acknowledge Professors Neil H. Borden, Paul W. Cherington, Paul R. Lawrence, Martin V. Marshall, Charles D. Orth, III, Fritz J. Roethlisberger, and Abraham Zaleznik for the encouragement and assistance I received from them at various points along the way. While my writing was in process, I participated in a faculty seminar concerned with research on consumer behavior — an experience which helped me develop my thinking about research methodology. Consequently, I am indebted to the other members of the group: Professor Samuel A. Stouffer, Director of the Laboratory of Social Relations at Harvard University, who spent the year with us at the Business School; Professors Cherington, John E. Jeuck,

Robert O. Schlaifer, and Lawrence E. Thompson; and Mr. Arthur Schleifer, Jr.

I wish to express my appreciation to Deans Donald K. David and Stanley F. Teele for making time available for me to undertake my study. I have benefited greatly from the expert editorial guidance of Miss Ruth Norton, and from the competent handling of many details as well as the typing of the manuscript by Miss Winifred Barnard.

While many people have contributed to the making of this book, the responsibility for what is said in it, of course, is mine.

J. W. N.

Soldiers Field
Boston, Massachusetts
September 1957

Contents

PART II. MOTIVATION RESEARCH: SELECTED CASE
EXAMPLES

PART III. WHAT MOTIVATION RESEARCH MEANS FOR MARKETING MANAGEMENT

PART I

Concepts of Buying Behavior and Their Development

CHAPTER I

Introduction

THIS BOOK, written primarily for the business executive, has two broad purposes. The first is to provide an improved basis for thinking about the nature and significance of motivation research. The second is to contribute to an understanding of management problems related to its use in marketing.

Motivation research, however, is not an "it" in the sense of being any one research approach or technique. Essentially, the term has come into popular usage to stand for a number of recent and expanding efforts to make greater use of the behavioral sciences. Viewed in this light, as a development rather than a thing, motivation research is a matter of great potential import because the main contribution the behavioral sciences can make to marketing is ways of thinking and learning about people and their wants.

The satisfaction of human wants, of course, is the basic reason-for-being of economic activity in general, and it is a matter of special interest to marketing which provides the vital link between the producer and the consumer. It is the marketing executive, for example, who typically is charged with all, or at least part, of such responsibilities as these:

Determining what products should be offered.
Determining what the characteristics of these products should be.
Determining how the products should be made available to people.
Determining what prices should be charged.

Determining how to communicate effectively with people about products and services offered.

Maintaining satisfactory relationships with customers.

Marketing's ability to do its job, then, depends heavily upon the amount and particularly the quality of its information about people as buyers and consumers. The success of the individual firm in a competitive economy depends, in turn, upon how well its personnel can use these data in creating products and marketing programs and in predicting consumer response to alternative offerings which might be placed on the market.

It certainly is not news that knowledge of wants is basic to marketing. Declarations to this effect have been repeated many times by practitioners, teachers, and observers. Yet, when it comes to identifying buyer wants in a given situation, or saying how this might be done, the voices lose their vigor. While notable progress has been made in supplying better products, it still is true that the unknowns in the area of why consumers behave as they do are of major proportions. In other words, marketing has many unanswered questions relative to its basic mission: what the wants are which can be satisfied through goods and services, the meanings of different products and brands, and how people select among them.

It is this situation which makes the appearance of new thinking and research approaches especially newsworthy. A few such efforts led by people trained in the social sciences began to attract attention soon after World War II. Growing in number and extent, although still relatively small scale, they had captured widespread interest by the 1950's. Together they represent what is now known as motivation research (also consumer motivation research and social science research in marketing).

ORGANIZATION OF THE BOOK

This book, based on intensive field visits with both researchers and their clients, is presented in three parts. In the first, an attempt is made to provide background useful for viewing the research development in perspective. Marketing's thinking about the consumer is examined, with special attention being given to the influences which have shaped the commonly used assumptions about the nature of buying behavior. The role played by marketing research, which represents an attempt to bring a scientific approach to the field, is reviewed in order to note its contributions and to identify the barriers which have stood in the way of further progress. The need for new ways of thinking is cited before a brief description is given of the motivation research development and a number of the concepts which have been associated with it.

In order that the discussion might be made as meaningful as possible, specific illustrations of marketing applications of behavioral concepts and research techniques appear in Part II. They take the form of six illustrative cases. In each one, detailed attention is given to the business considerations which led to the research, the thinking and methodology involved in the investigation, the findings, and, in some cases, the business action taken on the basis of the results. The examples were selected primarily for the ways of thinking and researching which they represent. All draw from one or more of the behavioral fields, particularly dynamic psychology, social and cultural anthropology, and sociology. The studies themselves are on the meanings to people of automobile insurance, coffee, automobiles, home sewing, dieting, and the route selling of grocery products.

Part III draws upon the background furnished by the case examples. Attention is given to the problems as well as the opportunities related to the growing use of behavioral specialists in marketing research. The more commonly used techniques are reviewed to note their advantages and limitations for producing useful data. What the marketing executive might do toward obtaining appropriate research of good quality and judging the findings to determine whether they should be accepted as a basis for action is discussed. Factors which seem to make for effective use of social scientists in marketing research are enumerated after the common administrative problems are described. The trends represented in the motivation research development are summarized in the concluding chapter which also looks to what the future may bring in terms of the character of marketing research groups, research activities, and education for marketing.

How Our Study Was Made

The field work upon which this book is based began with a two-month exploration in the summer of 1954. Our interest was in the newer uses of the social sciences in marketing. We attempted to find out what motivation research in this sense stood for in terms of specific examples, how much work was being done, who was doing it, and how we might best proceed in our investigation. We talked with 30 people in 20 companies, many of whom were regarded as leading research practitioners and observers.

From these interviews, lists were compiled of organizations reported to be engaged to any extent in this work and of client companies that had used their services. It soon became apparent that at least four commercial firms (two independent research groups and two advertising agencies) were regarded as leaders because of their early efforts and their substantial volumes of work. Several other names also were mentioned fairly frequently, but the total number, while it was to grow considerably in the next two years, was not large at this time. With one or two exceptions, manufacturing companies had done little work of this kind in their own research departments. Instead, the activity was centered in a few research firms and in advertising agencies.

Our field work continued on an intensive basis through 1955 with limited follow-up activity in 1956 and early 1957 when this book was being written. We contacted researchers to continue our check on who was doing what and to study selected examples in detail. We also learned much from them about administrative difficulties related to business attempts to make use of the services of social scientists. Detailed study of these problems was a major objective of our calls on client companies.

In our research approach, we relied heavily on qualitative interviews and detailed examinations of reports on motivational studies. The interviews frequently were very detailed, extending over several different sessions. We sat in as a silent observer on six research staff meetings at which investigations were being planned or field data were being discussed, and on 10 researcher-client meetings. We also attended 13 conferences of business and professional groups at which we listened to 80 speeches in the subject area of our interest. These programs and the informal contacts with others in attendance proved to be a valuable means of keeping in touch with what was going on and of observing changes in reactions to the concepts and methods characteristic of motivation research.

An important supplement to these activities was a program of outside reading in which we engaged for added background in the behavioral disciplines. Most of this was in the subject areas of psychology, psychoanalysis, anthropology, and sociology. All told it included some 40 books and a greater number of articles. Informal, after-hours discussions with people trained in these fields also were very helpful.

Our field work included calls on 20 marketing research and consulting firms (105 interviews with 55 people) ; 15 advertising agencies (75 interviews with 55 people) ; and 28 companies engaged in the selling of goods and services (94 interviews with 66 people) . We had at least some contact with 110 different researches and learned something of the nature of a good many more.

Thirty of the organizations had conducted at least one study which might be called motivation research, using their own personnel who in several instances were assisted by outside consultants. Among them were 15 research firms, 8 advertising agencies, 4 manufacturers, 1 radio network, and 1 newspaper. The figure is somewhat deceiving, however, because of the marked variation in the character of both the research staffs and their work. In 1955, no more than half a dozen of the firms appeared to be doing the great bulk of the commercial research which made any substantial use of dynamic concepts of behavior or of qualitative methods. In the 30 companies to which we have referred, the staffs ranged from those made up entirely of marketing researchers with little or no social science background to those consisting of a group of specialists who represented several behavioral disciplines. The research itself varied from largely conventional direct question surveys to multi-phased studies which emphasized qualitative methods and used several techniques in combination. In between were studies based primarily on the use of one technique such as qualitative interviewing by a psychologist or the use of one or more projective devices.

In terms of the major objectives of learning of the nature of the motivation research development and assessing its significance, by far the most important feature of our field work consisted of very intensive visits with several firms selected to represent the various research approaches. These visits ranged in length from several days to several weeks. During this time, we attempted to learn something about what specialized knowledge and training in the behavioral fields was, how it was used, and what it meant in terms of researching marketing problems. We became as well acquainted as possible with the researchers' ways of thinking and methods and the assumptions on which they were based. With eight organizations, we followed at least one and sometimes several individual studies through in detail, retracing the thinking and the steps which led from the research proposal to the presentation of the findings.

Intensive interviewing also was important in our study of user reactions to motivation research and the problems encountered in its use. Our usual procedure was to follow up on specific studies. We first would go over the report in detail, then conduct relatively nondirective interviews with the principal people concerned with it. In this way, we learned how much attention different persons had paid to the research, how they felt about it and often why, and what, if any, action had been taken. Multiple interviews in the same company were rewarding because they often revealed different interpretations and attitudes and, occasionally, internal conflicts relevant to the problem of getting research used.

We conducted as many as 10 to 15 interviews in each of five companies, including three advertising agencies which had a great deal of experience with motivational studies. In these organizations, reactions were obtained from account executives, creative personnel, and researchers. We had at least six interviews in seven other firms and at least two interviews in 15 more.

COMPANIES CONTACTED

In order to obtain information on what was going on in marketing research or to study examples of motivation research and its use, or both, we talked with people in the following organizations:

Advertising Agencies

Leo Burnett Company, Inc.
D'Arcy Advertising Company
Dancer-Fitzgerald-Sample
William Esty Company
Gardner Advertising Company
Grey Advertising Agency, Inc.

Henri, Hurst and McDonald, Inc.
McCann-Erickson, Inc.
Needham, Louis and Brorby, Inc.
Russell M. Seeds Company

Tatham-Laird, Inc.
J. Walter Thompson Company
Weiss and Geller, Inc.

Wherry, Baker and Tilden, Inc.
Young and Rubicam, Inc.

Research Organizations and Consultants

Advertising Research Foundation, Inc.
Alderson and Sessions
A. S. Bennett-Cy Chaikin, Inc.
Bureau of Applied Social Research, Columbia University
Institute for Motivational Research, Inc.
Institute for Social Research, University of Michigan
John Kishler
Harbridge House, Inc.
Market Facts, Incorporated

Market Research Corporation of America
McMurry, Hamstra and Company
National Analysts, Inc.
Nejelski and Company, Inc.
Alfred Politz Research, Inc.
The Psychological Corporation
Elmo Roper and Associates
George Horsley Smith
Social Research, Inc.
James M. Vicary Company
A. J. Wood and Company

Other Companies

Bureau of Advertising, Inc.
Cereal Institute, Inc.
Chicago Tribune
Colgate-Palmolive Company
CBS Radio
Consolidated Cigar Corporation
Donahue Sales Corporation
Ford Motor Company — Ford Division
Ford Motor Company — Mercury Division
General Electric Company
General Foods Corporation
General Mills, Inc.
Goodyear Tire and Rubber Company
Jewel Tea Co., Inc.

Lever Brothers Company
Oscar Mayer and Co.
The Maytag Co.
Miles Laboratories, Inc.
Pan-American Coffee Bureau
The Pharma-Craft Corporation
Pharmaceutical Advertising Club
The Parker Pen Company
Pillsbury Mills, Inc.
Scott Paper Company
Standard Oil Company (N.J.)
State Farm Mutual Automobile Insurance Company
Swift and Company
Tea Council of the U.S.A., Inc.
The Toni Company

Looking Ahead in Part I

With our introductory statement now completed, we shall turn our attention in the next chapter to how marketing typically has thought about buyer wants and behavior. In Chapter III we shall consider what might be done to make for greater progress on this front before describing in Chapter IV some of the behavioral science concepts which now are being introduced into marketing research.

CHAPTER II

Marketing's Thinking About Buying and Consumption

WHY IS IT that marketing often has been unable to explain satisfactorily why people buy what they do? — why they have marked brand preferences even when product offerings appear to be about the same?; why they frequently resist product innovations and improvements?; why they have gone in so heavily for such things as the do-it-yourself movement and longer and more powerful automobiles?

For a better understanding of the shortcomings in existing knowledge and what might be done about them, let us take a look at how marketing typically has thought about buying behavior. What has the marketing executive had to go on in making the judgments about human wants and probable consumer response which underlie so many of his important decisions?

MEASURES OF CONSUMER RESPONSE

A primary source of information, of course, is sales results. If a product or promotional offering actually has been tried out in the open market or in a well-executed market test, the executive may be in a favorable position to predict future response. In the absence of direct data, he may turn to other evidence such as sales figures for what appear to be similar offers made in comparable circumstances or statements of consumer reaction and intention to buy, perhaps solicited in connection with product tests.

Measures of response, however, are not themselves explanations of why the response occurred. When marked innovations are involved, the main reasons for a striking result may be fairly easy to identify. In some situations, such as exist in the mail order business, there may be an unusual opportunity to keep records on offers and response and to experiment. This, of course, provides an improved basis for thinking about the reasons for what happened.

Typically, however, inferences are much more difficult to make. The sales result is an over-all measure of response to the entire product offer and sales promotional program achieved over a period of time and under certain conditions. The number of influential variables is large, and it is no easy matter to discern cause and effect even under the best of circumstances. The drawing of incorrect conclusions from sales is commonplace. This is due not only to the difficulties already cited, but also to the tendency of businessmen to weave rational explanations for what they observe, even when such are inappropriate.

These are serious limitations. While it is essential to know what happened, it also is important to know why because the opportunity for constructive thinking is directly related to the extent to which there is understanding.

In attempting to interpret measures of consumer response, the marketing executive must reason the best he can just as he must in making judgments and predictions in the absence of such evidence. In doing this, he draws upon his background of impressions gained from both training and experience over the years. Whether he fully recognizes it or not, they have given him individual operating assumptions as to what people are like and what they will accept in the market place. Let us examine some of the main influences, other than sales results, which may have shaped his way of thinking.

ECONOMIC THEORY

Economists' concepts have had a marked impact on business thinking about the nature of buying behavior. Perhaps the most important has been that of the "economic man" which represents both what many economists have said, at least in part, and what many business people think economists have said. Stated in the extreme, the picture which has emerged is something like this: a consumer is a rational purchasing agent for himself and his family who carefully weighs the utility or want-satisfying properties of all available products, then allocates his limited income among them to get the greatest possible satisfactions for his (or his family's) wants.

The great emphasis placed on economy and rationality is due in part to the fact that this concept represented a direct application in the consumer area of the thinking used by economists to explain the behavior of the business firm. The firm theoretically used its resources to produce goods in order to maximize profits, and the consumer was seen as a small business firm, using his resources (income) to buy goods in order to maximize want satisfaction.

In addition to the over-all idea that people are essentially rational in their buying, several other assumptions are involved in the "economic man" concept: that the consumer knows what his wants are and maintains something like an inventory of them in his mind to guide his purchasing; that he knows of all available products and services which might meet his needs; and that he can discern the want-satisfying content of each product or service, at least in relative terms, so that he can decide which items to buy in order to get the most satisfaction for his money.

The above assumptions may make the consumer sound much more like a computing machine than a human being engaged in everyday living. Nevertheless, this picture reflects both the great emphasis our culture has placed on rationality and the fact that economists generally have not regarded it as their function to investigate the nature of man's wants. Instead, they have been concerned with explaining how man went (or should go) about spending his limited income in order to maximize satisfaction of his wants, whatever their character. Essentially, they have said: given a person's wants and given a number of products with known capacities for satisfying these wants, we can tell you how that person should go about deciding on his purchases if he is to achieve maximum want satisfaction. What is missing here is the very information which would be of most help to the marketing man who must decide what products should be in the first place and how to talk effectively about them to prospective customers: what are these wants and what are the satisfactions a given product provides?

While the "economic man" is an exaggerated and incomplete picture of the consumer, the ideas it represents can be useful if handled with caution. Most people do have incomes too limited to satisfy all of their wants and many appear to exercise at least some care in their spending. On the other hand, the concept can be misleading as businessmen often know from their own observations.

Traditional economic assumptions are being challenged more and more by results of research. A number of interesting findings of this kind have come from the University of Michigan's Survey Research Center which is engaged in studying economic behavior in terms of psychological as well as other variables. A study of purchase decisions for durable goods (TV sets, refrigerators, washing machines, and stoves), for example, provided evidence that people are not always careful buyers, that some are downright careless, and that there are wide differences in buying which cannot be explained in conventional economic terms.[1]

The same study indicated that people with the lower incomes and presumably the greatest economic need for information to guide them in their purchases are the least likely

---

[1] George Katona and Eva Mueller, "A Study of Purchase Decisions," *Consumer Behavior* (New York: New York University Press, 1954), p. 53.

to look for it. Sam Barton, President of the Market Research Corporation of America which conducts a national consumer panel, reports a number of instances of lower income families buying the higher, rather than the lower priced brands within categories where products would appear to be roughly similar in physical properties.

A number of experiences have served to question the reliability of the common economic assumption of the negatively sloped demand curve which states that more units of a product can be sold at a lower rather than a higher price. One company in the writing instrument field, for example, found in market tests that it could sell about as many units of a new product at $2.95 as at $1.95.

While economic thought has served to emphasize rationality and material wants, a number of economists have been careful not to impose this limitation. Kenneth Boulding has been among those who have stressed that things do not have an intrinsic worth. He has reminded us that:

> . . . "worth" . . . is not a physical property of an object like weight or volume, but is simply "how we feel about it." Things are "valuable" because somebody thinks they are and for no other reason whatever.[2]

The apparent inadequacies of the "economic man" concept of the consumer point to the need for learning more about how people make buying decisions and why they select one product or brand rather than another. Boulding's words suggest that this be approached by finding out how people feel about shopping and the things they buy.

LISTS OF BUYING MOTIVES

Emotional aspects of buying have received considerably more attention in the various lists of buying motives which

[2] Kenneth E. Boulding, *Economic Analysis* (New York: Harper & Brothers Publishers, Revised Edition, 1948), p. 24.

have appeared in marketing literature.[3] Some represent the work of psychologists while others have been compiled by marketers themselves.

Copeland's Early Work

One of the earliest of these was by Melvin T. Copeland. It appeared in 1924 in his *Principles of Merchandising*,[4] a pioneering work which has had a marked influence on marketing writings since that time. The book was notable in several respects. It emphasized that knowledge of buying motives and habits was the necessary starting point for thinking and planning in marketing. It enumerated buying motives for both consumer and industrial goods, and distinguished among "convenience," "shopping," and "specialty" goods on the basis of consumer buying habits.

The basic classification used by Copeland in presenting his list of 33 consumer buying motives was "emotional" and "rational." He saw emotional motives as those which "have their origin in human instincts and emotions and represent impulsive or unreasoning promptings to action," and rational motives as "those which are aroused by appeals to reason. . . . When influenced by a rational motive, a consumer carefully weighs the advantages and disadvantages of the purchase before acting." [5] He stated that a majority of buyers' motives for consumers' goods were "instinctive and emotional." [6]

Copeland's list of consumers' buying motives follows: [7]

[3] A summary of nine such lists appears in Malcolm P. McNair and Harry L. Hansen, *Readings in Marketing* (New York: McGraw-Hill Book Company, Inc., 1949) , pp. 58–61.

[4] Melvin T. Copeland, *Principles of Merchandising* (Chicago and New York: A. W. Shaw Company, 1924) .

[5] Ibid., p. 162.

[6] Ibid., p. 207.

[7] Ibid., p. 160.

Emotional Buying Motives

1. Distinctiveness
2. Emulation
3. Economical emulation
4. Pride of personal appearance
5. Pride in appearance of property
6. Social achievement
7. Proficiency
8. Expression of artistic taste
9. Happy selection of gifts
10. Ambition
11. Romantic instinct
12. Maintaining and preserving health
13. Cleanliness
14. Proper care of children
15. Satisfaction of the appetite
16. Pleasing the sense of taste
17. Securing personal comfort
18. Alleviation of laborious tasks
19. Security from danger
20. Pleasure of recreation
21. Entertainment
22. Obtaining opportunity for greater leisure
23. Securing home comfort

Rational Buying Motives

24. Handiness
25. Efficiency in operation or use
26. Dependability in use
27. Dependability in quality
28. Reliability of auxiliary service
29. Durability
30. Enhancement of earnings
31. Enhancing productivity of property
32. Economy in use
33. Economy in purchase

Copeland also differentiated between "primary" and "selective" motives. "A primary motive is one which imparts to consumers the major, initial impulse to purchase the kind of article offered for sale," he wrote, while a selective motive "is one in which the aim is to divert the consumer's expenditure away from other brands of the same article." [8] Another distinction made was that between a buying motive which "induces a customer to buy a particular commodity or type

_____
[8] Ibid.

of article," and a patronage motive "which induces a customer to trade with a particular firm." [9]

Copeland insisted that "analysis of buying motives be based on actual conditions, not upon *a priori* reasoning." [10] His approach was to examine 936 advertisements in then current general magazines, women's magazines, national weeklies, and farm papers. He decided to do this because the material was economically at hand. In addition, he believed that a field survey "would not have yielded equally dependable results, because a majority of the buying motives of consumers are not rational motives, and in many instances dependable answers could not have been secured from consumers." [11] He pointed out that his findings could not be regarded as final, but that they appeared to represent the collective experience of a large number of advertisers.

Copeland made a similar study of 756 advertisements in business journals, recognizing the possibility that there might be many buying motives which were appealed to in personal salesmanship, but which might not appear in advertising. He noted that all of his buying motives for industrial goods were "rational" which he considered logical "because an industrial firm makes its purchases for business reasons, not for the personal gratification of individual executives." [12] At the same time, however, he indicated that he was not completely at ease with this assumption by noting that "experience with the methods used by salesmen in the solicitation of orders for industrial goods has shown . . . that in personal interviews appeals frequently are made to the emotional motives of the buyers." [13]

Copeland's list of buying motives for industrial goods follows: [14]

[9] Ibid., p. 190.
[10] Ibid., p. 158.
[11] Ibid., p. 159.

[12] Ibid., p. 207.
[13] Ibid.
[14] Ibid. pp. 190–215.

(Product or Commodity) Buying Motives

1. Economy in use
2. Protection against loss
3. Enhancing productivity of plant
4. Dependability in use
5. Dependability in quality
6. Durability
7. Flexibility in operation or use
8. Simplicity in operation
9. Handiness
10. Facility of installation
11. Facility in making repairs
12. Enhancing salability of product
13. Facility in executive control
14. Aiding sales promotion
15. Safeguarding welfare and morale of employees
16. Sanitation of plant
17. Economy in purchase

Patronage Motives

1. Reliability of seller
2. Punctuality of delivery
3. Promptness in delivery
4. Securing exact fulfillment of specifications
5. Variety for selection
6. Engineering and designing service
7. Dependable repair service

Many years passed after the publication of Copeland's work in which little further progress was made toward understanding buying behavior. Until relatively recent times, marketing writers generally have failed both to share Copeland's interest in this area and to heed his warning against relying on *a priori* reasoning.

Hattwick's "Basic Wants"

An example of a more recent list of buying motives, which reflects a somewhat different approach, is that of Melvin S. Hattwick, a psychologist.[15] He listed "eight basic wants in life," which, he said, were common to all inventories of people's wants and desires which had been made by psycholo-

[15] Melvin S. Hattwick, *How to Use Psychology for Better Advertising* (New York: Prentice-Hall, Inc., 1950), pp. 18–21.

gists. They were represented as being those things which people desire most often and with the greatest intensity. Here they are:

1. Food and drink	6. To be superior
2. Comfort	7. Social approval
3. To attract the opposite sex	8. To live longer
4. Welfare of loved ones	
5. Freedom from fear and danger	

The basic wants were so named because they were believed to be based on "fundamental drives." It has been the opinion of some psychologists, which Hattwick shared, that people are born with the same fundamental drives or wants and satisfy them in about the same ways. According to this view, drives easily are aroused by appealing to the "basic wants," and once a drive is set in motion, the person wants to satisfy it almost immediately. Hattwick also identified the following nine "secondary wants" learned by people through experience: [16]

1. Bargains	6. Dependability, quality
2. Information	7. Style, beauty
3. Cleanliness	8. Economy, profit
4. Efficiency	9. Curiosity
5. Convenience	

Duncan's Study of Industrial Buying

Prevalent thinking about industrial buying is reflected in Delbert J. Duncan's study of the motivation of purchasing agents. He compiled a tentative list of motives on the basis of personal interviews in which executives were encouraged to talk freely of their purchasing experiences. The list later was submitted to members of the National Association of Purchasing Agents who were requested to indicate which

[16] *Ibid.,* pp. 23–25.

motives were the more important ones for heavy machinery, raw materials, and supplies.   The results follow: [17]

Heavy Machinery

Product Motives	Patronage Motives
1. Economy	1. Reliability of seller
2. Productivity	2. Cooperation
3. Dependability	3. Low prices
4. Time or labor saving	4. Quick repair service
5. Durability	5. Past services rendered; satisfactory relationships

Raw Materials

Product Motives	Patronage Motives
1. Right quality	1. Reliability of seller
2. Uniformity	2. Continuous supply under all conditions
3. Dependability	3. Accessibility of seller
4. Purity	4. Low prices
5. Ability to increase salability of user's product	5. Quick and reliable delivery of product

Supplies

Product Motives	Patronage Motives
1. Right quality	1. Reliability of seller
2. Dependability	2. Continuous supply under all conditions
3. Uniformity	3. Accessibility of seller
4. Economy	4. Low prices
5. Durability	5. Quick and reliable delivery of product

Duncan concluded that while both rational and emotional influences entered into the purchasing, the rational motives predominated and were, by and large, the governing factors.

[17] Delbert J. Duncan, "What Motivates Business Buyers," *Harvard Business Review,* Vol. XVIII, No. 4 (Summer 1940), pp. 448–454.

In commenting on his personal interviews, however, he observed that many purchases were made on a rational basis as a matter of habit or in accordance with past custom. He noted some cases where executives had difficulty in naming rational considerations which influenced their decisions.

Comments on the Lists of Motives

The lists of motives focus attention on the consideration of buyer wants and benefits and suggest factors which might be investigated in specific business situations.

At the same time, however, they have important limitations as bases for explaining and predicting behavior. One is their questionable accuracy and completeness as generalized statements of what people want when they buy. Copeland, for example, had to make the doubtful assumption in his study that advertisers knew from experience what appeals were most effective and that their ads reflected this knowledge. The marked tendency of people to rationalize is a major problem in studies like Duncan's which ask respondents directly for explanations of their actions. While Duncan took steps to minimize distortion, his final product still consisted of the traditional factors every good, rational purchasing agent should take into account, according to all conventional treatises on the subject. While these factors are of importance, they probably represent only a partial explanation. It is interesting to note that the purchasing agents did not report being greatly influenced by the fact that they liked a salesman or by a policy of reciprocity in buying.

The inadequacy of the list-of-motives approach has been noted by a few writers from time to time over the years. Arthur W. Kornhauser advocated its abandonment more than 30 years ago.[18] This viewpoint was largely ignored in

[18] Arthur W. Kornhauser, "The Motives-in-Industry Problem," *Annals of the American Academy of Political and Social Science*, September 1923, pp. 105–116.

marketing circles until relatively recent times when other writers and researchers began to reflect the more modern thinking on personality and motivation in which the motive concept has given way to other ideas. Sharing some of the opinions of Kornhauser, Douglas McGregor contributed another significant statement of the limitations of "motives" for marketing, writing in 1940.[19] Steuart Henderson Britt in 1950 wrote an article in a somewhat similar vein which has been widely quoted.[20] One of his main points was that there is no such thing as a universal set of explanatory motives.

McGregor pointed out, as had Kornhauser, that motives are terms of classification of observed behavior rather than forces which constitute explanations of behavior. By way of illustration, he wrote as follows:

> We arrive at the concept of motive by a process of observing, classifying, and naming abstracted similarities among different behaviors. For example, we observe that a variety of patterns of behavior tend to maintain and increase the individual's value in the eyes of his fellows. Then we name this class of behavioral patterns in terms of the abstracted common quality. We call it, perhaps "the desire for social approval," or "the desire for popularity." Then, when we are asked why people behave in these ways, we answer glibly: "because they have a motive to obtain social approval," or "because they have a desire for popularity." Obviously, the process of classifying a variety of observed phenomena under a common name does no explaining! . . . Yet this process of naming, and then attributing causal significance to names, has been the basis for practically all the theories of motivation which have been proposed until recently.[21]

[19] Douglas McGregor, " 'Motives' As a Tool of Market Research," *Harvard Business Review*, Vol. XIX, No. 1 (Autumn 1940), pp. 42–51.

[20] Steuart Henderson Britt, "The Strategy of Consumer Motivation," *Journal of Marketing*, April 1950, pp. 666–674.

[21] Douglas McGregor, op. cit., p. 44.

McGregor also pointed out that knowledge of a "motive" did not make prediction of behavior possible because a number of different forms of behavior were lumped together under each term or "motive" in the process of classification. More detailed knowledge of the individual concerned and the environment in which he behaves is necessary for explanations and predictions. As McGregor noted, this is why our most accurate predictions are made in connection with those persons we know best.

The thinking outlined above leads to a recommendation that consumer wants and reasons for buying be studied by investigating the factors in the total makeup of the individual and his environmental situation. McGregor expressed it by means of a formula: $R = f(S,I)$. He explained that "any given reaction (R) is a function of a complex pattern of relationships between factors making up the environmental situation (S) and the individual (I) as they exist at the moment of reaction." [22] An understanding of R must come from an analysis of both S and I. McGregor noted that the concept of motives was not needed in the point of view he expressed. Instead of explaining behavior in terms of motives as forces or drives which could be listed as entities, he saw reasons for action as consisting of "complex patterns of factors including such things as capacities, skills, habits, attitudes, knowledge, physiological state and personality traits." [23]

McGregor cited the need for developing research techniques which would get behind outwardly deceptive behavior or opinion. Britt emphasized the "tremendous importance of unconscious motivation" and advocated the use of the qualitative interview or the clinical approach to interviewing.[24]

At this point, we shall not go further into theories of

---

[22] Ibid., p. 45.
[23] Ibid.
[24] Steuart Henderson Britt, op. cit., p. 672.

motivation or methodology, except to say that the viewpoints expressed above gained much support in the past few years as we shall see later in this book.

The lists of motives are of interest to us here because they have been prominent on the marketing scene and therefore represent an influence on the way marketers have thought about buying behavior. The implied concept of the consumer is that of a person driven by a number of universal forces which can be enumerated. According to this view, understanding behavior is simply a matter of consulting "the" list of motives. This kind of thinking, which has been prevalent in marketing for some time, now is being increasingly recognized as an oversimplified theory of motivation. Whether or not such lists actually include the things strongly desired by most people, they provide no ready answers as to what satisfactions people get from the purchase and use of any given product or why they choose one brand over another. The lists cannot state what appeals would be most effective in a given situation.

ACADEMIC COURSES IN MARKETING

The nature of the influence academic courses in marketing have had on thinking about the consumer can be gauged by reviewing textbooks in current use. Comments first will be made on the general texts whose titles usually include the words "principles," "elements," and "methods." Later, attention will be directed to the case problems books which represent a different approach to the subject.

General Marketing Textbooks

These books have emphasized that knowledge of consumer wants is the starting point for planning and that marketers should learn everything possible about the buying motivation of those to whom they wish to sell. They have devoted very little space to buying motives and habits, however, — a revealing commentary on the lack of knowledge in this area. For example, one book of more than 900 pages had a consumer section of 25 pages, 5 of which dealt with buying motives. Another book of 800 pages devoted 65 of them to the consumer and 14 of these were on buyer wants and habits. The bulk of the consumers' sections was devoted to population statistics, living costs, buying power, and other factors which affect consumer expenditures.

The treatments of buying motives have represented no significant change from what Copeland had written nearly 30 years earlier. The same classifications (primary and selective; emotional and rational; product and patronage) and somewhat similar, though usually shorter, lists of motives have appeared and their value usually has been neither fully explained nor questioned.

The textbooks have been devoted principally to descriptions of marketing institutions, functions, industry and commodity groups, price economics, and the like. While their writers have noted the primary importance of consumer wants, they, like the economists, pretty much have left it there. In effect, they have said: you somehow supply the information about people's wants and offer products which will meet them and we will tell you about the marketing mechanism for moving the goods to the market place.

It is significant to note that it has been the advertising rather than the general marketing textbooks which have given the most attention to buying motivation and that this subject has received little systematic treatment as a source of product ideas. This situation reflects the prevalent attitude that new and different products and services somehow will be served up by ingenious producers and distributors and that the principal use of knowledge of consumer wants lies in developing sales appeals.

Case Problems Books

The purpose of the case books is not primarily that of providing information, but giving training in thinking, both
individually and in class discussions, which will develop a
capacity for management. The books present actual business
problems in merchandising, distribution channels, brand
policy, pricing, and the planning of sales programs for analysis by the student who must determine what action should be
taken in specific product and competitive situations. Consideration of the consumer is regarded as basic to this task.
"The consumer's needs, wants, desires, preferences, beliefs,
habits, foibles, and eccentricities constitute an important de-
terminant of the products which you offer, the channels
through which you sell them, the promotional efforts which
you will employ, and the price you will be able to obtain." [25]

In handling the material, the student must deal with such
questions as these, to mention only a few: Who will buy this
product? Why? How well does the product meet what the
market wants? What price will people pay? Should the
product be branded? How can people be induced to buy it?
The student, like the marketing executive, must think about
these matters the best he can, drawing upon his own background which will include influences such as those we are
examining in this chapter. This approach is reasonably
realistic and can provide very valuable training. At the same
time, however, it raises the question as to what extent it is
advisable to encourage reasoning about a subject as complex
as that of motivation, particularly in product areas with
which the student has little familiarity. There is a potential
danger of encouraging undue speculation which can lead to
bad habits of thought and "knowledge" that is not so. While
the student is thrown on his own resources, the latter repre-

---

[25] Malcolm P. McNair and Harry L. Hansen, *Problems in Marketing* (New
York: McGraw-Hill Book Company, Inc., 1949), p. 66.

sent both assets to be developed and barriers to the gaining of greater understanding of buying behavior.

In considering how far the marketing executive should go in his inquiry into buyer motivation, McNair and Hansen cautioned against both "the egocentric approach where the executive rationalizes consumer action in terms of his own motivations" and "a deep probing . . . which may involve a psychological analysis of the problem [which] may well offer real difficulties because of the present controversial state of these aspects of psychology." [26] They advocated a middle-ground approach "embracing both careful observation and intelligent appraisal of experience." This practical course has been useful in many marketing situations. It also has been necessary in view of the young state of development of marketing and its research. We should like, however, to regard it as a tentative conclusion pending advances which would make it possible to provide more guidance for the observation and appraisal of experience.

In the realm of research, the approach of studying in detail individual business situations has led to important contributions to thinking about behavior. A notable example is Neil H. Borden's study of how and why advertising affects demand,[27] the results of which played an important role in the planning of his advertising case problems book.[28] He emphasized that the potential effect of advertising on demand and the importance of brands as guides to consumer buying varied widely by products. He went a long way in explaining brand preferences by using the factors of objective product differentiation (on which he placed major emphasis), whether the product features were discernible or hidden to the buyer, and the presence of emotional buying motives

26 Ibid., pp. 67–68.

27 Neil H. Borden, *The Economic Effects of Advertising*, (Chicago, Illinois: Richard D. Irwin, Inc., 1944).

28 Neil H. Borden, *Advertising Text and Cases*, (Chicago, Illinois: Richard D. Irwin, Inc., 1950).

related to the main uses to which the product was to be put. "Where product differentiations are considered of no great consequence by consumers or are readily appraisable from inspection," he concluded, "brand means little." [29]

A notable change in the thinking about buying motives and habits characteristic of the marketing textbooks mentioned earlier is found in one of the most recent case problems books authored by Harry L. Hansen. After illustrating the difficulty involved in trying to distinguish between emotional and rational buying motives, he concluded that we have no clear understanding of the difference and that the terms might better be dropped. He went on to state:

> Instead, we would say that some purchases more than others are carefully weighed or considered. Whether this weighing is an intellectual or emotional process, if indeed a distinction is possible, seems beyond the point for the average marketer. . . . It seems in these questions of motives we might well beware of readily classifying them as emotional or rational — and especially beware when we have difficulty in defining or recognizing a decision as rational or emotional when we see one. . . . Frequently, what appears to be an emotional act to an observer may be a completely logical act to the doer.[30]

Hansen applied this viewpoint to industrial as well as consumer buying.

RESULTS OF INTROSPECTION

Economic theory, lists of buying motives, and academic offerings in marketing all have served to emphasize the importance of studying the consumer and to point to a number of general considerations. They have left the marketer largely on his own, however, in determining consumer wants

[29] Ibid., p. 151.
[30] Harry L. Hansen, *Marketing; Text, Cases, and Readings* (Homewood, Illinois, Richard D. Irwin, Inc., 1956), p. 30.

and predicting buying behavior in specific business situations. Among the bases widely used for more specific thinking has been the study of one's own wants and preferences. Self-examination unquestionably has been an important source of marketing ideas, but, of course, they have varied tremendously in quality. There are some sensitive, perceptive people who appear to be able to learn much of value by this means. Several top creative people in advertising have impressed us notably in this regard. Generally, however, the ability to successfully examine at length one's own behavior, thoughts, and feelings is rare indeed. There are a number of reasons for this. We cannot see what our own backgrounds of experience and training do not permit us to see, and we vary in our ability to infer meanings. Most of us were brought up in a culture which places high value on logic, reason, economy, and control over feelings — influences which constitute barriers to the development of self-awareness. To the extent we have been so indoctrinated, we are likely to think and see in these terms and to deny or overlook the presence of the more nonrational factors. All of us have our preconceptions which we often defend rather strongly without fully realizing it.

Even if one is able to observe and interpret his own behavior accurately, there is the danger of overgeneralizing and applying the results to a population of which the observer is not typical.

Business executives are likely to be both product-oriented and biased in trying to think about probable consumer reactions to their own merchandise. In this connection, Copeland warned against "sales egotism . . . the most prevalent malady that afflicts numerous sales and advertising departments." [31] He was referring to the marked tendency to overestimate salability.

In summary, the concept of the consumer which is implied

[31] Melvin T. Copeland, op. cit., p. 157.

in the use of self-examination is that "the consumer is like me." A basic assumption of this approach is that "I know what I am like."

INFORMAL STUDY OF PEOPLE ONE KNOWS WELL

Another important source of marketing ideas has been the informal observations one may make of the behavior of members of his family, close friends, and business associates, supplemented, perhaps, by their explanations of why they acted as they did or why they hold a certain opinion. The implication here is that "consumers are like these people," and necessary assumptions are "I can tell what they are like" or "they know and will tell me."

A number of the limitations cited in the preceding section also have a bearing here. There is, of course, the danger of overgeneralizing. In addition, a person may be a poor observer, either because he is careless in how he proceeds or because he is unable to see meaning in what is before his eyes. The nature of the latter limitation was well summarized by the noted psychiatrist, Harry Stack Sullivan, who explained that we cannot make any sense of our observations of another person "except on the basis of behavior that is meaningful to us — that is, on the basis of what we have experienced, done ourselves, or seen done under circumstances in which its purpose, its motivation, or at least the intentions behind it were communicated to us. Without this background, the observer cannot deduce, by sheer intellectual operations, the meaning of the staggering array of human acts." [32]

In regard to the dangers involved in relying on what the behaver has to say about his actions, Sullivan wrote:

A person can't tell you accurately how he acted in an important situation unless by almost sheer chance the way he

[32] Harry Stack Sullivan, *The Psychiatric Interview* (New York: W. W. Norton and Company, Inc., 1954), p. 19.

did act happened to coincide with his idea of how he should have acted — a rather uncommon coincidence. . . . In other words, everyone knows in a particular cultural situation just how he ought to act. If his behavior coincides with what he thinks he ought to have done, he can report the matter accurately. If, as is very much more frequently the case, there is no such coincidence between the act and the ideal, one finds that there is a truly astonishing decrease in the likelihood of the response being valid.[33]

Whether or not the people one knows well are typical, the approach of studying them does not in itself constitute a concept of the consumer which is of much help to the marketing executive who is left on his own limited resources to develop the picture.

EVIDENCE FROM MARKETING RESEARCH

Generally, marketing research has been much more active and successful in finding out what has been going on rather than in explaining behavior in terms of buyer wants and their satisfaction in specific product, brand, and competitive situations. Its role in large part has been shaped by its youth, most of its history being contained in two decades. Until recently, research has had to meet what business executives have considered to be more immediate needs than intensive explorations of why people buy.

One of the first major movements in the field consisted of compiling basic marketing facts such as those on population, retail sales, and income by geographical units. Later, store audits and consumer panels were launched to provide continuing reports on retail sales by brands, geographical regions, types of store, and certain consumer characteristics. The development of the survey technique for finding out how many people thought or acted in certain ways has been an important milestone. It has facilitated studies such as

[33] Ibid., p. 97.

those of advertising readership and the size and other characteristics of audiences of advertising media.

These developments represent notable progress within a short span of years in supplying badly needed data. They have provided important assistance to executives faced with such problems as the identification of markets, the allocation of sales and advertising efforts, the forecasting of sales, and the selection and the effective use of the advertising media. While information on what is going on does not in itself explain, it is an essential basis for thinking about the nature of the observed behavior.

In its efforts to explain buying behavior, marketing research has relied heavily on the direct question survey and on statistical analyses of sales data. With the latter, various attempts have been made to find what market factors such as income, age, education, city size, and geographical location seem to be correlated with, and, hence, presumably account for sales patterns. This level of explanation is important, but it usually does not in itself reveal why people buy in terms of the meanings the purchased product or brand has for them.

While direct question surveys can produce important information, they also have definite limitations which are discussed in some detail in Chapter XII. Generally, they are most useful for investigating the more tangible, rational factors which can be identified by the researcher in advance of the survey. The inability and the unwillingness of the respondent to give meaningful answers may be major limitations because people often do not consciously know important reasons for their actions or preferences. Even if they do know, they may rationalize or otherwise cover up the less socially acceptable influences.

Both statistical analyses of sales figures and direct question surveys by and large have dealt with the more objective factors and neglected the emotional aspects of buying behavior.

Contributing to this result have been the limitations of the techniques and the fact that the researchers employing them have been trained to think in terms of logic, reason, economy, and the like rather than in terms of people's feelings and the nonrational components of behavior. A consequence has been a marked tendency to assume that emotional factors were of relatively little importance in marketing.

A landmark in thinking about research to learn why people buy is Paul Lazarsfeld's article, "The Art of Asking Why," written in 1935.[34] Widely quoted, it has had a marked influence on marketing research books written since that time. The article is notable for its discussion of problems involved in direct questioning and for its emphasis on what Lazarsfeld called buying behavior determinants of the first degree. In this category he included conscious factors about which people were willing to talk such as product attributes, influences on buying action such as advertising and the advice of friends, the circumstances under which the decision for purchase was made, and the main use to which the purchased item was to be put.

Lazarsfeld included as determinants of the first degree emotional likes and dislikes for products, brands, colors, etc., but not the reasons for these feelings. The latter he classed as biographical determinants which represented a deeper level of explanation. He recognized their importance and the need for further progress in research methodology and interpretation in order to deal with them. Until very recently, however, marketing researchers and the writers of textbooks in the field generally have confined their attention to determinants of the first degree.

[34] Paul F. Lazarsfeld, "The Art of Asking Why," *National Marketing Review*, Summer 1935, Vol. 1, No. 1, pp. 32–43. The original source is out of print, but the article has been reprinted in Daniel Katz et al., *Public Opinion and Propaganda* (New York: The Dryden Press, 1954), pp. 675–686.

In Conclusion

In this chapter, we have reviewed influences on marketing's thinking about buying and consumption in order to better understand the existing limitations in knowledge. We conclude that in the past progress has been impeded by restricted ways of thinking and, as a corollary, by the limitations of techniques used in research.

While the marketer has been reminded on several fronts of the necessity of considering buyer wants, he has been left largely on his own limited resources for identifying and thinking about them in specific situations. Understandably, he has relied on narrow assumptions. His training and experience have given him a strong tendency to view buying as primarily a rational process involving the weighing of economic and material factors. While this may be appropriate in a number of instances, it often has proved inadequate. When an automobile owner explains his purchase of a Cadillac in terms of saving money in the long run, for example, one may well suspect an attempt to stretch the cloak of rationality too far. The same might be said for seemingly rational explanations of preferences for brands of cigarettes, gasoline, and other products where the consumer probably would have great difficulty in distinguishing among brands in an objective test in which brand names were concealed. While the marketer often has known that emotional factors are important, he has had no very systematic way of thinking about psychological and social meanings.

In spite of these limitations, marked progress has been made in supplying better products. It has come about to a large extent through the process of trying things out on the market and noting the results. Acceptance, or lack of it, presumably is indicative of a product's ability to satisfy wants, at least relative to competition, whether or not the wants can be identified. Ideas for new product and promotional offerings have been generated by technological advances, marked changes in ways of living, and reasoning about the important economic and material factors. These sources, of course, will continue to be important, and the market will continue to provide the practical test of a product's relative worth. The process of try and see, however, is accompanied by a great deal of waste; witness the large number of failures. While its results may contribute importantly to learning, the process itself is not a substitute for knowledge of how the human acts of buying and consumption are serving human purposes. It is greater understanding of this kind which is needed to cut waste and to enable marketing to do a significantly better job of designing and providing satisfying products and services and communicating effectively to people about them.

CHAPTER III

Needed: Conceptual Development

WHAT MARKETING needs for greatly accelerated progress is new, or at least much better developed, concepts of the things with which it deals. In other words, it must have more complete understanding for such basic questions as: "What is a consumer?" "What is a product?" "What is a brand?" "What is price?" "What is an advertisement?" and "What is selling?" The answers must be in terms of human wants and the elements that provide for their satisfaction, and they must be developed for specific situations.

How might such significant conceptual development come about? A requisite is freedom from the restrictive features of past ways of thinking and researching. While the latter have served useful purposes, they also inevitably carry limitations which can become rigid bonds if allowed to remain around unchallenged too long. A great deal more attention might profitably be given to conceptual development, viewing it as a process involving the following activities:

The development of a greater awareness of existing concepts and their underlying assumptions. This can come about through self-examination, experience, and discussions with others, perhaps in the course of planning of research.

The testing of existing concepts. This may be done in the course of business experience, through research, and, to some extent, in trading ideas with others.

The learning of the concepts of others. This can take place through reading, listening to lectures, participating in discussions, and research if new concepts are used by the researcher.

Creative thinking. This represents carrying forward one's

thinking from the background represented by the three steps already mentioned. It has to do with bringing into being images or ideas which previously were not in one's consciousness. This may be aided by data produced by research relative to the nature of things.

Ideally, these activities should be carried on in combination. The presence of any one of them does not automatically lead to improvement. Finding out what one's concepts are is an important first step. While this may stimulate thinking, it in itself is not dynamic. By testing, one may get evidence that a mental image is correct or incorrect, but this step in itself goes no further. For the concepts of others to be useful, they somehow must affect one's own thinking, either becoming integrated with ideas already present or stimulating new ones. As for creative thinking, it may give rise to new ideas, but whether they represent an advance over the old ones is yet to be determined. In any event, new ideas are essential for conceptual advancement and they may be either borrowed or created.

A Scientific Approach

Conceptual development should be an over-all process marked by general participation by all vitally interested in marketing. It should not be regarded as primarily the province of those formally engaged in research. On the other hand, research is essential. It can and should make tremendous contributions as it has elsewhere in the process of science which aims at improved understanding and the evolution of more satisfactory concepts. With this background, let us take a further look at marketing research which represents an attempt to bring the benefits of a scientific approach to the field.

Much has been written on "the" scientific method, although the latter has been viewed somewhat differently by different persons. For our purposes here, however, we shall state that a scientific approach has two essential elements: (a) getting ideas or hypotheses, and (b) testing them. This, of course, is to be regarded as a never-ending process which depends not only on checking of tentative ideas, but on stimulating thinking which will lead to still further investigations.

In our discussion of the process of conceptual development, we have indicated that research can be helpful in several different ways. Planning it can be useful for identifying current assumptions and clarifying thought. Research may test the validity of ideas. It may be undertaken by someone who has new concepts about what is being investigated, thereby introducing new thinking; and, of course, it may produce data useful in creative thinking by researchers and others who review the results.

Limitations of Research in Marketing

In view of the aims and potentialities of a scientific approach, what has served to limit the contribution marketing research has made to an understanding of consumer wants and buying behavior? A primary factor is that the great bulk of the attention has been given to the second step, that of testing, rather than the first, that of getting ideas to test. Marketing research textbooks, for example, have dealt almost entirely with the matters of research design, methods, and procedures while devoting only a handful of their pages to the topic of developing potentially fruitful hypotheses to guide explorations.

The emphasis on the mechanical aspects which has been so characteristic of marketing research generally has led to significant progress in this area. As a result, there now are well-developed sampling procedures for finding people to interview, improved questionnaire construction, better training and supervision of field interviewers, better ways of processing and interpreting survey data, and improved experimental design. The big need today is for better ideas by which greater advantage might be realized from the improved research machinery.

Hypothesis Formulation

The neglect of the function of formulating working hypotheses in marketing research can be attributed in part to the important technical needs of the young field and the fact that they, in turn, have attracted specialists in techniques and procedures. While this has had important benefits, it also has created problems which may assume sizable proportions when the technical specialists become directors of research. The danger has been that they, because of their basic orientation, tend to think more in terms of using and perfecting their techniques than of solving marketing problems. Their emphasis, in other words, is likely to be on methods rather than ways of thinking and ideas which could lead to new approaches to unanswered questions.

The tendency to fit problems to techniques rather than the other way around has plagued many fields. Its presence in the social sciences caused A. H. Maslow to write as follows:

> If scientists looked on themselves as question askers and problem solvers rather than specialized technicians, there would now be something of a rush to the newest scientific frontier, to the psychological and social problems about which we know least and should know most.[1]

In our opinion, the kind of situation which gave rise to the above statement now constitutes a major barrier to further progress in marketing.

Another reason for the neglect in marketing of getting good ideas for exploration is the assumption, widely though often implicitly held, that almost anyone with "common

---

[1] A. H. Maslow, *Motivation and Personality* (New York: Harper and Brothers, 1954) , p. 16.

sense" can think of the things research should investigate or measure. In other words, marketers and researchers, being consumers themselves as well as observers of the marketing scene, have tended to assume that they already know what the important factors for investigation are and that the really difficult step is that of carrying out the study of them. Actually, the assumption that the getting of worthwhile ideas for research is easy is a very dangerous one. Marketing's lack of knowledge and the limitations of its usual thinking about consumer behavior warn of this. So does the experience of the sciences. The much higher value placed on the process of formulating hypotheses by writers in some other fields is reflected in the following words of E. Bright Wilson, Jr., a chemist:

> The difficult part of the process of seeking the causes of observed phenomena is the construction of hypotheses to be tested. Thus, when it was suspected that the bite of an infected mosquito is the cause of malaria, this hypothesis could be rather easily tested. But the evidence for this cause and effect relationship has presumably always been available, and yet the link was only recently discovered.[2]

Exploratory Studies

The picture just given has been typical of marketing research in the past and, to a large extent, it holds for the present, too. In recent years, however, there has been an encouraging increase in the attention given to exploratory studies for guiding the main research effort. The trend is reflected in the more recent editions of marketing research textbooks.[3] The preliminary searches usually have included the examination of sales and other available marketing data

[2] E. Bright Wilson, Jr., *An Introduction to Scientific Research* (New York: McGraw-Hill Book Company, Inc., 1952) , p. 32.

[3] Harper W. Boyd, Jr., and Ralph Westfall, *Marketing Research: Text and Cases* (Homewood, Illinois: Richard D. Irwin, Inc., 1956) , pp. 53–56.

Lyndon O. Brown. *Marketing and Distribution Research* (New York: The Ronald Press Company, Third Edition, 1955) , pp. 123–124.

relevant to the subject of inquiry and the conduct of exploratory interviews with business executives, salesmen, dealers,
and consumers.

In so much of today's marketing research, the researcher is
called in only after the existence of trouble has been clearly
recognized and there is a sense of urgency about taking re-
medial action. Exploratory studies, then, typically have to do
with the immediate task of getting leads as to what is wrong.
They often can lead to spotting marked deficiences in product performance, price, distribution, and sales programs.
While this is a highly important function of marketing research, it is a somewhat different thing from what has been
our main interest thus far. It usually does not entail intensive investigation of buyer wants and the various functions a
given product or brand serves for its user; hence, it is not
likely to contribute substantially to marketing's conceptual
development.

It is one thing to hypothesize that Brand A is not selling
in a certain market because of poor retail distribution; that
Brand B's sales increase was due to a known product improvement; that the decline in sales of Brand C was due to a low-
ered price of Brand D; or that a given product is bought by
people of certain age and income levels. It is a more difficult
task to come up with hypotheses which will help determine
how a certain kind of product should be designed and styled
in order to best meet consumer wants; determine what it is
people really are buying when they purchase insurance, and
how they arrive at their choice of companies; and explain
why one brand outsells another when the two apparently
are about equal in the usual respects of objective product
characteristics, price, retail distribution, amount of promotion, and the like.

Exploratory studies, of course, are very much to the point
in research directed toward a deeper understanding of the
nature of consumer behavior, too. In such efforts, however,

the background restrictions of marketing personnel discussed in the last chapter are greater handicaps. Objective and systematic studies by researchers of technical competency cannot turn up ideas that the researchers themselves, because of limitations of experience and training, cannot recognize as they make their observations. It is this kind of obstacle that marketing needs to remove from its path.

Marketing research thinking typically has been confined too much to the usual market factors, and there has been a marked tendency to assume that one, or maybe two factors, could explain why all purchasers of a given product bought it. In addition, much research has been conducted in a hurry on a one-shot basis to meet immediate needs. A more systematic, continuous effort, guided by broader ways of thinking, would appear to be necessary for making further headway with the more difficult problems in marketing.

Turning Up Ideas

In emphasizing the need for greater development of the process by which hypotheses are evolved, we are not unmindful of the fact that the task of producing new ideas is an exceedingly challenging one. Much remains to be learned about how to do it.

F. J. Roethlisberger recently wrote on this subject as follows:

> . . . In the development of science the rules by which more fruitful hypotheses are reached have never been as clearly stated as the rules by which any hypothesis — no matter how barren — is verified. In fact the former has always been to some a deplorably nonlogical aspect of the scientific method. That some useful ideas capable of testing should arise from the subjective hunches, intuitions, guesses, skills, judgments, random observations, and even dreams of the investigator does not quite seem *comme il faut*. They should come only from more orderly, rational, and objective processes. But

on this point most scientists and philosophers of the scientific method seem to be agreed. They just don't.

It seems to be agreed that the quest for more fruitful ideas, questions, and hypotheses is not easily reduced to a formula. . . .[4]

While ideas cannot be ground out automatically according to formula, marketing appears to be in the position of having available to it potentially rewarding means of stimulating its thinking and imagination and, hence, improving its stock and flow of ideas.

Wilson reminds us that it is "often the case that an old problem is solved because some new tool, experimental or theoretical, has become available from another source." [5] The suggestion of borrowing from other fields is a particularly appropriate one for marketing. In the past decade or two, there have been important advances in both concepts and research methods in disciplines concerned with understanding the nature of human behavior. Some of the more likely sources from which significant borrowings might be made would appear to be psychology, psychoanalysis, social and cultural anthropology, and sociology. Marketing has barely opened the door to the opportunity represented here for taking a new and broader look at the consumer.

Roethlisberger's remarks, which we quoted earlier, were made in the foreword of a book which is of special interest because it grew out of work undertaken specifically to produce fruitful ideas, questions, and hypotheses. The subject was worker satisfaction and development. Noting the absence of a well-formulated technique for such effort, the question of "what should we do?" faced the human relations group led by Roethlisberger and of which A. Zaleznik, author of the book written subsequently, was a member. Writ-

[4] A. Zaleznik, *Worker Satisfaction and Development* (Boston: Harvard University, Division of Research, Graduate School of Business Administration, 1956), foreword, p. vii.

[5] E. Bright Wilson Jr., op. cit., p. 1.

ing about this, Roethlisberger explained that Zaleznik "proposed that we 'shoot the breeze' (a well-known method of producing ideas) in relation to some concrete data. It was this little addition of 'in relation to some concrete data' that lifted Zaleznik's idea out of the realm of Madison Avenue and the ordinary." [6]

The concrete data were obtained by an intensive investigation of workers in a machine shop made by a well-trained observer of human behavior. Few such intensive studies to get acquainted with the nature of consumer behavior have been undertaken in marketing. The possibility of conducting such investigations, using the ways of thinking and the skills of various students of human behavior, is an intriguing one. It represents a means by which marketing might be able to develop the conceptual schemes or ways of looking at consumers and products which it needs so badly in order to reduce its dependence upon learning by trial and error without the aid of a well-developed, over-all concept of what it is one is about. The following words of James B. Conant are appropriate in this connection:

> The process of "cut and try," of changing first one factor and then another without benefit of any over-all conceptual scheme or new idea, is clearly the essence of the empirical approach. This kind of planned but empirical experimentation is often confused with the scientific method, . . . but is obviously only an incomplete version of the procedure by which science developed in modern times.[7]

Conant emphasized that "the revolutionary advances in science are made in terms of new conceptual schemes (interlocked with controlled experiments), not in terms of improved methods, and not in terms of amassing data." [8]   He

[6] A. Zaleznik, op. cit., foreword, p. vii.

[7] James B. Conant, "Science and the Practical Arts," *Harvard Business Review,* Vol XXV, 4a (Autumn 1947) , p. 551.

[8] Ibid., p. 550

added that "when a new conceptual scheme is emerging, the applications of that scheme to the practical arts are most likely to be rewarding." [9]

In the behavioral sciences, new conceptual schemes have come into being (and, of course, continue to be developed) relative to the nature of man and how he lives. The use of these ways of thinking for more meaningful views of the consumer, the industrial buyer and marketing's own representatives, and the consequent development of improved marketing concepts has only recently begun.

[9] Ibid., p. 553.

CHAPTER IV

The Behavioral Sciences and New Concepts
for Marketing

IN THE LAST two chapters, we made observations of the thinking and research which have been typical of the marketing scene. In so doing, we purposely neglected, except for occasional references, some recent work of small but growing proportions which constitutes an important step toward making greater use of several of the behavioral sciences. This activity, popularly referred to as motivation research, is the main subject of this book. In chapters that follow, we shall present selected examples of studies of this kind and discuss some of the features and implications of the development they represent.

THE MOTIVATION RESEARCH DEVELOPMENT

Marketing, of course, has made some use of social scientists over a period of years. For example, we noted earlier that a few psychologists had supplied lists of buying "motives." Others have aided in developing survey questionnaires and other research techniques. Generally, however, this kind of activity has been limited. In recent years, there has been a change in both its extent and its nature. There has been a great upsurge of interest in seeking answers to why people buy, and this has been linked with looking for assistance to dynamic psychology which has come into its own in the past 10 to 20 years. Dynamic psychology is a broad term which has been used to include any field concerned primarily with the nature and development of the human personality and the social forces that act upon it. The principal fields contributing to the motivation research development have been psychology and psychiatry, including psychoanalysis, which approach behavior from the standpoint of the individual, and social and cultural anthropology and sociology which study behavior in groups. The boundary lines between some of these areas, never clearly drawn, are becoming less distinct as the trend continues toward integrating fields of common interest.

The lead in applying techniques and knowledge from the behavioral sciences to marketing problems was taken by a small number of social scientists. Some were on university campuses, others in research firms, and a few were in advertising agencies. It is impossible to fix any one beginning date for motivation research. This is due to both the broad way in which we choose to use the term and the fact that this kind of work develops over a period of time. For all practical purposes, however, it can be regarded as a post World War II development which did not attract wide attention until the early 1950's. The preliminary survey made by this writer in the summer of 1954 showed that a variety of studies had been made in the several preceding years, but that the total number was relatively small and most of them had been done by a handful of researchers.

A few events and dates will be mentioned to indicate when the subject came into the marketing spotlight. In 1951 the *Chicago Tribune* made public the first of five major motivational studies it was to sponsor over the next several years. The first was on beer, the others on cigarettes, detergents, automobiles, and gasoline.

In November 1952 the Advertising Research Foundation appointed a Committee on Motivation Research, noting "the recent remarkable increase of interest in the problems associated with applying the techniques which have been developed by the social scientists to investigate and determine the roots of people's unconscious and conscious reactions to advertising and products." [1]   The ARF proceeded to issue several publications on the subject, a bibliography,[2] a dictionary of psychological terms,[3] directories of research organizations [4] and social scientists,[5] and a book which described psychological techniques.[6]

The number of articles on the subject appearing in business journals increased notably starting in 1953 as did the number of business and professional meetings which gave attention to it on their programs.   The theme of the fourth annual Chicago Tribune Forum on Distribution and Advertising held in June 1953, for example, was "Why Do People Buy?"   In 1954 the subject of the University of Michigan Advertising Conference was "Improving Effectiveness of Advertising Through New Understanding of the Consumer."   In the same year the Boston Conference on Distribution had a panel discussion on "Consumer Motivation in Buying."   The subject was considered at various local and national meetings of the American Marketing Association.   The University of Illinois Marketing Symposium in October 1955 had as its central topic, "Consumer Behavior and Motivation."   A one-day clinic on motivation research, sponsored in July of that year by the Sales Executives' Club of New York, drew more people than could be accommodated in the ballroom of the city's Hotel Roosevelt.   One of the speakers who appeared before the group, Dr. Wallace H.

---

[1] George Horsley Smith, *Motivation Research in Advertising and Marketing* (New York: McGraw-Hill Book Company, 1954), preface, p. ix.

[2] Advertising Research Foundation, Inc., *An Introductory Bibliography of Motivation Research* (New York, 1953).

[3] Joseph W. Wulfeck and Edward M. Bennett, *The Language of Dynamic Psychology as Related to Motivation Research* (New York: McGraw-Hill Book Company, Inc., 1954).

[4] Advertising Research Foundation, Inc., *Directory of Organizations Which Conduct Motivation Research* (New York, 1954).

[5] Advertising Research Foundation, Inc., *Directory of Social Scientists Interested in Motivation Research* (New York, 1954).

[6] George Horsley Smith, op. cit.

Wulfeck, Chairman of the Advertising Research Foundation's Committee on Motivation Research, mentioned that he was on that day giving his fifty-third talk on motivation research. His first was made four and a half years earlier before the American Marketing Association. We have mentioned only a few of the meetings during this period which reflect the great amount of interest business people showed in the subject. Despite all the attention, however, the use made by marketing research of the social sciences, while growing, has been relatively small.

The most significant feature of the motivation research development is that it is supplying some of the need we cited earlier for new ways of thinking about buyers, consumers, and products. New concepts have led to the investigation of factors which had received little systematic attention before and to the use of research approaches relatively new to marketing. The research has done much to point up the importance of egoistic and social needs as determinants of behavior, adding them to the physical and economic needs which previously had received the bulk of investigative attention.

Before we get into research examples, we shall mention some of the broader new concepts which have played a part. Their influence can be seen in the selected studies which follow. In using the word "new" we recognize that nothing is brand new in a literal sense in that everything develops out of what has been done in the past. The ideas which interest us here are not necessarily new in the social science fields from which they come, and some of them, of course, are not entirely new in marketing. On the other hand, there has been a tremendous new emphasis on learning about the nature of human behavior. More research has been conducted in this area than ever before, and many of the more recent studies are much different in character from those of the past.

We already have indicated that motivation research has been characterized by somewhat different research approaches which reflect the varied backgrounds of the researchers concerned. There is no such thing as a single list of concepts or methods known and followed by everyone. Indeed, individual researchers cannot immediately produce on demand a full description of their ways of thinking and ideas just as you or I cannot readily identify some of the important ideas and assumptions which are basic to what we do in our everyday life. Nevertheless, the concepts are there and can be drawn out by detailed discussion and inferred from examining studies in which they exerted an influence. The ideas we shall point to below became apparent by these means, supplemented by this writer's background reading of books in the several behavioral fields. The following, then, represents a brief summary of a number of observations.

CONCEPTS RELATING TO THE CONSUMER

Self-Image

One of the more important concepts is that an individual's behavior is a function of his image of what kind of person he is and how he wants others to see him. This self-image is reflected to some extent in everything he does, including his buying of goods and services. Several of the studies to be presented in succeeding chapters make use of this concept. A marked example is the one on influences which govern the choice of a make of automobile.

The self-image idea is associated with the personal (or phenomenological) approach to the study of behavior from which many of psychology's more recent advances have come.[7] According to this school of thought, all behavior has a purpose, but to be understood, it must be observed not

[7] A useful presentation of the personal approach to the study of behavior is to be found in Donald Snygg and Arthur W. Combs, *Individual Behavior* (New York: Harper and Brothers Publishers, 1949).

from the point of view of an outsider, but from the point of view of the behaver himself. What a person does always has a reason in terms of how he views his universe, including himself, at the time he acts.

The view of self includes not only one's physical being, but "evaluations and definitions of self as strong, honest, good-humored, sophisticated, just, guilty and a thousand other ideas." [8] "Whether we have come to think of ourselves as being competent or incompetent, attractive or repulsive, honest or dishonest, has a tremendous effect on our behavior in different situations." [9]

The image one has of himself, of course, may not be accurate in terms of how he is seen by others. Nevertheless, it exists to serve certain needs and the person concerned acts to protect and enhance it. An individual develops his sense of self from his contacts with his parents and others during the course of his growing up. His psychological characteristics, which together with his physical make-up constitute his personality, are shaped by how he is treated, or, more specifically, whether and how his needs are met.

Basic Needs

Dynamic psychologists, on the basis of their clinical and other studies, have identified certain basic needs or goals toward which the behavior of man is directed. These are the needs with which all men presumably start. Their satisfaction, or lack of it, in one's early years determines in large measure what kind of person he will be as an adult. Just how an individual will act in order to satisfy these needs, or whether he will do so directly, will depend upon how they were handled in his childhood, how he reacted to this treatment, and various cultural and social restrictions on behavior.

[8] Ibid., p. 57.
[9] Ibid., p. 78.

The first comprehensive dynamic theory of personality centering about need gratification was developed by Sigmund Freud. Since then, considerable work has been done in this area and there have been a number of versions of basic needs as the thinking about human motivation has progressed. While the lists of needs presented by contemporary writers differ somewhat, they also have much in common. Their most important feature is the way of thinking they represent. It is used by a number of people with clinical training who are engaged in motivation research.

For purposes of illustration, we shall present a very brief summary of the basic needs used in the theory of human motivation developed by A. H. Maslow. It is one of the more recent contributions in the field. Maslow's basic needs, along with excerpted explanatory notations are: [10]

1. *The Physiological Needs:* There are any number of these, depending on how specific one wishes to become. They are the most prepotent of all needs which means that if all the needs are unsatisfied, the organism will be dominated by the physiological needs, all others being pushed into the background. When they are satisfied, however, other (and higher) needs emerge and they, rather than physiological hungers, dominate. Any of the physiological needs and the behavior involved to meet them may serve as channels for other needs as well. The person who thinks he is hungry, for example, may actually be seeking more for comfort and dependence than for vitamins or proteins.

2. *The Safety Needs:* These needs for protection and care emerge if the physiological needs are relatively well gratified. We can note the expressions of safety needs by adults in the common preference for a job with tenure and protection, the desire for a savings account, and for insurance of various kinds. More extreme examples can

[10] A. H. Maslow, *Motivation and Personality* (New York: Harper and Brothers, 1954), pp. 80–106.

be seen in the people who are the economic and social underdogs. Studies have shown that many children in our society feel too unsafe, reflecting a threatening family environment lacking in love.

3. *The Belongingness and Love Needs:* If both the physiological and the safety needs are fairly well gratified, there will emerge the love and affection and belongingness needs. The person will hunger for affectionate relations with people, a place in his group. The love needs involve both giving and receiving love. In our society the thwarting of these needs is the most commonly found core in cases of maladjustment. Love and affection are generally looked upon with ambivalence and are customarily hedged about with many restrictions and inhibitions.

4. *The Esteem Needs:* All people in our society have a need or desire for a stable, firmly based, usually high evaluation of themselves, for self-esteem and for the esteem of others. Needs related to self-esteem include the desire for strength, achievement, adequacy, mastery and competence, confidence, independence, and freedom. We also have the desire for reputation or prestige (respect or esteem from other people), status, dominance, recognition, attention, importance, or appreciation. Satisfaction of the self-esteem need leads to feelings of self-confidence, worth, strength, capability, and adequacy, of being useful and necessary in the world. But thwarting of these needs produces feelings of inferiority, or weakness, and of helplessness.

5. *The Need for Self-Actualization:* Man has a desire to become everything that he is capable of becoming. The specific form that this will take will vary greatly from person to person. The clear emergence of these needs usually rests upon prior satisfaction of the physiological, safety, love, and esteem needs.

6. *The Desires to Know and Understand:* These refer to the process of searching for meaning . . . a desire to understand, to systematize, to organize, to analyze, to look

foɪ relations and meanings, to construct a system of values.

7. *The Aesthetic Needs:* In some individuals there is a truly basic aesthetic need. They get sick (in special ways) from ugliness and are cured by beautiful surroundings.

Maslow believes that most people have the basic needs in about the order of importance indicated by the listing above, and that the gratification of the most basic need permits the emergence of the next most basic need and so on. He states that most members of our society who are normal are partially satisfied in all their basic needs and partially unsatisfied in all their basic needs at the same time — that a realistic description of the hierarchy would be in terms of decreasing percentages of satisfaction in going from the most to the less basic needs.

Maslow pointed out that the basic needs are either necessarily conscious nor unconscious, but that they are often largely unconscious. Any given behavior, he said, tends to be determined by several or all of the basic needs simultaneously rather than by only one of them. Our remarks thus far have been concerned with motivated or goal-seeking behavior. Maslow also recognizes expressive behavior which does not try to do anything but is simply a reflection of the personality.

The concept of basic needs or goals is of interest to marketing for several reasons. We note that an act is psychologically important in proportion to its contribution to the satisfaction of basic needs. This suggests that investigation of how a person feels about a product or brand, conducted with these needs in mind, may lead to an understanding of the character and strength of the meaning the product or brand has for him. Inasmuch as people often are not conscious of these needs, it is necessary to go behind the everyday conscious desires in order to add to our understanding of consumer wants and behavior.

Attempts along the lines indicated here will be seen in the studies that follow this chapter. In one of them, for example, coffee is shown to have many psychological values. Another, a study on automobile insurance, led the sponsoring company to conclude that the price appeal it had relied upon for years should be supplemented by strong emphasis on giving various assurances that the company could be relied upon to take care of the insured in time of trouble. Emotional support as well as the formal honoring of contractual obligations was involved. Many of the meanings of automobile insurance as revealed by this study seem to be related to what Maslow called the safety needs, and the latter showed themselves in various ways. A study of dieting refers to the psychological significance of eating and evidence that overeating is associated with feelings of dependency and depression (indicative of strong, unfilled love and belongingness needs, to use Maslow's terms).

The basic needs concept and attendant thinking also indicate an approach for learning more about brand preferences and brand loyalty. Preference may depend upon what the consumer feels to be the relative ability of a brand to satisfy one or more basic needs. One brand may have an edge over another in this respect even though the two are alike in the usual characteristics of ingredients, type of package, price, and the like. More will be said about this shortly in discussing the concept of brand image. The amount of loyalty to a brand may be related to the extent to which basic need satisfaction is involved. We have seen very little research which bears on the latter point.

Inasmuch as people differ in the extent to which their various basic needs have been gratified, differences can be expected as to which needs are the strong motivating forces as well as to how these needs manifest themselves. Different brands, then, may attract different people on the basis of the images people have of them. Indeed, it may be most difficult for a brand to appeal strongly to all prospective buyers. Studies in such product areas as gasoline, dentifrices, and cigarettes have provided evidence to support this point of view.

The concept of basic needs also is important to an understanding of projective tests of personality because the latter assume that all people have such needs. The function of the tests is to determine how a person has resolved his needs, what his main strivings and dispositions are. Therefore, they offer a means of differentiating among people on the basis of personality dimensions. The study on home sewing which will follow is an illustration of this.

Cultural and Social Influences

Thus far we have focused on the individual and his needs and basic dispositions. But people are reared in a certain culture and are members of social groups, informal as well as formal, which determine how individual needs are handled and otherwise influence behavior. There are a number of concepts in this connection with implications for marketing.

The term "culture" is used to refer to all social characteristics of a group such as thoughts, feelings, values, beliefs, standards, customs, and institutions. Ruth Benedict has written:

> What really binds men and women together is their culture — the ideas and standards they have in common.[11] . . .
>
> A culture, like an individual, is a more or less consistent pattern of thought and action.[12]

The above suggests that homogeneity might be expected within a culture or a cultural subgroup in regard to a num-

---

[11] Ruth Benedict, *Patterns of Culture* (New York: The New American Library of World Literature, Inc. A Mentor Book, 1934) , p. 14.

[12] Ibid., p. 42.

ber of consumer wants and attitudes toward products and even well-known brands.

Social class, a concept referring to status and broad patterns of social values, attitudes, and behavior within a culture, is being used in motivation research as a basis for differentiating among consumers. The dieting and automobile studies to follow are examples.

A narrower but somewhat similar concept is that of a reference group, a term used to denote any group to which a person relates his attitudes. The shaping of attitudes can take place through the setting and enforcing of standards or "group norms" to which the members may conform in order to gain acceptance or favor. The standards of a group also may be used as a reference point by an individual for making evaluations of himself and others whether or not he is a member.

The influence of group and interpersonal influences has been the subject of a number of studies. Columbia University's Bureau of Applied Social Research has done much work in this area. One of its reports published recently dealt with personal influences on decisions to buy foods and household goods, the selection of motion pictures to see, and the acceptance of fashion changes.[13] The findings challenged a commonly held assumption that opinions are formed by the elite in the community and are passed down from one social level to the next. The study demonstrated the existence of horizontal opinion leadership within each stratum. This was found to be most marked in relation to small consumer purchases.

The influence of the neighborhood social group on buying decisions of its members was emphasized by a study of ownership of air conditioners in Philadelphia.[14] The impor-

---

[13] Elihu Katz and Paul F. Lazarsfeld, *Personal Influence* (Glencoe, Illinois: The Free Press, 1955).

[14] William H. Whyte, Jr., "The Web of Word of Mouth," *Fortune*, November 1954, p. 140.

tance of group decision as a means of social change was illustrated by experiments in changing food habits conducted by
Kurt Lewin.[15]

Another concept is that of "social role." A role is a way
of acting one is expected to follow because of his social characteristics such as sex, age, marital status, social class, and
occupation. One study, for example, found that people had
definite ideas as to how a "good" insurance agent should act
in relation to the client or prospective client. Other studies
have shown the presence of commonly held opinions as to
what is expected of a "good" housewife and that they can
make for resistance to new products which involve different
ways of doing things, especially if they reduce or eliminate
work which has been regarded as part of her function.

Concepts Relating to the Product

A product may be viewed as a part of the culture. By
virtue of its cultural role, it may have acquired a number of
meanings varying in significance with the degree to which
the product is associated with important social interaction.
The product, then, serves as a symbol or a collection of meanings which it communicates to others when they look at it or
use it. Food products, beverages, and automobiles are
marked examples as we shall see in upcoming studies.

Closely related to the above is the concept of "brand
image." Broadly speaking, the brand image consists of everything people associate with the brand. These impressions
determine how one feels about it. Brands often acquire
certain meanings which tend to make them regarded as more
appropriate for some kinds of people than for others. These

[15] Kurt Lewin, "Studies in Group Decision," *Group Dynamics, Research
and Theory,* edited by Dorwin Cartwright and Alvin Zander (Evanston, Illinois: Row, Peterson and Company, 1953) , p. 287. Substantially the same article
appears as "Group Decision and Social Change," *Readings in Social Psychology,* revised edition, edited by Guy E. Swanson, Theodore M. Newcomb, and
Eugene L. Hartley (New York: Henry Holt and Company, 1952) , p. 459.

meanings, when revealed by research, often have come as a surprise to the manufacturer.

One of the important dimensions of a brand image may be the extent to which the brand itself has become closely identified with important meanings of the type of product it represents. A study of coffee brands, for example, showed one brand to be prominently associated with hospitality, entertaining, and good old-fashioned cooking while a competing brand, of comparable price and quality, had a relatively indistinctive image.

A brand image also may have dimensions of a more personal nature, and these are of interest in connection with earlier comments about people acting to express their self-images and to satisfy certain needs or goals. These dimensions may include the following:

Age — whether the brand is considered to be more for young people or for old.

Modernity — whether the brand is regarded as modern or old-fashioned.

Status — whether the brand connotes high or low social status.

Sex — whether the brand is seen in terms of those characteristics which in our culture identify it more with men or with women.

Security — whether it is considered to be sound, dependable, reliable, and well established.

The brand image concept has received considerable attention in motivation research. Learning more about images and their relationship to consumer needs appears to offer substantial potential rewards in terms of understanding buying behavior. Burleigh B. Gardner and Sidney J. Levy have written on this as follows:

These sets of ideas, feelings, and attitudes that consumers have about brands are crucial to them in picking and sticking to ones that seem most appropriate. How else can they decide whether to smoke Camels or Lucky Strikes; to use Nescafé or Borden's instant coffee; to drive a Ford or Chevrolet or a Plymouth?

Justifying choice is easier with the cars; there at least the products have clearly visible differences. But the reasons people give for choosing a brand of cigarettes (and soap and bread and laxatives) are pretty much the same. Thus you find drinkers of any brand of beer justifying their preference in identical terms: "Schlitz is better because it's dry." "I like a dry beer, so I prefer Bud to Schlitz."

Something must make a greater difference; the conceptions of the different brands must be compounded of subtle variations in feelings about them, not necessarily in product qualities. A big problem in this area, then, is what kind of symbol a given brand is to consumers.[16]

The brand image concept implies a way of viewing an advertisement which has gained favor in the past few years, displacing to some extent the commonly held belief that a given advertisement or campaign should make immediate sales. Speaking before advertising agency executives, David Ogilvy, president of Ogilvy, Benson and Mather, confessed to changing his mind on this subject and coming to this view:

> We now hold that every advertisement must be considered as a contribution to the complex symbol which is the brand image — as part of the long-term investment in this reputation of the brand.[17]

Descriptions of images for different makes and types of cars will be found in the automobile study to which reference already has been made.

[16] Burleigh B. Gardner and Sidney L. Levy, "The Product and the Brand," *Harvard Business Review*, Vol. 33, No. 2, March–April 1955, pp. 33–39.

[17] Mr. Ogilvy's speech, "The Image and the Brand — a New Approach to Creative Operations," was given before the central regional conference of the American Association of Advertising Agencies in Chicago in October, 1955. The text was carried in full by *Advertising Age*, November 14, 1955, pp. 113–114.

A Concept of the Buying Process

The above comments relative to the consumer and the product suggest a concept of the buying process, namely, that it is a matching of a person's self-image with the image of a product or a brand. This suggests that users of different brands may tend to have different personality characteristics and that a product or brand may serve somewhat different purposes for different people.

A Concept of Personal Selling

A concept similar to the above can be applied in the realm of salesman-customer relationships. The buyer can be viewed as wanting two broad categories of things from the salesman:

(1) A satisfactory offer in terms of physical properties of the product, price, service, and other important rational requirements.
(2) A satisfactory personal relationship in terms of the buyer's emotional needs. This has to do with the buyer's being allowed by the salesman to establish and maintain the favorable ideas about himself which constitute his self-image or the way he wants to be seen by others.

The second point has gone almost untouched in writings on selling even though it would appear to represent the essence of personal salesmanship. There have been a few studies in this direction made by trained observers who have followed salesmen for several days or so, noting in detail what went on, including, in some cases, verbatim notes of conversations. In some instances, there also have been personal interviews with both the salesmen about what he thought went on and why he did what he did and with customers called on to learn more about their reactions.

One of the earlier efforts of this kind with which the writer is familiar was conducted in 1952 by Professor Albert H. Dunn, III, when he was on the Harvard Business School faculty. He observed a number of salesmen for the H. J. Heinz Company, taking full notes on all conversations. His material, consisting largely of transcripts of sales calls, was used as a basis for class discussions of the nature of the salesman's job. No written analysis of it was presented. Similar material was prepared by Philip Borden, a member of the Harvard Business School faculty at the time, on the basis of observations he made in 1953 of salesmen of a large electric company.

The Jewel Tea Company has had two studies made of its route selling. The reports of findings emphasized the importance and described the nature of the routeman-customer relationship. The research made use of observations of sales calls and detailed interviews of salesmen and customers conducted independently, the latter being supplemented in one case by the use of some projective techniques. The first study was made in 1949, the second in 1953.

SOME CONCEPTS WITH IMPLICATIONS FOR RESEARCH METHODOLOGY

At several points we have referred to the difficulties which may be encountered in attempts to get motivational information from people. Below we mention a few concepts which relate to this problem and ways of meeting it.

The concept of the unconscious — that the mind contains ideas and urges which influence behavior even though they are not consciously recognized — was one of Freud's most important contributions. Inasmuch as much motivation is not conscious, people will not be able to explain fully the reasons for their buying behavior. This means that indirect research approaches are needed.

The psychiatric concept of rationalization helps us understand what research is up against when it seeks explanations of behavior. This term refers to the process, which may or may not be conscious, of making irrational acts appear rational by giving intellectual reasons for behavior that really is the result of personal desires one does not wish to acknowledge to himself or to others. In our culture, this is likely to mean that people will explain their buying in seemingly logical, rational terms rather than admit to emotional forces.

The concept of projection has given rise to projective techniques which now are being adapted for marketing research purposes. Projection is an unconscious mechanism by which an individual takes part of himself and puts it onto something else. For example, when one who is afraid criticizes others for cowardness, he is projecting. In a projective technique, a person may tell a story about a picture and give information about himself without realizing it in so doing. There are two main characteristics of these techniques: the test material is relatively ambiguous or unstructured so that it will not suggest a certain kind of response, and the purpose of the test is disguised.

The principle of free association was discovered by Freud and is used as a major tool in psychoanalysis. The basic idea is that if a person gives up the usual logical controls he exercises over his thoughts and says whatever comes to his mind at the moment in the presence of a skilled listener, unconscious feelings and thoughts can be discovered. This is a product of a free-flowing chain of words or ideas which are consciously or unconsciously associated with one another so that one calls up the next which, in turn, calls up the next and so on. This idea has led to depth or detailed interviewing in marketing research as a means of giving the respondent favorable conditions for telling of his ideas and feelings.

In this chapter, we have attempted to mention briefly some of the main concepts used thus far in motivation research so that the reader might have this background as an aid in viewing the detailed descriptions of studies that follow. This is not intended as a complete listing. Other ideas, of course, will be noted in the researches. The purpose here was to focus attention on concepts of potential importance in the task of learning more about consumer wants.

PART II

Motivation Research: Selected Case Examples

Introduction to the Selected Case Examples

THIS SECTION of the book consists of detailed case descriptions of work done by research firms or departments whose staffs include persons with social science training. The studies were selected for their ways of thinking about people as consumers and their ways of learning about what people want when they buy. All borrow to some extent from one or more behavioral fields, particularly dynamic psychology, social and cultural anthropology, and sociology. Variety will be noted due to the differences in backgrounds and thinking of the researchers concerned and the nature of the research problems at hand. Considered together, the examples constitute as useful an answer as we can give to the question: "What is motivation research?"

The following cases are presented in the chapters that follow:

State Farm Automobile Insurance Company (Research conducted by Needham, Louis and Brorby, Inc., Chicago.) A direct question survey and a psychological study were undertaken concurrently in an effort to learn how the company, the largest in its field, might increase its business.

Pan American Coffee Bureau (Research conducted by the Institute for Motivational Research, Inc., Croton, N.Y.) This consumer research was undertaken to learn more about how coffee consumption might be increased.

Automobiles — What They Mean to Americans (A study sponsored by the *Chicago Tribune* with research done by Social Research, Inc., Chicago.) The investigation was directed to obtaining an improved understanding of the meanings of automobiles to people and why they choose one make over another. The information was used as a basis for recommending ways in which automobile advertising might be made more effective.

Donahue Sales Corporation (Research conducted by Mc-Cann-Erickson, Inc., New York.) The purpose of the study was to provide a basis for determining how home sewing might be promoted and how the retail sales of Talon zippers might be increased.

Dieting Study (Research conducted by Young and Rubicam, Inc., New York.) The goal was an understanding of the importance of overweight as a problem, what women were overweight and why, what women would diet and why, and how their dieting would affect the use of selected foods.

Jewel Tea Company (Studies conducted at different times by the Institute for Motivational Research, Inc., Croton, N.Y. and Social Research, Inc., Chicago.) Research was directed to improving the sales effectiveness of the company's home route service.

The studies are presented in the context of the business situation to which they were addressed because our first concern is with marketing problems and their solution. Our primary interest is not in concepts or techniques in the abstract, but in their application to provide help to the marketing executive in the making of decisions.

A commentary will appear after each of the cases for the purpose of noting and discussing some of the principal features. In this connection, however, we wish to point out that it is not our intention to pass technical judgment on the individual researches. Our concern here is with broader matters. Our main purpose is to observe the kinds of things which have been going on. In later chapters, we shall give additional attention to concepts, research techniques, and administrative problems related to making use of the social sciences in marketing.

CHAPTER V

State Farm Mutual Automobile Insurance Company

FORENOTE

In the case which follows, the largest company in the automobile insurance field, feeling competitive threats to its leadership, turned to marketing research for the first time. Past success had been achieved by following a certain program which, among other things, included emphasis on low rates and little consumer advertising. The relative importance of elements of the program was largely a matter of opinion, and executives differed in their views as to what should be done in the future. Research was expected to resolve these differences and supply any information which would help the company determine how it might strengthen its position.

There was the question, then, as to what kind of research would be most useful under the circumstances. Two studies were undertaken concurrently by the company's advertising agency, Needham, Louis and Brorby, Inc. One was a market survey employing a questionnaire of direct questions. The other was a psychological study which used group interviews and adaptations of several projective techniques. Both studies proved useful for somewhat different reasons. To a large extent, their missions were not the same, but they had enough in common, particularly in the question areas of how and why people buy insurance, to permit contrasts to be drawn between the research approaches they represented and the findings they produced.

STATE FARM MUTUAL AUTOMOBILE INSURANCE COMPANY

A Descriptive Case

EARLY in 1954 executives of the State Farm Mutual Automobile Insurance Company of Bloomington, Illinois, consulted with executives of their advertising agency, Needham, Louis and Brorby, Inc., of Chicago, regarding the advisability of undertaking marketing research to help the company maintain its position of leadership in the face of growing competition.

Since its founding 35 years ago, the company had grown to where it served 3,300,000 automobile insurance policyholders in 1954, the thirteenth year it had insured more automobile owners than any other company. In 1954 State Farm operated in 40 states (omitting New York, New Jersey, and the New England states) and Ontario, Canada.

The company had achieved its position by following policies which made possible rates lower than those charged by many of its competitors. One of the most important was that of insuring "careful drivers only" in order to minimize the cost of claims. State Farm computed its rates from the accident record of its own policyholders instead of charging "book rates" computed by national rating bureaus from the accident experience of other insurance companies.

Other features also contributed to lower rates. State Farm agents received commissions only on new business (not on renewals) plus a fee for service rendered in subsequent years. Policyholders, therefore, paid selling cost only once and this took the form of a membership fee. State Farm did all the bookkeeping, billing, and collecting from its 11 regional offices. Relieved of this detail work, the agents had more time to devote to selling. Agents who had been with the company five years averaged $14,000 in annual income. State Farm also issued a "continuous policy" rather than writing up a new one each year. The policy, kept in force by renewal payments every six months, was not changed unless changes occurred in the car insured, the address, or the conditions of risk.

The company had attained its lead among automobile insurers without large expenditures for consumer advertising. Its advertising appropriation, however, had been increased from $200,000 in 1950, to $1,000,000 in 1954. Consumer advertising early in 1954 stressed cost savings and the careful driving theme.

Inasmuch as State Farm had the largest number of policyholders of any automobile insurance company, the emphasis in its sales strategy had been placed on retaining present customers. While the company's business was continuing to expand, its leading competitor, Allstate, was growing at a somewhat more rapid rate, posing a threat to State Farm's leadership. In 1953 Allstate's earned premiums were about $132,000,000 compared with State Farm's $175,000,000. The totals for both companies were up about $43,000,000 over 1952.

Allstate insurance was competitively priced with that of State Farm. Allstate was also an aggressive advertiser, and operated in eastern states where State Farm was not represented. Allstate enjoyed the advantages offered by the reputation of Sears, Roebuck and Company and was able to sell in Sears retail stores at locations where adult male floor traffic was heavy.

The competitive situation prompted a review of basic selling strategy and led to consideration of undertaking a large-scale marketing research project for the first time in State Farm's history. There were some differences of opinion among company executives regarding advertising policy. One executive believed that women were important in the making of the decision to buy insurance and thought that more advertising should be directed to them. Another executive questioned the advisability of continuing to stress price in the advertising, fearing that this might connote cheapness and would work against building a reputation for quality. There also was a question as to how much advertising the company should do.

As a basis for determining sales and advertising strategy, Mr. T. C. Morrill, Vice President, believed that the company needed to know more about its competitive position in its various marketing areas, why some policyholders left State Farm, and why people bought State Farm in the first place. Mr. Morrill had joined the company in 1950 as Director of Research. In 1954 his responsibilities included public relations and advertising, and he approached State Farm's advertising agency regarding a market survey. Among those at the agency with whom the matter was discussed were Mr. William Ohle, Vice President and Account Supervisor; Dr. Steuart Henderson Britt, Vice President and Director of Research; and Dr. Dik Twedt, Research Supervisor for the State Farm account.

Under the leadership of Dr. Britt, the research department at Needham, Louis and Brorby had been utilizing the social sciences in developing approaches to its research problems.[1] Dr. Britt and Dr. Twedt were two of the three psychologists in the department which had a professional staff of people with graduate degrees in such fields as psychology, economics, statistics, marketing, business administration, agriculture, and library science.

The agency, working closely with representatives of State Farm, developed plans for two studies which would complement each other and which would be conducted simultaneously. One was to be a basic survey of the market for auto-

[1] Dr. Britt received his Ph.D. in psychology at Yale. He had written and edited several books and also had written a number of articles for various professional journals. Among his publications: *Social Psychology of Modern Life*, Revised Edition (New York: Rinehart & Company, Inc., 1949) ; *Selected Readings in Social Psychology* (New York: Rinehart & Company, Inc., 1950) ; *Advertising Psychology and Research,* co-authored with Dr. Darrell B. Lucas (New York: McGraw-Hill Book Company, 1950).

mobile insurance in which a prepared questionnaire was to be used in personal interviews to be conducted among a probability sample of 7,500 respondents within State Farm's forty-state operating area. The other was planned as a psychological analysis of the market for automobile insurance which would use group interviews with about 50 men and interviews with approximately another 50 men in which projective techniques would be used. Evidence from the market survey indicated that men were the primary target for insurance. The ones to be interviewed were to be drawn from various walks of life. The plans were approved and work began.

THE MARKET SURVEY

The stated purpose of the survey was to obtain information about attitudes toward State Farm and attitudes toward certain other automobile insurance companies so that comparisons might be made. Information was sought about car owners, both insured and noninsured, which might help explain why people buy automobile insurance, why and how they choose a particular company, why they sometimes lapse, and what their general attitudes toward automobile insurance coverage are.

The survey was planned to answer these questions, among others:

1. What proportion of new business comes from former customers of other companies, and what proportion comes from people not previously insured?
2. Which members of the family influence the decision to buy automobile insurance, and who actually chooses the particular company?
3. What per cent of automobile owners carry any insurance?
4. Why do people change insurance companies? Are there differences in this respect between mutual and stock

companies? Between State Farm and its competitors?

5. Why and how often do people give up insurance altogether?
6. How much shopping around do people do before buying automobile insurance? How are people influenced by insurance advertising?
7. To what extent is the State Farm name known? What are the attitudes toward the name and the company? How does attitude vary as a function of experience with the company?
8. To what extent are members aware of all the advantages offered by State Farm? How many people know that State Farm also sells life and fire insurance?
9. How important is the Bank Plan as a competitive advantage? (I.e., How many people buy their insurance and finance their car in one "tie-in" deal?)
10. What does the average automobile owner know about his state's financial responsibility law, if any?
11. What do people think about the cost of their present insurance?
12. How important is an "easy pay" plan in the automobile owner's decision to buy from a particular company?
13. What do people think about the idea of putting an insurance insignia on their cars? How many of them actually do it?
14. How are State Farm members different from buyers of other automobile insurance?

Answers to the above questions were to be obtained by asking respondents direct questions (see Appendix A, pages 107–117 for the complete questionnaire) and analyzing their answers statistically. The questions varied somewhat in nature as the following selected examples illustrate:

Does anyone in this household happen to have an automobile? (Yes or no)

How did you get in touch with your present company — that is, how did you first hear about it?

What reasons were most important to you in choosing the company you did? Any others? (Probe)

In general, how well satisfied are you with the way your present company handled your claims? Would you say that you were *very well satisfied, fairly well satisfied,* or *not at all satisfied?*

(If not at all satisfied) Why?

People give different reasons for taking out auto insurance. Which one of these do you think is most important to most people? Which one do you think is least important to most people?

— To cover yourself against damage to your car
— To cover your responsibility for damage to the other fellow
— Because it is required by law
— Other (explain)

Here are some of the things about auto insurance companies that some people feel are important. (Interviewer: Show set of yellow cards) Now can you tell me which one of these is most important to you personally? (Record "1" below and ask:) And of these left, which one is the most important? (Record "2" and proceed until all cards have been ranked)

— Quick settling of claims
— Low cost of insurance
— Good service from local agent
— Well-known company
— Claim adjusters in all parts of the United States
— Fair treatment by company
— Installment plan for payment
— Other (explain)

The interviewing and the tabulation of data was done by Market Facts, Inc., of Chicago, working under the supervision of Dr. Twedt of the advertising agency's research department. The final report, completed in October 1954, con-

sisted of 96 charts based on a similar number of tables. The
type of information contained in the tables is indicated in
Appendix B, pages 118–120.

Selected questions dealing with how and why people buy
automobile insurance, with tabulated answers, appear in
Appendix C, pages 121–124.

THE PSYCHOLOGICAL STUDY

The purpose of the second study was to uncover basic psychological attitudes which influence the purchase of automobile insurance. There were two major questions to be answered: Why do people buy automobile insurance? What
qualities do they look for in an automobile insurance company?

Research into motives underlying consumer behavior had
been of special interest to Dr. Britt who had emphasized in
speeches and articles that little was known about why people
do as they do.[2] He had pointed to the difficulties of identifying and classifying motives, concluding that there is no such
thing as a universal set of motives, and had urged that greater
use be made of the clinical approach to interviewing and that
more qualitative research be undertaken.

The psychological study attempted to find out just how
people look at automobile insurance. By using their own
categories and expressions of feeling about the subject, an
assessment was made of why they had such attitudes. Data
were gathered in two ways: by a series of tape-recorded "snowball" interviews conducted among small groups of men, and
by individual interviews in which projective testing materials
were used.

THE "SNOWBALL" INTERVIEWS

Needham, Louis and Brorby had used tape-recorded
"snowball" interviews for several years to give account ex-

[2] Steuart Henderson Britt, "The Strategy of Consumer Motivation," *Journal of Marketing*, April 1950.

ecutives and copy writers a direct picture of customer thinking.[3]   The interviews, nondirective and conversational in
nature, were a means of getting a small group of people into
a relaxed, informal frame of mind so that they would talk
freely.   The name "snowball" referred to the cumulative
effect of the continual stimulus of one respondent on another
which often resulted in expressions of opinion of greater
depth and breadth than might be obtained in individual
interviews.

There was no interviewing in the usual sense of the word.
Instead a discussion leader, preferably a person with dress,
manner, and speech similar to the rest of the group, served
to create a favorable setting, help the discussion along when
this was needed, help to bring out pertinent points being
made by respondents, and introduce certain topics near the
end so that they would not be overlooked.   The object was a
natural, candid discussion and generally the less the leader
interrupted the better.   (See Appendix D, pages 125–129 for
a description of the "snowball" interview supplied to discussion leaders for the State Farm study.)

The leaders were given a list of topics to be covered, but
they were cautioned that this was to be used only as a discussion guide rather than as a questionnaire.   (See Appendix E, pages 130–132.)   They were told that it was not necessary or even desirable to take the points on the guide in order
as they appeared on the list, and that they probably would
not ask the questions on the guide directly.

Tapes of the interviews recorded not only what was said,
but captured the general feeling as was indicated by the
quality of expression, phrasing, and emphasis.   (See Appendix F, pages 133–139, for excerpts from interviews.)

In the State Farm study, eight group interviews were conducted among working class men, including farmers, the

[3] Perham C. Nahl, "The Snowball Interview — New Tool for Market Research," *Printers' Ink,* March 23, 1951, p. 35.

groups ranging from four to six men each. Fifty-two men participated in the interviews, each of which was held in a different area of the country.

THE PROJECTIVE DEVICES

In addition to the "snowball" interviews, 52 individual interviews were conducted with men from the same geographical areas to get data on the attitudes of auto owners toward auto insurance and auto insurance companies. Three projective devices were used for this purpose: incomplete sentences, narrative projection, and balloon tests. The questions, though focused upon specific areas related to auto insurance, were intentionally phrased to allow the respondent a good deal of latitude in terms of his interpretation and response.

The interviewer was instructed to read the incomplete sentence and have the respondent complete it with the first thing he thought of whether it was a word, a phrase, or a whole sentence. There were 20 sentences in all. The interviewer was cautioned against suggesting answers and was asked to write down the respondent's exact words because a slight difference in wording might be very important.

In using the narrative projection device, the interviewer described four imaginary situations, one at a time, asked the respondent to tell what he thought about each, and wrote down verbatim what was said. The interviewer was instructed to get as many comments on each situation as possible by probing and to follow up on each lead given by the respondent.

Seven pictures were used in the balloon test. In each, one person was saying something to another. The respondent was asked what he thought the second person might reply. One of the pictures used appears as Exhibit 1. Typical replies to the picture appear in Appendix G, pages 140–141.

One interview report, showing both the questions and one

Exhibit 1

A Balloon Test Used to Study Reactions to a Price Appeal

Here's an ad that says you can save as much as 40% on your auto insurance. Do you think we ought to look into it when ours expires next month?

person's responses to all 20 incomplete sentences and all four narrative projection questions and two of the seven balloon tests used, appears in Appendix H, pages 142–145.

The field work for both the "snowball" interview and the interviews employing the projective devices was handled by

Gould, Gleiss & Benn, Inc., of Chicago. The work was under the direction of Dr. Donald L. Kanter who also analyzed the data.

The Findings of the Psychological Study

The qualitative analysis of the responses obtained in the "snowball" interviews and in the interviews where projective techniques were used resulted in a 34-page report dealing with these general topics:

— The psychological meaning of automobile insurance
— The characteristics of a "good" automobile insurance company
— Attitudes toward the different kinds of automobile insurance
— Things to consider in buying insurance
— The function of the agent; how he should act and talk

While much of the feeling and meaning of a report such as this is lost in condensation, a digest of some of the findings is presented in Appendix I, pages 146–152.

Presentation of Findings

After the research had been completed in November 1954, Mr. Ohle, Dr. Britt, and Dr. Twedt of the advertising agency went over the findings in detail in an all-day session with Mr. Adlai Rust, President, and the other top executives who made up State Farm's executive council. The objective was to get well acquainted with the findings and to discuss their significance.

Near the end of this session Mr. Rust outlined some of his thoughts on what the company should do to retain its position of leadership. He mentioned three main points: (1) State Farm must be highly competitive pricewise with no sacrifice of standards of quality; (2) in rendering service, State Farm should be prompt and provide needed emotional

◆▶ *Traffic laws say:* **"Full Stop Stop Signs."** If you always stop, it can help you...

save up to 40% on your auto insurance!

Read why careful drivers get top-notch protection at rock-bottom rates with
STATE FARM MUTUAL

If you drive carefully, like the man in the picture (and his small friend on the sidewalk) ... you're already well on your way toward reducing the cost of your auto insurance.

Now, all that's left to do is contact your State Farm agent. He will tell you how we seek to insure *careful drivers only* ... how we save money on their accident-free driving ... how we pass this saving back to our members in the form of *rock-bottom rates.*

If you qualify, he will quote you rates that are *as much as 40 percent lower* than the cost of equivalent protection from other good companies.

More than 3 million car owners (more by far than any other company insures) already save on our "careful driver" insurance. They buy it on a convenient semi-annual payment plan. If they *do* have an accident, they get prompt, courteous "round the clock" service from State Farm's 7000 agents and 700 claim expediters.

Want more information? Call the agent listed under "State Farm Insurance" in your classified directory, or write: State Farm Mutual, Dept. G-9, Bloomington, Illinois.

Can you qualify?

State Farm aims to insure careful drivers only. Drivers who can be counted on to:

☐ **Make full stop at stop signs**
☐ **Heed crossing signals**
☐ **Obey speed laws**
☐ **Be extra careful on slick pavements**
☐ **Keep car in good shape**
☐ **Avoid passing on hills or curves**
☐ **Avoid mixing alcohol and gasoline**
☐ **Yield pedestrians the right of way**

STATE FARM MUTUAL

"the careful driver insurance company"

STATE FARM
Auto · Life · Fire
INSURANCE

FREE TO MEMBERS!
New State Farm insignia (like above) in bright red headlight-reflecting Scotchlite. Identifies you as "careful driver, soundly insured".. provides emergency reflection when parked or if taillight fails.

State Farm Insurance is written only by the
State Farm Mutual Automobile Insurance Co.
and its wholly owned affiliates:
State Farm Life Insurance Company
State Farm Fire and Casualty Company

Home office: Bloomington, Illinois. Field claim offices in 300 principal cities. 7,000 agents in 40 states, District of Columbia, and Canada

Hear "Jack Brickhouse Sports News" Saturdays and "Cecil Brown News Commentaries" Sundays over Mutual Stations. Check local radio listings.

See "Panorama Pacific" (CBS-TV) 7-9 A. M., Tuesdays and Thursdays on KNXT, KPIX and KFMB-TV

EXHIBIT 2. A Pre-Research Advertisement

Mr. E. M. Poirot, Golden City, Missouri, say

"Ownin
is like havin
when yo

After a recent auto accident, Mr. Poirot — who has been insured with State Farm for 26 years — also stated in an unsolicited letter to his State Farm agent:

"The check from State Farm meant more than the money involved. It meant I had insurance when I needed it. I came to the conclusion that when State Farm says protection, it means protection. And it looks like you leaned over backwards to give it to me."

...*and the cost is rock-bottom low!*

For example, Mr. Poirot carries Liability (50/100/5), MAX Medical Payments, Comprehensive and $25 Deductible Collision coverage on his 1954 Ford 2-door sedan.

At State Farm rates,
he pays each year **$69.14**

At ordinary rates,
he would pay each year $114.75

Naturally, insurance rates depend on several factors — such as the area in which you live. These figures refer to rates in effect in Golden City, Missouri, as of June 15, 1955, for car owners in Mr. Poirot's insurance rating classification.

88

EXHIBIT 3
State Farm Mutual Automobile Insurance Company

tate Farm auto insurance
friend at your side
eed a friend"

▶ **More than 3,400,000 Americans carry State Farm Mutual auto insurance.**
And for the same reasons Mr. Poirot does: fast, fair, friendly service when they have
an accident or a claim . . . low "careful driver rates" that save them money.

   ▶ **State Farm Mutual keeps its rates low by aiming to insure careful drivers only.**
By deliberately avoiding accident-prone drivers, State Farm holds accident costs to
a minimum. It then passes savings back in the form of low rates. Independently
calculated rates that save policyholders ten . . . twenty . . . even forty percent, compared to the cost of ordinary auto insurance.

▶ **Can you qualify?**
Not everyone can, of course. But if you use good judgment, common sense and
courtesy behind the wheel, it should be easy. For complete information, talk to any
State Farm agent this week. For the name of the agent nearest you, look in the
yellow classified pages of your local phone book under State Farm Insurance.

STATE FARM MUTUAL

"the careful driver insurance company"

State Farm Insurance is written only by the
State Farm Mutual Automobile Insurance Company
and its wholly owned affiliates:
State Farm Life Insurance Company
State Farm Fire and Casualty Company

Home Offices: Bloomington, Illinois
Field claim offices in 325 principal cities
7,000 agents in 41 states, District of Columbia, and Ontario, Canada

If your phone book does not list a State Farm
agent, write directly to Dept. E-5, State Farm
Mutual, Bloomington, Illinois.

89

A Post-Research Advertisement

Topnotch service..

---

rock-bottom rates

STATE FARM
Auto Life Fire
INSURANCE

Read how 3,400,00 with State Farm

Here are statements from typical members and the actual savings they enjoy with State Farm Mutual

Mr. Milton E. Nollau, St. Louis, Missouri

"Shortly after I joined State Farm Mutual, I had an accident while driving in a blizzard near Kansas City. I got in touch with a State Farm agent there who not only handled the case for me but made me feel I had a friend. I'm glad I switched to State Farm and hope to remain permanently."

Mr. Nollau carries Liability (15/30/5), MAX Medical Payments, Comprehensive, and 80% Collision coverage on his 1954 Oldsmobile 4-door sedan. He pays $136.90 a year with State Farm. At ordinary rates, he would have to pay $319.50 for the same coverage.

Miss Mildred Sullivan, Butte, Montana

"When I had my accident, your agent immediately responded to my call and gave me every courtesy. I now have more faith than ever in your company and will do all on my part to let other people know of its fairness."

Miss Sullivan carries Liability (10/20/5), MAX Medical Payments, Comprehensive, 80% Collision, and Emergency Road Service coverage on her 1951 Chevrolet 2-door sedan. At State Farm rates, she pays $95.50 a year. At ordinary rates, this coverage would cost $225.80 a year.

Reverend W. E. Opie, Fresno, California

"I appreciate the wonderful way your Fresno, California, people took care of me after my very serious accident. The agent and the adjuster were very solicitous of my welfare and went to no end of trouble to assist me in the minutest details. The handling of my case has certainly stirred me to a new height of enthusiasm regarding State Farm and the way it takes care of its policyholders."

Reverend Opie pays State Farm $105.48 a year for Liability (50/100/5), MAX Medical Payments, Comprehensive, $50 Deductible Collision, and Emergency Road Service coverage on his 1955 Pontiac 4-door sedan. At ordinary rates, he would pay $129.90 a year.

Mr. Bert Spencer, Minneapolis, Minnesota

"At the time of a serious accident, when a member of your family is injured, you have plenty to worry about. It is good to know that you have insurance with a company that is so reliable. After my recent claim with State Farm, I have peace of mind knowing that I am covered by a company whose agents give good service and do everything they say they will do when they sell you a policy."

Mr. Spencer carries Liability (25/50/5), MAX Medical Payments, Comprehensive, and $50 Deductible Collision on his 1954 Oldsmobile 4-door sedan. He pays $107.58 a year with State Farm. At ordinary rates, he would have to pay $230.44 for the same coverage.

EXHIBIT 4
State Farm Mutual Automobile Insurance Company

ar owners get <u>both</u>
careful driver insurance"!

The simple fact that State Farm Mutual insures more automobiles than any other company in the world proves one thing: *that U. S. car owners want the best in protection and service at minimum cost.* And that's exactly what they *get* with State Farm.

State Farm Mutual does not charge the same rates as other companies. State Farm calculates its own rates from the accident records of its *own* members—and not from industry figures compiled by rating bureaus.

State Farm's unique "careful drivers only" plan keeps rates low. In the long run, careful drivers have fewer accidents than reckless, irresponsible drivers. By deliberately seeking to insure careful drivers only, State Farm holds down accident costs. It then passes savings back to its members in the form of low rates. Rates that save policyholders ten . . . twenty . . . even forty percent, compared to the cost of ordinary auto insurance.

State Farm Mutual provides fast, fair, friendly claim service in case of accident. And this service is just a phone call away. There are now more than 7,500 State Farm agents

strategically located in the United States and Ontario, Canada, to come to your assistance day or night . . . wherever you live or travel. And agents are backed by 1,000 claim experts who work only for State Farm members. This is the largest full-time, salaried staff of adjusters in the automobile insurance business.

The record shows that State Farm claim offices pay 90% of routine collision and comprehensive claims within 48 hours of receipt of bills. Every claim is processed with the utmost speed. The objective: to pay *promptly* every dollar that's due —with a minimum of red tape and inconvenience.

Can <u>you</u> qualify for State Farm's "careful driver insurance"?

Not everyone can, of course. But if you use good judgment, common sense, and courtesy behind the wheel, it should be easy. For complete information, talk to any State Farm agent this week. For the name of the agent nearest you, look in the yellow classified pages of your phone book under "State Farm Insurance."

STATE FARM MUTUAL

"the careful driver insurance company"

State Farm Insurance is written only by the
State Farm Mutual Automobile Insurance Company
and its wholly owned affiliates:
State Farm Life Insurance Company
State Farm Fire and Casualty Company

Home Office: Bloomington, Illinois
Field claim offices in 325 principal cities,
7,500 agents in 40 states, District of Columbia, and Ontario, Canada.

Insurance (cont'd)
STATE FARM INSURANCE

Famous careful-driver auto insurance at rock-bottom rates. We insure more cars than any other company.

Fast, fair claim service. 7500 agents in U. S. and Canada. Also life and fire insurance; residence liability.

"FOR INFORMATION CA...

If your phone book does not list a State Farm agent, write directly to Dept. E-3, State Farm Mutual, Bloomington, Illinois.

Insuran...
Brown
Brown
Comis
Ernst
Fox F
Hartf
K

Another Post-Research Advertisement

Busy girl earns a "Coffee-break"

Fingers beat staccato on the keys. The phone interrupts. Then back to the typewriter. Check for spelling. Mark each "Air Mail—Special Delivery." Now it's finished, the boss signs and says, *"Time for coffee!"* She smiles. A cheerful cup of good, hot coffee! What a wonderful way to ease the strain of concentration. Coffee! Nothing else offers such a friendly lift. Coffee—it's always so much pleasure, and only pennies a cup. During *your* day, too, isn't it frequently "time for coffee"? Enjoy coffee often and make it right. Use 2 level tablespoons (or 1 Standard Coffee Measure) to every cup. Give yourself a "Coffee-break"! Think better, work better, feel better. PAN-AMERICAN COFFEE BUREAU, 120 Wall St., New York 5, N. Y.

Exhibit 1

Pan-American Coffee Bureau

A Pre-Research Advertisement

It's a good day with Coffee!

morning! Start the day with the -up aroma of good, hot coffee—then the coffee itself (*extra*-strong, way folks like it for breakfast).

Good neighbor. It's the friendly thing to do — having a mid-morning "Coffee-break" with your neighbor. (Your husband's probably having coffee at work.)

Good eating. Good coffee makes even the simplest lunch taste better. Coffee seems to go just right with *everything* — and every time, too.

feeling. What a relief to be off feet a few minutes during the mid-noon. Your "Coffee-break" perks p so pleasantly!

Good evening. Perfect finish to supper — *coffee* made the way the experts do: 1 Standard Coffee Measure to each 6 ounces of clear, cold water. Delicious!

Good idea! Treat guests to simple Caffè Cappuccino: add steaming milk to strong coffee (half and half). Dust cinnamon over the top. Superb!

©1956

There is nothing so satisfying as a cup of good coffee

PAN-AMERICAN COFFEE BUREAU, 120 Wall Street, New York 5, N. Y.

EXHIBIT 2. Pan-American Coffee Bureau: A Post-Research Advertisement

support to the client; (3) steps should be taken to make more people more aware of the company.

Two weeks later the same executives met in another all-day session at which the agency proposed an advertising program for 1955. The emphasis was to be on attracting new State Farm members, although the past objectives of conserving present membership and stimulating the agency force would continue to receive important attention.

The agency proposed that emphasis continue to be placed on the low cost of State Farm insurance because price stood out in the research findings as the most important reason for changing companies. Continuation of the "careful driver insurance company" theme was also recommended, research having shown this to be in the insured's mind an easily understood reason for low cost.

The agency proposal then dealt with points that research had indicated were in need of additional emphasis. The first of these was to make the public aware of the size and stature of the company. The studies had shown that car owners want a large, well-known company and that too many of them were unaware of State Farm's true position in the industry. The second point dealt with emphasizing and documenting prompt, expert, courteous service rendered by both the agent and the company. This was viewed as essential not only because of the interest in service but because this was the surest way to get people to look on State Farm insurance as a "good buy" and not as "cheap insurance."

Toward the above objectives, the agency recommended the following for State Farm's print advertising in 1955:

1. Long copy. Long enough to cover all points and leave no important questions unanswered.
2. Big space. Big enough to hold the copy and to make the message look important.
3. Factual presentation in black and white editorial format which the agency had found effective for copy dealing

with new concepts. The State Farm story was essentially "news" to many car owners.

4. Case histories and testimonials to prove the claims and make the advertising believable. State Farm should tell about policyholders who had realized significant savings and experienced good service.
5. Illustrate the State Farm trade-mark heading from the classified phone book as part of the signature to clarify how prospects could get in touch with a State Farm agent.
6. Aim the advertising primarily at adult men.

The agency outlined the following strategy which would guide selection of media: (1) Retain present business which meant holding current leadership in small town, rural, and farm areas in which half of State Farm's policyholders were located. (2) Improve the company's position in urban markets where 60% of all car owners reside. (3) Concentrate on the mass market, especially the 25- to 50-year-old age group and the $3,000 to $7,000 income group. (4) Make the car-owning public much more aware of State Farm. The major market survey showed that 40% of all car owners in State Farm's operating territory had never heard of State Farm. (5) Devote special attention to those areas where State Farm's share of the market was below the company's average.

State Farm's first major use of television was recommended. "Red Barber's Corner," a program of late sports news, was to be carried by 51 stations for 39 weeks. The audience composition for this show had averaged 58% men, 35% women, 7% children.

Life and *Look* magazines were to be used because they had large audiences and were considered to be well suited for the news-type sales message. The campaign would start with a five-page section to run in *Life* on January 10. A series of double-page spreads running at three-week intervals, alternately in *Life* and *Look*, would follow in the remainder of the year.

Use of the following rural, farm, and small-town magazines would be continued: *Farm Journal, Successful Farming, Town Journal,* and *Progressive Farmer.* Special newspaper advertising was recommended for the West Coast in order to get greater coverage and impact there.

The agency recommended an advertising budget of $1,750,000 to carry out the proposed program, this representing an increase of about $750,000 over 1954.

The agency's proposal was accepted by the client.

MR. MORRILL'S SUMMARY OF FINDINGS

In talking with the writer of this case in June 1955, Mr. Morrill summarized what he considered to be the principal findings from the research. He listed the following points from the consumer survey:

1. Public awareness of State Farm was not as great as we thought it was. More people knew of Allstate than of State Farm even though State Farm was the larger.
2. Price appeared to be an important reason for buying State Farm, but many people didn't know how low cost State Farm was. The company had not put this story across as well as it could have.
3. Of the people who dropped out as members of State Farm, many did so simply because they didn't have the money when the premium was due. State Farm billed semi-annually, but extended no credit, offered no grace period. Policies lapsed ten days after the premium was due unless the agent himself helped finance his client.
4. It's the man who makes the buying decision on automobile insurance.

Mr. Morrill named the following main points gained from the psychological study:

1. The study showed that the company must sell more than price. We might have missed this point if it were not for the psychological study.

2. The study told us something of the emotional state of persons when they are filing claims, pointing up the need for the company to be "on their side." Persons who have had an accident are emotionally upset and the insurance agent is about the only person many of them can turn to.

3. In dealing with agent and claim adjusters, many people have about their only contact with "big business" and and they act like *they* think big business people act or should act. This explains much of the "strange" behavior which we have observed in these relationships.

4. People are quick to believe unfavorable things about an insurance company.

Mr. Morrill went on to mention the principal things the company had done as an outgrowth of the research:

1. We doubled the advertising budget (going from $1,000,-000 in 1954 to $2,000,000 in 1955).

2. We ran a five-page ad in *Life* as the starter in the new advertising campaign. The response was terrific. I think we got more good from that ad than from any one thing we had ever done promotionally. We received many favorable comments. The ad had a very beneficial effect within the company as well as with people generally.

3. We bought the national TV show, "Red Barber's Corner." The show was chosen primarily to reach men. On the basis of the research, we were able to talk more understandably to persons who in the past had urged more advertisting to women.

4. With the 1955 campaign, we began presenting the low cost story directly. Before, we had soft-pedaled it because some believed that connotations of cheapness might have a harmful effect.

5. We are selling more than price — service "on your side," etc. We are using testimonials to do this. (See Exhibits 3 and 4.)

6. We are trying to add to the understanding of our agents and claims people on how to handle clients filing claims.

We are trying to help them see that they should expect emotional upset, understand it, and act accordingly.

7. We have undertaken further investigation of the reasons why some people drop out of State Farm.

8. We are now experimenting with a payment plan. This had not been necessary in the low premium areas, but we are moving into New Jersey and New York where premiums are relatively high.

9. A number of our claims grow out of accidents involving two State Farm policyholders as is inevitable when you insure one out of 11 cars in your operating area. We are now working on ways to help people understand how these claims are handled to help keep both parties to the accident happy even though the accident is always the fault of "the other guy."

The "selling more than price" to which Mr. Morrill referred represented a major change in advertising approach. The earlier ads talked in terms of savings with medium emphasis. The ad reproduced as Exhibit 2 is an example. Its headlines:

Traffic laws say: "Full stop at stop signs." If *you* always stop, it can help you . . . save up to 40% on your auto insurance! Read why careful drivers get top-notch protection at rock-bottom rates with State Farm Mutual.

The new approach stressed low rates more directly but at the same time gave major emphasis to providing assurances about the company's dependability and service. Emotional support figured prominently in this as can be seen in the following headline which was based on a testimonial of a man whose picture was featured in the the ad (See Exhibit 3):

"Owning State Farm auto insurance is like having a friend at your side when you need a friend."

This ad also gave attention to the "rock-bottom cost" by comparing State Farm's rates with the "ordinary rates" which would be applicable to the man featured in the testimonial.

The new approach also is illustrated by the advertisement reproduced as Exhibit 4. Its main headline follows:

> Topnotch service . . .
> _____
> rock-bottom rates!
> Read how 3,400,000 car owners get *both* with State Farm's "careful driver insurance"!

The ad emphasized "It's this 'personal touch' that's helped make State Farm service so famous. In case of accident, just phone the nearest State Farm agent. He goes to bat for you. . . ."

Testimonial statements from four State Farm members emphasized friendly service. A picture of each of the people quoted appeared along with information of their insurance coverage, State Farm rates, and what they would have had to pay at "ordinary rates."

REACTION OF MR. RUST, THE PRESIDENT

Mr. Rust's first response to a question as to what he considered to be the principal values obtained from the research was in terms of findings from the psychological study. He spoke particularly of the part which highlighted the importance of the agents and claim men having what he called "a good bedside manner" when handling clients emotionally upset after having had an accident.

Mr. Rust had quoted from the studies at meetings of State Farm executives, agents, and claim adjusters. He had held a number of meetings with his executives at which the research findings were discussed and plans were made for transmitting principal findings to men in the field through speeches and written material.

An example of how the findings were used in the field was a speech entitled "On Your Side" given by Mr. Morrill before meetings of State Farm agents. The theme of the speech was that the company wanted people to see in it the image of a good company and a good agent; that good public relations depended most of all on what the men and women who represented the company did in their daily contacts with people. The theme was developed by quoting extensively from the psychological study report on what insurance meant to people, what they wanted from their insurance company and agent, the functions of the agent, how the agent should act and why. (Excerpts from Mr. Morrill's speech appear in Appendix J, pages 153–155.)

A lecture on the research was made a part of the training course for field claim adjusters. Findings were made a part of the basic instructional material for both claim adjusters and agents and were used to guide the writing of letters and the preparation of other printed materials that went from the company to the policyholder. The company regarded the application of the findings as a long-term educational process and was at work on additional projects designed to get the findings into the hands of its employees and agents in an effective way.

In reply to a question relative to possible limitations of the research, Mr. Rust said: "We've been so busy concentrating on the findings of value that we haven't undertaken any thorough study of the limitations."

Mr. Morrill's Reactions to the Research

"To be frank with you," Mr. Morrill said, "I was lukewarm about doing the psychological study. Some of the psychological stuff — balloon tests, narrative projections, etc. — seemed like nonsense to me. The idea of group interviews seemed like a difficult one to sell. I didn't know if I could buy the results of a psychological study. If I was not enthusiastic, I wouldn't be able to sell it to anyone else.

"The agency said it would pay for the psychological study, so we went ahead with it on that basis. We paid for the major market survey.

"Now, I'm very much sold on the psychological study. We got more practical value out of it than out of the fact-finding study. I'll want to do more of this kind of thing. The psychological study had a broader impact on our business as a whole. Many things in the fact-finding study were interesting but prompted you to ask: 'So what?' The findings of the psychological study were an extension and broadening of our thinking. They seemed so right in terms of what we knew about our business.

"In regard to handling claims, for example, we learned from the psychological study what a fellow is thinking about when he has a claim and what he is like inside. We didn't know these things before. We learned what attitudes meant in terms of relationships between people — and this was an eye-opener."

STATE FARM AUTOMOBILE INSURANCE COMPANY

Commentary

The Market Survey

Findings

In noting the nature and importance of the market survey, we shall start with the findings which received special mention for their usefulness by Mr. Morrill. They included the discovery that State Farm and its low rates were not nearly as well known as company executives had assumed that they were. Inasmuch as a major question facing the executives was how much consumer advertising should be undertaken, this finding was of special importance. To resolve differences of opinion within the company as to whom the advertising should be directed, Mr. Morrill pointed to the survey's evidence that it was the man of the family who makes the automobile insurance buying decision. He also cited the finding that half of the State Farm members who let their insurance lapse said they did so because they did not have the money at the time the premium was due. This point raised a question as to whether the company should institute a special payment plan.

We note that the above findings which were regarded as particularly helpful related to questions executives knew they wanted to ask. In addition, the results represented direct checks on key assumptions underlying the company's promotional planning and, therefore, had rather clear implications. The disclosure that 40% of the people interviewed had not heard of the company, for example, figured prominently in the decision to double the advertising budget. The expression of findings in terms of how many people responded in certain ways was useful for indicating the magnitude of problems. All dealt with relatively tangible factors which also was true of the striking results to the effect that most people did not shop around to get prices from different companies, that they contacted the agent rather than vice versa, that they first heard about their present company through friends, and that they thought the most important reason for taking out automobile insurance was to cover responsibility for damage to the other fellow.

We note that among the survey findings cited by Mr. Morrill there was none that dealt directly or extensively with such questions as why people bought insurance in the first place and what they wanted from an insurance company. The survey included questions aimed at these targets, but the latter are more complex matters with which less progress was made by the approach employed.

The Research Approach

The survey's results were obtained by asking people directly for what was wanted. The respondent's task was to supply brief answers of his own to a number of very specific questions or choose among or rank items prepared by someone else. The value of the survey results, then, depended upon whether the researchers knew what things were important to ask about, and whether accurate information could be obtained by the means described.

The results cited by Mr. Morrill represent information which probably can be obtained reasonably accurately and readily by asking direct questions. For example, here are some of the questions upon which they were based:

> Here is a list of eight insurance companies. Which ones have you ever heard of?
> Of the eight companies, which company would you say probably offers insurance at the lowest cost?
> Which member of the family would you say knows most about choosing automobile insurance?
> When you take out automobile insurance, do you usually discuss it with your wife (or husband)?

Most people probably would be able to respond to these questions and would have no reason to conceal or mislead in so doing. This comment is applicable also to the variety of questions relating to car ownership and driving, insurance carried, claim experience, and the like. There may be some question as to the adequacy of the question, "Why did you drop the insurance?", asked of people who had carried automobile insurance in the past 12 months but who did not carry it at the time of the interview. More than half of them replied that they didn't have the money when the premium was due. This may be too easy and simple an answer here, and more intensive interviewing might reveal additional information of importance. The company planned further research into this matter.

We already have referred to limitations of this survey for obtaining an understanding of why people buy insurance or why they select certain companies. Let us consider this matter further by looking at a few of the questions used, starting with this one: "What reasons were most important to you in choosing the company you did?" It produced the following results (figures are percentages of total respondents who gave the indicated response) :

24% — Save money, cheaper
18% — Good company, reputable, reliable, good service
17% — Agent is a friend, relative, neighbor
17% — Heard about company through friends, relatives
12% — Better coverage, different types
12% — No reason given
9% — Settle claims promptly, fairly (No other reason was mentioned by more than 2% of the respondents.)

There are several observations we can make. Answers to open questions can be a valuable source of ideas for further research and there appears to be at least one such clue here. We refer to the strong showing of interpersonal influences which suggests the possibility that many people rely heavily on the word of others in buying insurance and do not concern themselves very much with technical details.

One good idea, of course, can make the question (indeed, the whole survey) very much worth while. It is probable, however, that the researchers had in mind an additional objective, namely, that of identifying the important factors which influence the selection of a company and measuring their importance. While the question furnishes evidence in this direction, it also has several major limitations. The value of the answers listed in the table is impaired by a lack of clarity. We do not know just what was meant by such terms as "good service," "good company," and "better coverage." Another possible limitation has to do with the wording of the question. While the respondent presumably was free to answer whatever he wanted, the emphasis placed on "what reasons were most important" would seem to imply that he arrived (or should have arrived) at his decision through a conscious reasoning process. Many of the responses were in this vein. There is the possibility, then, that the factors named, even though they may be of importance, are what people think they are supposed to be concerned about when buying insurance and that they do not represent the whole story. Their very conventionality creates suspicion.

Another reason why the figures in the table should not be taken too seriously is their questionable comparability. Inasmuch as some of the responses were in terms of how people first heard of their companies while others dealt with features of the service, there may have been different interpretations as to the intent of the question. The fact that some people chose to interpret it one way and some another may in itself be significant. It would be dangerous, however, to conclude that low rates are the most important factor in the choice of an insurance company just because saving money was mentioned by more people than any other factor.

Another question used to learn of factors influencing the choice of an insurance company asked people to rank in order of importance to them seven features named by the interviewer. The percentage ranking each of the features first was as follows:

23% — Quick settlement of claims
18% — Fair treatment by company
17% — Well known company
15% — Low cost of insurance
13% — Good service from local agent
 7% — Claim adjusters in all parts of the U.S.
 2% — Installment plan for payments

Presumably, State Farm intends to do the best it can in offering all the things named, but would like to know what to emphasize in its advertising. Perhaps the main point of interest here is that no one of the seven items ran away with the first place votes. Instead, five came in for considerable attention. Whether the figures mean much more than this is debatable because of the assumptions underlying this type of question. One is that people will be able to rank the factors in a meaningful way. If the respondent thinks in terms of a pattern of interrelated factors, all of which have to be present, or if he did not think much at all, the forced ranking will distort the true picture. Certainly there is doubt as to whether items like "low cost" can be meaningfully considered in the abstract. There also is a question as to whether "fair treatment by company," "well-known company," "good service from local agent," etc., mean something specific enough to be useful for either the respondent or the person who will have to interpret the results. If the purpose was to determine the main influences in the selection of a company, the most important assumption made was that the significant factors appeared as items on the list in the first place.

The influence of price was a matter of primary interest to company executives, and a number of survey questions had some bearing on this question. However, they left a mixed picture for anyone intent upon establishing its relative importance. We already have mentioned some of the relevant answers. When people were asked what reasons were most important in their choice of a company, saving money was mentioned by more respondents (24% of the total) than was any other factor. On the other hand, when they were asked to rank seven factors about insurance companies in order of importance to them, only 15% ranked low cost first and this answer came in fourth on the basis of first place votes. Half of the people who let their State Farm insurance lapse said they did so because they didn't have the money at the time. About half of the respondents believed that there was at least a small difference in rates charged by different companies, and 73% of this group believed that they had low cost insurance. Another half of the respondents either believed rates charged by the different companies were about the same or said they did not know. Eighty-two per cent of all respondents said they did not shop around to get prices from different companies. When asked for main sales points made to them by their agent, only 14% of the people mentioned cost. Thirty per cent said that no sales talk was necessary because they either trusted the agent or the person who recommended the company concerned.

The above responses may be confusing to an executive trying to decide how much emphasis should be placed on a price appeal, but they at least should serve to raise questions in the minds of those inclined to hold extreme opinions on the matter. While they can be regarded as useful evidence, they clearly leave a difficult task for the interpreter as do the tables of figures discussed earlier. Clarification would seem to depend on somehow developing a more complete understanding of just what insurance means to people, and, therefore, what is important to them when they buy it.

We have noted that the direct question approach employed in this survey was most helpful for obtaining answers to specific questions which executives knew they wanted to ask and which sought answers people would be both willing and able to give. They were less helpful for learning why people buy insurance and why they select certain companies. Our comments on the several questions no doubt appear overcritical. After all, no one question can be expected to do everything, especially in a difficult research area. Our purpose here, however, was to point to limitations which have led to other approaches, some of which were included in the psychological study to be discussed next.

THE PSYCHOLOGICAL STUDY

Findings

State Farm executives were particularly impressed with the psychological study as a contribution to their thinking.

We shall attempt to explain this reaction by noting some of the characteristics of the study and how it contrasts with the market survey.

The psychological study focused on the meanings of insurance to people and the nature of their relationships with insurance company representatives. These, of course, are matters of major importance. Assumptions about them, whether explicit or implicit, underlie basic policies. New insight into them therefore can have significant consequences as is seen in connection with the findings mentioned by Mr. Morrill. The latter had to do with what the company should say in order to attract new clients as well as retain old ones, and what agents and claim adjusters might do to increase client satisfaction.

On the basis of findings of the psychological study, a new advertising approach was developed and put to work in a $2 million campaign. It represented a major departure from the rather mild copy of the past on savings. Low rates were featured more directly along with giving prospective customers strong assurances about the company and its service, including the element of emotional support. The training programs for agents and claim adjusters were modified to include consideration of human relations aspects of dealings with clients. The potential reward here would seem to be great because of the number and frequency of client contacts (State Farm handled a million applications and settled a million claims annually) , and because these experiences are the basis of personal information, passed along by word-of-mouth, which was found to be of such great importance in the building of an insurance company's reputation.

Several reasons help explain why the psychological study was able to contribute as much as it did to understanding of basic matters. Perhaps the most important was the detailed attention it gave to emotional aspects which often have been overlooked or neglected by both business executives and marketing researchers. Early explorations into this area, then, are likely to be fruitful. The researchers believed that insurance, by its very nature, had deep psychological meanings for most people, and they proceeded to find out more about them. The study was very much concerned with how people felt about insurance, insurance companies, and agents and employed means of learning what these feelings were from the people themselves.

The final report was an attempt to describe a reasonably integrated and complete picture of the meanings of insurance. This meant that it was able not only to present conclusions, but, to a large extent, explain why they were so. The explanation was in the over-all picture of insurance which included many factors in such a way that their relationship, if any, could be seen. There was a unifying core, namely, the essential nature of insurance itself.

To illustrate the above point, let us consider one of the main conclusions: that the company must sell more than price. A few of the many things which supported this conclusion will be cited here for purposes of illustration. There was the point that while people are interested in cost, they first of all are buying a guarantee which they find difficult to evaluate. Hence, they want assurance that a company can be depended upon to provide both the protection against financial loss and the emotional support they seek. The latter has to do with the feeling by the insured person that he is not alone in facing uncertainties, but that someone will be on his side in the event of trouble. Several reasons were given as to why people find it difficult to evaluate the promises an insurance policy represents. They feel that they cannot really understand insurance and its complex language. In addition, they tend to be suspicious because of stories they have heard about companies not paying off because of unsuspected technicalities. Hence, the need for assurance is especially great. The study showed that price is used to some extent as a gauge of quality, and that cheap insurance is suspect. Exclusive use of a price appeal, then, might be ineffective. In seeking assurances, people ask others about their experiences because they believe that only experience will really reveal whether a company will keep its promises. This helps to explain why word-of-mouth was found to be such an important medium of information. Factors already mentioned also help to explain why the study found that the major criteria for selecting an automobile insurance company were: (1) large size, and (2) a well-known, favorable reputation among one's friends.

We note that these findings were not produced by the market survey. While the latter contained clues as to some of the points developed in the psychological study, the meanings of them were far from clear. Mr. Morrill commented that the conclusion that the company must sell more than just price might have been missed had it not been for the psychological study. In the latter, this point could hardly have been missed because the research started out to develop a picture of all the important meanings of insurance. In some of the market survey questions, the goal seemed to be to find "the" most important factor so that it could be used in advertising rather than others. The thinking was not in terms of the meanings of insurance or the possibility of a pattern of interrelated factors. This "either-or" type of thinking has been common in marketing, reflecting an assumption that there is only one right button to push for hitting the sales jackpot. The results of the psychological study on automobile insurance seem to challenge this idea.

As the above remarks have indicated, the psychological study provided more specific explanations than did the market survey. For example, it included sections on what people meant by "the good automobile insurance company" and "good service," and what the functions of the agent were and how he should act. While these descriptions confirmed many of the beliefs of executives, they also introduced new ideas, particularly in the psychological realm. A striking example was the point that people who turn to their insurance agents after an accident often are emotionally upset. Their need for emotional support as well as other assistance and the implications of this for the agent had not received detailed attention in the past.

Before leaving the psychological study, we should note that the findings were presented in descriptive terms. The lack of tables of figures such as characterized the market survey represented an assumption that most people share many of the same feelings about uncertainty, the insurance they buy to protect themselves in the face of uncertainty, and what they want from agents and claim adjusters. Indeed, these were the conclusions of the psychologist who interpreted the interview data. For the purpose of identifying and understanding the more important meanings of insurance, measurements aside from the qualitative judgments of the interpreter would seem to offer little of practical value. Attempts at applying these findings, however, might well give rise to more specific questions where more precise measurement would be helpful. Copy testing of alternative advertisements is an example.

Research Approach

We have noted the importance and the nature of the psychological study. An important observation is that, to a large extent, it dealt with factors which had not been identified as important ones for investigation by company executives before the research began. In other words, new considerations entered the picture via research and they were developed in some detail. We now shall turn our attention to how these results came about.

The research approach featured two important elements. First, it employed the services of a psychologist trained to think in terms of meanings and relationships. It was natural, then, that these matters received attention. Second, certain techniques were used which were regarded as especially appropriate for getting ideas from people and learning how they felt about insurance and related matters.

In the market survey, people were asked direct questions about what the researchers thought were important factors. In the psychological study, the researchers thought it useful to assume that they did not know what was important to people about insurance. To find out, they decided to listen to small groups of people discuss the subject in a natural, informal way free from preconceptions of outsiders. While certain assumptions about useful topical areas were made in the preparation of the discussion guide, the emphasis was on letting both the topics and the development of them come from the respondents themselves.

This approach assumes that people can tell you a lot under favorable conditions and that the conditions of the group interview are favorable. It was believed that people will be both willing and able to talk freely and honestly in a group setting; that the effect of the participants on one another will be a beneficial one. It is important that the interviewer be skillful so that he does not inadvertently color the proceedings as he gets others to express themselves.

The interviews were recorded and later interpreted by the psychologist who inferred meanings from what was said, the way in which it was said, and what was omitted. The analysis of the data was qualitative. There was no counting of literal responses. Instead, the emphasis was on discerning meanings. The psychologist, then, was a most important part of the effort because the findings were determined to a large extent by what he was able to make out of the interview data.

In addition to the group interview, the psychological study featured the adaptation of several projective techniques to the task of learning about attitudes and feelings about automobile insurance. They were relatively unstructured so that the respondent would be on his own to a large extent in responding, and they represented an indirect approach in that their specific purpose was not apparent.

These characteristics can be seen in the incomplete sentence: "Mutual auto insurance companies. . . ." It attempts to find out whether people distinguish mutual companies from others, and, if so, something about the nature of this distinction. The sentence does not indicate that the researcher is interested in any particular aspect of the topic, nor does it imply that the respondent should have knowledge or opinions. It is up to him to determine what, if anything, he says. In so doing, he presumably will talk of what is significant to him and reveal his attitudes.

Let us take another example, the narrative: "A friend of yours has just bought his car. He asks you what he should do about getting insurance. What would you tell him?" Here, again, the question avoids putting words in the respondent's mouth and implying that he should have a reasoned-out approach to the subject. In this respect, it contrasts with two of the survey questions mentioned earlier: the one which asked what reasons were most important in the choice of a company, and the question asking for a ranking of seven factors of presumed importance about insurance companies. The narrative question seeks a natural response with the respondent more at ease than he might be under direct questioning.

Let us consider one more example, the balloon test which shows a woman telling her husband: "Here's an ad that says you can save as much as 40% on your auto insurance. Do you think we ought to look into it when ours expires next month?" The respondent was asked what the man might reply. In so doing, he presumably would give his own reactions more accurately than if he were asked for them directly. One object was to learn about the importance of price by confronting the respondent with a specific situation in which price played a part. It is of interest to note that the responses showed considerable skepticism and reluctance to investigating the advertised savings, indicating limitations of a straight price appeal.

The projective devices were not unusually demanding of the interviewer. His job was to present the projective questions and record responses verbatim.

In Summary

The market survey was most helpful when it produced answers to specific questions identified in advance as important by company executives and when there was reason to believe that people would be both willing and able to give accurate information in the interview situation. For example, it was more effective when it sought to measure how many people had heard of State Farm than when it tried to identify or determine the importance of factors influencing the selection of an insurance company. The survey can be characterized as dealing with the more tangible and rational considerations relative to automobile insurance. The selection of a company was seen by the researchers as a matter-of-fact affair in which practical criteria such as cost, coverage, speed of claim service, and the like played a decisive role. Implicitly, the meaning of insurance to people was defined in these terms.

Other meanings were an important feature of the psychological study. This came about because such basic matters as the meaning of insurance and the nature of client-company relationships were investigated for their emotional as well as more rational qualities. Indirect techniques were used to find out from the people themselves what was important to them and to learn of feelings and attitudes which are not consciously recognized by those who hold them. The final report was an attempt to present a reasonably complete picture of the meanings of insurance, the functions of the agent, what people regarded as "good service," "a good company," and the like. The result was something which company executives felt increased their understanding of the nature of their business.

Some Administrative Aspects

A notable feature of this case is that the research findings became an important part of the thinking of the top executives and that significant action followed on several fronts. This is uncommon enough in marketing research to merit our interest in how it came about. We note that it happened in a company which had no market research department.

The willingness of top executives to re-examine their thinking on which company policies were based was essential. Without this, the research could not have resulted in "an extension and broadening of our thinking" as was reported here. Several factors contributed to the willingness. The research was undertaken against the background of a tightening competitive situation and the company desired to retain its leadership. The research had the support of the president who actively participated in the meetings of top executives held for the purpose of thoroughly discussing the findings. A key top executive was instrumental in having the research undertaken in the first place and had the overall responsibility for it. This meant that research had a spokesman who was a regular member of the executive council, and that the wide gap which often separates research and those who make the decisions did not exist.

Another very important factor was the close liaison maintained between the advertising agency people connected with the research and company executives. Special care was taken with the presentation of findings: witness the scheduling of two full-day meetings for discussion of the results attended by all members of the company's executive council. The presentation itself was the responsibility of an account executive who was acquainted with the company's problems and the thinking of key personnel.

Another feature of the case represents a common problem in connection with using the social sciences in marketing. We refer to the initial resistance to the psychological study which was undertaken only because the advertising agency agreed to pay for it. When company executives first considered research, they quite naturally thought in terms of the familiar market survey. They wanted a "fact-finding study" as they called it. The term reflects the customary preference of the businessman for the tangible and the feeling that a psychological study is suspect because it does not deal with "facts." Once the research had been completed, however, the attitude changed. The executives were especially impressed with the psychological study as being the more helpful to them in their thinking. The change in thinking noted here is not uncommon among companies which have gone in for research of this kind, although the frank admission to such a change is distinctive.

Appendix A

AUTOMOBILE QUESTIONNAIRE

RESPONDENT IS

M   F

Head of
Household _____
Other _____

Census
Region _____
Area _____
City _____
State _____
Cluster # _____

Appendix A

Job. No. 4–879

Market Facts, Inc., 39 S. LaSalle St., Chicago, Ill.

AUTOMOBILE QUESTIONNAIRE

Date _____

Market Facts Representative _____

City and State _____   Cluster No. _____

How do you do? I'm with Market Facts, Inc., and we're doing a national survey about automobiles. May I ask you some questions please?

(ASK QUESTIONS 2–5 FOR EACH CAR OWNED — IF MORE THAN ONE CAR OWNED, USE THIS INTRODUCTION: Would you please give me some information about each of these cars? Let's take any one of them first . . .)

1a. Does anyone in this household happen to have an automobile?

Yes _____   No _____

1b. (IF "YES" TO 1a) How many cars do you have? (CIRCLE ONE)   1   2   3   4   or more

2a. What make and year is this car?

2b. Do you use this car mainly for business, for pleasure or both?

2c. About how many miles would you say the car is driven each year?

Qu. 2a		Qu. 2b			Qu. 2c	Qu. 2d	Qu. 2e		Qu. 3a		Qu. 3b	Qu. 4a through 4f				Qu. 4f	
		Use (X ONE)					Under 25		Insured		Cost of Ins. Per Year	Coverage			Insuring Company	How Long Carried	
Make	Year	Business	Pleasure	Both	No. Miles This Year	No. Driving Car	Y	N	No	Yes		Type of Coverage					
												Liab.	Coll.	Comp.			

2d. How many people drive this car?

2e. Are any of these people under 25 years old?

3a. Is this car insured? (IF "YES," ASK QU. 3–4; IF "NO," GO ON TO QU. 17)

3b. In round figures, about how much does insurance for this car cost you each year?

4a. Does this car have the kind of insurance that pays for damage to other people if you have an accident — that is, *liability* insurance?

4b. With what company is this insurance carried?

4c. Does it have the kind of insurance that pays for damage to your car if you have an accident — that is, *collision* insurance?

4d. With what company is this insurance carried?

4e. Does it have the kind of insurance that pays for loss from fire, and theft of your car — that is, comprehensive?

4f. With what company is this insurance carried?

4g. (FOR EACH COMPANY MENTIONED) How long have you been carrying insurance with this company? (SPECIFY YEARS OR MONTHS)

(FOR EACH CAR)

5a. Which member of the family drives this car the most?

5b. How old is (he) (she)?

5c. Which member of the family would you say knows the most about choosing auto insurance?

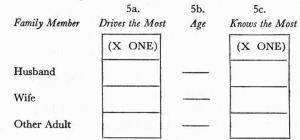

Family Member	5a. Drives the Most (X ONE)	5b. Age	5c. Knows the Most (X ONE)
Husband		——	
Wife		——	
Other Adult		——	

(QU. 6–16 — ASK ONLY IF CAR NOW INSURED)

6a. How did you first get in touch with your present company — that is, how did you first hear about it? _____

6b. The last time you bought auto insurance did you "shop around" — that is, did you get prices from different companies?   Yes _____   No _____

6c. (IF "YES") How did you go about finding the names of companies to contact? _____

6d. What reasons were most important to you in choosing the company you did? . . . Any others?   (PROBE) _____
_____

7a. With what company did you carry auto insurance before this one? _____

7b. (IF COMPANY NAMES) Why do you no longer carry your car insurance with this company? _____
_____

8a. Do you think there is a big difference in what different companies would charge you for the same kind and amount of auto insurance, or a small difference, or do you think that they all charge about the same?

Big difference _____   Small difference _____
About the same _____   DK _____

8b. (IF DIFFERENCE BETWEEN COMPANIES INDICATED) Do you think that the cost of *your present car insurance* is higher than most companies, lower than most other companies, or about the same?

Higher _____   Lower _____
About the same _____   DK _____

8c. (IF "HIGHER" OR "LOWER") Why do you say that? _____

9a. When you bought your present policy, did you contact the agent, or did he contact you?

He contacted me _____   I contacted him _____

9b. (IF RESPONDENT CONTACTED AGENT, ASK:) How did you first get his name? _____

10a. What were the main sales points the agent made about your present insurance? _____
_____

10b. Did the agent show you any printed material?

Yes _____ No _____ Don't remember _____

10c. (IF "YES") Do you remember what it was about? _____

11a. Did you get any kind of insurance company identification to put on your car?

Yes _____ No _____ Don't remember _____

11b. (IF "YES") What was it? _____

11c. Did you put it on your car? Yes _____ No _____

11d. Why? _____

12. How would you prefer to pay for your automobile insurance? Would you rather pay the whole amount *once a year,* pay half the amount *twice a year,* or make smaller payments *more frequently?*

Yearly payment _____ Twice a year _____

More frequent payments _____

13a. Are you satisfied with the evidence of auto insurance coverage that you now get from the company — such as the policy itself, a file card for your wallet, and so forth?

Yes _____ No _____

13b. (IF "NO") Why not? _____

14a. Have you ever had any occasion to use the insurance you carry with your present company — that is, have you ever had any claims with this company?

Yes _____ No _____

14b. (IF "YES") About how many times would you say you've dealt with this company on a claim? (CIRCLE ONE)

None 1 2 3 4 5 6 7 8 or more

14c. In general, how well satisfied are you with the way (PRESENT COMPANY) handled your claims? Would you say you were *very well satisfied, fairly well satisfied,* or *not at all satisfied?*

Very well _____ Fairly well _____ Not at all _____

14d. (IF "NOT AT ALL") Why? _____

15a. Is there anything you would like to see changed in your present auto insurance company?

Yes _____ No _____

15b. (IF "YES") What would you like to see changed? _____

16a. What other types of insurance besides auto insurance does
   your present company sell?   (x ALL MENTIONS)
   _____ Life   _____ Health and Accident
   _____ Fire   _____ Liability
   _____ Other (EXPLAIN) _____

16b. When you take out auto insurance do you usually discuss it
   with your wife (or husband)?
              Yes _____   No _____   Does not apply _____

(ASK OF ALL RESPONDENTS)

17a. What do you think is the principal difference between a
   mutual insurance company and other kinds of insurance
   companies? _____

   _____

17b. In general, would you prefer to insure your car with a *mutual* insurance company or a *stock* insurance company?
              Mutual __   Stock _____   No difference _____
              Don't understand the difference _____

17c. (IF ANY PREFERENCE IS EXPRESSED) Why do you say this?_____

   _____

18. People give different reasons for taking out auto insurance.
   Which one of these do you think is *most* important to most
   people? Which one of these do you think is *least* important
   to most people?

	Most Important (X ONE)	Least Important (X ONE)
To cover yourself against damage to your car		
To cover your responsibility for damage to the other fellow		
Because it is required by law		
Other (explain)		

19a. Do you think there should be a law requiring anyone who
   drives to have some kind of auto insurance that protects the
   other fellow?
              Yes _____   No _____   No Opinion _____

19b. Does (YOUR STATE) have any special law that makes drivers carry auto insurance?

        Yes _____   No _____   Don't Know _____

19c. (IF "YES") Briefly, what are its provisions? _____

_____

_____

19d. Would you say that the law that (YOUR STATE) has is a good law or a poor law?

     Good law _____   Poor law _____   No Opinion _____

20. Here are some of the things about auto insurance companies that some people feel are important. (SHOW SET OF YELLOW CARDS.) Now can you tell me which one of these is *most important to you personally?* (RECORD "1" BELOW AND ASK) And of these left, which one is the most important? (RECORD "2" AND PROCEED UNTIL ALL CARDS HAVE BEEN RANKED)

_____ Quick settling of claims

_____ Low cost of insurance

_____ Good service from local agent

_____ Well known company

_____ Claim adjusters in all parts of the United States

_____ Fair treatment by company

_____ Installment plan for payment

Other (explain) _____

21. Besides your present company, what auto insurance companies can you think of offhand? . . . Any others? _____

_____

_____

22a. Of all the auto insurance companies you have ever heard of, and regardless of cost, which one do you think gives the *best service in settling claims quickly and fairly?* _____

_____

22b. Why do you happen to think so? _____

_____

23a. Of all the auto insurance companies you have ever heard of, which one do you think gives the *poorest service in settling claims quickly and fairly?* _____

_____

23b. Why do you happen to think so? _____

_____

24a. Here is a list of eight insurance companies (SHOW SIDE 1 OF GREEN CARD). Which ones have you ever heard of before? (CHECK ALL MENTIONS)

24b. Have you ever bought insurance from any of these companies? (CHECK ALL MENTIONS)

24c. (FOR EACH COMPANY BOUGHT FROM PREVIOUSLY, BUT NOT NOW CARRIED) Why do you no longer carry (EACH COMPANY) insurance on your car? (FOR EACH COMPANY HEARD OF BEFORE)

24d. What do you think of this company? (INTERVIEWER RATE RESPONDENT'S ATTITUDE) Why?

24e. Does (EACH COMPANY HEARD OF) sell other kinds of insurance besides auto insurance? What other kinds?

24f. One of these companies sells more auto insurance than any other company in the world. Which company would you guess that is?

25a. Of the eight auto insurance companies, which company would you say probably offers insurance at the lowest cost?

	24a.	24b.	24c.	24d.						24f.	24e.	25a.
				Attitude						Sells more	What Other Kinds	Lowest Cost
Company	Heard of	Bought from	Why not carried now?	Poor	Fair	Good	DK		Why?	(X ONE)	(WRITE IN)	(X ONE)
Allstate												
State Farm Mutual												
Travelers												
Liberty Mutual												
Hartford Accident												
Farmers' Insurance Group												
U.S. Fidelity & Guaranty										No Difference Don't Know		
Farm Bureau Mutual												

25b. (IF RESPONDENT HAS INSURANCE, BUT NOT WITH COMPANY MEN-TIONED ABOVE IN 25a) How does it happen that you don't carry (LEAST EXPENSIVE COMPANY) insurance on your car?

_____

26a. Have you ever heard or seen advertising for any of these four companies? (SHOW SIDE 2 OF GREEN CARD)

26b. (FOR ADVERTISING HEARD OR SEEN) Where did you hear or see the advertising for (COMPANY NAMED)?

26c. What did the advertising say?

26d. How does that strike you?

26e. (FOR ALL FOUR COMPANIES) You probably don't know ex-actly, but just as a guess, what per cent of (EACH COMPANY'S) policyholders would you say are *farmers?*

CHECK ALL MENTIONS

Company	26a. Heard or Seen any Adver.	26b. Where								26c. What did advertising say?	26d. How does that strike you?	26e. % Farmers
		Direct Mail	Magazines	Newspapers	Radio	TV	Car Cards	Billboards	Other (Explain)			
Allstate												%
State Farm Mutual												%
Travelers												%
Liberty Mutual												%

27a. In the last four years have you ever driven your car without any insurance for any length of time — that is, as long as 6 months?

Yes _____ No _____

27b. (IF "YES") What was the main reason you did not carry in-surance at that time? . . . Any other reasons?

_____

_____

_____

28a. (ASK IF CAR INSURANCE NOT CARRIED NOW) Have you had any auto insurance in the past 12 months?

Yes _____   No _____

28b. (IF "YES") What company was it with? _____

28c. Why did you drop this insurance? _____

---

29. About how many years do you usually keep a car before trading it in?   (CIRCLE ONE)

1 year   2 years   3 years   4 years   5 years

More than 5 years

30a. When you first got the car you are now driving, did you sell or trade in another car at about the same time?

Yes _____   No _____

30b. (IF "YES") At that time, when you changed cars, did you also change insurance companies?

Yes _____   No _____   Don't Know _____

30c. (IF "YES") Can you tell me why? _____

_____

_____

_____

CLASSIFICATION DATA — ALL RESPONDENTS

31a. How many people are there in your family? _____

---

31. How old are they?

	AGES	
	Male	Female
Head of Household:	_____	_____
Children or other Adults	_____	_____
	_____	_____
	_____	_____
	_____	_____
	_____	_____

32. (X AGE OF RESPONDENT BELOW)

16–20 _____   21–24 _____   25–30 _____   31–40 _____

41–50 _____   51–60 _____   61 and over _____

33a. In what business, trade or profession does the head of the household work? _____

33b. What is his or her exact job? In other words, exactly what kind of work does he do? (GET OCCUPATION OF PRESENT LIVING HEAD OF HOUSEHOLD. IF RETIRED OR UNEMPLOYED, RECORD FORMER OR REGULAR OCCUPATION.)

34a. Can you receive television in this area?
                           Yes _____   No _____

34b. Do you have a television set?   Yes _____   No _____

34c. What is your name, please? _____

34d. What is the address? _____
     City_____   State_____

35a. Income class: (SHOW INCOME CARD AND ENTER LETTER HERE)

35b. How was this obtained?
         From respondent _____   By observation _____

36. This respondent is: White _____   Non-white _____
                           (BY OBSERVATION)

                                       A.M.

Date _____ Time Interview Began _____ P.M.

                                       A.M.

                Time Interview Ended _____ P.M.

Appendix B

INFORMATION CONTAINED IN TABLES
BASED ON SURVEY

The final report of findings of this study consisted of ninety-six tables giving the following information:

Car Ownership — by occupation, income, age of respondent, family age composition, TV ownership, census divisions, city size, and State Farm territories.

Insurance Coverage — by occupation, annual family income, age of respondent, family age composition, TV ownership, census divisions, city size, State Farm territories, miles driven per year, number and age of drivers, and value of car.

Why noninsured car owners dropped their previous company.

Types of insurance coverage carried.

Number of cars presently insured by each company.

Who (in the family) knows the most about automobile insurance and who drives the most?

How long has respondent been insured by present company?

The reported yearly cost of present insurance.

The most important reasons for choosing present company.

Number of respondents by company with which they had insurance immediately preceding present insurance company with breakdowns by preceding company by occupations, annual family income, age of respondent, family age composition, TV ownership, census divisions, city size, State Farm territories, use of car, and miles driven per year.

Reasons for dropping immediately preceding company.

Do people think there is a difference in insurance charges?

Reasons why people think there is a difference in insurance charges.

Do buyers shop for insurance?

How names of companies were found by those who shopped for automobile insurance.

Do buyers contact the agent first?

What do buyers remember about the agents?

Memory of printed materials shown by agents.

Did present company give emblem or other identification for car?

Do buyers discuss purchase of auto insurance with their spouses.

Preference for timing of payments.

Satisfaction with evidence of insurance and opinion of it.

Number of claims with present company.

Opinions of claims handling.

What policy holders would like to see changed.

Knowledge of other types of insurance sold.

Opinions on the main difference between "mutuals" and "stock" insurance companies.

Preference for types of insurance companies.

Relative importance of reasons for taking out automobile insurance.

Knowledge and opinions of safety responsibility laws by present company.

How people describe their state's safety responsibility law.

Number who think "there should be a law requiring anyone who drives to have some kind of automobile insurance that protects the other fellow." By states and by present insurance company.

Relative importance of features of automobile insurance.

What companies are believed to be best on claims service and why? By present company, total insured car owners, total car owners, and previous experience with company.

What companies are believed to be worst on claims service? By present company, total insured car owners, total car owners and previous experience with company.

Opinions about claims handling of eight leading automobile insurance companies.

Leading companies, believed lowest in cost. By present company, by previous experience with company.

Reasons for not carrying automobile insurance with company thought to be lowest cost.

Car owners' knowledge of and attitude toward State Farm and other insurance companies.

Reasons why former policyholders of eight leading companies no longer carry insurance with those companies.

Car owners' knowledge of State Farm and other insurance companies. By types of insurance respondents believe each company sells; by number believing which company sells the most automobile insurance; by number having heard or seen each company's advertising; by respondents' description of what each company's advertising said.

What percentage of each company's policyholders are thought to be farmers?

Number who have driven six months without insurance with reasons.

How long is the car usually kept before trading?

Is insurance traded when the car is traded?

Appendix C

SELECTED STUDY QUESTIONS WHICH DEALT WITH WHY AND HOW PEOPLE BUY AUTOMOBILE INSURANCE [1]

Question 6a: How did you first get in touch with your present company — that is, how did you hear about it?

- 46% — Through a friend, neighbor, or relative
- 23% — Know the agent (good friend, neighbor, relative)
- 8% — Don't remember
- 4% — Through car dealer or person who sold respondent the car
- 4% — Saw or heard company's advertising and called company
- 3% — Agent called on respondent
- 3% — Other agent recommended it
- 2% — Friend or relative worked for the company
- 2% — Carried other kinds of insurance with company
- 1% — Through bank or loan company where car was financed
- 7% — Other sources

Question 6b: The last time you bought auto insurance did you "shop around" — that is, did you get prices from different companies? (Yes or no)

- 18% — Did shop
- 82% — Did not shop

Question 6c: (If "yes" to previous question) How did you go about finding the names of companies to contact?

- 8% — Friends, relatives, neighbors
- 2% — Phone book
- 2% — Advertising
- 3% — Went to different insurance offices
- 2% — Other
- 3% — Don't remember

[1] All percentages are State Farm members. Comparable figures for all insured car owners and for other companies are not shown here.

Question 6d: What reasons were most important to you in choosing the company you did: . . . Any others?   (Probe)

24% — Save money, cheaper

18% — Good company, reputable, reliable, good service

17% — Agent is a friend, relative, neighbor, etc.

17% — Heard about company through friends, relatives

12% — Better coverage, different types

12% — No reason given

9% — Settle claims promptly, fairly

2% — Insured through finance company — no choice

2% — Conveniently located

2% — Heard about agent through friends

1% — Insurance in connection with job

1% — Offered payment plan

1% — Wanted all insurance with one company

6% — Other reasons

Question 8a: Do you think there is a big difference in what different companies would charge you for the same kind and amount of auto insurance, or a small difference, or do you think that they all charge about the same?

38% — Insurance charges are about the same

24% — There is a big difference in insurance charges

21% — There is a small difference in insurance charges

17% — Don't know

Question 8b: (If difference between companies indicated) Do you think that the cost of your present car insurance is higher than most companies, lower than most other companies, or about the same?

73% — Lower than most companies

21% — Don't know

5% — Higher than most companies

1% — About the same as most companies

Question 9a: When you bought your present policy, did you contact the agent, or did he contact you?

25% — He contacted me

72% — I contacted him

3% — Don't remember or question not appropriate

Question 9b: (If respondent contacted agent, ask:) How did you first get his name?

    31% — Through friends, relatives, neighbors
    19% — Knew agent
    6% — Saw advertising
    6% — Don't remember
        All other reasons accounted for 3% or less each.

Question 10a: What were the main sales points the agent made about your present insurance?

    39% — Don't remember
    18% — Trusted agent, didn't have to give sales talk
    14% — Costs less
    12% — Trusted person who recommended agent
    10% — Better coverage, more protection
    6% — Company has good reputation
    4% — Fair handling of claims
    1% — Insured through finance company or bank
    5% — Other reasons

Question 18: People give different reasons for taking out auto insurance. Which one of these do you think is *most* important to most people?

    89% — Cover responsibility for damage to other fellow
    5% — Required by law
    3% — Cover against damage to own car
    3% — Other and none

Question 20: Here are some of the things about auto insurance companies that some people feel are important. (Show set of 7 yellow cards) Now can you tell me which one of these is most important to you personally? (Record "1" below and ask:) And of these left, which one is the most important? (Record "2" and proceed until all cards have been ranked.)

    Per cent ranking feature as number 1:
    23% — Quick settlement of claims
    18% — Fair treatment by company
    17% — Well known company
    15% — Low cost of insurance
    13% — Good service from local agent

7% — Claim adjusters in all parts of the United States

2% — Installment plan for payments

Question 24c: (For each company bought from previously, but not now carried) Why do you no longer carry (Each company) insurance on your car?

Of those switching from State Farm, the following reasons were given:

50% — No reason given

18% — State Farm rates too high; present company cheaper

16% — Agent is personal friend (State Farm agent died, got sick, left the town, switched companies, etc.)

10% — Poor claims handling

9% — Poor service — did not bill promptly

9% — Other company had better coverage

6% — Let insurance expire

5% — Insured through finance company, loan company, insurance payments made with car payments

24% — Other reasons

Of those switching to State Farm, the following reasons were given:

47% — No reason given

21% — Rates too high, State Farm cheaper

7% — State Farm has better coverage

6% — State Farm agent is personal friend

3% — Let insurance expire

3% — Insured through finance company, loan company, bank — company selected, included with car payments, etc.

3% — Poor claims handling by other company

2% — Poor service from other company

11% — Other reasons

Appendix D

THE SNOWBALL INTERVIEW

The "snowball" interview is a recorded discussion between four or five people all of whom have a common interest. It is not an interview in the usual sense but approaches an "over the back yard fence" conversation which is guided and helped along by a discussion leader. The subject for the interview can be any topic that people know enough about to discuss. The name "snowball" interview perhaps sounds unusual — it comes from the fact that after a few minutes talking in one of these interviews, the people get to know one another well enough to talk freely, the conversation becomes more animated, and more and more pertinent comments come out. With five people each comment adds to the one made just before it and the interview "snowballs."

This technique is used to get material that would be very difficult if not impossible to obtain in any other way. While they're talking each person's comments stimulate the others in the group and it is possible to get material in five minutes that might take hours in any other way. Five heads are better than one and the agreements and disagreements among the members of the group bring out ideas and suggestions that would not appear if each person were interviewed separately. Usually the more informal the conversation the better — they should be like a group of women talking across the back yard fence or several men talking at the bowling alley.

Because the snowball interview is a group interview, it is not at all like a conventional interview with a single respondent, and the discussion leader has a different role from that of an interviewer. The discussion leader's job is to create a setting that is favorable to the discussion and to start the talk off in the right direction. From then on she makes sure that all points are followed through but the less talking the interviewer does the better as long as all the topics are covered. When necessary the leader introduces new topics to make sure that nothing will be overlooked.

Little things that might be relatively unimportant for a conventional interview are extremely important when conducting a snowball discussion. The way you talk with the people as they arrive and the way you get the discussion started may determine the way the group approaches the topic. Then the way the discussion leader helps the conversation along also has a definite effect. As a general rule the fewer times she interrupts the group the better, but sometimes it's necessary to cut in to bring out pertinent points that are about to be glossed over. More often though, it is better to listen quietly, and *even the way the discussion leader listens has an effect.* She should always at least *appear* alert and friendly and she should appear to be listening carefully and with great interest to everything that is said, even though the conversation may actually seem dull to her. It cannot be over-emphasized that the group watches her and her attitude toward the interview determines the final value of the discussion more than any other thing.

There are two things to do immediately when you need to do one or more snowball interviews. The first is for you to find out just as much as you can about the subject the group will talk about so you'll be prepared in advance.

Then you'll have to find your respondents. These will always be selected according to some common interest such as the fact that they all own dogs or they all have new cars, or they all have automatic washing machines.

The fact that there is something in common between the people makes it much easier to get the group to meet — and usually they like to talk about something that they know something about.

If you need women for your group then it is possible to schedule the interview almost anytime during the day; however, if you need men for something like a discussion of auto insurance you will have to try to get them all together at a time when they are not working and a time that is convenient to all of them. This is pretty important for groups of either men or women — set the time for the discussion whenever it is easiest for the people you want to participate, and moreover try to make all arrangements as simply and as quickly as possible. Just one change in schedule from what was first planned may endanger the group discussion because it makes people less willing to participate freely. By leaving the time when the discussion will be held up to the people that you want to talk, you are making things just as easy for them as you can.

Of course, the interview can be conducted either in the interviewer's house or in the home of one of the respondents. If the interview is to be at a respondent's house, you should arrive a little early to set up the recorder and be ready to go with the discussion as soon as everyone is there. Choose a placement for the microphone where it's about 5–6 feet from the center of the group. Probably at one side of the group is best. Avoid anything like a coffee table because usually these have ashtrays on them so that every time someone taps a cigarette on the tray the noise will appear on the recording. Adjust the volume control on the recorder by trying it out and you're all set for the group to arrive.

We have been requested that the interviews be made with the absolute minimum of background noise of any kind. These are the sorts of things we would like to avoid on the recording; clocks ticking, electric fans, refrigerator noises, jangling keys, coughing, humming, drumming of fingers on tables, squeaky chairs, obvious echoes in the room where you're recording.

Now, needless to say it will take the utmost in tact when you set up your interview to be able to control all sources of extra noise. For instance, it's pretty hard to get the man in whose home you are doing the interview to have his children be absolutely quiet for the discussion. However, by talking it over with him carefully and explaining that the mikes are very sensitive you should be able to control at least a large part of the noise. When the group arrives, you might tell them about the noise problem and ask for their cooperation.

As soon as everyone is there get them together where you're going to do the talking. The arrangement is not at all formal. It is important that everyone be as comfortable as possible though because an uncomfortable person affects other people in the group and their twisting or rustling of papers or something like that can cause quite a lot of extra noise. When people are all together you're ready to begin. Before you turn the recorder on it is best to explain briefly what the discussion is to be like. Here's what has always worked pretty well for us: "What we have in mind here is sort of an informal discussion about _____. Go right ahead and tell me everything that you know about it, just in the way you'd talk it over with your neighbors or friends when you get together. It's sort of a back yard fence conversation that we'd like to hear. Now, I can't take notes fast enough to keep up with you I'm sure and anyway I want to spend all of my time listening to you so I have the recorder set up to do the job for me. Don't worry about it — it won't bite. Once in awhile people ask what we do with the recordings. We just send them in to the office and they sit down and listen to them for ideas on improving products and services. There is just one problem in using a recorder. It is pretty hard on a recording to pick out the separate comments if more than one person is talking at a time. So please — only one at a time. If during the conversation I hold up my finger and wave it, you'll know that too many are talking at once. So now let's go ahead."

Now turn the recorder on and start out something like this for the recording: "As I said what we have in mind here is a general discussion on _____. Just tell us all about it. How about you Mrs. Jones, what kind of _____ do you have (or use)?" Then go around the group one by one. The conversation may "take off" after you have asked only two or three people in the group. This is fine; however, be sure to come back to the people that you have missed so that each person has had a chance to talk near the beginning of the conversation. One reason for this is that it gives you a chance to call each person by name for the recording and the voices will be identified for the remainder of the conversation. Also it is important that everyone be encouraged to participate at the beginning, though there are wide differences between groups of people and you will have to use your own judgment. Often someone will remain silent for half of the interview and then suddenly begin to talk and give some very important and interesting points.

It is rather hard to know just when to step into the discussion to guide it or bring out points, but it is safe to say that whenever it looks as if a point is about to be missed or if you can get more information by asking something like: "What's your opinion of it?", "Why did you do that?", "What happened then?", be sure to do so. However, it is extremely important that the conversation does not seem to the group to be a quiz. You, as discussion leader, should know as much about the subject of the discussion as possible, but it should not show. You must be dumb but smart.

As the discussion goes along use the topic guide list to bring in succeeding topics for discussion. It is not necessary or even desirable to take these in the order that they appear on the list. It is much better to take topics which are close or following from the topics that are being discussed at the moment. Incidentally, don't let the people in the group see the topics on the list before or during the discussion. As soon as each topic on the list is covered, check it off. Then near the end of the discussion you can see at a glance what topics have not been covered and can go back to them. However, don't rush this because usually only a few topics will remain if the discussion throughout has gone along smoothly.

Remember that the list of topics is a guide only. It is not a questionnaire. Although the topics are in question form, you probably won't have to ask them directly. Do try to have as many people in the group as possible give opinions on general topics. You can do this by following up a comment that has just been made with, "How about *you*, Mrs. Smith? What do you think?"

After the discussion is over if the respondents in the group want to listen a few minutes to the playback to hear their voices. this is all right, but don't take up too much time with it. At the same time you should make out a list of the people's names and addresses, their occupations and any other classification data that we may need. Then as soon as you are through, mark the tape box with the tape in it with the survey title and the names of the people in the group so that we will be able to identify it.

Appendix E

SNOWBALL INTERVIEWS ON AUTOMOBILE INSURANCE

Guide for Interviews

I. Do you have insurance on your automobile now?
  A. (for those who do have it) Why?

   What are the most important reasons why you have automobile insurance?

   What are some other reasons?

   What reasons have you heard — for instance advertising — that you think are *not* important?

   Have you ever driven without insurance?

   How did that happen?

   Would you do it again?

   What do the others in the group think; would they do it?
  B. (if insurance not carried) Why not?

   Have you ever had it?

   Why did you drop it?

   Do you expect to get some; when?

II. Turn the discussion to types of auto insurance coverage.
  A. What is collision insurance?

   (try to get the group to define it, but make sure they know that it means insurance that pays for damage to the owner's car as a result of an accident no matter whose fault.)

   Do you have collision insurance?

   Why? (probe) — Have you always had it? (if not) Why did you get it?

   (if collision insurance not carried)

   Why not? (probe) — Have you ever had it? (if yes) Why did you drop it?

   Do you expect to get it again?

   Encourage discussion between those who do have it and those who don't on the merits of this type of insurance.
  B. (repeat the preceding discussion for:

Liability Insurance (Bodily Injury and Property Damage) — that which pays for damage done by a driver to other cars or property or to other people. Comprehensive Insurance (Fire, Theft, etc.) — that which pays for loss or damage to a car as a result of fire, theft, natural hazards, vandalism, etc. Medical Payments — that which pays medical expenses of guests in the car.)

III. Turn the discussion to insurance companies.

A. Why did you pick your present company?

What company is it?

What things about your present company — or what it offers — do you like?

How important was the *cost* of the insurance to you?

How did you hear of the company?

Did you buy through an agent, a broker, or direct? Did he call you, or did you call him? How did you find out about him? What did you ask about?

What did the agent or broker tell you? Which is more important in buying insurance, the agent or the company itself?

Before you selected your present company did you shop around? How much?

What did you try to find out about each company?

What sales arguments did you hear? What did you think of them?

Do you buy other forms of insurance (fire, life, etc.) from the same agent or broker? From the same company?

B. What differences are there among insurance companies? (be sure that cost, service, trustworthiness of the company, number and type of agents are mentioned.)

How big are these differences?

How important are they?

(if there are big, important differences) How do you choose between companies?

Which companies are good; which are bad?

C. Is there anything about your present company you don't like?

D. What actual experiences, besides just buying a policy and paying bills have you had with insurance companies?

Have you ever tried to collect money from somebody else's company — for instance, someone who ran into your car? What happened? What did you think about it?

Have you ever tried to collect money from your own company? What happened? What did you think about it?

E. Have you ever changed insurance companies? Why? (if dissatisfied with former company, find out why. If the new company seemed better, find out why.)

Any other changes? Why?

How many changes have you made altogether?

In general, do you change more out of dissatisfaction with the old company or because you feel that the new company is somehow better?

What are the dissatisfactions?

How have the new companies seemed better?

F. What could auto insurance companies do to keep their customers? (probe)

IV. What do you think about the advertising for automobile insurance?

How much have you seen or heard?

Where have you seen or heard it?

Can you think of any *good* example?

How about *bad* examples?

What kind of auto insurance advertising would you like to see more of?

How many auto insurance companies can you name?

Appendix F

EXCERPTS FROM THE STATE FARM
SNOWBALL INTERVIEWS

(Key to abbreviations: N — Narrator who introduces the various excerpts. L — Group discussion leader. Numbers — Discussion participants.)

N — This is a series of excerpts taken from our tape recorded snowball group discussions on automobile insurance. The excerpts illustrate some of the highlights in our study and give an idea of how the automobile owners in our sample talked about insurance. Naturally, some of the topics that they are talking about overlap from one excerpt to another. The first excerpt is taken from our Chicago group where the men are discussing why they have insurance at all.

L — Why did you get insurance?

1 — Why did I get insurance? Insurance is just like your right arm. Anybody who doesn't have insurance today is crazy. Not that I go for the song and dance that some of these brokers give you that they can sue you for every penny you have. It is just something you have to have. You've got to be protected. It takes a load off your mind. That's one thing.

L — It protects you (pause) or — ?

2 — Well, I think that primarily I carry insurance because it frees me of certain worries. If something should happen, I'm covered. The insurance company will take the rap. I won't. That's what I think, I've never — (pause)

3 — Well, for protection against any possible expenditure that would come up, if I was involved in an accident, and with the tremendous number of cars on the street it's easy to get into an accident that I'd hate to have the risk on my own shoulders without having insurance. However, I sometimes wonder if it's necessary to have as much insurance as I have because probably the most expensive portion of the insurance is the collision.

L — Have any of you ever been without insurance?

3 — Yes, for two days, and I had an accident.   (group laughs) I hit a woman.

4 — Oh, no!

3 — You think I'm kidding, don't you? I'm not kidding. In California I bought a car . . . and I was going to get the insurance the next day. I drove the car home. Bam! I hit a woman.

4 — In California?

3 — In California. My fault, too.

L — Let me ask you this —

4 — So what happened?

3 — So what happened? It cost me about $300 the whole thing.

5 — Let me answer that question in this way. In between, you know when I was going from company to company about two or three months ago, there was one day when my insurance ran out, and I wasn't sure I had a company. I usually leave the house at 8:30, and I wouldn't leave the house until I got a hold of my broker and found out I was covered or else that car wouldn't move from my house! Cause I wouldn't drive a block without insurance —

3 — I'd take a cab —

2 — Who would want to take a chance? I would never drive —

5 — Never.

L — How about you, Mike?

6 — No, I definitely wouldn't.

7 — Nowadays just any kind of an accident, people sue you for $10,000, $50,000. It don't mean a thing to them.

8 — You've got to have insurance —

6 — The only insurance that I can think of that I wouldn't be without, I mean life insurance, you can go, (pause) even hospital people go without, but when you drive a car, that's one thing you have to have.

5 — That's right. Absolutely.

1 — Any responsible person has got to have it. It's a must.

.   .   .

N — The next excerpt, from our Detroit group, shows some of the confusion about types of insurance.

L — What is — (pause) you talk about public liability and collision and that. What comes under collision insurance for instance?

1 — Well, that's damage to your car, damage to the other car, but your public liability takes care of that.

2 — Yeah.

L — Take care of what?

1 — Damage to the other party.

3 — Now, if you have an accident, and you hit a car and you bounce and hit a home and say you knock the front of the home out, that's public liability. That will take care of that and take care of the car. And then your collision — (Several men talked at once for a few moments, then participant 3 continued) You see now, Allstate has 20 and 40. Most of the others only carry 10 and 20 — (pause) or 5 and 10.

1 — I carry 10 and 20, see —

2 — I have 10 and 20. That's $20,000 — (Several men talked at once for a few moments)

4 — And — (pause) and (repeated in strong voice to gain attention) why most of us carry insurance is because we own a home and you have a family. So if you are involved in an accident, and you didn't carry any insurance, the people turn around and sue you and won the case and take your home away and take everything away.

(Several brief comments overlapped at this point)

L — Got any other reasons you carry it?

5 — Well, I carry it more to protect the other fellow than myself. I don't carry collision.

2 — Well, that's what public liability is.

5 — That's right. I'm making sure that if I hit anyone, I'm protected there as far as the other party's concerned. I'm not going to worry about my own damage —

3 — You are not liable for any damage suit.

5 — That's right.

4 — It's not the part that you're smashing the cars, it's the part that human people, human beings are involved and you happen to cripple one —

2 — That comes under personal liability again.

4 — If you cripple him up and he is in the hospital for six months, where would you get the money to pay it?

L — That's a good question.   (Group laughs)

4 — Yeah, it's with the insurance company.   It's their worry.

L — What is the difference between the public liability and the bodily injury, then?

3 — Well, that's a separate write-up there.

6 — You have two different coverages, public liability and personal liability.

L — Oh.

6 — Any injury to persons would be under personal liability.

3 — That's a separate premium there whereas public liability would be injury to the other car or a public utility of any kind or home, anything.

L — Umm, humm.

(Several talked at once for a moment.)

L — What's the comprehensive?

2 — That covers all breakage of glass, fire and theft and anything that is stolen on a car.

7 — That's full coverage, sir.

L — Didn't I hear someone say that if people in the car got hurt or something —

(Several brief comments overlapped.)

1 — If I pick you up and we have an accident and your — say runs $1,000 and I only have $500, well, I have to stand the cost of $500.   If I have $1,000, that will cover you, but they ask you to take $2,000 or $2,500.   That only costs what? Seven dollars.   That's good protection, too.   A man of the family today has to spend a little money and protect himself.

.   .   .

N — The following excerpt from Birmingham illustrates the need for prompt claim settlement.

1 — I think we can all boil it down — it costs too much for what it's worth — (pause) so I think we'll all agree that insurance companies seem to be prospering — as far as I can see.

2 — They are building an awfully big building, I know that,

over there on the south side. Looks to me like it's worth a lot of money. (Laughs and several overlapping comments.)

L — One of the questions here is what could auto insurance companies do to keep their customers?

3 — (Speaking deliberately and seriously) In my opinion, make the settlements promptly. That is the biggest thing that they could do to influence people and make friends. Just to show their good spirit, they should serve your case just as honestly and just as promptly as they do when they want to serve you a policy.

N — The next excerpt from a group of farmers illustrates again the need for good claim handling.

1 — Good claim handling is the best single thing —

2 — Just like I was saying about this State Farm agent. Now, he makes his own claims, the agent himself. Where before you had to wait for an adjuster and he come when he felt like it.

3 — I don't think we have that trouble. Adjusters are always on the job the next day or maybe the same day.

2 — That's according to how far away his office is, yeah. And you usually have to wait for him to make out the check and now the agent can make it out himself.

4 — If you have good claim service and you never have to use it, why that's all you need in an insurance company.

5 — If you've got a good agent, you can talk with him. Now I think you could talk with Ken —

2 — Yeah, he's a good guy.

5 — Because he is a nice fellow.

1 — Who was the fellow ahead of him?

2 — Bob Bond. He went farming.

4 — So now you get back to good claim service again. If you've a reputable company and good claim service, you are all right.

N — The next excerpt from the South Bend farmer group again shows the effect of the attitude of the agent and his procedures on the prospective insurance buyer.

1 — . . . but like I say, some of these insurance companies, they sell you a big bill of goods and you get nothing for it.

2 — Yeah, that's right, you —

3 — Especially somebody who doesn't understand about insurance. Why they can do a lot of talking —

1 — The average man don't know anything about insurance. You got to learn the hard way. The average man can take out a life insurance policy, the agent will come in here and explain a policy to him and could give him another one and he'd never know the difference because he never reads his policy.

2 — No (agreeing). You got to know Greek —

4 — A man came out and I thought a lot of his insurance and he went over it pretty good. But when I told him that we wanted to look around I thought he'd know — (pause) then he started this line that he had a quota to make and all that, you know.

1 — Yeah, he started selling you a big bill of goods.

4 — Yeah, I chased him out. I liked his insurance. It sounded good to me.

1 — Well, I think that's why if you got a good reputable agent, he wants you to shop around. Take your Farm Bureau. Your Farm Bureau has a good thing. Now so has my insurance company. Now they don't try to push it off. They'll tell you, go ahead and look around and see what you can get that's any better. Compare it.

5 — They don't have to, because it sells itself.

1 — That's what I say. They got a good fool proof insurance, as good as you can get, and if a company is good, I don't care where you shop, you can't beat it. You can't even come up to their standards. That's one thing they should do with insurance is standardize it.

6 — Well, there is a lot of difference in the salesmen, though. We had one salesman for the Farm Bureau and I chased him out of the house. But I went to the other fellow and took my insurance out because I liked Farm Bureau. But the way he was putting it on, I wouldn't have it. He was just

trying to high pressure me. I know what I want and that's what I want. He doesn't have to tell me what I got to take.

3 — That's the only reason I changed insurance. I got provoked with the insurance company I had, with the dealings, the way they did business —

.   .   .

N — Finally, from Detroit we have a discussion on rates and any possible rebates.

1 — . . . advertising, that's mostly come-on anyway. But that's their business, if they want to throw their money around —

2 — Well, I say they spend too much money for advertising.

3 — They should use that money to lower their rates.

2 — That's right.

4 — What they should do, I say, as far as the insurance companies are concerned is to give the man that don't have no accidents and don't draw any money out of the company, give him a rebate. I mean dividends —

2 — Yeah. I thought about that long ago.

4 — We're paying a lot of money for these hot rodders . . . that go around and bang up all these cars. We're paying for that.

5 — I don't believe I have collected a penny in the last seven or eight years from insurance company. I figure if a man doesn't have an accident in five years —

4 — They could make themselves a savings, so if you didn't have an accident in three years, you'd get a rebate of $25. Say if you didn't have an accident in three years, then, everybody would be more caution, more careful driving and everything, too.

6 — Well, I've collected $21 in 18 years. Now you beat that.

Appendix G

SOME REPLIES TO BALLOON QUESTION 4:

"HERE'S AN AD THAT SAYS YOU CAN SAVE AS MUCH AS 40 PER CENT ON YOUR AUTO INSURANCE. DO YOU THINK WE OUGHT TO LOOK INTO IT WHEN OURS EXPIRES NEXT MONTH?"

I'll look into it — of course, with reservations.

They'll have to prove that to me. I don't think there's much difference between one and another.

If we can save 40 per cent, we had better look into it.

If it's an old established company with a good past reputation for claims and gives the coverage we need, let's look into it.

I don't think we should. I don't think there's that much difference in insurance.

Yes, but be sure it's good and that we'd get the same benefits for less money.

Sure, but we must see just how good it really is before we do anything about it.

I would be suspicious of that ad — 40 per cent off is quite a bit.

No. Any company that saves you 40 per cent isn't paying out full coverage.

Forty per cent is quite a saving. Yes, we'll look into it and see just how they can do it.

Sure. It doesn't hurt to look as long as we're not obligated to buy if we don't like it.

I don't believe there's any such company — can't be a reliable one.

Yes, we should look into it and compare the new policy with the one we now have as to coverage.

Well, I would try looking in on it.

By all means.

No, that ad is just a come-on.

No. We have a good agent. Let him take care of it.

I don't believe there's such a thing as a company offering such a big discount as rates are regulated by federal and state government.

I wouldn't bother with it to save a few cents because I know my own company and agent.

I think we should check into it.

Sure, look into it if you can save 40 per cent.

No harm in looking into a saving on anything. You can't buy a pig in a poke and in insurance you must accept some on trust and the agent's trust.

I'd say no. I don't want to change our insurance. Am very satisfied with it just as it is.

You pay according to your protection and 40 per cent wouldn't be an inducement to me. You get what you pay for in the policy.

There must be a catch in it.

I should think so. Save as much as you can on premiums.

I would investigate carefully. Forty per cent is too much. Does it give same coverage?

We ought to look into it now before it expires.

Yes, let's look into it. We don't have to buy it if it doesn't sound good.

Couldn't see a 40 per cent cut in premium without cutting the coverage — something wrong somewhere if they can cut 40 per cent.

No, I think we should keep what we have.

I think she'd better. I had insurance with several companies and have been cheated as much as 60 per cent from them. It's a good idea to look for the right company.

He ought to look into it, I suppose.

It's a blame good savings and worth looking into. But let's be sure to read the fine print and the hidden clauses.

No. When someone advertises a savings of 40 per cent — it can't be very good insurance.

I don't believe it. Forty per cent, that's pretty near half.

Maybe so. There's not too much difference in cost. They should look into it all right, but it might be expensive in the long run. The company may be questionable.

Good common sense, but you'd want to know if you get good coverage first.

Appendix H

AUTO INSURANCE PROJECTIVE TEST

I. Sentence Completion

I have a group of sentences here. I'd like to read the first part of them to you then tell me what you would add to them to complete the thought. Just tell me the first thing that comes into your mind. For instance, I might start a sentence, "On Sunday afternoons . . ." and you might complete this by saying, "I just like to relax." So the complete sentence would be, "On Sunday afternoon I just like to relax." In other words just tell me the very first thing you think of to complete the sentence, no matter what it is — a word, a phrase, or a whole sentence.[1]

1. Insurance of all kinds is_____(very important.)_____

2. The whole insurance industry____(is very necessary.)_____

3. The most important thing about auto insurance is____(the protection in case of accident.)

4. Auto insurance that protects the other fellow____(is most important of all.)

5. Auto insurance that protects my own car____(is good in the long run.)

6. Anybody who drives without auto insurance____(is crazy.)___

7. The one thing I dislike about auto insurance____(is the red tape to collect claims.)

8. The largest auto insurance company in the world____(is A.A.A.)

9. I would never buy auto insurance from____(couldn't say.)___

10. The best thing about my auto insurance company____(the peace of mind when I am driving.)

11. Mutual auto insurance companies____(don't know anything about them.)

* Respondent's answers appear in parentheses.

12. Trying to save money on auto insurance_____(is foolish in long run.)

13. Most insurance agents who sell auto policies_____(are OK.)

14. Insurance agents commissions are_____(good.)

15. When it comes to settling a claim, most auto insurance companies _____(do settle claims fairly.)

16. Extra careful drivers_____(should not have to pay as high premiums as others.)

17. Auto insurance companies that accept only careful drivers (should have lower premiums than others.)

18. Most advertising for auto insurance_____(is done by A.A.A.)

19. Auto insurance companies cancel your insurance when (you have too many accidents within a period of time.)

20. When I have an auto insurance claim_____(my company is prompt in acting.)

II. NARRATIVE PROJECTION

I have here a few imaginary situations I'd like to tell you about and have you tell me what you think. For instance, suppose your neighbor has just asked your advice about what kind of car he should buy. You might tell me you would advise the neighbor to buy either a Ford or Chevrolet because the repair costs are low on these cars. Just tell me what you honestly would think in each situation.

1. A friend of yours has just bought his first car. He asks you what he should do about getting insurance for it. What would you tell him?

   (*By all means get insurance from a good company. I wouldn't want to suggest a company. I've only had insurance with my company a short while.*)

2. A close friend of yours wants to buy the least expensive auto insurance he can get. Which insurance company would you recommend to him?

   (*I think Allstate is less expensive from what I've heard.*)

3. Every year a man shopped around very carefully for the least expensive auto insurance he could find. How much do you suppose he saved by this practice?
(*He might save $10.00 at the most. I don't think there's a lot of difference.*)

4. Another man buys all his insurance, including fire, life and automobile insurance, from one agent who handles all the details. This man doesn't even know exactly which companies get his money, but he trusts his agent. How many people do you think buy their auto insurance this way?
(*I'd say 60% or so. I think people should take more interest in their companies.*)

III. BALLOON TESTS

I have here a group of pictures. Before we look at them I'd like to give you an example of the sort of thing it is. The pictures show one person saying something to another person. I'd like to have you tell me what you think the second person might reply. This doesn't have to be what you would say, but just what you think the other person probably would say. For instance, suppose I show you a picture of two men talking. The first man is saying, "What should we do tomorrow?" You might possibly look at the picture and tell that the second man would reply something like, "Well we could go to the ball game, we could go swimming, or maybe we could get in some golf. What do you think?" Just give me ordinary, every day comments — the sort of thing that you think the people in the pictures might say. It could be most anything, so give me the first answer that you think of.

(SHOW PICTURES ONE AT A TIME IN ORDER. RECORD ANSWERS BELOW.)

(Two of the seven balloon questions used, and the responses to them, appear below.)

4. Woman and man. "Here's an ad that says you can save as much as 40% on your auto insurance. Do you think we ought to look into it when ours expires next month?" Answer:
(Look into it before ours expires. If we get the same coverage for less we could try it.)

5. Two men. "Yes, that company's auto insurance is not as expensive as some, but what kind of satisfaction do they give you if you have an accident?" Answer: (Well, I know from past experience they take care of claims fairly.)

CLASSIFICATION DATA

NAME_____Mr. Ray Donahue *_____

ADDRESS_____3881 Lee Street_____

CITY____Detroit____ESTIMATED AGE____29____SEX__Male__

OCCUPATION_____Machine Operator_____

MAKE AND YEAR OF CAR_____Ford — 1950_____

What type of auto insurance do you carry?

① Collision ② Fire and Theft ③ Public Liability and Property Damage

④ Other _____ (specify)

Company insurance is with____(American Insurance)____

(Show Income Card and Ask:) Here are 8 income groups. Would you mind indicating by letter which group comes closest to equaling the total income of all the members of your household?

__(Q)__ Income Letter

INTERVIEWER____A. Jones____Date____July 22, 1954__

* Name and address of respondent have been disguised.

Appendix I

A DIGEST OF THE REPORT OF FINDINGS OF "A PSYCHOLOGICAL ANALYSIS OF THE MARKET FOR AUTOMOBILE INSURANCE"

Some Generalizations About Automobile Insurance

Insurance is essentially a guarantee (in return for a fee) against loss. . . . By its very nature, insurance has a deep psychological meaning for most people. Much of this meaning is not at a level of conscious awareness — but it still exerts a powerful influence upon the way that people feel about insurance. Some of the generalizations that have come out of the study:

Insurance is Fatherly. It assumes responsibilities and reduces the tensions associated with being subject to the perils of the universe. Insurance is like the father who says to his son, "You may get into trouble but in case you do, I'll be there." The man with insurance has the feeling that he is not alone; something strong and dependable is with him regardless of "trouble."

Insurance is a Threat. At the same time, insurance is also a threat. Taking out insurance is a recognition that the world is a dangerous and unpredictable place to live in. This is not pleasant for most people to contemplate. . . . Thinking about accidents and how contingent one's life is upon the next fellow makes for a great deal of anxiety, and threatens the feelings of serenity that most people like to have about their environment.

Insurance is a Ritual. To insure is one concrete way that people have of warding off the anxiety connected with thoughts of disaster. Many people *feel* that if they do something concrete then things will be changed. . . . In some respects insurance is like "knocking on wood." . . . By paying something (an offering) trouble might be avoided. Insurance is a way of giving up something to gain assurance that the forces in the universe will be considerate.

Insurance Provides a Means of Control over the Future. Psychologically speaking, insurance is a means of controlling or reducing the uncertainties of the future. People are better able to plan if they feel that an accident will not come along and alter everything they have tried to do. . . . Insurance is a way of influencing, to a degree, one's personal destiny.

Insurance is Begrudged. Paying for nothing is resented. . . . The feeling of relief that nothing has happened is only partially balanced by the feeling that the insurance protection has been needless.

An Automobile is Psychologically Meaningful to the Owner. In some respects an automobile is an expression or reflection of its owner. For example, certain kinds of people prefer convertibles, others prefer sports cars, and others prefer more utilitarian models. A car is usually more than a means of transportation; it is a manifestation of its owner's personality. Also, for this reason an automobile is more significant to a man than a TV set or some furniture. The car is, aside from its money value, one of a man's more important and personal possessions. The automobile is worth insuring.

Every Man is a Good Driver. Whether a man is courteous, inconsiderate, cautious, truculent, or careless as a driver depends a great deal upon his personality. But most men consider themselves to be good drivers. It is always the other person who causes the accident. A man consciously insures himself against the "other guy" when he takes out insurance. It would be hard on his ego to think otherwise. The feeling of personal blamelessness for any trouble to come is a source of much fundamental resentment toward insurance companies. Many men feel that they must pay for protection against the other driver's recklessness.

The Dangers of Driving Are Recognized. . . . Regardless of who may be at fault, the fact that one can be involved in costly, serious trouble is clear. There is little or no choice; insurance is necessary to protect one from the very real dangers that can befall any driver.

The Meaning of Automobile Insurance

Certain attitudes about automobile insurance were held by most of the men interviewed. Some of these attitudes, viewed psychologically to bring out their broad implications of meaning, follow:

Insurance Has an Intense Social Sanction . . . automobile insurance is a *good thing.* It is something which is almost taken for granted . . . most people feel queasy and vaguely immoral when they think about *not* having any automobile insurance . . . automobile insurance is "sound and knowledgeable" business practice . . . "only a sucker would go unprotected." . . . There is a pronounced righteousness towards those people who do not carry automobile insurance. . . . Carrying insurance means to most men that they are responsible, stable citizens who meet their obligations to society. . . . Automobile insurance is considered a "good thing that everyone should have in order to do his duty."

Insurance is a Business. People see themselves in a business relationship with the insurance company. . . . Essentially people . . . want to be treated as customers, not as individuals who are trying to get something for nothing. They feel that they pay plenty for what they get and should be handled accordingly. Too often, they feel, they are treated peremptorily, discourteously, and remotely. In a business that is so intimately connected with "personal protection," this is especially disquieting. More than anything else, the customer wants to feel that the company is "involved" with him personally. . . . By and large it is very ego-enhancing for . . . people . . . to "do business" with large insurance companies. . . . There is a proud and constant allusion to "my company" or "my agent" from the respondents. . . . Although there are real gratifications in associating with "big business," there are also fears connected with it. . . . Many people have attitudes of uncertainty about large insurance companies.

Insurance is Technical. For the most part, insurance is not clearly understood by those it covers. There is a good deal of confusion about the kinds of automobile insurance (what each type covers) and also the meaning of specific policies. Much of this confusion centers around the very *language* of automobile insurance. . . . The uncertainty that surrounds the meanings of automobile insurance makes for *resentment.* . . . The complexities of insurance language, and the fact that insurance is a big business, are enough to produce a good deal of skepticism about the intentions and reputability of the industry. Most peo-

ple feel that it is possible to express ideas in "simple language";
they wonder why insurance companies rarely do so. . . . The
fact that companies often do not communicate the meaning of
their coverage to clients results in cynicism and hostility. People
feel that a service which involves protection to life, savings, reputation, and family should be understandable.

Insurance is a Protector. . . . Insurance means that no one
can come and "wipe you out" if you should happen to have an
accident. But automobile insurance acts as a protector in another sense also. In some respects automobile insurance *takes
care of you emotionally.*

> One man said: "The shock of having an accident is
> enough. You need someone with you. Not a whole
> bunch of legal mumbo-jumbo that scares you half to
> death so you don't know where you're at."
> Another example is this statement from a young man:
> "The point behind insurance is that we'll take care of
> you if something happens. That's what you want to
> know . . . don't worry, you're protected. You can get
> help."

One way of conceiving of insurance is that it assuages the anxiety connected with "going it alone." The insurance company is
there not only to pay off but to do battle for you. In the case of
an emergency the company is there *on your side.* It is as if the
insurance company acted like the strong if distant "father" who
patches up all of the complexities involved in accidents. The
image of the insurance company as a paternalistic figure helps to
explain some of the expectations that people have of the companies. It is not enough simply to pay the debts; the good insurance company must provide other things, too. (See Appendix H, sentence completions 1, 2, 3, 4 and 10).

Insurance Companies Create Resentment. A conscious source
of resentment and hostility toward the company is the fact that
there is *no reward for good driving* . . . the no-accident driver
feels . . . that he deserves some sort of a rate change as a result
of his "good driving." . . . Outside of the very practical consideration of getting a rebate for his good behavior, there is an

almost child-like need on the part of many no-accident drivers for *recognition* of some sort. An acknowledgment of their "value to the company" seems to be important to them.

THE IMAGE OF THE AUTOMOBILE INSURANCE COMPANY

The Good Automobile Insurance Company. . . . The good company must be large, reputable, well-known, paying, on your side, initially selective, and emotionally supporting. . . . Largeness . . . is consistent with solvency. . . . The major criterion for selection to the average man is to select one that is large, and preferably one that is well and favorably known by his friends. . . . Reputability is built largely upon *personal* information about the company. Word-of-mouth is the medium which is highly respected with reference to choosing an insurance company. . . . People are eager to be with a company which does not insure "just anybody." . . . Perhaps the most important criterion for reputability is the manner in which a company reacts in case of "trouble." The interviews are studded with examples of "stalling," "getting cars fixed in one certain place," and sudden discoveries of "hidden clauses." . . . The company must function as an *advocate* for its client. . . . One of the most critical functions of the insurance company is protecting the client in his feeling of "aloneness." . . . The company is expected to assume that the client is "in the right" and treat his "case" with the dignity it deserves. People feel that they have *sympathetic* courteous treatment coming. They resent very much the company which is "grudging" and which appears to stall in any way. This delaying action (real or fancied) threatens their sense of belonging to a large benevolent protector and assaults their self-pictures as good drivers who never get into trouble.

THINGS TO CONSIDER IN BUYING INSURANCE

You Get What You Pay For. This is a theme that runs throughout the interviews. Repeatedly the men . . . talked about "cheap insurance." "Cheap insurance" is suspect — it may or may not pay off; the company won't back you; there's a catch to it somewhere; you don't get something for nothing. . . . Associating dependability, protection, and service with low rates is something that the people of the sample found hard to do.

Service is Important. Service means many things. It means *prompt* settlement: . . . a gap between the trouble and "atten-" tion" from the company creates anxiety as to whether one is being "deserted" or is being given the "run-around." . . . It means *expertness:* the general attitude . . . is that "I'm paying you well to tell me what I need." It means *emotional support.* . . . The feeling seems to be one of, "You have got to see that no one pushes me around in the event of trouble." . . . It means *professional interest:* People want to be treated as clients. . . . They want to have time given to them for purposes of explanation and for the underlying reasons of emotional assurance.

The Agent and the Company Are Both Important. Most of the people in the sample feel that "you can't have a good company without a good agent and vice versa."

THE FUNCTION OF THE AUTOMOBILE INSURANCE AGENT

He Serves a Practical Purpose. The function of the agent according to the respondents is not only selling; it is to explain the complications of insurance coverage and it is to "go to bat" for the client in case of trouble. (He) is the expert who is paid to take care of problems. . . . He is the man on whom the client depends most of all for concrete assistance when things go wrong.

The Agent Has Psychological Functions, Too. He reduces the distance between the client and the remote company. He is reassurance that the client will not be abandoned in time of trouble. The agent is a further guarantee that the client will not be swallowed up in a maze of red tape or left to operate indecisively if something should happen. The agent symbolizes the "first step" in meeting trouble and the ultimate resolution of any trouble. The agent, as a representative of "big business," carries a certain amount of prestige. For many of the people (particularly working class people) . . . he is one of the very few contacts they have with a "business relationship." The agent-dealings are a source of esteem and pride; he is one of the few people with whom lower income people can "negotiate." Having a business relationship which satisfies all of the preconceptions and stereotypes held by people unfamiliar with such things is a source of gratification. A successful contact with business is a very meaningful experience. . . . One man phrased the notion this way: "A company and its agents should be dignified. They shouldn't try to get buddy-buddy."

The Agent Should Act in Certain Ways . . . the agent is a "professional" man; he should, therefore, act with dignity, courtesy, "detachment," and interest. Insurance is essentially a matter of having *confidence* in the ability of the company to solve one's difficulties as they arise. One of the most derogatory things said of insurance agents is that they are "salesmen." People want them to be more than that . . . the ideal agent is conceived to be more of a counsellor than he is a glad-hander. Insurance is buying something serious and costly; its very complexity makes it threatening, too. The agent is the man to translate the protective needs of the individual into an actual policy. A serious business demands a serious approach.

The best selling techniques are those which reflect the notion that the agent is a counsellor. Pressure . . . is resented. Insurance is not a matter of "salesmanship"; it is considered to be a matter for rational consideration. Positive values, what insurance does specifically for the client, is what the prospective buyer wants to know. . . . Comparisons should be encouraged by the agent. The idea that the agent has a good service and that it will stand comparison with any other is something that many . . . consider the opposite of pressure. Selling service is as important . . . as selling the policy benefits. A dignified, concrete, professional approach is the one that most people want from agents.

Appendix J

"ON YOUR SIDE"

(Excerpts from a speech given by Mr. Morrill before State Farm Mutual Automobile Insurance Agents)

A few months ago State Farm Mutual made a survey. It wasn't just an ordinary survey — it was the biggest ever attempted in the automobile insurance business. . . . In a moment, I want to give you some highlights of that survey. But to set the stage, here is a direct quotation from a man we interviewed in Alabama:

> "If you're insured," he said, "they ought to give you
> all the courtesy that's due you. Just like when you hire
> a lawyer. Like he's on your side."

"On your side!" Doesn't that phrase sum up the real heart of our business? In these words, it describes what it is about our relationship with our customers that sets us apart from other businesses. . . . Our business . . . involves us deeply with people — people who want to feel that they have paid their money not just for a legal contract but to enlist an ally who will be on their side in case of trouble. . . .

Getting along with people is the key to our success as a business. If we are to get along with them, we must measure up to what they expect of us. We must compare favorably with the image they have of the good automobile insurance company and agent. That image, more than that of any other business with which they deal, is, they tell us, an image of an ally that is "on your side." . . .

Good public relations begin with a sound product. They depend on fair play and a genuine interest in the customer. Most of all, they depend on what the men and women who represent us do in their actual daily contacts with people.

The opportunities that we have in State Farm for good or bad public relations stagger the imagination. Our offices put out seven and one-half million pieces of correspondence last year.

Agents wrote almost a million new and reinstatement applications.   Agents and adjusters handled more than 1,100,000 claims. . . . In every one of these millions of contacts with people, we will either add to or subtract from the sum total of the good will which people have for our organization — everything we do adds a plus or a minus.

It seemed to us that the very scope of our relations with people justified spending some time and money in a field survey. . . .

[At this point, Mr. Morrill cited findings from the "fact finding" study on how many car owners had left another company to join State Farm and why; the same information for people leaving State Farm; how many people had claims experience and how satisfied they were with it.   He then described briefly how the psychological study was conducted and then presented findings, these comprising a little more than one-half his speech.   See Appendix I for a digest of principal findings.]

Doesn't all of this [referring to the psychological study findings] underscore the importance of careful, thoughtful, and considerate dealings with people at all times?   This is the very foundation of good public relations.

One concept of this survey struck me with much greater force than ever before: The fact that a policyholder who comes in with an accident report or a claim is in an *emotional* situation.   He has had an accident.   Something disturbing has happened to him.   Now he turns to his insurance agent, perhaps a little embarrassed or confused or fearful.   Now is the time that he puts to the test his theory that "if you haven't tried to collect then you don't know anything about a company."   He finds out whether we pay off.   He also finds out whether the agent who was so agreeable when he made the sale is just as agreeable when it comes time to deliver the product.

After all, what we sell are promises.   It isn't like selling a man a bar of soap or a can of beans.   In our business we take a man's money, and all we give him in return is a promise.   Any company which takes money in exchange for its promise and then defaults on the promise is close to fraud.   The agent who is warm and interested when making the sale but cold and indifferent when a claim is presented is scarely in an admirable position.   Such a company or such an agent can not hope to keep the confidence of its customers.

Ours is a service business, one that is made up of literally millions of experiences with customers and the public in the course of a year. Good relations with these people cannot be mass produced. We have no mass transactions, but instead a mass of individual transactions — each one with a human being who expects to be treated like one and be recognized as an individual.

In large part, the keeping of our promises, and the way in which we keep them, depends on our agents. To your hands has been entrusted a large share of the responsibility for building and maintaining our public relations. . . .

[Mr. Morrill concluded by asking the agents to join enthusiastically in the company's "Big New Drive for '55."]

CHAPTER VI

Pan-American Coffee Bureau

FORENOTE

The Pan-American Coffee Bureau had sponsored various research over the years relating to its purpose of promoting coffee consumption. There had been no intensive investigation of why people bought and drank coffee, however, until 1955 when research of this kind was conducted for the Bureau by the Institute for Motivational Research, Inc. It served as the basis for planning the Bureau's advertising and sales promotion for late 1955 and 1956.

The study is of interest for its concepts relating to the social and psychological functions of coffee and for its use of informal, detailed interviewing. The research started with highly unstructured interviews and then proceeded to a structured questionnaire in successive stages. It also employed coffee taste tests and tests of consumer reactions to advertisements. It was addressed to the task of learning more about how coffee consumption might be increased — the same assignment which had been assumed by a market survey in 1939. The latter is described briefly so that the contrast between the two approaches may be noted.

PAN-AMERICAN COFFEE BUREAU

A Descriptive Case

EARLY IN 1955 executives of the Pan-American Coffee Bureau, New York City, approached Dr. Ernest Dichter, President of the Institute for Motivational Research, Croton, New York, about the possibility of undertaking consumer research to learn more about how coffee consumption might be increased.

The Bureau, managed by Mr. Charles G. Lindsay, was supported by coffee growers of 11 Latin American countries to promote the use of coffee. It had run substantial consumer advertising campaigns toward that end for a number of years, and had sponsored research to learn about coffee buying and consumption. Research efforts, described by Dr. James E. Wood, Director of Research, included the following:

1. A survey of coffee consumption in the United States, conducted by an advertising agency in 1939. A number of direct questions were asked of a sample of nearly 5,000 housewives to find out such things as who drank coffee, how much they drank, when and where they drank it, how they made coffee, how often they bought it, and whether they regarded coffee as good or harmful.

   While this study has been superseded, it is cited here as an example of early research. Among its findings: about 80% of all adults drank coffee, the average daily consumption was three cups, 88% of the housewives said their husbands liked the coffee they made, and 40% of the women used less than two level tablespoons of coffee per cup, the amount considered by the Bureau as necessary for a good cup of coffee. (See Appendix A, pages 185–190, for questionnaire and summary of findings.)

2. Annual surveys of amount of coffee drinking in winter, conducted by The Psychological Corporation of New York starting in 1950. This information was obtained in personal interviews in which people were asked how many cups of coffee they drank on the preceding day.

3. Starting early in 1954 the Bureau received weekly, monthly, quarterly, and annual reports on purchases of coffee, both regular and instant, by families in the national panel of the Market Research Corporation of America, New York City. The Bureau converted these figures into their green coffee equivalent in which terms total demand was expressed.

4. Two studies of the number of cups extracted from a pound of coffee had been made for the Bureau by National Family Opinion, Inc., of Toledo, Ohio, one in 1953 and the other in 1955. For them, housewives reported the amount of coffee used for a specified meal and the number of cups made from that amount.

A need for consumer research which would add to understanding of the nature of the demand for coffee and how it might be increased was felt even more keenly in 1955. Per capita consumption of coffee in the United States had been declining since 1946. Executives wanted to know how effective the Bureau's consumer advertising had been and whether its "coffee break" theme used since 1950 should be continued or modified in some way. The outlook was for more coffee being offered on the market several years hence as the price increases of 1953 had prompted new plantings of trees which would start producing when five years old. Increases in coffee supply in the past always had been accompanied by substantially more than proportionate decreases in price.

The Bureau also hoped to learn of sales appeals for coffee which could be used more effectively by companies selling coffee at retail than the "more cups per pound" claims a number of them had been making for their brands. It was feared that these claims might lead to the making of weaker coffee and further reductions in per capita consumption. The Bureau in its advertising had been urging the use of two level tablespoons of coffee per cup, believing that many people drank less coffee than they might because they made it too weak for maximum enjoyment.

Research conducted prior to 1955 had consisted of quantitative surveys of coffee use and preference and of economic studies of the total demand for coffee. There had been no studies of why people bought and drank coffee. Believing that research of this type was needed, executives of the Bureau called in Dr. Dichter to talk about the possibility of undertaking a motivational study. They discussed research which would seek to learn what coffee meant to people, believing that once such an understanding had been gained, objectives and ideas for future advertising and public relations approaches would become clearer.

Dr. Dichter, a psychologist born and trained in Vienna, had been active in urging that business make greater use of psychology. In recent years he had become prominently identified with motivation research, and frequently appeared as a speaker on this subject before business and professional groups.[1] The staff of his Institute for Motivational Research included about 30 people, more than half of whom had formal training in the social sciences.

In early conferences, executives of the Bureau and the Institute for Motivational Research prepared a number of questions to serve as a preliminary definition of the research assignment.

Later, the following motivational research areas were identified as most likely to yield the desired information:

1. What is coffee's "cultural label"? What should be coffee's cultural status in the future?
2. What are the attitudes toward coffee by age, income, and social groups?
3. What are the personality patterns of the coffee drinker?
4. Under what circumstances is coffee bought and used? Is it bought and consumed in a certain "coffee mood"? Is coffee purchasing really an established part of a living pattern or does it yield to impulsive purchases?
5. How can noncoffee drinkers be converted into coffee drinkers? How rigid are people about their coffee habits? Is it possible to increase consumption among coffee drinkers?

[1] Articles written by Dr. Dichter include the following: "Psychology in Market Research," *Harvard Business Review*, Summer 1947: "A Psychological View of Advertising Effectiveness," *Journal of Marketing*, July 1949; and "What Are the Real Reasons People Buy Today?", *Sales Management*, February 1 and 15, 1955.

6. Does coffee evoke specific childhood associations? If so, how do they influence teen-age and adult coffee habits?
7. Do people have definite pictures of coffee which include specific good and bad qualities?
8. How important is price? Is coffee really expensive or only psychologically so? What is the correct psychological price of coffee?
9. Is there an ideal coffee? Does this vary by region, economic, social, and cultural background?
10. How do employees view the "coffee break"? Employers? Is there a conflict? If so, how can it be reconciled?
11. Is there a new attitude toward coffee because of new nutritional concepts?

The proposal also contained descriptions of the research method, sample and procedure, time and cost estimates, and information about the Institute's staff.

The proposal was accepted and the study got under way.

Factors of probable importance to coffee consumption were identified and discussed in staff conferences. Available literature on coffee was searched and one book, which described how coffee had fitted into various cultures, was particularly helpful to early thinking.

In describing the planning of the research, Mr. Ernest Angel, a psychologist who served as director of the coffee study, said:

> You know certain things from your training in the social sciences, from doing other research (the Institute had done five studies for individual coffee companies), and from talking with people. For instance, we knew that strength of coffee was likely to be an important area to investigate — some people drink coffee "straight" like some people do whiskey. Also, we knew that the utility vs. pleasure and social aspects probably were important. Some people drink coffee as a "must" to get started; others do it for pleasure. They like the aroma, variety, etc. We also knew that coffee had some connection with maturity and that it was an issue

between parents and children, doctors and patients, teachers and pupils. While we knew some of these things, we did not know the detailed implications, why certain things were true, or what should be done about them in writing advertising copy.

Two waves of depth interviews were conducted to develop points such as those indicated above and to learn of others of importance. Concepts arrived at by this process then were tested by the use of projective questions, coffee taste tests, and tests of reactions to advertisements which had been run by the Pan-American Coffee Bureau.

THE DEPTH INTERVIEWS

In the depth interview, the basic research technique used, a trained interviewer encouraged the respondent to talk freely about his associations and feelings related to coffee. Direct questions seldom were asked. Instead, the interviewer attempted by skillful probing to learn of what was important to the respondent and to investigate the emotional factors which often determined apparently rational behavior.

For the first wave of 36 depth interviews, for example, the interviewers were given instructions which included a brief description of the general objectives and a list of broad areas for investigation. (See Appendix B, pages 191–192.) They were told that it would be most helpful if they could just get people to talk freely for an hour or so on all of their feelings about coffee. At the start, interviewers were to encourage maximum free association to get everything that came into people's minds when they thought of coffee. Then the respondents would be encouraged to be more specific by talking about their last few cups of coffee — how they felt from the moment they thought of coffee through the drinking of it and how they felt afterwards. Interviewers were instructed to probe in detail for all sensory impressions such as smell, taste, and appearance.

Research areas which were suggested for probing after free association had been exhausted included kinds of coffee, coffee drinking occasions, what the respondent considered to be the best cup of coffee he had tasted, childhood impressions of coffee, attitudes toward children drinking coffee, frequency of coffee drinking, and feelings about coffee and health.

The interviewers also were given instructions about choosing respondents so that the sample would include men and women, "dark strong" and "light weak" coffee drinkers and "heavy" (6–8 cups a day) and "light" (2–3 cups per day) coffee drinkers.

Persons with some training in the social sciences were preferred as interviewers because they were more likely to be able to make the respondent feel free to talk, skillfully probe to get at the roots of feelings, and avoid leading questions. Among those regarded as top interviewers were a number with some training in clinical psychology. Interviewers were instructed to take as nearly verbatim notes as possible. If they wished to report any observations or interpretations, they were asked to do so only after they had completed their verbatim notes as to what was said. Occasionally interviews were recorded on tape. Frequently, new interviewers had to be trained to learn to distinguish between their own feelings and what others said. It was common for them at first to unconsciously project their own feelings into interview write-ups.

In reading the write-ups of the interviews, the study director searched for new ideas, noted patterns of response, and developed concepts. By this process, it became clearer what areas should be explored further, and a guide was prepared for the second wave which included 93 depth interviews. (See Appendix C, pages 193–196.)

Spontaneity of response was encouraged in the second wave of interviews as it had been in the first, but the interviewer also was to be sure to cover in detail areas suggested by the guide. The first area, for example, was that of the coffee stereotype, and questions which illustrated how the topic might be developed included the following. What comes to mind when you hear the word coffee? What pictures come into your mind? What associations do you have with coffee? Why do you think people drink coffee? What does coffee do for them? Why do women drink coffee? Men? What are the major functions that coffee fulfills? How important do you think coffee is in American life?

The second wave interviews were apportioned by geographical region and by several groupings of respondents: parents of children 5 to 10 years of age; people 50 years of age and older; newlyweds; teachers; pediatricians; employers who did and employers who did not have a coffee break for their employees; employees who worked at plants or offices which did and which did not have coffee breaks. A separate guide was used for interviews with unmarried college students.

Half of the interview reports in the second wave were read by the study director and half by an assistant. Both looked for ideas which suggested theories to be tested in further field work. Their qualitative analyses were supplemented by statistical tabulations of responses by broad content groupings.

The repetitive nature of the responses was regarded as evidence that the depth interviews had served to identify most of the ways people thought and felt about coffee and its use. The remainder of the field work, therefore, was devoted to three different tests of the importance of these factors.

THE QUESTIONNAIRE

One test employed a questionnaire with a variety of direct and projective questions devised so that the results could easily be quantified.   (See Appendix D, pages 197–210.)   Information about the respondent (name, address, sex, age, marital status, number and ages of children, ethnic origin, occupation, income) was recorded on the cover sheet.

Part I of the questionnaire included questions dealing with the frequency, amount, time, and place of coffee drinking; what people usually took in their coffee; whether coffee was regarded as a necessity, a regular use item, or a luxury as compared with other foods for which the same information was obtained; and how well the respondent thought he liked coffee as compared with other people.

In Part II the respondent was asked to tell about his own coffee history.   While he was to be encouraged to talk in his own way, the interviewer was instructed to look for changes in coffee consumption, and when and why they occurred. A form was provided so that coffee consumption in cups per day could be plotted against age as the respondent talked. The dots could be joined to give a coffee use profile.   Space was provided for detailed explanations of the occasions for starting to drink coffee and for changes in coffee consumption.   The respondent also was questioned about what strength of coffee he used when he started drinking it; his parents' attitude toward his early coffee drinking; and his opinion as to whether coffee was habit-forming, whether it was a good or bad habit and why.

The next part sought the respondent's feelings about coffee by asking his ideas as to what kind of a personality would drink coffee in different strengths and amounts and with varying amounts of cream and sugar.   For this purpose, the respondent was told that four women were having lunch together: a clergyman's wife, a nursery school teacher, a lady senator, and a department store buyer.   After lunch each woman ordered her coffee exactly the way she wanted it.   The respondent was asked what each women would order.   For example, the clergyman's wife would order (a) strong coffee,

(b) average coffee, or (c) weak coffee. She would use (a) lots of cream, (b) a little cream, or (c) no cream, etc.

The respondent also was asked to compare the usual cup of coffee with the best she could imagine; and the usual cup with the cup she got in her favorite restaurant. She also was asked about her knowledge of various kinds of coffee (coffee as served in various foreign countries etc.) ; causes of bad coffee; her image of coffee-growers; and her knowledge of coffee growing and the Pan-American Coffee Bureau.

Part III consisted of multiple choice questions about the respondent's reasons for drinking coffee and for not drinking it more often.

The questionnaire was used in interviews with about 200 people.

COFFEE TASTE TESTS

Taste tests were conducted with 128 respondents living in four different regions of the country to learn of the acceptability of coffee of different strengths and to determine whether it might be possible to increase consumption by getting people to drink coffee in different forms on different occasions.

Respondents were chosen so that half were women, half men, and half were "coffee-sophisticated" (exposed to a variety of different coffees before) and half were "coffee-naive." They were invited in groups of four to interviewers' homes where the tests were conducted in a relaxed, informal atmosphere, but in a way to avoid one respondent influencing another.

Comparisons were made of different strengths of conventional American coffee and of a different or "exotic" coffee. Each test group tasted two of the alternatives, the respondents being asked which they liked the better and why. Two brands of coffee were used for all of the tests, one representing conventional coffee and the other the different or "exotic" coffee. Strengths of coffee were according to Coffee Brewing Institute specifications. Comparisons were made of the following in the series of tests:

1. Conventional American coffee: standard strength vs. strong. (The strong coffee was rejected by more than three-fourths of the respondents.)
2. Conventional American coffee: standard strength vs. weak. (The weak coffee was rejected.)
3. Conventional American coffee of standard strength vs. "different" coffee of strong coffee strength. (The different coffee was preferred by more than two-thirds of the respondents.)
4. Same as No.3 except that the different coffee was introduced with a prestige-promoting remark: "This is the coffee the coffee people themselves consider best." (The number favoring the stronger coffee was increased slightly by the prestige introduction.)

While the numbers involved in the tests were not large, results were strongly consistent. They were interpreted as confirmation of people's readiness to accept change when it was offered as "variety," while they would reject it if offered only as the same thing but stronger.

THE AD TESTS

The ad tests, administered to 217 respondents, provided a further check on earlier findings by obtaining reactions to 11 Coffee Bureau ads which had appeared in *Life* and *The Saturday Evening Post* from 1952 to 1955. Only three of the ads were used in each interview. The interviewer started by asking for general impressions of coffee advertising and detailed comments on any ads the respondent remembered. (See Appendix E, pages 211–212, for detailed instructions to interviewers).

The respondent then was shown the first of the three ads. She was asked to look over the ad, return it to the interviewer, and tell about everything that ran through her mind when she looked at the ad — her recollections, associations, impressions, images, or questions. This was repeated for the other two ads. This information was to be obtained by encouraging maximum spontaneous association as was done in the depth interviews. The purpose was to get comments which would reveal the respondent's reactions and explain why she liked or disliked an ad or parts of it. The interviewer was instructed to probe for these explanations and to guard against the respondent assuming a role of ad expert. Whether the respondent considered one ad to be a good ad and another poor was viewed as largely irrelevant.

In the next stage of the interview, the respondent was given each ad once more. As she looked at it, the interviewer probed in detail for associations to each part of the ad: the illustration, heading, color, slogans, and each section of the copy. The interview concluded by asking the respondent what she would do to improve the ad.

While over-all reaction to many of the ads was favorable, a number of feelings were expressed which indicated how improvement might be made. For example, 80% of the respondents expressed dissatisfaction with the way coffee was portrayed in the ads (dull and cold rather than hot) ; 20% objected to being told how to make coffee (two level tablespoons per cup) and preferred to be free to make coffee in their own way; generally people accepted the message of the ad much more readily if they did not feel that they were being "sold"; and many pointed out that the spirit of the coffee break was negated when the ad showed people having coffee at the actual place of work (beside a machine or at a drawing board) .

Reactions to one of the ads are given in more detail here for illustrative purposes. The ad showed a father, mother, and daughter seated in the front seat of a car stopped for a coffee break. The parents were drinking coffee, the daughter nothing. Everyone liked the idea of the family being out together, but they commented adversely on several things as is shown in the sample comments which follow:

Comment #1: Well, I like it, but I'm disappointed that the child didn't have anything. You would think she would have ice cream or a coke but she doesn't have anything in her hand. As for the rest, I like the family scene. It seems a typical family.

Comment #2: I have a feeling that someone ought to tell the group to get out of the car and then they could relax even more. It's good to have the family group, but the little girl ought not to be left out of things.

Comment #3: In a sense the ad is not realistic. What about the little girl? She seems as though she doesn't belong in the picture. Everybody's enjoying a drink, but not she. I would give that poor child something to drink, or take her out of the car to relax even more. You can't really relax all stuffed in the front seat.

REPORT OF FINDINGS AND RECOMMENDATIONS

Findings and recommendations were presented in a 150-page report, the main theme of which was that coffee had become a utilitarian staple and that it must be rediscovered as an exciting beverage of pleasure if consumption is to be increased. (See Appendix F, pages 213–222, for digest.) Several specific objectives were cited in line with accomplishing this task:

1. Change coffee from a sinful and escapist beverage to a positive, life-accepting product. Coffee was seen by some as a drug which promoted addiction, as a dangerous stimulant to the heart, and as an aid to laziness. While many people liked coffee, they also were afraid of drinking too much of it or of giving it to young people. The conflict that coffee represents was indicated by the fact that people also see powerful factors in favor of its use. Many feel

that it aids in better self-control, that it relaxes and serves to bring back one's natural resources. Coffee is used by many as a reward for hard or long work.

Some steps which could be taken to change sin to morality for coffee: make coffee a helper in coping with life; purify it morally by showing it as a natural product; dramatize its help in self-control; and reassure about the universal acceptance of coffee by pointing out that all the world loves coffee and by citing what poets and writers have said about it.

2. Help coffee catch up with the cultural changes which are represented by the desire for more gracious living, the moving away from earlier restrictions imposed on enjoying sensory pleasures, and the trend toward expression of personality by more individualized consumption and appreciation and enjoyment of differences and variety. Coffee has become too utilitarian and "frozen" psychologically. People feel that most brands do not reflect varieties of flavor and that shopping for coffee is not rewarded by discovery. At the same time, taste tests show a willingness to accept change in coffee when it is offered as variety. Coffee is seen by some as a symbol of a better, more leisurely life, and many people also realize and appreciate its contribution to their emotional health. The coffee break gratifies deep and often deeply hidden emotional needs in workers as well as their bosses.

These findings point to the need to change coffee from a utilitarian to a pleasurable beverage, to stress its sensory pleasures, and to make it more of a food for emotional health. Variety should be introduced in many ways. The coffee break should be proof of creative considerateness by the employer and a reward for hard work.

3. Change from an authoritative to a permissive approach regarding the making and serving of coffee. (Pan American Coffee Bureau advertising had been telling people to

use 2 level tablespoons of coffee to every cup.) People are proud of their individual rights to coffee once they have been gained from parental authority and they reject any prescription of rigid rules as to strength or brewing methods as being correct for all coffee drinkers. The interviews showed a widespread diversity in the way coffee affects people and the ways in which they prefer coffee. Many expressed great pride in their individual art of coffee brewing and serving and indicated their receptivity to trying new and different kinds of coffee flavors or brewing methods.

Almost all parents expressed sharp rejection of any outside suggestion relating to children drinking coffee. They were willing to allow coffee drinking to start at varying age levels, but they wanted to retain control over this expression of their children's growing up. Mothers frequently reported putting a little coffee in milk as an aid in getting children to drink the latter. Coffee also is used as a special treat or as a reward for "being good."

Findings suggest that people should not be ordered to make coffee in any one way; instead, they should be invited to experiment and discover for themselves. Individual feelings about coffee should be respected. Advertising could let more parents know about other parents' success with coffee as a way to get children to drink milk, and good-humored approaches could help parents introduce coffee to children as a part of growing up.

The study showed that people regard coffee as an intimate beverage associated with closeness, warmth, and good fellowship. Coffee is seen as an aid to removing barriers and promoting understanding between people. For many, it is a measure of interest in homemaking and in receiving friends in a warm and appreciative fashion. Good, strong coffee expresses abundance and generosity while poor, weak coffee is identified with poverty and skimping. The aroma of coffee frequently is connected with nostalgic feelings about childhood pleasures and security. Coffee is a symbol of grown-up relaxation. Advertising should be in keeping with this image. Coffee should be shown in social surroundings which include the elements of intimacy and closeness.

The interviews indicated that the American housewife represents a good potential for increased coffee consumption. Her job is one of monotony, drudgery, and few rewards. Coffee can be the needed excuse for relaxation, be an inviting reward, and provide her with a sense of security by heightening her alertness and sense of mastery over the situation. As a symbol of sociability, coffee can provide comfort by serving as a substitute for a companion when it is not possible to relax over a cup of coffee with a neighbor. It was recommended that housewives be encouraged to experiment with different blends, roasts, and methods of preparing coffee with the primary goal being to extend pleasures. Increased use of coffee by the housewife might lead to greater consumption by her family.

Coffee served in most restaurants was not regarded favorably, the restaurant situation usually being one which tends to deny coffee as a symbol of closeness and hospitality. When special emphasis is given to the type or quality of coffee, however, it meets with favorable response. Coffee commonly is regarded as an index of a restaurant's quality, a finding of significance for coffee advertising to the restaurant trade.

CHANGES IN ADVERTISING

Prior to the motivation study, the Coffee Bureau had been running full page ads which promoted the "coffee-break" and called attention to coffee's role as a stimulant. Typical was an ad which showed a somewhat weary looking secretary drinking coffee at her desk. (See Exhibit 1, between pages 82 and 83.) It suggested hot coffee as "a wonderful way to break the tempo of work and ease the strain of concentration. Nothing else offers such a friendly lift." The ad also stressed "Enjoy coffee often — and make it right. Use two level tablespoons (or 1 standard coffee measure) for every cup."

Findings of the research were reflected in later advertisements which moved from "stress and strain" situations to pictures of people happily enjoying coffee and departed from telling people to make coffee in one "right" way. Instead of showing black coffee in ordinary cups, the ad for October 1955 featured attractive cups of coffee with a dash of whipped cream on top. The copy talked about "good, full-bodied delicious coffee — made just the way *you* like it best." It suggested that the "next time *you* serve coffee, why not try it this different way? Top it off with a swirl of whipped cream — the way they do in old Vienna!"

The copy of some advertisements stressed that it was socially acceptable for a woman to drink coffee black or for a man to drink it with cream or sugar. This was done by talking about the "figure-conscious girl who drinks hers black," "the businessman, cream, two sugars," "the driver, black with apple pie," "the motherly-type woman, light, one sugar."

In the process of developing advertising for early 1956, twenty different ads were prepared on the basis of the motivation study findings. Six were selected for tests of consumer reactions conducted by the Institute for Motivational Research to see whether they seemed to accomplish their purpose. The results suggested changes which were incorporated in a new series of three ads in color which appeared in *The Saturday Evening Post* and *The Ladies' Home Journal* starting in March 1956.

In the new series there was a gradual change in emphasis from the "coffee-break" to the new theme of helping people rediscover coffee. The headline of the first ad was "Good time for a 'coffee-break'!" The headline of the second ad was "Get all the 'breaks' of coffee!" Both ads included six pictures to show coffee served attractively in different ways at different times of the day and used the slogan, "There is nothing so satisfying as a cup of *good* coffee." The reader was invited to try given brewing directions.

In the third ad, "coffee-break" was dropped from the headline which read "It's a *good* day with coffee." (See Exhibit 2, between pages 82 and 83.) Six illustrations featured the use of coffee at different times in the day. One of them urged the reader to treat guests to a special coffee, Caffee Cappuccino.

The findings of the motivational study also were used in the development of a promotional campaign for iced coffee which many people in the industry felt could not be sold successfully. Coffee consumption in the three months of June, July, and August had been 16% below the average for the other three quarters of the year and Dr. Wood estimated that this slump cost the coffee industry about $100 million in sales annually.

To start the campaign for iced coffee, a three-page, gatefold ad was run in the June 2, 1956, issue of *The Saturday Evening Post*. Using colored photographs, the ad featured six different ways of serving iced coffee; (1) "Coffee Float — drop a generous amount of your favorite ice cream into good iced coffee"; (2) "Iced Coffee Mocha — add a teaspoon of chocolate syrup or cocoa per cup"; (3) " Spiced Iced Coffee — pour 3 cups of hot, double-strength coffee over 2 cinnamon sticks, 4 cloves, and 4 allspice berries"; (4) "Iced Coffee Junior — sweeten the youngster's milk a little and color it with the cold coffee — you're the best judge of the amount"; (5) "Coffee Julep — add a dash of mint flavor and serve in silver or aluminum cups, well-frosted"; and (6) "Iced Coffee Viennese — topped with a snowy swirl of whipped cream." The ad also featured "three ways to make delicious iced coffee every time!" because it was felt that improperly made and served iced coffee had been a major barrier to increased consumption in the past. A similar single-page version of this ad appeared in *Look* magazine late in June.

The Bureau's director of consumer services prepared a 48-page booklet, "Fun with Coffee," which represented a collection of "the world's finest coffee recipes — 100 different ways to enjoy America's favorite beverage." The iced coffee advertisements described above contained a coupon which readers could use to send with 25 cents for a copy of the recipe booklet.

Various point-of-sale material was prepared for use in food stores including a colorful "Cool off with Coffee" mobile with glasses of iced coffee hanging from it, and pads of recipes for making iced coffee.

Various steps were taken to inform the trade of the motivational study and to invite roasters to make use of the findings in advertising their own brands of coffee. The research and the Bureau's advertising and promotion plans were among the topics emphasized at regional seminars for coffee roasters and others of the industry held early in 1956 in New York, Chicago, New Orleans, and San Francisco. Several articles relating to the promotion of iced coffee appeared in the February 1956 issue of *Coffee and Tea Industries,* a trade publication. The summer slump in coffee consumption was discussed by Dr. Wood in one article, and in another Mr. E. E. Van Horn, the Bureau's director of advertising, described the 1956 advertising and promotion plans for iced coffee. In a third article, entitled "The Conflict of Iced Coffee," Dr. Dichter wrote about consumer attitudes and how they might be turned into promotional assets for iced coffee.

In addition to printing the complete report of findings of the motivational study, the Bureau prepared a 12-page summary of it for distribution within the coffee industry. Entitled "New Horizons for Coffee Promotion," the summary was organized around these recommendations for promotion "to help people rediscover coffee in all its many aspects:

1. Feature coffee as a beverage to heighten the pleasures of life; give it the variety required by modern living.
2. Dramatize coffee's role of helping people to meet with everyday problems.
3. Promote the 'coffee-break' in all of its implications.
4. Remove consumer doubts about coffee drinking.
5. Change from a dictatorial to an invitational approach in recommending coffee brewing methods.
6. Approach the teen-age market with care and consideration."

Pan-American Coffee Bureau

Commentary

The advertising agency study of 1939 was an early part of the Coffee Bureau's continuing research program. Nevertheless, it is typical of a great many market surveys of today and its inclusion here permits us to contrast it with the 1955 motivational research. The studies started with the same general objective of finding out how to increase coffee consumption, but they differed markedly in approach. In part this reflected the different stages of the research history at which they came. Some of the information sought in 1939 was available from various sources in 1955. Another reason, however, was that the studies were planned by people with different backgrounds and ways of thinking about consumer behavior and research. It is these differences which are of particular interest to us.

The survey's approach to the problem was primarily in terms of gathering objective data on such things as coffee purchasing, making, and drinking. That this was appropriate is not questioned here. Instead, we are noting that the researchers thought largely in these terms rather than others.

In the effort to find out who drank how much coffee, "who" was defined by geographical region, city size, age, and income. Information on these familiar market factors usually can be ascertained fairly easily and groups of people based on them can be approached more or less selectively by certain advertising media. Presumably, a major purpose was that of identifying segments of the market to which promotional effort should be directed. Special mention is made of the market factors because recent studies have used others as well, including some relating to personality and social status. This suggests the possibility that dimensions other than those used in 1939 might be even more useful for differentiating among people on the basis of their coffee consumption. The problem, of course, is how to go about finding out what they are.

In order to determine what else might be done to sell more coffee, the researchers, drawing on their experience in advertising and market research, made several assumptions as to what was related to the amount of coffee consumed. It apparently was not the purpose of the survey to check these assumptions. Instead, the questionnaire sought information on what extent assumed favorable conditions existed. This included finding out whether people used as much coffee per cup as the Coffee Bureau recommended; whether they thought coffee had good or harmful effects; whether they liked restaurant coffee; and whether the husband liked the coffee served at home. (It is interesting to note that 40% of the women were found to be making coffee weaker than Coffee Bureau standards, that subsequent Bureau advertising made a point of telling people to use two level tablespoons of coffee per cup, and that this practice later was abandoned upon a recommendation growing out of the 1955 motivational research.)

These items, as far as they went, represented background information which could be helpful to thinking, but the study's direct contribution to an understanding of how coffee consumption might be increased was a limited one.

In regard to research techniques, the survey relied on direct questions, assuming that people would be willing and able to give the information desired. Most questions were of a restricted answer variety in that they called either for very specific information or presented several alternative answers. The respondent had little control over either the topic discussed or how his response was expressed and recorded.

Whether structuring of responses is desirable depends upon the objective, and advantages and limitations of different types of questions will be considered more fully in a later chapter. For our purposes here, we shall agree that the questions pertaining to habits of coffee drinking and buying and the kinds of utensils employed in making coffee probably were satisfactory. Some of the other questions, however, may have shut off helpful information when it was not the intention to do so. Two examples of where this may have happened are given below to call attention to assumptions implicit in questions:

Question: "What is your recipe for making coffee?" (Questionnaire included check lists for types of measuring instruments and measurements plus several lines for "details of method and comments.")

The question assumes that people can tell you how much coffee they use, expressing it in the terms appearing in the check lists. If they "just pour coffee in up to here" or do it more or less "by feel," the question runs into trouble. If the purpose included finding out how careful and consistent people were in making coffee, the question has limitations.

The use of the word "recipe" may suggest to the repondent that she should be precise in making coffee. If she is not, she may hide the fact from the interviewer.

Question: "When you make coffee yourself, what one thing is most important?"

This question appears to assume that there is one thing which is most important to the repondent, that she is aware of what it is, and that she can talk about it meaningfully in isolation from other factors. If these things are not true, the responses will not be very enlightening. (Only one blank line was provided, so responses of only a few words appear to have been expected.)

In summary, the survey focused on objective rather than subjective data. The emphasis was on finding out who drank how much coffee rather than why they did. Questioning was direct, the questionnaire controlling to a large extent the topics discussed and the character of the response. This implies the assumption that the researchers knew what aspects of the subject they wanted dealt with in the interviews, that they could anticipate the kinds of responses well enough to provide adequately for recording them on the questionnaire form, and that the questions were sufficiently in accord with the way people usually think to be intelligible and answerable.

The 1955 Study

The 1955 study employed a number of concepts and methods developed in the social sciences, particularly dynamic psychology. The approach to finding out how to increase coffee consumption was to develop a greater understanding of why people drank it. The focus was on the consumer as a human being and what coffee meant to him in terms of his emotional and other needs. A variety of psychological as well as other factors were considered. Coffee was seen to have many meanings because of its inherent characteristics and its role in our culture. Some of the meanings are consciously recognized by people, others are not. To learn about them, heavy reliance was placed on indirect methods of questioning.

The general approach reflects the ways of thinking of people with specialized backgrounds. On a more specific level it is of course difficult to show adequately how a person's training contributed to his performance in any single enterprise. To a large extent, the individual concerned cannot explain this. His background includes many things which have become integrated parts of him. Together they influence how he thinks and how he goes about his work. An important part of this influence for people engaged in consumer research stems from concepts which seem to aid in understanding human behavior and which serve as important sources of ideas as to what should be investigated. In the 1955 study, for example, aspects of coffee behavior were considered which had not received attention earlier. In order to illustrate the use of concepts, we have attempted to identify below a few of the ideas which figured in the planning of the study and the interpretation of the data:

The concept that a product (coffee) has a role in a culture and that the importance of the role depends, among other things, on how well the product keeps up with cultural changes. Coffee was seen as losing its rich meanings and becoming more utilitarian at a time when there was a growing desire for more gracious living. These observations led to investigating people's willingness to accept change in coffee when it was offered as variety. The result was one of the major recommendations of the study: that different blends, roasts, and methods of coffee be promoted.

The concept of a product as a symbol, a collection of meanings which enable coffee, in this case, to contribute to people's emotional well-being. Some of the symbolic meanings of coffee mentioned in the study were pleasure, leisure,

luxury, intimacy, hospitality, sociability, relaxation, adulthood, an interest in homemaking. It also was recognized as
an aid to promoting conversation and understanding between people, as a stimulant and an aid in self-control of
feelings.

The psychological concept of conflict — a recognition that
people often have opposite feelings about the same thing
at the same time. This led to seeing whether this was true
for coffee. It was. While people enjoyed drinking it for a
number of reasons, they also were afraid to drink too much
of it, to give it to young people. They connected it with
addiction, overstimulation, laziness, a fear of punishment
for enjoyment of sensory pleasure — associations which represented barriers to consumption.

Recognition that parents desire to retain control over
(some even to prevent) their children's growing up. This
idea, plus the concept of coffee as a symbol of maturity, had
several implications. One was that parents rejected outside
suggestions relating to the drinking of coffee by children.
Another was that once a person had gained permission from
parental authority to drink coffee, he guarded his "coffee
freedom." Investigation of how coffee was used with children in the home demonstrated its use as a symbol of initiation into adulthood. Mothers added a few drops of coffee
to a glass of milk for their young children, the proportion
of coffee often increasing as the child grew older.

Recognition that resentment of authority is common as
an outgrowth of experience with parents, teachers, and
other authority figures, and that it often is associated with
developing and taking pride in individual preferences.
This led to questioning the advisability of the Coffee Bureau's use of an authoritarian approach in telling people to
make coffee "right" as defined by Bureau standards. Consumer reactions were investigated and the findings led to a
recommendation that the approach be abandoned.

Related to the above point was recognition that many
people, often unconsciously, feel resentment toward their

working situation. The coffee break was pictured as offering a socially acceptable outlet for this resentment.

The concept of a product being considered as masculine or feminine. By this is meant that people identify it as being more appropriate for a man or for a woman because of characteristics which in our culture are seen as masculine or feminine. The cultural stereotype of coffee was found to be dark and strong (masculine). There were indications that people who preferred weaker coffee or coffee with cream tended to avoid drinking coffee because they did not wish to be considered as feminine or "sissy." This led to a recommendation that advertising promote the idea that coffee preference is an individual matter, cutting across the sexes.

Recognition that childhood experiences often color a person's feelings for a lifetime. This led to investigating the influence of these experiences on the formation of attitudes toward coffee.

Dynamic psychology also strongly influenced how the researchers went about gathering data. Reference already has been made to the concept that people are not conscious of many of their feelings about coffee, and therefore they cannot tell about them in response to direct questioning. This was one reason why indirect, free response questioning was used, especially in the initial stages. Another was the idea that the people themselves, if approached correctly, could be a valuable source of clues as to what was important to them about coffee and hence what factors should receive attention in the study.

The first interviews represented an attempt to get people to talk about coffee fully and in their own way, free from preconceptions of the researcher or leading or evaluative comments by the interviewer. The object was to allow the respondent to follow her thoughts with no effort being made to enforce a rational pattern on the material. The spirit was reflected in this instruction to interviewers: "It would be most helpful . . . if you could just get people talking freely on all their feelings about coffee for an hour or so."

The approach relies upon the principle of free association. The objective was to provide the respondent with the most favorable circumstances possible for recalling and telling all she knew, consciously or unconsciously, about the meaning of coffee to her. The first interviews started with an attempt to get all the respondent's spontaneous associations to coffee. Then the respondent was encouraged to talk in certain broad topical areas suggested by the researchers' knowledge of human behavior as likely to be rewarding.

The researchers' backgrounds also played a highly important part in the interpretation of verbatim reports of the responses. It should be noted that the findings were not limited to a literal interpretation of what people said. Instead, the important feature was what the psychologists, drawing upon their knowledge of human behavior, made of the data. Meanings often had to be inferred.

The use of indirect, free-response techniques involves several assumptions. One is that people will talk both freely and honestly. A great deal depends upon the interviewer's skill in establishing rapport and in probing. Another is that the responses will be recorded accurately in the words of the respondent, not those of the interviewer. A crucial assumption, of course, is that the interpreter will be able to make something out of the interview reports and avoid the temptation of seeing things in the data that are not there.

An important feature of the research was that it included several different phases. Interviews in the first wave were very exploratory and open, the main effort being to give the respondent a free hand so that important aspects of coffee behavior could be identified. As this was accomplished, the interviewing could become somewhat more focused. The guide for the second wave of interviews, for example, was more complete than the first in suggesting topical areas for investigation. The coffee questionnaire which followed, designed largely to check on earlier findings, was highly structured. While some of the questions may have been indirect in that their ultimate purpose was not apparent to the respondent, for the most part they called for limited, specific responses. The latter could be counted and analyzed statistically. The taste tests and the ad tests represented somewhat different approaches to learning about people and coffee and checking on earlier findings.

The 1955 study had a marked impact within the Coffee Bureau which was faced with immediate and difficult promotional problems. It served the valuable functions of introducing new ideas and serving as a rallying point for fresh promotional efforts which were undertaken with renewed enthusiasm. Within the organization it was regarded as "an imaginative study representing a very important new approach," to use the words of one executive. Another pointed to its value in crystallizing ideas and centralizing thinking at a time when this was needed. The research, which reflected ways of thinking which had not been tried in previous studies for the Bureau, led to major changes in the advertising approach for hot coffee and a new promotional attack on the difficult problem of stimulating sales for iced coffee. It also gave the Bureau something to talk about with coffee roasters and others in the trade in efforts to encourage their promotional cooperation.

In summary, the 1955 study contrasts with the 1939 survey as to the kinds of things considered and in the ways of gathering and interpreting data. The focus was on the meanings of coffee to people in terms of their emotional as well as other needs. Research techniques were chosen which would permit the tapping of unconscious as well as conscious material. Skillful interpretation of qualitative data is crucial to the successful use of these techniques which also place heavier than usual demands on the interviewer. The research approach included going to the people themselves to get ideas as to what factors should be researched. Suggestions as to fruitful areas for investigation also were a product of the backgrounds of the researchers, which included knowledge of human behavior developed in other fields, particularly dynamic psychology. The research was conducted in several stages, tentative findings of early interviews later being tested further by more specific means, including a structured questionnaire.

QUESTIONNAIRE AND SUMMARY OF FINDINGS FROM "A NATIONAL CONSUMER SURVEY OF COFFEE CONSUMPTION" CONDUCTED FOR THE PAN-AMERICAN COFFEE BUREAU, 1939

Name _____ City Size Group:

Post Office Address _____ 250,000 or more _____

50,000 to 250,000 _____

City _____ State _____ 10,000 to 50,000 _____

2,500 to 10,000 _____

CLASS: A ____ B ____ C ____   Rural nonfarm _____

Farm _____

1. COMPOSITION OF FAMILY AND COFFEE DRINKING HABITS (Write in number of people in each group under each heading.)

	Total in Family	Drink Coffee Reg.	Do Not Drink Reg.	Reasons for Not Drinking Regularly (After each reason, indicate number of people to whom that reason applies)	No.
Women (Over 16)	___	___	___	_____	___
Men (Over 16)	___	___	___	_____	___
Children 6 to 16	___	___	___	_____	___
Children under 6	___	___	___	_____	___
TOTAL	___	___	___		

2. What beverages do you serve at various times of the day?

	None	Coffee Reg. Occ.	Decaff. Reg. Occ.	Coffee Subst. Reg. Occ.	Tea Reg. Occ.	Cocoa Reg. Occ.	Milk Reg. Occ.	Other (Specify)	Reg. Occ.
Breakfast	___	___	___	___	___	___	___	___	___
Mid A.M.	___	___	___	___	___	___	___	___	___
Lunch	___	___	___	___	___	___	___	___	___
Mid P.M.	___	___	___	___	___	___	___	___	___
Dinner	___	___	___	___	___	___	___	___	___
Evening	___	___	___	___	___	___	___	___	___
Other (Specify)	___	___	___	___	___	___	___	___	___
	___	___	___	___	___	___	___	___	___
	___	___	___	___	___	___	___	___	___

(IF NO ONE IN THE FAMILY DRINKS COFFEE REGULARLY, SKIP TO QUESTION 17)

3. Do you ever serve iced coffee? Yes _____ No _____
(If yes) On what occasions?

	Summer		Winter		Comments
	Reg.	Occ.	Reg.	Occ.	
Breakfast	—	—	—	—	
Mid-morning	—	—	—	—	
Lunch	—	—	—	—	
Mid-afternoon	—	—	—	—	
Dinner	—	—	—	—	
Evening	—	—	—	—	
Other (Specify)					
——————	—	—	—	—	
——————	—	—	—	—	

4. At what times during the day does each member of the family *usually* drink coffee (either at home or away from home)? (Write in numbers, accounting for *every* member of the family *who drinks coffee regularly*.)

	Women (over 16)			Men (over 16)			Children 6–16			Children under 6		
	Drink	Do Not Drink	Tot.	Drink	Do Not Drink	Tot.	Drink	Do Not Drink	Tot.	Drink	Do Not Drink	Tot.
Breakfast	—	—	—	—	—	—	—	—	—	—	—	—
Lunch	—	—	—	—	—	—	—	—	—	—	—	—
Dinner	—	—	—	—	—	—	—	—	—	—	—	—
Bet. meals	—	—	—	—	—	—	—	—	—	—	—	—

5. About how many cups of coffee does each person in the family *usually* drink at each meal? (Opposite each meal, both at home and away from home, account for *every* member in the family *who drinks coffee regularly*.)

	Meals	Women (over 16) Cups						Men (over 16) Cups						Children 6–16 Cups				Children under Cups			
		0	1	2	3	4	Tot.	0	1	2	3	4	Tot.	0	1	2	Tot.	0	1	2	Tot
1.	Breakfast At Home																				
2.	Away Fr. Home																				
3.	Lunch At Home																				
4.	Away Fr. Home																				
5.	Dinner At Home																				
6.	Away Fr. Home																				
7.	Between Meals At Home																				
8.	Away Fr. Home																				

6. About how often do you buy coffee?

	Coffee	Decaff.		Coffee	Decaff.
3 times a week or oftener	_____	_____	Once every 10 days	_____	_____
Twice a week	_____	_____	Once every 2 weeks	_____	_____
Once a week	_____	_____	Less often (Specify)	_____	_____
Seldom or never serve any coffee at home	_____				

(IF SELDOM OR NEVER SERVE COFFEE AT HOME, SKIP TO QUESTION 13)

7. How many pounds of coffee do you usually buy at a time?___

8. How do you buy your coffee?

GRIND	PACKAGE
Already ground: _____	Vacuum can _____
Drip grind _____	Paper bag _____
Percolator grind _____	Glass jar _____
Universal grind _____	Plain tin can _____
Other (Specify) _____	Other (Specify) _____
Whole bean; have	
grocer grind _____	_____
Whole bean; grind	
at home _____	_____
Other (Specify) _____	

9. What kind of utensil do you usually use for making coffee?

Old fashioned coffee pot _____	Glass vacuum _____
Percolator _____	Other (Specify) _____
Drip pot _____	_____

Comments: _____

_____

10. (If old fashioned coffee pot or percolator) How long do you brew it (after it has started to boil or "perk")?

_____ minutes   Until it boils or "perks" _____

Other (Specify) _____

11. What is your recipe for making coffee?

Coffee measurements:

Use: Tablespoon _____   Measurements: Level _____

      Dessert spoon _____   Rounded _____

      Teaspoon _____   Heaping _____

      Other (Specify) _____

Water measurements:
Use: Standard kitchen measuring cup _____
      Coffee serving cup _____
      Other (Specify) _____
Quantity: _____ measurements of coffee and _____ cups of
        water to make _____ cups of coffee
Details of method and comments: _____
_____
_____

12. When you make coffee yourself, what one thing is most important? _____
_____

13. How do you judge a good cup of coffee?   (Be specific) _____
_____

14. When you eat in a restaurant or other public eating place, do you drink coffee?

          Usually _____   Occasionally _____
          Seldom _____   Never _____
(If not usually) Why not more often? _____
_____

15. What do you think of coffee served in public eating places?

Generally very good _____   Generally poor _____
Generally good _____   Some good; some poor _____
Generally fair _____   Don't know _____
Comments: _____
_____

16. What does your husband think of the coffee served in your home?

Generally very good _____   Generally poor _____
Generally good _____   Sometimes good; sometimes
Generally fair _____   poor _____
                     Don't know _____
Comments: _____
_____

17. Do you feel that there are any good effects to be derived from drinking coffee?

Yes _____   No _____   Don't know _____
(If yes) What are they?   (Describe in detail) _____

_____

(If no, or don't know) Comments: _____
18. Do you or any members of your family feel that coffee has any harmful effects?

Yes _____   No _____   Don't know _____
(If yes) What are they?   (Describe in detail) _____

_____

(If no, or don't know) Comments: _____

_____

19. Have you or any members of your family *ever* been forbidden to drink coffee?   Yes _____   No _____
(If yes) On what grounds? _____

_____

General comments:

Investigator _____
Date _____

HIGHLIGHTS OF THE SURVEY [1]

1. Assuming that one heaping tablespoon or two level tablespoons are adequate for eight ounces of water, approximately 40% of the women do not use an adequate amount of coffee.
2. How women brew coffee: 46% use a percolator; 39% a drip pot; 11% an old-fashioned coffee pot; 7% a glass vacuum.
3. Few women are willing to admit they don't make good coffee. 88% claimed that their husbands liked the coffee they made, although many of the replies were tempered with "he don't complain," or "he'd better like it."
4. The average housewife buys coffee three or four times a month. Her average weekly purchase is slightly over a pound. 49% of the housewives bought coffee in a paper bag; 45% in vacuum tin; 6% in slip tin; and 4% in glass. 56% of the upper-class

[1] Percentages based on nearly 5,000 interviews. Since miscellaneous replies are not included, percentages do not necessarily add up to 100. Where total exceeds 100, some women gave more than one answer.

families buy vacuum packed coffee; 41% paper bag coffee. Among the lower-class families, 42% buy in vacuum tins and 52% in paper bags.

5. Coffee is consumed by 82% of all men over 16 years of age; 81% of all women over 16; 15% of all children between 6 and 16; 4% of all children under 6 years of age.

6. The average adult drinks a cup and a half of coffee twice a day or 3 cups a day. Coffee is all but universal at breakfast, about half of the people have it for dinner and 43% have it for lunch. Coffee is by far the most popular beverage in the home with two regular servings per family per day. Milk is its nearest competitor with $1\frac{1}{2}$ regular servings. Tea averages only half a regular serving per family per day. Coffee is served regularly every day in 92% of all homes. Coffee drinking is spread evenly over all income classes.

7. Adult per capita consumption of coffee by geographical regions: New England, 16.1 pounds; Middle Atlantic, 18.7; East North Central, 21.7; West North Central, 24.0; South Atlantic, 19.7; East South Central, 16.7; West South Central, 18.9; Mountain, 21.6; Pacific, 20.7; United States as whole, 19.9.

8. Iced coffee is served by 37% of the families in the New England and Middle Atlantic states, 14% on the Pacific Coast and 10% to 12% in all other districts. It is served by 27% of the families in income class A, 21% in class B, and 16% in class C. Only 10% of farm families serve it, but the figure rises to 15% for villages and ranges from 20% to 30% for cities.

9. 32% of all housewives have a definite fear of coffee's possible harmful effects; an additional 6% say they think coffee has harmful effects if used "in excess"; and 23% say that at least one member of their family has been forbidden coffee at some time. The usual ailments leading to the ban were reported to be stomach trouble, high blood pressure, heart trouble, and nervousness. 51% of all coffee consumers see only good wholesome effects from coffee.

Appendix B

COFFEE INTERVIEWERS' SUGGESTIONS

(Used for first wave of depth interviews)

Sample Note: Of your two respondents, please make sure that you have represented one male, one female; one "dark strong" coffee drinker, one "light weak" coffee drinker; one "heavy" drinker (6–8 cups), one "light drinker" (2–3 cups per day).

Just for Your Information

There are 4 major practical questions which we want to answer in this study:

1. What is the real role of coffee drinking in people's lives today?
2. Why people drink coffee more frequently, or less?
3. Why people prefer stronger, or weaker coffee brewing?
4. At what age levels and why is coffee drinking morally possible? Any special feelings about coffee on the part of older people?

To answer these questions, we need to probe for the whole range of people's feelings about coffee and its real role in their lives. Encourage maximum spontaneity and feel free to probe any area that seems likely to be significant.

It would be most helpful for these initial interviews if you could just get people talking freely on all their feelings about coffee for an hour or so.

The research areas suggested on the next page are to be probed only after fullest possible rambling free association is exhausted.

SOME SUGGESTED RESEARCH AREAS

Among others, try to probe the following areas which we have found helpful in our preliminary field testing:

1. *Spontaneous Associations* — First try to encourage maximum free association with coffee, *everything that comes into people's minds as they think of coffee.* Then, get them to talk about their last few cups of coffee, from the moment they thought of coffee, through the drinking and all about how they felt afterwards. Probe in detail for *all sensory* impressions, smell, taste, appearance, etc.

2. *Kinds of Coffee* — All impressions about different types of coffee — strong, weak, black, etc., difficulties in making coffee, how he brews coffee, etc. Are some friends specially "proud" of their brewing skills, etc. What kinds of people seem to like "strong" coffee? What kinds prefer "light" coffee? Which friends drink a lot of coffee, which a little?

3. *Coffee Drinking Occasions* — When respondent drinks coffee, and attitudes to coffee at all these specific occasions — when it is most wanted, best liked. Respondent's feelings about the first cup in the morning, the break, the last cup at night, etc.

4. *Best Cup* — The *best* cup of coffee — how it tasted, etc. When and where he had this cup, his associations, etc. How about *worst* cup of coffee?

5. *Childhood* — Impressions of coffee in childhood — when first asked for some — parents' attitude — when he and friends first started drinking coffee — all impressions of that first cup, taste, smell, etc.

6. *His Children* — Any comments about or requests for coffee by his children — what he said — at what age will they be allowed, or were they allowed, to drink coffee?

7. *Frequency* — Average number of cups per day — most cups he drinks — how he feels about friends who drink more, etc.

8. *Health* — All feelings about coffee and health — what harm or good coffee does — how it acts on system, any hesitations about coffee using he might have.

Appendix C

COFFEE STUDY INTERVIEWING SCHEDULE

(Used for second wave of depth interviews)

For this assignment, please use the following type of respondent as indicated below. *The category of respondent used should be indicated on the face sheet under "Additional Data."* Wherever possible, please use American born respondents and be sure to indicate country of origin on face sheet.

_____ parents of children 5–10 years of age
_____ older people — 50 years plus
_____ newlyweds — joint husband and wife interviews (see below)
_____ teachers
_____ pediatricians
_____ employers whose operation is large enough to warrant a coffee break. Get half who have a break at their business and half who don't.
_____ employees who work at a plant or office large enough to justify a coffee break. Get half who have a break at work and half who don't.

There are special research areas in the interview schedule which are especially pertinent to each of the above groups. Make sure that you cover these areas fully.

Special Note: Joint Husband-Wife Interviews: Interviewers who are assigned these interviews are asked wherever possible to interview both husband and wife together. When joint interviews are conducted instead of single wife or single husband interviews, an additional bonus of $2.00 will be paid. Treat these joint interviews as a single interview indicating only whether a response is given by husband or wife; try to avoid duplication of responses by husband and wife, but record all divergent responses.

1. COFFEE STEREOTYPE: What comes to mind when you hear the word coffee? What pictures come into your mind? What associations do you have with coffee? Why do you think people drink

coffee? What does coffee do for them? Why do women drink coffee, — men? What are the major functions that coffee fulfills? How important do you think coffee is in American life?

2. CHANGING STEREOTYPE: Tell me about the coffee drinking habits of your parents? When did they drink coffee, how often? What did they think about coffee? How do your coffee drinking habits differ from theirs? What do older people get out of drinking coffee as compared to other people? Why do younger people drink coffee? How have attitudes to coffee changed over the years? Why do you think people today drink more — less coffee than a generation ago? Than in other countries?

3. COFFEE MOOD: What are the different times of the day when you drink coffee? How do you feel about these different cups of coffee? What is your breakfast coffee like, mid-morning coffee break? What does it feel like to have coffee at lunch, dinner, in-between meals? What are your feelings about coffee at different times? Which cup do you enjoy most? Tell me about it. Do you feel that you need any cup more than any other? What does coffee do for you when you drink it at home? In the office? At a restaurant? At work, at play?

4. CHANGING COFFEE HABITS: How much coffee do you drink now? Have your coffee habits changed since you started to drink coffee? Do you drink more or less now? When did you notice a change? Do you like your coffee now prepared differently than you did before? Heavier, weaker, sweeter, lighter, etc.? What made you change your tastes in coffee? When did these changes occur?

5. CHILDREN'S USE: (*Pay special attention to this area if you are interviewing teachers, pediatricians, or mothers of children 5–10 years of age*) When did you start drinking coffee? At what age? Tell me about your first cup. How did your parents feel about it? How did you feel about coffee? Do your children drink coffee? What do you feel about their requests for coffee? At what age were they allowed, or will they be allowed to drink coffee? (For teachers, pediatricians, parents of kids especially.) Do you think there are any negative effects of coffee on children — what are your feelings about this? How would you classify coffee as compared to Coca-Cola for children, coffee as compared

to tea, coffee as compared to cocoa and chocolate? How does coffee rate as a children's beverage compared to other beverages available?

Pediatricians: Do parents ever ask your advice regarding allowing children to drink coffee? What advice do you give them? What is your opinion regarding the health and nutritional value of coffee? What is your professional opinion regarding the common attitude that coffee is bad for children, that it is bad for their nerves?

Teachers: Do you know if any children in your classes drink coffee? Have you noticed any behavioral differences between these children and other children? Do children ever ask about coffee in the classroom? Has the use of coffee as a beverage been brought up by children in connection with any classroom discussion on South America and coffee bean?

6. HEALTH: What are respondents feelings about coffee and health? What harm or good does coffee provide? How does it act on the system? Please describe. Are there any hesitations which respondent has about using coffee? What does respondent feel about the nutritional value of coffee? Its chemical makeup? Are there any age limits above or below which coffee might be especially harmful or beneficial? What are these limits? Why? What does coffee do in these cases? (Especially for respondents over 50 years of age.) What is the maximum amount of coffee people should drink in regard to health? What are the results of drinking coffee in excess of this amount? Are there any minimum amounts of coffee which the body should have — what are they, and what are the effects on the body if this minimum is not reached?

7. FAMILY DETERMINER OF COFFEE HABITS: (Pay special attention to this area if you are interviewing newlyweds.) What are the differences in the type of coffee you and your wife (husband) prefer? What types do you each like, how do you each like coffee prepared, how do you each like to drink your coffee — black, light, with sugar? What changes have been made in your coffee drinking habits since your marriage? Has your spouse influenced your coffee habits and preferences — how have they changed? Who brews coffee in your family? How is it brewed? Have you ever

brewed coffee by any other method? Why did you change, and who was most influential in making the change? Who is the greatest coffee drinker in the house? Who is the most fussy about the way coffee tastes? Who shops for coffee and tries different brands? Who knows most about coffee blends and roasts?

8. COFFEE BREAK: Do you take a "coffee break" (coffee between meals) in your home during the day (or for office worker, etc.)? Do you have a coffee break during the day at your place of work? How do you feel about the coffee break? What feelings and thoughts come to mind about the coffee break? How important is it to you and the people you work with? Do you ever not take a coffee break because it is an interruption in your work — or do you find it helps you do your work much better? What feelings do you have regarding the coffee break as a regular part of everybody's working day? What does it mean for the employer? for the employee? What is the effect of the coffee break on all parties concerned?

(FOR EMPLOYERS) Do you have a coffee break at your plant? When was this instituted as a regular company policy? Was it your own innovation or was it done by request of the employees? Do you feel that it has an effect upon their work? Their morale? How do you feel about a coffee break? Has the coffee break at your plant been misused? What do you think about all the positive and negative aspects of the coffee break as an industrial institutional custom?

9. COFFEE KNOWLEDGE: Where do you think coffee comes from? How does it grow — where does it grow? Do you know of any differences in coffee on basis of growing? What makes one coffee different from another? Who are the people who grow coffee? How do you think they live and work?

Appendix D

COFFEE STUDY QUESTIONNAIRE

COF–4
May 10, 1955

INTERVIEWER'S NAME _____

Address _____

Regions

NE _____

NW _____

SO _____

West _____

Data on Respondent:

Name _____

Address _____

Place _____

Age _____ Sex _____

Marital Status _____

Number of children _____ Ages _____

Ethnic Origin _____

Occupation _____

Occupation of Spouse _____

Years of Education completed _____

Income Level   Under $3,000 _____

$3,000 to $5,000 _____

$5,000 to $7,500 _____

$7,500 to $10,000 _____

Over $10,000 _____

Respondent

Single 20–25 _____

Married 20–25 _____

Single 30–35 _____

Married 30–35 _____

Married 40–45 _____

Married 60+ _____

Male _____

Female _____

Town _____

(Under 50,000)

Small City _____

(50,000 to 500,000)

Large City _____

(over 500,000)

(Leave Blank)

Part I

1. Here is a list of foods and drinks that most people use at one time or another. Please tell me:
    a. Which of them you need every day   (Necessity)
    b. Which are not really necessary but
       which you use fairly regularly   (Regular)
    c. Which you use only occasionally   (Luxury)
    d. Which you don't like or never use   (Don't use)

(Take each food or drink one at a time and check it under appropriate column)

	Necessity	*Regular*	*Occasionally*	*Don't use*
Bread	_____	_____	_____	_____
Milk	_____	_____	_____	_____
Olives	_____	_____	_____	_____
Tea	_____	_____	_____	_____
Hot chocolate	_____	_____	_____	_____
Potatoes	_____	_____	_____	_____
Coffee	_____	_____	_____	_____
Butter	_____	_____	_____	_____
Coca-Cola	_____	_____	_____	_____
Cheese	_____	_____	_____	_____
Whipped cream	_____	_____	_____	_____
Steak	_____	_____	_____	_____

2. Do you drink coffee?   Yes _____   No _____

NONUSERS:

3. Have you ever drunk coffee more or less regularly?
                      Yes _____   No _____
4. If so, what made you stop? _____
   _____

5. If no, have you ever tasted coffee at all?
                      Yes _____   No _____
6. If so, what made you avoid it? _____
   _____

USERS:

7. How often do you ordinarly drink coffee? If you regularly drink a cup or more each day, estimate the number of cups you drink on the average day. If less frequently, estimate the approximate number of cups you drink in a typical week, or month.

Daily cups   Number: _____

Weekly cups   _____

Monthly cups   _____

8. If you are a regular coffee drinker — that is, if you usually or invariably drink your coffee at specific times or places, indicate which:

	Usually	*Invariably*
a. With breakfast	_____	_____
b. Before breakfast	_____	_____
c. With lunch	_____	_____
d. With dinner	_____	_____
e. At breaks in the working day	_____	_____
f. At home, in the evening	_____	_____
g. Out after a show	_____	_____
Specify others: _____	_____	_____

9. Do you ever use "Instant Coffee"?   Yes _____   No _____
   If yes, how often do you drink instant coffee in comparison to regular coffee? _____

10. What brand (s) of regular coffee do you regularly use? _____
    _____

11. What brand (s) of "Instant Coffee" do you regularly use?
    _____

12. As compared with most other people, do you like your coffee:
    a. A lot stronger than average   _____
    b. A little stronger than average   _____
    c. About average strength   _____
    d. A little weaker than average   _____
    e. A lot weaker than average   _____

_____ Black	_____ Milk alone
_____ Sugar alone	_____ Milk and sugar
_____ Cream alone	_____ Canned Milk alone

_____ Cream and sugar   _____ Canned milk and sugar
_____ Just a touch of _____

14. Do you ever drink your coffee any *other* way — just as a "change," for example?   Yes _____   No _____
14a. How do you drink your coffee then? _____
15. On what occasions, and at what times do you drink your coffee this way? _____

_____

_____

Note: Ask either question 16 or 17, whichever is appropriate. If respondent is single, ask neither.

MARRIED MEN:

16. Does your wife drink coffee?   About how many cups does she
    drink?   Daily _____
                                              Weekly _____

MARRIED WOMEN:

17. Does your husband drink coffee?   About how many cups does
    he drink?   Daily _____
                                              Weekly _____

USERS AND FORMER USERS:

Note: In getting the respondent's coffee history use the suggested question only in getting started; let the respondent tell you about it naturally.   You are looking for three things:

(1) The changes (up and down) in his coffee consumption, in cups per day

(2) The times (i.e., ages) at which these changes occurred; and

(3) Something about the occasion (marriage, job changes, group influences, maturation, etc.) of each such change.

On the following page you will find a graph.   The respondent's coffee career can be plotted on this graph in terms of age and cups per day as he tells it to you.   Make an "x" on the graph for each datum he gives you ("At fifteen I began drinking, oh, about a cup a day."   This is an "x" at the intersection of the "15" age line and the "I" cups-per-day line.)   Connect these "x's" with reasonably straight lines.   (No drafting is necessary) If your respondent is at all typical his coffee drinking will go up by jerks — that is, your graph will proceed from left to right by steps, not diagonally. Each vertical line in this step-like graph will be a period of relatively constant coffee-usage. Each horizontal line will represent a relatively abrupt change. It is these changes we are looking for. Record any truly gradual change diagonally if they do occur.

Number these changes from left to right starting with the first change *after* starting. After the respondent has told you the main outlines of his story, go back and fill in the details on each circumstance (occasion) under which the changes occurred. Write these up, as much as possible in the respondent's own words, in the lines provided at the bottom of the graph.

Try to get the numerical details (cups per day and approximate ages) as unobtrusively as possible *while* the respondent is telling his story. If he is troubled by failure to remember details, reassure him that the exact figure (cups or age) is not necessary: we're more interested in the "why" of each change than the "what." On the other hand, be as accurate as possible in entering these results. If a datum is questionable, mark it with a question mark on the graph.

18. Now I'd like you to tell me how you got started drinking coffee, how your coffee habits have changed, and so on:

Age

65

60

55

50

45

40

35

30

25

20

15

10

Age (cont.)

5

0

| None | Sips Only | 1– | 1 | 2 | 3 | 4 | 5 | 6–7 | 8–9 | 10–11 | 12–13 | 14–15 | 15+ | *cups per day* |

Occasions

Started: _____

_____

1st Change: _____

_____

2nd Change: _____

_____

3rd Change: _____

_____

(continue over if necessary)

19. When you first started drinking coffee, did you:
    a. Take a little coffee with your milk and increase strength gradually; or   _____
    b. Take occasional sips of regular-strength coffee and increase the amount gradually; or   _____
    c. Start immediately with full cups of regular strength coffee   _____
20. What was your parents' attitude toward your early coffee-drinking?
    a. They thought it was wrong and tried to get me to stop   _____
    b. They expressed some disapproval but didn't try to stop me   _____
    c. They didn't care one way or the other   _____
    d. They approved of my drinking coffee   _____
    e. I don't remember that they expressed any attitude at all about it   _____
21. Do you think that coffee is habit-forming?

    Yes _____   No _____

IF "NO" SKIP ITEMS 22, 23, 24.

22. Coffee is generally-speaking a good habit _____; or a bad habit _____ (check one)

IF BAD HABIT SKIP ITEM 23.

23. Coffee-drinking is a *good habit* because:
    a. It perks you up when you're tired _____
    b. It provides a break in the work routine _____
    c. It is the ideal drink with a good meal _____
    d. It is nice to drink with other people _____
    e. It relaxes you when you're tense _____

IF GOOD HABIT SKIP ITEM 24.

24. Coffee-drinking is a *bad habit* because:
    a. Too much of it can be harmful _____
    b. All habits one becomes a slave to are bad _____
    c. Drinking too much of it becomes an expensive luxury _____
    d. It is an unnecessary interruption of people's working habits _____
    e. It is an artificial stimulus _____

PART IIB

25b. Do you think that coffee is stimulating? Yes_____ No_____
Four women are having lunch together. They are a clergyman's wife, a nursery school teacher, a lady senator, and a department store buyer. After lunch each woman orders her coffee exactly the way she wants it. This is a very special restaurant and serves coffee any way the customer wants it. What do you imagine each woman would order.

Order of Administration: _____ _____ _____ _____

26b. The clergyman's wife would order . . .	Clergyman's Wife	Nursery Teacher	Lady Senator	Dept. Store Buyer
a. strong coffee				
b. average coffee				
c. weak coffee				

	Clergyman's Wife	Nursery Teacher	Lady Senator	Dept. Store Buyer
"What about cream?" She would probably use . . .				
d. lots of cream				
e. a little cream				
f. no cream				
"What about sugar?" She would probably use . . .				
g. lots of sugar				
h. a little sugar				
i. no sugar				
She would probably ask for a second cup.				
j. yes				
k. no				

27b. The nursery teacher would order . . .
28b. The lady senator would order . . .
29b. The department store buyer would order . . .

Note: Repeat all parts of item 25b for items 27b, 28b, and 29b, going through the whole list for each occupation before going to the next. Alternate the order of the professions for each new respondent; that is, ask about the buyer, senator, nursery teacher, and clergyman's wife with every *other* respondent. Record the order of administration used in the blanks provided at the column headings.

Note: In administering the next two items, record all responses in the scoring form which follows item 31b. Take each comparison one at a time and finish the entire list before going on to the next. Alternate the order in which you ask items 30b and 31b with each respondent. Indicate the order used in the blanks above each column of the scoring form.

30b. Compare the usual cup of coffee you drink in your home to-day with the *best* or most ideal cup of coffee you could imagine.

31b. Compare the usual cup of coffee you drink in your home to-day with the cup of coffee you get in your favorite restaurant.

Which is . . .	Order: 30b ___		31b ___	
	Home	Ideal	Home	Rest.
stronger				
richer				
blacker				
more bitter				
weaker				
more watery				
more oily				
generally fresher				
more distinctive				
more aroma				
sweeter				
fuller flavored				
heavier				
more pungent				
more substantial				
more luxurious				
harsher				
more flat-tasting				
milder				

32b. **Have you ever heard of . . .**

		Heard	*Drunk*
(Check "yes" responses	Cafe Expresso	_____	_____
only in appropriate col-	Cafe Royale	_____	_____
umn.)	Viennese Coffee	_____	_____
	Demitasse	_____	_____
	Mocha	_____	_____
	Capuccino	_____	_____
	Turkish Coffee	_____	_____
	Brazilian Coffee	_____	_____

33b. **Have you ever actually drunk . . .** (re-read list and check responses in column above.)

34b. **Sometimes you have a bad cup of coffee, or a cup of coffee that you feel has been improperly prepared. What do you think are fairly frequent causes of this?**

(Check any that apply; permit respondent to take his time and hear whole list first if he so desires.)

_____ impure water

_____ cooked too long

_____ not enough coffee

_____ not cooked enough
_____ too much coffee
_____ not hot enough
_____ coffee served cold

_____ wrong type of cup

_____ not freshly prepared

_____ reheated (even once is too much)

_____ coffee was boiled (it should never boil)

_____ poor brand of coffee was used

_____ wrong grind of coffee used
_____ coffee used was not fresh
_____ utensils not properly cleaned
_____ wrong method of preparation used

_____ utensils not properly preheated

35b. **Suppose you are traveling in a foreign country and a friend of yours introduces you to a resident of that country who is a coffee-grower. In what country would you be most likely to be traveling?**

(write in) _____
                            coffee-grower

Now, try to imagine what this _____ (repeat nationality given, e.g., "Brazilian coffee-grower") would be like. If you don't know anything at all about _____ coffee-growers, just guess. Answer "yes" or "no" as quickly as you can.

36b. He would be:

fat _____	wearing white clothes _____
lean _____	wearing dirty clothes _____
rich _____	wearing business clothes _____
poor _____	wearing over-alls _____
wearing a mustache _____	smoking a cigar _____
unshaven _____	not smoking _____
wearing shoes _____	driving a modern car _____
wearing a big hat _____	riding a spirited horse _____
not wearing a hat _____	riding a burro _____
	wearing a blanket _____
	wearing a pistol _____

Note: If the respondent has made inconsistent responses and wishes to change any, let him. In these cases add a question-mark (?) to the original entry, but do not erase the check-mark. Give each respondent this opportunity. This applies to items 37b and 39b as well.

37b. His farm would be:

called a ranch _____	a piece of jungle _____
called a finca _____	an upland valley _____
a small patch of	thousands of acres _____
mountain side _____	hundreds of acres _____
a flat piece of grassland _____	a few dozen acres _____

38b. He would be growing his coffee on:

trees _____	large bushes _____
small bushes _____	vines _____

39b. The color of the coffee bean when picked is:

black _____ brown _____ green _____ red _____

40b. He does _____ does not _____ roast the coffee before selling it (check one.)

41b. He does _____ does not _____ grind the coffee before selling it (check one.)

42b. The Pan-American Coffee Bureau is:
(Write in): _____

_____

_____

_____

43b. A student is having coffee just before an important examination to sharpen up his wits. It will also make him more:
a. relaxed _____   b. jittery _____   c. no effect _____

PART III

Note: Only two of the following 8 questions are to be asked each respondent, on the basis of the previous information (item 7 — respondent's coffee drinking habits) you have obtained on his coffee-drinking habits.

Each question consists of two parts. In administering the first part, make sure the respondent has heard and understood *all* lettered alternatives before making his choice; his choice is his *primary* reason for drinking coffee. Force a choice between these alternatives if you have to.

In administering the second part of each question (except that for "Nonusers") — that is, the part after the "BUT . . . ," read each alternative one at a time getting the respondent to indicate "yes" or "no" for each before going on to the next. Check only "yes" responses.

NONUSERS:

44. I don't drink coffee primarily because:

(check one)
a. when I've tried it, it seems too strong   _____
b. when I've tried it, I just don't like the taste   _____
c. I know it's harmful without trying it   _____
d. It's too expensive   _____
e. I don't want to get the habit   _____

OCCASIONAL USERS (*Less than one cup daily*):

45. I drink coffee primarily because:

(check one)
a. there are times when coffee perks me up   _____
b. sometimes I want a change from other beverages   _____
c. I like the taste   _____

d. I like to be sociable when I am with other people who are drinking coffee _____ _____

BUT:

(1) I don't really like the taste _____
(check (2) I don't particularly like its effect on the body _____
any) (3) I think too much coffee is bad for you _____
(4) I don't want to get the habit _____
(5) It's too expensive as a regular thing _____

REGULAR DRINKERS *(1 to 5 cups daily)* :

47. I drink coffee primarily because:
a. It is simply part of a good meal _____
b. I need it to get started right in the morning _____
(check c. It is a pleasant social custom _____
one) d. It is an institution in my household _____
e. It is just a habit _____
f. It helps me get through the work-day _____

48. BUT:
(1) I really don't like the taste _____
(check (2) I don't like its effect on the body _____
any) (3) I think too much coffee is bad for me _____
(4) I don't like having the habit _____
(5) It really costs too much _____

HEAVY DRINKERS *(6 or more cups daily)* :

49. I drink coffee primarily because:
a. No meal is complete without it _____
b. It is especially important in getting the day started _____
(check c. It is a social necessity _____
one) d. It is an institution in my household _____
e. It is just a habit _____
f. I need it to get through the day _____

50. BUT:
(1) I really don't like the taste _____

(check
any)

(2) I don't like its effect on the body _____

(3) I think I drink too much coffee _____

(4) I don't like having the habit _____

(5) It costs too much _____

Appendix E

AD TEST PROCEDURE

1. The interviewer might initiate the Ad-Test by asking the respondent something like, "What is your *general impression* of coffee advertising?" If the respondent replies with a comment about the advertising of a particular BRAND of coffee, the interviewer might indicate that we are not interested in any special brand, just coffee advertising in general. When the respondent has expressed herself fully, if this has not already come up in the conversation, the interviewer might ask directly, "Do you remember any coffee ad where NO BRAND is mentioned?"

Elicit her impressions, her reaction to these ads. Have her describe the ad. How vividly does she remember the various components of the ad. Was it a single unit or part of a series? etc.

2. After this preliminary part of the interview, show your respondent the first of the three Coffee Ads which are enclosed. Ask her to look it over and then return it to you.

Then ask her to tell you all her recollections, associations, and impressions both favorable and unfavorable, and anything else that runs through her mind when she looked at the ad; and any images or questions that she had or have since occured to her.

You must be careful to keep the respondent from judging the ad or acting the expert. We cannot use information which tells us that the respondent likes or dislikes the ad. We need to know her reactions to the ad, what it is that makes her like or dislike it. Material in your interview that tells us your respondent considers one ad a good ad and another a poor ad is also irrelevant for our purposes. We are interested, however, in any comments which reveal the respondent's reaction to any part or to the whole of any of the ads.

3. After the maximum spontaneous association has been elicited, give your respondent the ad once more. In this third step the interviewer probes for all associations with each section of the ad as the respondent looks at it; the impressions and associations evoked by the pictorial representation or various parts of

it; by the heading, color if any, slogans, each section of the copy.

Repeat steps two and three for each of the five ads enclosed.

4. The final step in your interview might be to ask your respondent, "If you were the advertiser, or in charge of this advertising campaign, what would you do to improve this ad?"

Please return the ads with your interviews.

Appendix F

A DIGEST OF FINDINGS AND RECOMMENDATIONS

Findings and recommendations growing out of the research were presented in a 150-page report. Its main theme was that coffee had become a utilitarian staple in this country and that for consumption to be increased coffee must be rediscovered as an exciting beverage of pleasure, one more appropriate to life in contemporary America. This point was summarized as follows:

Something has happened to coffee. Because of its universal acceptance and the fact that most people like coffee, we have at the same time been lulled into a complacency about it. Many of the coffee advertisers, because of their great emphasis on convenience, economy, brewing techniques, have helped accelerate the change from coffee as an exciting, luxurious beverage to a commonplace utilitarian staple. Thus, when we are asked how we can increase coffee consumption, our answer is: By helping people to rediscover coffee in all its many facets. The very reason for the existence of coffee is that it is not a utilitarian product. By making it one, the coffee roaster is barricading its road to progress. . . . We feel that every one of the specific questions, such as how to get people to drink more coffee, to take more coffee breaks, to start drinking coffee at an earlier age, etc., are all in one way or another dependent upon this revitalization of coffee which we have set forth as the most immediate task.

Several specific objectives were cited. One was to change coffee from a sinful and escapist beverage to a positive, life-accepting product. While many people liked coffee, they also were afraid of drinking too much of it or of giving it to young people. A second objective was to introduce greater variety into coffee flavors, to make coffee not just an adjunct on a restaurant's menu, but to give it the status of a full-fledged course by listing four or five varieties of coffee. A third recommendation was that people

be left free to decide how to make and drink their coffee. Interviews showed that people were proud of their individual tastes
and that some resented being told in an authoritarian manner
how to make coffee.

A summary of findings which led to the above conclusions is
presented below:

I. The First Change: From "Escapism" to "Coping"

Strong remnants of puritanical attitudes are still alive in the
American consumer and they influence his feelings towards coffee.
He enjoys coffee but is at the same time convinced that coffee has
many drawbacks. Thus, he is caught in a coffee conflict. Contributing to this conflict is a punishing attitude toward pleasure,
especially sensory pleasure. Any feeling of "sinning" usually is
followed by an expectation and fear of "punishment" although
the "sinner" may not always be aware of this.

Of 125 coffee drinkers, 67% expressed concern about their
coffee habit (55% worried about drinking too much coffee, 12%
about the habit-forming and dependence aspect). In another
test, 55% of 129 respondents expressed their belief in coffee's ill
effects on health and sleep. Lingering feelings of "sin" and "punishment" in coffee drinking were spontaneously expressed again
and again in the depth interviews.

Three principal aspects of coffee's "sinfulness" emerged from
the research:

1. Coffee was seen by some as a drug-provoking addiction. The
words "habit" and "dependence" appeared frequently in responses. Coffee often was compared to liquor. The two principal notions that supported the coffee-drug-liquor identification
were that heavy coffee drinkers are nervous, neurotic people, and
that coffee drinking promotes loss of control over one's appetite.

2. Coffee was felt to be a dangerous drink tending to over-
stimulate the heart and other organs of the body in an artificial
and detrimental way.

3. Coffee was accused of aiding in laziness. Many respondents
said that coffee provided an excuse to get away from the requirements of modern life. The words "excuse," "postponement,"
"procrastination," frequently were connected with coffee, some-

times revealing apology or guilt, sometimes amounting to accusation.

The conflict which coffee represents was indicated by the fact that in each of the three areas itemized above coffee also had on its side powerful factors pointing in the opposite direction. For example, many felt that coffee, unlike liquor, aided in better control. In responding to the following incomplete sentence: "A doctor receives a call at 3 A.M., and first gets himself a cup of hot coffee. The coffee will _____," 65% agreed that it will "wake him up and give him control." People also felt that coffee relaxed while it stimulated; that it served to bring back one's natural resources. If coffee is used by some as an "excuse" for dodging work, it is used by many more as a reward for hard or long work, punctuating successful work completion.

In summary, one of the major tasks for the coffee industry is to help in changing coffee from a sinful and escapist beverage to a positive and life-accepting one. The modern consumer has gone partly in this direction. He is, however, still caught in conflict. He likes coffee and yet is afraid of drinking too much of it or of giving it to young people.

How to change sin to morality is a big task and we cannot state exactly what the creative translation will look like. We have attempted, however, to indicate a number of steps we feel should be taken. Among these: make coffee a helper in coping with life and coexistence with stress; purify coffee morally by showing it as a natural product; dramatize its help in independence and self-control; associate it with well-known, realistic "copers" in life; present the coffee bean as nature's magic treasure chest; reassure about the universal acceptance of coffee by pointing out that all the world loves coffee and by citing what poets and writers have said about it.

II. BRIDGE THE SOCIAL LAG

In the last few years, people have become aware of several cultural changes with which coffee has not kept pace: 1. A desire for more gracious living. People are tired of patterns of living and working that entail continuous tension, haste, and push. They feel that they have to learn to relax and desire to develop ways

of living more pleasurably and graciously. 2. Americans are moving away from earlier restrictions imposed on enjoying sensory
pleasures. Recent examples of this trend are two-tone cars, more
color in men's clothing, and a growing receptivity for more re-
fined and new types of food. 3. A new kind of individualism
which has as its goal the expression of one's personality by more
individualized consumption and appreciation and enjoyment of
differences and variety.

Coffee has lagged behind these trends. It has become too utilitarian; it is related more to nutritional rather than emotional
health; and coffee drinking has become routinized. Such phrases
as "I must have it . . ." and "I can't do without it . . ." re-
curred frequently in the interviews. People were aware of coffee's
role as a remedy and aid in emergencies (a help in cases of shock,
cramps, and overdose of sleeping pills; it makes aspirin act faster;
stimulates regularity; etc.). Many also mentioned coffee as an
eye opener in the morning "to make them feel alive . . . human." Men appeared to be more luxury minded about coffee
than did women in answering this incomplete sentence: "I drink
coffee primarily _____." Forty-four per cent of the men as
contrasted with 16% of the women mentioned drinking coffee
primarily as a part of a good meal. Forty-four per cent of the
women as opposed to 26% of the men mentioned drinking coffee
primarily to get started in the morning. This finding suggests
appealing to the woman as a coffee consumer and not as a coffee
maker for men. If she sees coffee as part of a good meal herself,
she would be more inclined to pay more attention to it.

Coffee has become "frozen" psychologically. People feel that
most brands do not reflect varieties of flavor, and that shopping
for coffee is not rewarded by discovery. The advertiser has contributed to this result by stressing economy and convenience.

At the same time, taste tests indicated that people are willing
to accept change in coffee when it is offered as variety. Three-
fourths of the respondents rejected a "strong" conventional American coffee when comparing it with the same type of coffee in
standard strength. However, 69% preferred a different or "exotic" coffee of stronger than standard strength when it was compared against average coffee of standard strength.

The depth interviews showed that coffee could be made to heighten the pleasure of life. Respondents frequently expressed a desire for more gracious living and saw coffee as a symbol of a better, more leisurely life. Coffee was credited with making a variety of pleasures more pleasurable: cigarettes, music, a picnic, etc. There were 129 spontaneous references in the depth interviews to the pleasure, leisure, and luxury roles of coffee. These referred to taste, flavor, aroma, its social role in helping conversation, and coffee as a symbol of leisure. It is significant that these references were almost equal in number to the 140 spontaneous references to the utilitarian functions.

A high percentage of respondents had heard of and tried varied types of coffees such as demitasse, Cafe Royale, and Turkish coffee. This is an indication of a trend toward taste individualism and experimentation with new sensory pleasures. Many respondents made coffee in different ways for different times of the day. They told of numerous ways of serving, preparing, blending, and roasting coffee, and were eager to learn more about more and different coffees.

Coffee is widely regarded as a beverage without nutritional value other than that of the cream or sugar put in it. From a nutritional health point of view, it is tolerated as a necessity of modern life. However, a large majority of consumers also realize and appreciate coffee's contribution to their emotional health. Our modern pace of living not only exhausts many people physically, but also fills them with bitterness and anger at the world and themselves. For such moods, from grouchy and morose to aggressive, coffee is a great "healer" that makes life appear worth living again.

The findings indicate that the coffee break is assuming a much more important role in our culture than that of a rest or relaxation period. It gratifies deep and often deeply hidden emotional needs in workers as well as their bosses. Almost everybody has some smouldering resentment against duties, work, the boss, the drudgery of necessary routine. The coffee break offers a harmless, socially acceptable outlet for such resentment; it provides the housewife with an excuse to get away from her "drudgery" for a while without feeling guilty about it; it permits the worker to indulge in a legitimate breach of discipline and to get "something for nothing"; and it serves every kind of "rebellion" against rut and routine, even the routine of marriage and family life. The most positive reactions to coffee breaks by employees referred to the intention of the employer rather than to the break itself. Allowance of some time off for coffee seems to be almost taken for granted. But the warmest spontaneous comments related to the way the break was provided, to any little actions that show the employer going out of his way to make his employees happy. Employees are sensitive to management's feelings about the coffee break and resent it if they notice that the break is considered a "necessary evil."

In summary, this section has pointed to the need to change coffee from utility to pleasure of life, to stress its sensory pleasures, and to make it more of a food for emotional health. Variety should be introduced in many ways. The coffee break should be proof of creative considerateness by the employer and a legitimate breach of discipline and a reward for hard work. Coffee consumption should be increased by encouraging a "fill 'er up" psychology dramatizing the completion of the second cup: "it is the second cup that counts."

III. CHANGE FROM AUTHORITATIVE TO PERMISSIVE APPROACH

Once a person, usually in adolescence, obtains permission from parental authority to drink coffee he is proud to retain his individual rights to coffee. The authoritative origin of coffee drinking and the reaction against it appeared in the interviews in a number of ways. The most important finding was the rejection by the overwhelming majority of respondents of any conception of someone's "right" way to make coffee. The feeling expressed seemed to be composed of the following main elements:

A. There was a widespread expression of diversity in the way coffee affects people and the ways in which people prefer coffee. The underlying assumption reflected by most respondents is their personal need to discover just the right amount of coffee, just the right strength, just the correct brewing method, just the right flavor, and just the right number of cups per day or per meal for themselves personally. This is accompanied by a recognition that other people, even other members of the family, may have varying preferences.

B. Many respondents expressed great pride in their individual art of coffee brewing and serving. Their "coffee freedom" was seen as a precious expression of individuality.

C. Most respondents reported some change in their brewing method or taste preference or quantity of coffee they liked over the past years. More important, they indicated their receptivity to trying new and different kinds of coffee flavors or brewing methods when they were offered these varied taste experiences by friends or by restaurants.

D. People tend to reject any prescription of rigid rules as to strength or brewing methods as being correct for all coffee drinkers. Our evidence indicates rejection of any advertising tone or slogan that sounds like "coffee authoritarianism." This was reflected in negative reactions to the injunction to "use two tablespoons full."

Most people still tend to think of coffee as masculine. A new trend was indicated in the interviews, however, by the existence of a small number of men who prefer light coffee and a larger number of women who have come to prefer strong or black coffee. To some degree they seem defensive about their preferences when they do not conform to the expected cultural stereotype of their sex and feel the need to justify them. Coffee advertising could resolve some of these conflicts by promoting recognition of the idea that coffee taste preference is an individual matter, cutting across the sexes, rather than being sex-related. This should reduce the danger of people turning to tea because they can't get coffee on their own terms.

Almost all parents express sharp rejection of any outside suggestion relating to children drinking coffee. While they are willing to open the door to coffee drinking at varying age levels, they desire to retain control over this expression of their children's growing up. In the most strongly voiced rejections, respondents referred to coffee as something parents whom they did not respect might give to their children instead of milk.

Mothers frequently were receptive to coffee as a milk vehicle and reported results occasionally achieved in getting children to drink milk more readily when it was flavored with just a drop of coffee. Nearly 30% of the respondents first tasted coffee as children when they got a little coffee with a lot of milk. Coffee frequently is used with children as a special treat or as a reward for "being good," particularly when the latter takes the form of an approved kind of mature or adult behavior.

The role of coffee as a symbol of initiation into maturity for children was reflected in two ways. A child on his own initiative might drink coffee in a friend's home or in a restaurant, expressing rebellion against his parents and his desire to be treated as a grown up. Another example is when parents for the first time offer to a child a cup of coffee which contains more coffee than milk rather than more milk than coffee. This is recognized as an expression of the child's movement to maturity and adulthood.

Recommendations based on the findings in this section include changing from an authoritative to a permissive approach in all communications about coffee with the public. Do not order people; instead, invite them to try and experiment and discover for themselves. Respect people's individual feelings about coffee; give them permission to brew and drink coffee as they like. Let more parents know about other parents' success with coffee as a milk vehicle and use good-humored approaches to help them introduce coffee to children as part of growing up. Provide moral permission for women as well as men to prefer strong coffee and for men to like weak coffee.

IV. The Image or Personality of Coffee

Coffee's image in the minds of consumers is reflected in their talking about coffee in the depth interviews. Some of coffee's characteristics follow:

A. Coffee is intimate. When speaking of people meeting over a cup of coffee, respondents use such words as "close," "closer together," "feeling warmer toward people." Closeness and warmth are conducive to a feeling of good fellowship.

B. Coffee removes barriers and promotes understanding between people. It stimulates talk and makes it easier to be silent, too. Coffee talk is described as relaxed talk through which you get to know people. Business talks tend to lose their competitive coldness when carried on around the coffee table.

C. It appears from our study that coffee, even more than food, is for many people a measure of interest in homemaking, in receiving friends in a warm, appreciative fashion, and in their ability to give. Good and strong coffee expresses abundance and generosity, while poor and weak coffee is identified with poverty, skimping, and stinginess.

D. Whenever people talk about coffee they mention its strong, masculine character. As a parallel, weak, poor coffee is considered a symbol of poverty and skimping.

E. Our responses strongly suggest that many people are eager to enjoy pleasures of the senses and have a desire to develop a sense of flavor and taste discrimination if properly aided and stimulated. Thus, coffee has a good chance to become an outlet for those who do not get sufficient sensory gratification from their daily food due to American mass food production and preservation (canned, iced, artificial flavoring, etc.).

F. Our findings indicate strongly that aroma is still more prevailing in the experience of coffee than flavor. Childhood experiences, which often color a person's feelings toward coffee over a life-time, are particularly marked by impressions of odor; they often connect with nostalgic feelings about childhood pleasures and childhood security. Hence, coffee for many stands as a symbol of "Paradise Lost," a paradise that can be revived by similar sensory experiences of odor and aroma.

G. Coffee is a symbol of grown-up relaxation.

Advertising copy and art should follow this image of coffee. Coffee should be shown in social surroundings with the elements of intimacy and closeness. Wide open spaces as background would be wrong. Even cowboys when drinking coffee pick a protected spot, an oasis of intimacy.

V. OTHER FINDINGS

The interview and test responses indicated that the American housewife represented the best potential market for increased use of coffee. Her job is one of monotony and drudgery and few rewards. It calls for an excuse for interruptions and relaxation. Coffee can supply this and also be an inviting reward for her dull and lonely work. Coffee can provide her with a sense of security by heightening her alertness and sense of mastery of the situation. While most housewives look forward to relaxing over a cup of coffee with a neighbor, there are many times when this is not possible. It is at these times that coffee, as a symbol of sociability, can provide comfort and relaxation by serving as a substitute for a companion.

The report recommended that the housewives be encouraged to experiment with different blends, roasts, and methods of preparing coffee with the primary goal being to extend her pleasures in having and drinking coffee. Increased use of coffee by the housewife likely will be reflected in the general consumption of her family. As a coffee drinker, she will be more careful to keep a supply on hand, and will be more inclined to offer it to her family and guests and to think in terms of using coffee in new ways.

Respondents repeatedly commented that coffee tastes better at home than in a restaurant. Most restaurant situations, often accompanied by serving of mass-produced coffee, tend to deny coffee as a symbol of closeness, hospitality, and relaxation. When special emphasis is placed on the type or quality of coffee, however, it meets with favorable feelings of luxury. Coffee is seen by many people as an index of a restaurant's quality, a finding that could be of considerable significance for coffee advertising to the trade.

The report also presented findings (not summarized here) on consumer attitudes toward price, the Pan-American Coffee Bureau, and the Latin American coffee-growing countries, and uses of coffee in addition to its major role as a hot beverage.

CHAPTER VII

Automobiles — What They Mean to Americans

FORENOTE

This study illustrates ways of thinking about the product, the brand, and the buying process which appear to have important implications for advertising, selling, and product design. It uses several different approaches to develop material on product and brand images. The basic research technique was the depth or detailed interview. This was supplemented by projective techniques, including incomplete sentences, cartoons and adaptations of the thematic apperception test, and a number of attitude and opinion question devices. The concept of social class is employed in connection with the selection of the sample of people to be interviewed. The research, conducted by Social Research, Inc., was sponsored by the *Chicago Tribune* as a means of encouraging thought about improving the content of automobile advertising.

AUTOMOBILES — WHAT THEY MEAN TO AMERICANS

A Descriptive Case

THE CHICAGO TRIBUNE, through its Research Division, made available in 1954 the results of qualitative research undertaken to show how automobile advertising might be made more effective. As a basis for improving advertising content, greater understanding was sought as to the meanings of automobiles to people, the factors which led to the choice of one brand over another, and the role of advertising in the making of car sales.

The study developed the thesis that for most people the

automobile was considerably more than a means of transportation, that it was a source of much pride and pleasure. Preferences for accessories, models, colors, and make of car, it was believed, had important psychological as well as practical roots and particular attention was given to exploring underlying personal and social meanings.

Earlier research had served to focus attention on the problem of improving the advertising message. For a number of years studies had been made to determine the amount of readership received by advertisements appearing in the *Tribune*. In addition, in 1948 the *Tribune* established a panel of Chicago area consumers who reported their purchases in various product categories so that information could be compiled on sales movements and share of the market held by the different brands. Analyses of readership and panel data had shown many cases of high advertising exposure with no significant change in sales volume. Such observations contributed to a growing interest by Mr. Pierre Martineau, Research Director, in social-psychological research as a means of learning more about buying motivations. The belief was that the effectiveness of newspaper advertising would be greater if important buying motivations were appealed to than if they were not.

The automobile study was the fourth in a series of motivation research projects sponsored by the *Tribune* in an effort to stimulate interest among advertisers in improving the content of their advertising. The first, undertaken in 1951, was on consumer attitudes toward beer and beer advertising. The second came a year later and was on the role and function of cigarettes. Motivations relating to soaps and chemical detergents were explored in 1953, and in 1957 a study was made of gasoline, gasoline companies, and their symbols.

To plan and conduct the motivation studies, the *Tribune* employed Social Research, Inc., a Chicago firm whose staff of psychologists, anthropologists, and sociologists specialized in research directed toward defining and understanding motives and attitudes which influence behavior. The executive director was Dr. Burleigh B. Gardner, a social anthropologist who had become prominently identified with the application of social science research to problems in human relations and marketing. He formerly had been on the faculty at the University of Chicago and had done anthropological studies for that school and for Harvard University.[1] Serving as senior consultant to Social Research, Inc., was W. Lloyd Warner, Professor of Sociology and Anthropology at the University of Chicago, who was well known for his Yankee City Series of studies in which the American social class system was defined.[2]

THE RESEARCH APPROACH

The task of learning about motivations for owning an automobile and selecting a particular brand was recognized as a difficult one because behavior usually represented the influence of a number of interrelated factors. Many were not consciously known to most people and some would not be considered socially acceptable. For these reasons, people could not or would not give full or accurate information in response to direct questions. To meet this problem, Social Research, Inc., combined several techniques in its research approach. Some asked directly for desired information,

[1] Some of his publications: *Deep South: A Social Anthropological Study of Caste and Class* (with Allison Davis and Mary R. Gardner) (Chicago, The University of Chicago Press, 1941); *Human Relations in Industry* (with David G. Moore) (Homewood, Ill., Richard D. Irwin, Inc., 1955); "How the Social Sciences Are Used in Advertising," *Printers' Ink,* December 11, 1953; "The Product and the Brand" (with Sidney J. Levy), *Harvard Business Review,* March–April 1955.

[2] Some of his publications: *Yankee City Series I: The Social Life of a Modern Community* (with Paul S. Lunt) (New Haven, Yale University Press, 1941); *American Life: Dream and Reality* (Chicago, The University of Chicago Press, 1953); *Social Class in America* (Chicago, Science Research Associates, Inc., 1949).

while others were indirect in character in that they sought responses from which attitudes and motives could be inferred.

Of basic importance was the depth interview, an informal and detailed conversation in which the respondent was encouraged to talk fully in his own way. As a preliminary step, about 30 interviews lasting from two to four hours each were made to identify important factors relative to automobiles which should be explored in the study. There were no prearranged questions for these early interviews. Responses were recorded as completely as possible and later discussed by staff members as they worked out the research plan and prepared the first interviewing guide. (See Appendix A, pages 242–245 for depth interview questions.)

The later interviews were similar to those already described except that guides were used which indicated subject areas in which the respondent was to talk and included questions to help start and maintain conversation. The earlier questions were general in nature to allow the respondent freedom to introduce new ideas and talk in his own way. More specific questions were used later to check certain points. While all topics listed on the guide were to be covered, the questions did not have to be asked in any set way. Instead, the interviewer was instructed to let the interview develop naturally and to probe for full response on points of particular interest.

Three interview guides were used in succession, the second and third guides incorporating changes which appeared to be appropriate as interviewing progressed. The second and third guides put more emphasis on projective techniques and more direct research devices. Some sought new information, others provided for a check on earlier findings.

Projective Techniques

Most people are not fully aware of their personality characteristics and attitudes which are relevant to their choice of automobile. They reveal something about these factors, often without realizing it, in depth interviews. In an effort to learn more about them in this study, several projective devices were used. All such techniques confront an individual with a relatively ambiguous situation which he has to structure. A person is pretty much on his own in responding and presumably will disclose something of his private world of meanings, values, attitudes, and feelings. Brief descriptions of projective devices used follow:

Incomplete Sentences (see Appendix B, pages 246–247) — They represented a relatively quick means of obtaining a wide range of information relative to automobiles. As each incomplete sentence was read by the interviewer, the respondent was to complete it with the first thing that came to mind. Examples of sentence stems used:

> People who drive a convertible . . .
> Factory workers usually drive . . .
> Most of the new cars . . .
> When I drive very fast . . .

Selected responses are given below to illustrate how two sentence stems served to bring out differences between the attitudes of men and women toward a new car:

Sentence Stem: When you first get a car . . .

Women's responses:
. . . you can't wait 'till you take a ride.
. . . you would go for a ride.
. . . take rides in it, naturally.
. . . you put gas in it and get places.

Men's responses:
. . . you take good care of it.
. . . I want to make darn sure it has got a good coat of wax.
. . . check the engine.
. . . how soon can I start polishing it?

Sentence Stem: A car of your own . . .

Women's responses:

. . . is a pleasant convenience.

. . . is fine to have.

. . . is nice to have.

Men's responses:

. . . I would take care of.

. . . is a good thing.

. . . oh, absolutely a necessity.

The women's responses indicated that for them a car is something to use and that pride of ownership stresses being seen in the car. For men a car was something for which they should be protective and responsible. Their emphasis was on examining the car and doing things to it. Men appeared to feel closer to their car and regarded it as more of a necessity than did women.

Cartoon (see Exhibit 1) — A cartoon defined the situation of a father's being asked by his son for advice about getting a car. The respondent was told to imagine he was the father and asked what he would tell the boy.

Thematic Apperception Test (see Exhibits 2 and 3) — Two adaptations of this psychological test were included. Each consisted of a picture for which the respondent was asked to tell a story about what was going on. He had to decide what to talk about and how to go about it. The telling of a story required more organization and thought than was necessary in responding to incomplete sentences and cartoons. The answers were seen as depending as much or more on the personality of the respondent as on the situation shown.

One picture showed the open highway as seen from the driver's seat of a moving automobile. Hands were shown on the steering wheel and the speedometer reading was between 60 and 70 miles per hour. While the respondents were instructed to put themselves in the position of the driver, most people did not do so. Instead, they had someone else doing the driving. While they told stories about how much fun it would be to go fast on an open road, they said or implied that the driver should not be driving that fast. In this

way, the picture brought out contradictory attitudes toward speed, among other findings. Responses were interpreted to mean that speed involves both pleasure and fear. While high speed is wrong, a car nevertheless must be capable of high speed.

A second picture showed a car stopped along a road with a man looking at the engine under an opened hood. The respondent was told to make up a story about what was going on, how it came to happen, how things would turn out, what kind of people were in the car, and what kind of car they were driving.

ATTITUDE AND OPINION QUESTIONS

Supplementing the methods already described for learning about people's images of the different cars were several

EXHIBIT 2

A Thematic Apperception Test Adaptation Used in the Study
of the Meaning of Automobiles

PUT YOURSELF **HERE**

techniques which represented a more direct approach to attitudes and opinions. The devices were structured which meant that responses could be counted easily and the results expressed statistically.

One device was designed especially to learn whether certain kinds of people were associated with certain kinds of cars. Summary descriptions of people of different psychological and social roles were prepared. (See Appendix C, page 248) — Sample descriptions:

A middle-aged man, rather set in his ways. He's settled down and follows a routine life, pretty much.

A hard-boiled businessman, an executive; he's ambitious, energetic and smart.

She's a housewife whose home is always in perfect order.

As the interviewer read each description, the respondent was asked to pick from a list handed him a car of the make, model, body type, and color which he thought went best with each kind of person.

EXHIBIT 3

Another Thematic Apperception Test Adaptation Used in the Study of the Meaning of Automobiles

In an effort to learn more about opinions, people were asked to list both the best thing and the worst thing about each of 18 makes of cars. They also were asked to indicate whether they thought each car was for people of above middle class, middle class, or below middle class status. (See Appendix D, page 249.)

Another question asked for brief comparative descriptions

of automobile companies.   (See Appendix E, page 250.)
Another, called a comparimeter, asked them to check the
brand among those listed which they thought went best with
each of 19 descriptive terms such as "most reliable," "best
engineering," "flashiest," "ugliest design," and "most improved."   (See Appendix F, page 251.)   A somewhat similar
technique consisted of reading a number of descriptions of
automobiles and asking the respondent to name the make of
car he thought best matched each description.   (See Appendix G, page 252.)   Some of the descriptions: "A powerful,
swift, sleek-looking car," "It's conservative. A sturdy, reliable car," "Looks like a boat. It's clumsy, but it's well engi-
neered."

Another device consisted of reading a number of current
advertising claims and asking the respondent which brand of
car he associated with each of them. He also was asked to
rate each claim as to whether he didn't like it, thought it was
okay, or thought it was pretty good. (See Appendix H,
page 253.)

THE SAMPLE

The study was interested primarily in purchasers and potential purchasers of new cars — people who were attentive
to developments in the automobile field. With this in mind,
a sample was selected which gave more than proportionate
representation to men and to the middle to high social
classes. Of the 352 people interviewed, 62% were men, 38%
women. Five-sixths of the total owned automobiles. A
check was maintained on the representation by make of car
and year of model. All respondents lived in the metropolitan
Chicago area.

The interviews were distributed by age groups as follows:

15 to 20 years	18%
21 to 35 years	38%
36 to 50 years	32%
51 and over	12%

The distribution of interviews by social classes:

Upper middle class	24%
Transitional upper middle and mobile lower middle	10%
Lower middle class	34%
Mobile upper lower class	3%
Upper lower class	29%

Social class was used as a basis for sample selection because it referred to patterns of social attitudes and behavior of probable importance in the purchase of automobiles. The concept of social class had been developed in social anthropological studies of American communities on the basis of how people explained the different ways of thinking and acting of their neighbors and acquaintances. The class designations, therefore, were made or implied by themselves in referring to each other.

Social class was not strictly a matter of economic status; instead, it represented a way of living. Social status was determined by education, family background, who one's friends were, type of home and neighborhood, and occupation as well as the amount and type of income. There were five social classes: upper (3% of the total population), upper middle (12%), lower middle (30%), upper lower (35%), and lower lower (20%). The lower middle and upper lower classes, which accounted for 65% of the population, representing the "common man" level, were referred to as the "middle majority." (See Appendix I, pages 254–255, for brief descriptions.)

To help interviewers find respondents of the desired social classes, they were directed to selected residential areas. A Social Data Sheet was filled out to provide information on each respondent which was used later by a staff member in determining his social class by means of the Index of Status Characteristics. This was a rating system based on four social characteristics: occupation, source of income, house type, and dwelling area. A respondent was given a numerical rating on each characteristic. The numerical value then was weighted in accordance with the predetermined importance of the characteristic and the total of the weighted values was the basis for determining the social class. The I.S.C. method had been developed and validated by W. Lloyd Warner and others.

Other information from the Social Data Sheet was used to ascertain whether the respondent was mobile, i.e., whether he was moving up or down in social status. A number of transitional families were included so that the relevance of mobility to the questions being investigated could be checked.

The sample of 352 respondents was considered large enough to give adequate representation to the principal subgroups. It was believed that there were relatively few core answers to the question of how people felt about their automobiles and that people could be meaningfully grouped on these points. If this was true (as it was found to be), it would be revealed by a relatively small sample.

A small sample also was found to be adequate for establishing the public reputations of different brands of cars. Dr. Sidney Levy, director of the study, explained that this was possible because people are "social informants" as well as individuals. They live in groups. When they talk about brands, they reflect not only their own ideas but those of others with whom they associate. The study did not go into detail about the characteristics of the owners of different makes of cars. A larger sample would have been necessary for this purpose.

INTERVIEWING

Interviewers were selected for their ability to develop good rapport with respondents, to get them to talk fully, and to record what was said as nearly verbatim as possible. The interviewers were not expected to interpret what was said, this function being reserved for staff members with experience and special training in the social sciences. Many of the interviewers were housewives. Some were psychiatric social workers.

THE FINDINGS

Various members of the staff read interview reports and participated in discussions which guided the interpretive work and organization of results. The final report of 97 pages discussed the mechanical, personal, and social aspects of automobiles, categorized kinds of cars by their character attributes, and gave recommendations for automobile advertising. A summary report was prepared for more general distribution and is reproduced in Appendix J, pages 256–263. Some of the main findings are discussed briefly below.

An automobile must satisfy certain practical requirements of transportation and cost, and these considerations are important in people's thinking. The study showed, however, that for many people economy and value are not the most important reasons for choosing a particular car. Most people have no real interest in the complex technical features of automobiles.

The findings highlighted the role of the automobile as a social symbol and a means of expressing individual personality. It often serves as a sign of the owner's social status and the nature of his social participation. Certain cars are generally recognized as being more appropriate than others for particular groups of people. The socially impelled motives tend to make people concerned not only with cost, but with size, style, color, and reputation of the make and model. These elements also are important in the expression of the owner's character, temperament, and self-concept. People buy cars they think are especially appropriate for them.

Some of the broad patterns of characteristics people may express through their cars are summarized by the wish to appear conservative or reserved, the wish to be sociable, and the wish for attention.

The report described the process of buying a car as an interaction between the personality of the buyer and the personality of the car. Descriptions of the images people had of the different makes of cars were presented, and makes, models, colors, and other features of cars were classified as to whether they expressed conservatism (Plymouth, Dodge, DeSoto, Packard), middle-of-the-road moderation and participation (Chevrolet, Pontiac, Buick, Chrysler), some showiness (Ford, Mercury, Oldsmobile, Lincoln), and unusual status or individual needs (Cadillac, Studebaker, Hudson, Nash, Willys).

Thumbnail sketches of the images people had of the three popular, lower priced cars (when the research was conducted in 1953) are given below for illustrative purposes:

Chevrolet — Sales leadership; stability and responsibility; excellent value; reasonably attractive; high trade-in value; universal service facilities. The attitudes toward Chevrolet did not have quite the animation of those toward Ford. People evaluated Chevrolet in a more factual tone. Everyone knew it as a good reliable car and regarded its appearance as satisfactory, but the car was weighted in people's minds toward stability and responsibility.

Ford — Most distinctive of the three low priced cars; particular reputation for fastness, flexibility, and hard use; least social class bound; strong appeal to young people; for single people and hot-rodders; much improved; action car, nicely styled; too light; not too durable; high trade-in. There was wide-spread interest in the way Ford had changed the character of the car in recent years.

Plymouth — Most conservative of the three low-priced cars; inexpensive and dependable; small but neat; outstanding economy; sensible car for stable average people; neutral styling. The attitudes expressed toward Plymouth had a mild tone. The car was considered a good value, a sensible car for people who don't have much to spend. Economy is an attribute that seemed to be strongly attached to Plymouth. The car received very little criticism, but neither did anyone get wildly excited about it.

RECOMMENDATIONS

The report recommended that automobile advertising take into consideration both the basic motivations for car ownership and the personality of the make of car advertised.

Motivations for car ownership were summarized as follows: "to acquire and demonstrate participation in society; to extend one's life boundaries; to acquire a sense of power; to accomplish transportation; to feel pride of skill and mastery; to assert adult prerogatives and capabilities; to demonstrate status; and as an outlet for aggression."

Advertising should be planned with knowledge of how it relates to the character of the car as it currently is known to the public and how it contributes to building the image the advertiser wishes to create in the long run. [Advertising is likely to be most effective, the report stated, when it is in keeping with the car's personality. While the latter can be expanded successfully, people will not believe blunt denials of widespread stereotypes. They believe what agrees with their previous conceptions. In interviews in which reactions to selected advertisements were solicited, most people talked about the car itself first and their established beliefs usually overrode what the ads themselves said.

While everyone has some interest in styling and design, the study indicated that advertising giving central emphasis to appearance is not the most effective in the broad sense. While it is fitting for cars with real appearance reputations, generally it was considered better to combine appearance themes with the popularly valued ideas of dependability, performance, durability, economy, and safety. Appearance themes were seen as being most effective with the individualists, the young, the egocentric, and women. People will not believe unrealistic social status claims; they tend to resent attempts at either marked upgrading or downgrading of the prestige of a car.

Many advertising themes, when used singly, have a narrow appeal. The practical theme of reliability, durability, and dependability, for example, has strength when used alone among only the most reserved people. Similarly, the straight economy theme creates a cheap reputation, and a safety theme attracts mostly people with extreme fears. The use of a variety of themes was recommended for building broader personalities. Advertising should be planned in terms of an over-all governing conception of the car rather than in terms of single appeals.

Automobiles — What They Mean to Americans.

Commentary

This study, like the preceding ones on automobile insurance and coffee, takes a broad view of the product. The automobile, for example, was seen not only as a mechanical object which must meet certain practical standards, but also as a symbol of social status and participation and as a means of expressing one's personality. There is a real danger that the study's contribution in highlighting the last two functions may not be fully appreciated. This is due to the human tendency in many of us to react by saying, "Sure, but I already knew that cars had social values, that people buy them to impress others," etc. There is enough truth in this statement so that we are not taken completely by surprise by evidence on the subject. But it also is true that we actually have known very little about it and that the psychological and social meanings have been almost completely neglected by research.

Most market research in the past has related to engineering matters — the things the manufacturer is accustomed to thinking about. It is, of course, important that such investigations continue. But this study challenges the wisdom of limiting research to this area. We note not only the findings relating to the importance of social and personal aspects, but also the evidence that many people have no real interest in the complex technical features and do not give them detailed consideration in deciding which of several competitive and technically comparable makes to buy.

The use of the brand image concept warrants emphasis because of its apparently important implications for research in marketing. The automobile study found widely held images of the different makes and types of cars and made the point that some are seen as more appropriate for some kinds of people than for others. This led to viewing the buying process as a matching of the personality of the buyer and the personality of the car.

It was not within the scope of the research to actually compare owners of different cars as to social and personality characteristics. Its findings, however, seem to emphasize that this could be rewarding. They show that a given make of car selects its potential customers, and at the same time limits its market, by the brand image it has and builds and by the product and style features it offers. Therefore, information on just how it does so in terms of the numbers and kinds of people who are attracted by various characteristics could be most valuable to the manufacturer. This suggests the use of research into consumer wants for creative purposes in connection with designing and styling the product, an intriguing and challenging possibility about which virtually nothing has been done.

For advertising, the study offered a number of interesting thoughts which have not been typical of the field in the past. The main purpose of advertising, for example, was seen to be that of building an over-all image or character of a car consisting of a number of important and integrated ideas. In order for this objective to be met, it would be necessary for the advertiser to think in terms of an over-all image and to be acquainted with its possible dimensions for his product. There has been relatively little research undertaken to identify the main elements of existing images, and it has been common for advertising thinking to be in terms of one or a few main appeals without long-range image planning.

Of interest in this connection is the evidence that many advertising themes, when used singly, have a narrow appeal because they have different strengths for different people. This led to the recommendation that a variety of themes be used to build broader brand personalities. Much advertising thinking has been characterized by the opposite emphasis. Also of interest is the warning that care must be exercised in expanding existing images because people will not believe claims or ideas which bluntly deny their previous conceptions.

While this study differed somewhat in techniques from those described in preceding chapters, it shared the major feature of going to the people to learn what factors were important for investigation rather than to rely entirely on arm-chair hunches of researchers. It used indirect, relatively nonstructured means, especially at the outset when hypothesis formulation was the principal concern, to give the respondents plenty of freedom to express their thoughts and feelings. The techniques were adapted specially to the purposes of the study, recognizing that people are not conscious of a number of their buying motivations or of many of their attitudes and feelings about the various makes and types of automobiles. A variety of means were used to approach the matter in different ways so as to develop a full picture and provide internal checks on responses.

The research organization was made up of people representing several social science fields, and this variety of backgrounds of training and experience was brought to bear in staff discussions.

The study serves to illustrate the use of the concept of social class. While people within a given social class are not all alike, they tend to have much in common. They share patterns of thinking and living which are the product of social forces. This extends to personality characteristics which are the result of the impact of social influences on personality development. A number of studies in the behavioral sciences have shown the effects of social influences on attitudes, values, tastes, expectations, and habits of interpersonal relations. A recent study by Lee Rainwater showed a deeper effect on personality than had been demonstrated previously. It indicated that "social class influences also permeate the patterning of psychic drives, the kinds of need tensions which press most in the personality, and the way emotional controls are organized by the ego." [3]

What this means to marketing is that social class may represent a more useful dimension for differentiating among people of different buying behavior than some of the more conventional market factors such as income, age, and place of residence, although several of these may be important. Whether this is true in a given situation is a matter for research. The concept of social class is of potential value not only in connection with selecting a sample of respondents. Information on social class characteristics can be valuable background for suggesting hypotheses about buying behavior and for interpreting field data. Research in the social sciences has contributed data of this kind, and more detailed information is now being accumulated as marketing research is conducted with the social class dimension in mind.

[3] Lee Rainwater, *A Study of Social Class Factors Influencing the Personality Characteristics of Middle and Lower Class Adolescents* (Chicago: unpublished thesis submitted at the University of Chicago, December 1954) .

Appendix A

DEPTH INTERVIEW QUESTIONS USED IN AUTOMOBILE STUDY [1]

1. Do you have a car? _____ Yes _____
   What make is it? _____
   What model? _____
                                     (year, type, body)
   How long have you had it? _____
   Where buy it? _____
                             (dealer, friend, lot)
   What did you have before? _____
                              (make, model, type, etc.)

2. How did you come to buy your present car? What were the circumstances; what things entered into your decision? Did anyone help you decide? Were there any objections; any special problems? Why did you choose that type (sedan, convertible, etc.) Why 2 or 4 door? What color is it; how did you come to choose that color?

3. What do you think about your car since you've had it? Do you think it was a good buy? How does it run? What's best about it, what could be improved?

4. What accessories came with your car? Were there any you didn't want, but got anyway? Which would you like to have? (Spotlight, bumperguards, radio, heater, seatcovers . . . other extras, whitewalls, undercoating.)

5. How do you use your car mostly — for work, for pleasure?

6. Who else uses the car? Who uses it most? Who is proudest of it; most possessive about it; how do they treat it? How do you feel about letting other people use the car?

7. Where do you generally park the car? How do you take care of it — check-ups, flat tires, washing, winterizing, etc.

---

[1] This is a composite list of questions from three depth interview guides. Questions used for the first wave of interviews in the order in which they appeared on the guide: 1, 2, 16, 17, 18, 19, 20, 21, 22, 23, 24, 25, 26, 27, 28, 29, 30, 31, 32, 33, 12, 13, 14, 15. Questions used in the second guide: 1, 2, 3, 4, 5, 6, 7, 8, 9, 10, 11, 12, 13, 14, 15. Questions used in the third guide: 1, 2, 3, 11.

8. What plans do you have — or wishes — for another car?

9. What kinds of things do you think influence people most when they buy a car?

10. What kind of cars do most people at work drive? What kind of cars do your friends have? What do they say of them?

11. I'd like you to think of the most satisfying things about owning and driving a car. What would you say they are?

12. When people talk about cars, what do they talk about mostly? What about the new cars this year? Ever discuss the mechanical advantages? Design improvement? Horsepower? Power-steering? Kind of engine, transmission, brakes, differential, carburetor, clutch, gear, etc.

13. How do people find out about the technical changes in cars; where have you read or heard about them? (Magazines, newspapers, radio, TV, friends, get ideas on each.)

14. Think of some ad you saw recently in the newspapers about automobiles; what claims, mechanical improvements, advertisements; for which cars, in which paper? What did you think of the claim?

15. What is your opinion of the automobile ads in the newspapers? What is their particular value? How do they compare with auto ads in magazines, TV, radio?

16. What do you think about your car now that you've had it this long? Do you think it was a good buy? How does it run? What are its drawbacks; what could be improved; what do you like especially about it?

17. Is your car useful to you in your work? In what ways?

18. Now let's talk about how you use the car otherwise. How does it give you most pleasure? (Explore in terms of travel, Sunday trips, social visits, long drives, any other use.)

19. What about the others in the family? Who uses the car most; how does your family enjoy the car; what do they complain about; do wife or kids use it for any special occasions — shopping, schools, etc.? Who is proudest of the car, or most possessive about it; how do they treat it?

20. Now, about taking care of your car. Where do you generally park? Do you use public garage facilities?

21. How frequently do you get check-ups? What sorts of things

do you or could you fix yourself? When do you take it to a mechanic? What about flat tires, washing, greasing, winterizing, etc.? What was the most unusual or outstanding experience you ever had with car breakdown or repair?

22. What kinds of things have you found get most out of order in a car? What do you think cars don't have that they could use?

23. Have you thought about buying a new car (another car)? What are your plans? (If a used car, when a new one?) What make, model, body type (brand, year, coupe, sedan, victoria, etc.). Why do you want that kind? What are some of the most important things to consider in getting a new car? (Discuss this thoroughly.)

24. Suppose money were no obstacle; what car would you get then? Why?

25. Suppose you lived way out in the country? Which then? Why?

26. What would you want if you have a larger (or smaller) family?

27. If your last car had been a "lemon," would you consider the same make? Why? Why not?

28. (If had cars before now) What was the first car you ever had? What kind was it and how did you come to get it? How did you feel about it at the time? — the family?

29. Many people feel that there are tricks to breaking in a car. How do you feel about that? What kinds of problems does this involve? What breaking-in experiences have you ever had?

30. How often do you think cars should be traded in? What are the advantages of that?

31. What kind of cars do most of the people at work drive? Do you recall one of them who was especially enthusiastic about his car? What did he say; what kind was it?

    Do most of your friends have cars? What kinds do they have? What do your best friends think of their cars? (Get individual instances not vague "okays.") What are some criticisms of particular cars that you have heard?

32. Think of a friend who is a very good driver. What kind of a person is he (she)?

    Now think of the worst driver you know. Describe the kind of person he is; what he's like (or she).

33. What do you think about letting other people drive your car? What are the advantages, the disadvantages? How do (would) you personally feel if a friend asks to borrow your car?

    How do you feel about riding with other people; in the front seat, in the back seat? What usually goes on when you are driving and other people are riding with you?

Appendix B

INCOMPLETE SENTENCES USED
IN THE AUTOMOBILE STUDY

Now I have some incomplete sentences. I will read them to you one at a time, and I'd like you to finish them for me with whatever they make you think of.

From First Interview Guide:

1. A woman likes a car that _____
2. A Ford is the car that _____
3. A good second car is _____
4. The new Mercury seems rather _____
5. Cars would be safer if _____
6. Buick claims that _____
7. They advertise cars more in _____
8. I would buy a Plymouth if _____
9. In order to own a Cadillac, you _____
10. Dependability in a car means _____
11. If I could have any car I wanted _____
12. Kaiser-Frazer ought to _____
13. The nice thing about a Willys is _____
14. The best car for hot-rodding _____
15. When you own a Chrysler, you _____
16. A car that needs to be traded in less often, usually, is _____
   _____ because _____
      (make)
17. I think that Studebaker _____

From Second Interview Guide:

1. A car of your own _____
2. Financing a car _____
3. Most of the new cars _____
4. When I drive very fast _____
5. The best color for a car _____
6. A station wagon _____
7. People can now _____

8. I'd rather own _____ than a car _____
9. We named our car _____
10. A car with a high center of gravity _____
11. People who drive convertibles _____
12. The worst thing about having a car _____
13. It's best to trade in a car _____
14. I'd rather own a car than _____
15. My father had _____
16. Driving a car without a clutch _____
17. I would never get a _____

Appendix C

KINDS OF PEOPLE AND KINDS OF CARS

We often think of certain cars as especially suitable or unsuitable for different kinds of people, the way it seems funny for a very big man to drive around in a very tiny car. I will describe some people and I'd like you to pick out a car from this list (on card) that goes with each person the best. Even if you think any car would do, name one that seems to come closest, in your opinion, in make, model, body type, color, etc.

1. "A middle-aged man, rather set in his ways. He's settled down and follows a routine life, pretty much."

   _____

2. "A college co-ed — she's sort of spoiled, wanting everything her own way, and doesn't care much about other people."

   _____

3. "A hard-boiled businessman, an executive; he's ambitious, energetic, and smart."   _____

4. "She's a housewife whose home is always in perfect order."

   _____

5. "He's a thin, nervous man, high-strung, and pretty temperamental."   _____

6. "He's a lively joe — he's strong, fast, likes his liquor hard and a good brawl."   _____

7. "She's a gal with a career; snappy, energetic, and very capable about running things."   _____

8. "He's a family man and a hard worker; he bowls on Wednesdays in the league."   _____

9. "He's a young guy, just starting out, bright and hopeful."

   _____

(Used in Third Interview Guide)

Appendix D

ATTITUDE AND OPINION STUDY

Below are listed the main American cars. What is the best thing and the worst thing about each?

Best Thing	Make	Rank	Worst Thing
_____	Nash	_____	_____
_____	Chevrolet	_____	_____
_____	Mercury	_____	_____
_____	Cadillac	_____	_____
_____	Dodge	_____	_____
_____	Ford	_____	_____
_____	DeSoto	_____	_____
_____	Hudson	_____	_____
_____	Plymouth	_____	_____
_____	Kaiser-Frazer	_____	_____
_____	Packard	_____	_____
_____	Pontiac	_____	_____
_____	Willys	_____	_____
_____	Studebaker	_____	_____
_____	Buick	_____	_____
_____	Oldsmobile	_____	_____
_____	Chrysler	_____	_____
_____	Lincoln	_____	_____

Now go back and rate each car as to whether you think it is A, B, or C; with A for people above middle class, with B for average middle class people and C for people below middle class.

(Used in Second Interview Guide)

OPINIONS OF AUTOMOBILE MANUFACTURERS
AND BRANDS

Now, I'd like to get your opinions about the various makes of cars, thinking about them from different points of view. First, how would you compare the different companies that make the main American cars? What would you say about the general quality, engineering, durability, and so on of

The Chrysler Corporation —
    (Dodge, DeSoto, Plymouth, Chrysler)
Packard Motor Company
Nash-Kelvinator Corporation
Ford Motor Company
    (Ford, Mercury, Lincoln)
Kaiser-Frazer Motor Corp.
    (Henry J. Frazer)
Hudson Motor Company
Studebaker Corporation
General Motors Corporation
    (Buick, Pontiac, Chevrolet, Cadillac, Oldsmobile)
Willys-Overland Motors

(Used in Third Interview Guide)

Appendix F
COMPARIMETER

Buick	Plymouth	Oldsmobile	Mercury	Nash	DeSoto	Pontiac	Chrysler	Kaiser-Frazer	Dodge	Ford	Studebaker	Lincoln	Chevrolet	Cadillac	Hudson	Willys	Packard	
																		Best for city driving
																		Most reliable
																		Most highly powered
																		Best for hard use
																		Best engineering
																		Flashiest
																		Least changed
																		Best for a family
																		Most conservative
																		Best gas mileage
																		Most beautiful
																		Preferred by men
																		Cheapest
																		Most improved
																		Ugliest design
																		Preferred by women
																		Most luxurious
																		Most popular
																		Least worth the money

(Used in Second and Third Interview Guides)

Appendix G

BELOW ARE SOME DESCRIPTIONS OF AUTOMO-BILES. WHICH CAR–MAKE DO YOU THINK FITS CLOSEST TO EACH DESCRIPTION?

1. A powerful, swift, sleek-looking car. _____

   (make)
2. This car is perfect for long trips. It hugs the road, drives smoothly and has good mileage. _____
3. A small, neat car. It's comfortable and not flashy.

   _____
4. It's conservative. A sturdy, reliable car.

   _____
5. A regular bull-dozer of a car. No matter the weather or the road, it gets you there safely. _____
6. This is the car of the future; it looks like a jet plane. Ultra-modern in all details. _____
7. A quality car. Expensive, impressive, but not flashy. It's built to last. _____
8. It's a light-weight car . . . looks almost flimsy.

   _____
9. Looks like a boat; it's clumsy, but it's well-engineered.

   _____
10. This is a safe, solid car; the kind you can really depend on.

    _____

(Used in Third Interview Guide)

Appendix H

ADVERTISING CLAIMS

Following are some of the claims made for various cars nowadays. Try to identify which makes the claim, and then rate them 1, 2, or 3 whether 1 — you don't like the idea, 2 — it's okay, or 3 — it's pretty good.

1. "The one fine car designed for modern living . . . completely powered for modern driving."

    _____   _____
    (make)   (rating)

2. "The new standard of the American road."

    _____   _____

3. "The new classic for '53."   _____   _____

4. "We've gone your dreams one better."

    _____   _____

5. "The new American car with the European look."

    _____   _____

6. "In a class by itself; dollar for dollar you can't beat a

    _____   _____

7. "Beautiful. A new inspiration for the automotive world."

    _____   _____

8. "The action car for active Americans."

    _____   _____

9. "Ruggedness combined with superb styling."

    _____   _____

10. "The first truly balanced car in the low-priced field."

    _____   _____

(Used in Third Interview Guide. Another list of advertising claims was used in Second Interview Guide.)

BRIEF DESCRIPTIONS OF SOCIAL CLASSES
IN AMERICA [1]

Social anthropological studies in American communities have identified and described five social classes which are definable levels of social attitudes and behavior. The class designations were arrived at on the basis of how people explained the different ways of thinking and acting of their neighbors and acquaintances. While people of the same social class are not all alike, they have many common characteristics which are important in how they live and what they buy.

Social classes are not strictly economic classes. While economic factors are very important, social status is determined by education, family background, who one's friends are, type of home and neighborhood, the kinds of problems of survival, and occupation, as well as the amount and type of income. Brief descriptions of the social classes follow:

Upper Class (3%) — The aristocracy of birth and wealth represented by the "old families" and, just beneath them, the families with newly gained economic and social power. Much of their income is from invested wealth.

Upper Middle (12%) — Professional people, successful executives, owners of large businesses. The respectable, achieving, solid citizens who emphasize civic action, highly moral principles, personal integrity. Income largely from salaries and fees. Live in the better suburbs.

Middle Majority (65%) — The "common man" level. The middle majority world is restricted physically and socially, centers in the home, is highly moral. There are two groups within the middle majority:

Lower Middle (30%) — White collar workers, tradesmen, and a few skilled workers. Have fewer interests and live more closely regulated lives in smaller geographical

[1] Based on material prepared by Social Research, Inc.

and social worlds than those of the upper and upper middle classes.

Upper Lower (35%) — "Poor but honest" workers in skilled and semiskilled occupations. Spend most of their limited incomes from wages on food and shelter. Limited participation in educational advantages of the community.

Lower Lower (20%) — Impoverished. Lack concern for a routine pattern of life. Considered by classes above them to be lazy, shiftless, irresponsible. Do little reading.

Appendix J

HIGHLIGHTS OF THE REPORT ON AUTOMOBILES: WHAT THEY MEAN TO AMERICANS

Section I: Practical, Personal, and Social Meanings

1. *Automobiles Are Mechanical Objects With Many Important Practical Functions*

A minority of the population (mostly men, and mainly in the lower class) have any real interest in the technical aspects of cars. Much broader is the group who want to know and to be able to talk about the gadgets and gimmicks and latest innovations of the new cars — not the complex technical features.

Still on the "realistic," practical side is attention to the functional uses of cars. By and large, a car is intended for particular concrete purposes; these are fundamental, even if taken very much for granted.

In the total pattern of attitudes toward automobiles, realism and the satisfaction of practical goals and needs are human motives met by the car as a mechanical object and vehicle of transportation.

2. *Automobiles Are Sharply Related To The Economic Life Of The Individual (And The Family)*

A man's economic situation is likely to set sharp limitations on what he can do about his automotive wishes.

In general, initial cost is important in influencing people in their choices, and in the place they give a car on the price scale; but probably more real, continuous consideration is given to the economy factors of gas mileage and upkeep — and this seems true for owners of expensive cars as well as cheap ones.

Nevertheless, the role of economy as a limiting factor should not be exaggerated. The limits set can be quite sharp — but for many people they are not the center of concern; they are not the most important reasons for choosing a particular car, and they may often be a minor consideration.

In the complex pattern of attitudes that people have about cars, their acquisition and their use, economy, and value (economy as influenced by other considerations) stand out as prominent ideas.

3. *Automobiles Are Heavily Laden With Social Meanings — Relating To Social Status, Aspiration, Participation, Etc.*

Cars have many social meanings and implications. They are very valuable in facilitating social interaction, being a means of camaraderie, courtesy, intimacy, etc.

The automobile is notable in the way it operates as an informative symbol in the status system of America, as a sign of social position and the nature of one's participation.

There are many kinds of cars; and they have many different qualities. These are identified and evaluated in one's thinking, ultimately with the implication "for me" or " not for me." There is a general recognition that certain cars are more appropriate than others for particular groups of people.

Socially impelled motives tend to make people concerned not only with cost, but with size, style, color (less utilitarian and more visible features), and particularly with the reputation of the make and model.

4. *To Signify Personal Mastery And Control of Major Human Impulses*

A. *Self-Assertiveness* — Because the driver is controlling a mass of tremendous energy, he knows the pleasures and also the fears of handling powerful human drives. He identifies not only with the car's power, but also its capacity for destruction.

Everyone knows that cars have a potential for bursting the bounds of human control and taking their destructive toll. This frightens many people very much — and it's also exciting and provocative.

B. *Affiliation* — This is the expression of human companionship — friendship — sex — people being together. Cars play a vital part in our mating and dating customs.

A major part of the car's intense value is that it provides much emotional stimulation, and at the same time concretely symbolizes the control of fundamental impulses.

Everyone develops some mastery of his drives. This is self-control. Cars are especially successful in feeding the important desires of Americans who want to be somebody. Wanting to be somebody is the basic desire every human being has for being important and effective, in some way that other people recognize.

For many reasons in many ways having an automobile gives people the feeling of being somebody, of being more substantial and capable than the nonowners.

5. *Automobiles Provide Avenues For The Expression Of (And Testimony To) The Character, Temperament, And Self-Concept Of The Owner And The Driver*

Automobiles are one of the means of revealing and satisfying — to an extent — some of the characteristic feelings and individual motives that typify each person.

Because the differences in people have so much to do with the way they express themselves in car selection, it is important to single out some of the broad lines of what essentially different people want to be:

A. *The Wish to be Conservative or Reserved* — This is the solid citizen who emphasizes conformity — wants to be considered reliable and stable, draws back from drastic innovations, doesn't want to be conspicuous or to experiment.

B. *The Wish to be Sociable or a Participant* — These are the people who want to be up to date, to do what is popular. If people are moving toward informality and color, they want to be in the swim.

C. *The Wish for Attention* — These people want to be different, they are looking for the newest things — they are innovators and style setters, and will take a chance on novelty. They enjoy being talked about. There are 4 main directions of this attention-getting wish.

C-1. *Substantial Brightness* — Big, bright costliness in cars, loud impressive display, everything the best, the most expensive, widely recognized high status symbols.

C-2. *Conspicuous Reserve* — They want people to know their

status, but simultaneously express modesty. They go in for dignified display, large dark cars with expensive appointments or deliberate downgrading.

C-3. *Sophisticated Flair* — These people prize individuality; smartness, not gaudiness; brightness, not drabness; forefront of style; try anything.

C-4. *Youthful Impulsiveness* — These are all the people of any age who express their youthful yearnings through automobiles. The car demonstrates daring and vigor in the way it looks and how they drive it. Brightest colors! Showiest gadgets!

SECTION II: THE BUYING PROCESS IS AN INTERACTION BETWEEN THE PERSONALITY OF THE CAR AND THE PERSONALITY OF THE INDIVIDUAL

Any well-known product acquires a personality of its own — a character, reputation, or image. This is a composite of the attitudes that people have toward it.

The car purchase is comparable psychologically to building a house. It is a composite of many things.

To select one particular make, people buy the cars they think are especially appropriate for them.

Any human is a complex of many motives: practical aims, economic limitations, personal characteristics, social position, and ambitions. These different motives should be seen as patterns with predominant or subsidiary meaning.

A. *Cars and Features that Express Conservatism* — These help people express such ideas as dignity, reserve, maturity. They appeal to people who want to tell the world that they are very responsible, serious in their work and family outlook. They emphasize practicality and dependability.

Plymouth	4-door Sedan
Dodge	Dark colors, especially black,
DeSoto	green, blue
Packard	Minimum accessories
	Very few gadgets, if any

B. *Cars and Features that Express Middle-of-the-Road Moderation and Participation* — These people want to avoid being too

conservative or too extreme.   They don't want to be conspicuous
by being too reserved or too flashy.   They want to keep up to
date, being neither stodgy or very "advanced."   They think about
practicality and realism, too, but give a more active interest to
looks, to getting on the bandwagon.

Chevrolet	2-door Coupe
Pontiac	Light colors
Buick	"Ordinary" accessories
Chrysler	Commonly the current fad in gadgets

C. *Cars and Features that Express Some Showiness.* — These
help people to express their interest in what's new, to exhibit
their modernity and individuality.   They show an interest in
some flashiness, more emphasis on appearance.   They are alert to
change and experiment.   Individualism is highly stressed.

Ford	Hardtop
Mercury	Two-tones
Oldsmobile	Bright shades and hues
Lincoln	A range of "extras" and gadgets
	Often new fads

D. *Cars and Features that Express Unusual Status or Individual Needs* — These help people to express extreme attitudes or
most special needs.   The particular wishes vary from notable os-
tentation (Cadillac, Studebaker) to marked safety fears.   Apart
from Cadillac, attitudes toward them tend to be quite mixed, or
insufficiently known and organized to perceive their real character in a broad way.

Cadillac (high status, ostentation)	Convertible (impulsiveness)
Studebaker	Very bright colors, red, yellow, white
Hudson	The latest gadgets and accessories
Nash	
Kaiser	
Willys	

Section III: Advertising Should Utilize Two Basic Sets of
Motivation

1. The basic wish for car ownership.
2. What the personality of a particular car expresses.

Product-dominated copy assumes that the car is bigger than the
buyer. It doesn't consider the owner is using the car for practical expressive purposes. It assumes he is latching on the car to
acquire its character.

It doesn't address itself to the humans and what urges them to
auto row.

1. Motivations for car ownership.
    — To acquire and demonstrate participation in society.
    — To extend one's life boundaries.
    — To acquire a sense of power.
    — To accomplish transportation.
    — To feel pride of skill and mastery.
    — To assert adult prerogatives and capabilities.
    — To demonstrate status.
    — As an outlet for aggression.
2. The advertising problem of car personality:
    A. What is the current character of the car in the minds of
       its audience,
           And what does the campaign do to build, mod-
           ify, or contradict this character?
    B. What is the long-run character the advertiser wants to
       establish,
           And how does the campaign contribute to this
           image?

The advertising is most effective when it is in terms of the
car personality, and when it is successfully exanding this character.

           Advertising must fit car personality, although it can
           be widened.

People rate believability in advertising in terms of their attitudes toward the car.

People believe what agrees with their previous conceptions of
the car. When asked to evaluate auto ads, they talk about the

car first, and their established beliefs override completely what the ad says.

Practical themes are most popularly valued.

— Dependability	— Economy
— Performance	— Safety features
— Durability	

Value themes have wide appeal.

Appearance themes most effectively appeal to the individualists, the young, the egocentric, and to women.

For the average person — appearance is secondary to performance and value.

Social status themes can easily create unbelievability.

Some degree of upgrading is expected. Nevertheless everyone is quite realistic about where cars stand in prestige. People resent either market upgrading or downgrading.

Many themes should not stand alone.

1. Just dependability — durability — reliability appeals only to the most reserved people.
2. Just economy creates a "cheap" reputation.
3. Just safety appeals only to people with extreme fears.

Broad proclamations of superiority or newness lack real content.

Difficult themes. In the widest audience, these themes had a generally negative reception.

   — Very unusual advances in style or design.
   — Something alien.
   — Fantasy of the audience.
   — Extremity of power.

Cars that are narrowly defined either because of extreme features or singleminded advertising definitely limit themselves.

Varied themes build broader personalities and wider appeal.

A car can sell itself to different people by presenting different facets of its personality.

The problem in countering definitions is more than just saying the opposite of what people think.

Don'ts for advertising

Don't bluntly attack or deny widespread stereotypes.

Don't put modest cars in upper class settings if you want to sell them.

Don't appeal just to snobbery.

Don't talk about just mechanics.

Don't get caught up in European, international, or otherwise alien and exotic claims, jargon, and prestige if you want widest audience appeal.

Do's for advertising

I. Show situations that lend themselves to personal identification.

II. Show cars in realistic backgrounds. Otherwise the advertising tends to reinforce and narrow the existing image because this is a reminder rather than teaching.

III. Find the best combination of realism and fantasy.

IV. Use clear-cut people with character.

V. Upgrade or downgrade not too far.

VI. Plan advertising in terms of an over-all governing conception of the car rather than in terms of single appeals.

VII. Consider the car personality as well as the basic aims of the audience.

CHAPTER VIII

Donahue Sales Corporation

FORENOTE

In this case the general objective for which a research approach had to be developed was that of learning what might be done to increase both the amount of sewing in the home and the use of zippers as a form of closure. The study was planned and conducted by McCann-Erickson, Inc., which had pioneered in developing means of differentiating among users and nonusers of various types of products and brands on the basis of personality characteristics. A prominent feature of the research described here was the use of selected personality tests to explain differences in sewing behavior. Their inclusion gives an emphasis and systematic attention unusual in consumer studies to the belief that what a person does reflects what he is like psychologically. In addition to the personality tests, the approach relied heavily upon the use of the detailed or depth interview supplemented by a series of cartoons and word association questions.

DONAHUE SALES CORPORATION

A Descriptive Case

THE DONAHUE SALES CORPORATION was under contract as the sales agent responsible for all retail sales of Talon zippers. While the Talon Company sold direct to garment manufacturers, Donahue's sales force of 30 men called on department stores, chain stores, and wholesalers who sold to small retailers. Donahue supported these selling efforts with a promotional program to encourage home sewing and the use of zippers.

The Talon line was the most complete offered at retail.

It consisted of 1,000 different zippers in eight types: dress, neckline, skirt, trousers, upholstery, corset, purse, and jacket. For each type, there were several weights, 1 to 15 lengths, and up to 25 different colors. Most retailers carried only one manufacturer's line of zippers.

Donahue had achieved wide retail distribution. For expansion of sales, the company looked primarily to increases in the amount of home sewing and in the use of zippers as opposed to other closures. The major element of Donahue's program directed toward these objectives was the Talon Educational Service through which sewing teachers and their students were supplied teaching aids and information on zipper applications. In addition, Donahue's research department worked to develop new and simpler ways of sewing in zippers, and the company's fashion director consulted with the leading pattern companies to get zippers specified among the findings needed for garments. She assisted with design and sewing problems and with the preparation of sewing instructions.

The Talon Educational Service had been developed under the guidance of Mr. Walter Salmon, Director of Sales, who had joined Donahue in 1947. Formerly, he had been in charge of sales and exports for the Simplicity Pattern Company, Inc., where, in the 1930's, he had helped launch an effort to boost pattern sales by offering assistance to sewing teachers. The program grew and contributed to Simplicity's marked rise to sales leadership in the pattern industry.

The Talon Educational Service was directed primarily at junior and senior high school classes in which, it was believed, most of the learning to sew took place. Miss Rajean M. Codish, the director, had a staff of five field representatives who gave more than 1,500 lectures to 60,000 students annually in schools over the country. They also participated in an adult educational program by conducting demonstrations in department stores.

Various materials were supplied free of charge. In one year, 18,000 prints of a strip film on zipper applications had been issued for classroom use. In response to advertising in home economics, clothing, and 4-H Club publications, 20,000 to 25,000 requests were received annually from teachers for such materials as wall charts, zipper designs, student lesson books, "practice packets" for students, and leaflets describing new closures and telling how to apply them. In the past seven years, 14,000,000 student leaflets had been distributed.

In recent years Mr. Salmon had become increasingly concerned over a lack of reliable information on the size and nature of the home sewing market. While a figure of 40,000,000 home sewers had been quoted in the industry, its accuracy was questionable. Mr. Salmon guessed that 5,000,-000 persons accounted for the great bulk of skilled sewing, such as the making of clothes, and he noted signs that this group might not be getting larger. While Donahue's zipper sales had enjoyed increases, Mr. Salmon believed that the amount of home sewing was not keeping pace with population growth.

Mr. Salmon became interested in undertaking research to find out more about how home sewing and the use of zippers might be promoted. He discussed the matter with Mr. J. Stahlin, account executive at McCann-Erickson, Inc., the agency which handled all of Talon's advertising. After several conferences with members of the agency's research department, a motivational survey was proposed to investigate the motives and attitudes of women toward sewing and zippers. Heavy sewers, light sewers, and nonsewers were to be interviewed. Their responses would be analyzed to learn why some women sewed more than others, what the major appeals as well as drawbacks and resistances to sewing were, and how the productive output of the light sewer might be increased. A number of teen agers, sewers, and nonsewers were to be interviewed to learn whether their attitudes were different from those of adults. The research approach would include depth interviews, projective questions and cartoons, and personality tests.

Late in 1954 company approval was given to Mr. Salmon's recommendation that the study be undertaken.

McCann-Erickson's research department, which at the time of the study was headed by Mr. Donald B. Armstrong, Jr., Vice President, had used psychological techniques for a number of years to determine consumer motivations and attitudes toward various products. These surveys were used to guide creative planning and to help with various aspects of sales strategy including merchandising, dealer relations, and product design. Much of this work had been supervised by Dr. Herta Herzog, a psychologist who had received her formal training in Vienna. As a member of the staff of Columbia University's Bureau of Applied Social Research, she had used depth interviewing techniques in her work there as early as the 1930's. She had employed depth interviews in advertising research since joining McCann-Erickson in 1944 and a few years later she began the use of personality tests. A number of studies had been made of personality characteristics of consumer groups such as users vs. nonusers of a product or brand.

As Director of Creative Research, Dr. Herzog was responsible for the work of three departments: motivation research and two copy research departments, one for printed media and the other for radio and television. Dr. Virginia Miles, who received her Ph.D. in psychology from Columbia University, headed the motivation research staff of several persons trained in psychology and other social sciences. In her four years with McCann-Erickson she had completed more than 100 motivational surveys for about 60 clients representing 15 product fields. She formerly had served as Associate Director of Research and Planning for R. H. Macy, Inc., and Advertising Research Director for Alexander Smith, Inc.

PLANNING THE STUDY

After discussing the problem with Mr. Salmon, Dr. Miles began planning the survey by consulting available market studies on home sewing. The latter suggested areas for questioning and ways of categorizing home sewers, and provided information on the size of the home sewing market, its growth compared with population growth, and the number of garments sewed.

With this background Dr. Miles and her assistants began the development of a tentative depth interviewing schedule. Certain areas for questioning were immediately apparent from the problems mentioned by Mr. Salmon and the goals of the survey. It was essential to have the respondents discuss why they sewed, what satisfactions they got from sewing, why they did not sew more, and what difficulties or dissatisfactions there were in sewing. It also was necessary to include questions about zippers: how the respondent decided what closure to use, what she thought of zippers versus other closures for various functions, and what problems she had encountered with zippers.

After the more obvious question areas were included, additional topics were added as a result of thinking through the problem and its ramifications. Certain question areas were included in order to test hunches about sewing behavior. In addition, more than 100 previous motivation surveys had indicated topics which generally should be explored for certain types of products. For example, surveys had indicated that a woman's own view of her role as a housewife and her satisfactions and dissatisfactions with housework and family had an important bearing on attitudes toward products used in the home.

As the tentative depth interviewing schedule was constructed, it became apparent that certain underlying factors of disposition probably would be important in influencing surface attitudes, particularly those toward housework and womanly chores like sewing. This led to the decision to supplement the depth interviewing with certain personality tests which will be described later. It also was decided to use a cartoon technique to get at underlying attitudes toward sewing which are not readily voiced, particularly the respondent's feelings about the reactions of other members of the family to her activities. A short answer questionnaire also was prepared to supplement the depth interview with top-of-mind responses to various key points.

The depth interviewing guide and the other research materials were tested in 25 pilot interviews conducted by highly skilled interviewers. The results were analyzed to see where the interviewing procedure could be sharpened up, whether any subjects spontaneously brought up by respondents had been slighted in the guide, whether the topics included were yielding useful material, and whether more detail and probing were needed on certain points. For example, the pilot interviewing revealed that some of the structured questions had been used too soon and had tended to cut off spontaneous response. This was corrected. A few of the questions used with the cartoons had to be structured a little more to keep the responses within the subject area of home sewing.

THE DEPTH INTERVIEW

The depth interview was aimed at spontaneity of response and coverage of surface attitudes and emotional undercurrents of prejudice and disposition. Respondents were encouraged to express their feelings in a free, conversational manner. The interviewer, using the guide list of relevant question areas, brought up each aspect of the subject and gave the respondent every opportunity to talk herself out. Whenever spontaneous response ceased, the interviewer probed to get the respondent to talk further, to explain, to look beneath the surface. Remarks were noted verbatim so far as possible to preserve the respondent's own way of talk-ing. The adult interviews lasted about an hour and a half. Because of the length, each woman was given a chromium cigarette lighter for her cooperation.

McCann-Erickson had a staff of 250 depth interviewers who worked regularly on a contracted free-lance basis. They lived in various parts of the country, representing all regions, rural as well as urban and suburban areas, and large cities as well as small towns. Most of the interviewers were house-wives who had academic training in the social sciences. Ex-perience had shown that such women, properly trained by McCann-Erickson's field personnel, made most satisfactory depth interviewers. Interviewing quality was checked con-tinually and interviewers whose work was not of high caliber were dropped. Each interviewer was provided with a de-tailed instruction booklet to serve as a constant review of the purposes and problems of depth interviewing.

The interviewer's job was to get the respondent to talk about the various subject areas and to probe significant re-sponses. She was not to interpret, but to act as a sounding board and to take notes on what was said. For training pur-poses, a sampling of interviews was recorded on tape and later compared with the interviewer's actual write-ups.

Instructions for interviewers who worked on the sewing study appear in Appendix A, pages 293–295.

Each interview opened with a series of short questions de-signed to find out how home sewing and the several forms of closure were regarded. (See Appendix B, pages 296–297.) Some questions were projective in nature, taking the form of incomplete sentences and words to which associations were elicited. The woman's attention was focused on sewing or a form of closure, otherwise no answer was indicated. In completing a sentence, such as "A woman who sews at home . . . ," the respondent was on her own and presum-ably would project her own feelings and attitudes in responding. The same held for giving associations to words like "zipper," "buttons," and "snaps."

Several open end questions also were used to learn which closure was preferred for a dress and why. In an effort to learn of the respondent's image of each of four forms of closure, she was asked which form ranked first on each of several given qualities (which was the prettiest, most feminine, easiest to make, most durable, most practical, etc.) .

The regular depth interview followed the short questions, separate interviewing schedules being used for women who sewed, women who did not sew, teen-age sewers, and teen-age nonsewers. Interviews with adult sewers opened with the respondent's personal history of sewing, the social context of sewing and her sewing ability. They also covered sewing gratifications, sewing machines, reading about sewing, and zippers. (See Appendix C, pages 298–301.)

The schedule for adult nonsewers explored resistances to sewing, what influenced the respondent's attitudes toward sewing, why she thought some women sewed, whether she had access to a sewing machine, whether she read about sewing, and what attitudes she had toward zippers. (See Appendix D, page 302.)

The depth interviews concluded by asking for responses to an advertisement which pictured a woman struggling with a skirt zipper which had jammed. The brand name was deleted to avoid bias. The ad was included as a projective technique to get women to talk about zippers sticking in order to assess the real importance of this problem. It was suspected that there was more talk than serious concern about the matter.

The interviewing schedules for teen agers were shorter but similar to those used with adults.

EXHIBIT 1
A Cartoon Used to Study the Meanings of Home Sewing

EXHIBIT 2

Another Cartoon Used to Study the Meanings of Home Sewing

THE CARTOONS

After the depth interview, six cartoons dealing with sewing or zippers were shown, one at a time. Facial expressions and the emotional tone of the cartoons were neutral. The respondent was asked to say what a designated person in the cartoon was thinking. In answering, she presumably would project her own attitudes and feelings about sewing. Brief descriptions of the cartoons follow:

1. A woman shown working at a sewing machine. (See Exhibit 1.)
2. One woman showing another a dress. Sewing machine in background. Respondent was asked what the second woman was thinking.
3. A woman shown zipping up a jacket worn by a little girl who was carrying two books. Respondent was asked what the woman was thinking.
4. A woman, dressed in hat and coat and with a handbag over one arm, was shown by a rack of dresses in a store. She was holding up and looking at one of the dresses. Respondent was asked what the woman was thinking.
5. A woman was shown standing just outside but looking into a room in which a young girl was sewing at a sewing machine. Respondent was asked what the woman was thinking.
6. A woman was shown at a sewing machine in a room in which a man, pipe in mouth and newspaper in hand, was sitting in an easy chair. Two young children were playing in the room. Respondent was asked what the man was thinking. (See Exhibit 2.)

THE PERSONALITY TESTS

Special tests were used to probe into factors of personality and disposition of which the respondent might not be aware. It was felt that the various research techniques used together would lead to an understanding of sewing behavior, each technique contributing a part to the whole picture.

Personality measures appropriate for this study were selected by Dr. Norbert Freedman, a clinical psychologist who taught and conducted clinical research at a hospital in New York City and who also served as a member of McCann-Erickson's research staff. The selection was governed by the interview time available for the tests (about 15 minutes) and the psychological variables of probable importance to sewing. The latter were discussed by Dr. Herzog, Dr. Miles, and Dr. Freedman who formulated questions to be answered by testing. The pilot interviewing helped in the refinement of the personality tests as it did in the development of the depth interviewing schedule.

The personality tests were directed at several psychologically different levels of behavior to search for explanations of why women become heavy, light, or nonsewers and to determine which level would differentiate among them most effectively. They also sought to find out as much as possible about attitudinal differences so that as clear an idea as possible would be had about the characteristics of persons to whom advertising might be directed.

Some of the hypotheses formulated for testing follow: Since sewing takes time and requires planning of various life activities, are heavy sewers more apt to be planful personalities who organize and regulate their lives than light sewers or nonsewers? An affirmative finding would not explain how women became heavy sewers, but it would say something useful about what they were like. Because of the psychological meanings of planning, advertisements for women who were careful planners probably should appear to be well planned, orderly, and clean. Inasmuch as sewing involves making things, are heavy sewers more creative and more original than light or nonsewers? Do sewers differ from nonsewers in the way they feel about clothing and other objects in their environment? Do sewers get more or less pleasure from their environment? Unconscious feelings were investigated in an effort to identify and describe those which tended to make some women heavy sewers. Questions such as these were raised: Do sewers differ from non-sewers in their feelings of femininity (i.e., in characteristics which, in our culture, are assigned to the female and are considered feminine)? Are sewers more or less secure and satisfied with themselves and their surroundings?

By viewing the depth interview material in the light of the results of the personality tests, it was believed that the relationship among sewing behavior, attitudes, and motives could be established.

Brief descriptions of the four measures of personality selected for the sewing survey follow:

The Planning Scale: (See Appendix E, page 305.) This was designed to measure to what extent the respondent planned her daily life, whether she was over-organized or haphazard. Six statements varying in the degree of planning from "I plan everything down to the last detail" to "I just don't bother with making plans" were arranged under a line extending across a sheet of paper, thus forming a scale. The respondent was asked to put an "X" at the point on the line which she felt described her best. Numerical values were given to various positions so that the results could be scored. In effect, the test sought to take a sample of the respondent's behavior. Developed by Small in a doctoral thesis at Columbia University, it had been validated by comparing its results with those obtained from other tests known to give results related to social planning.

Unusual Purposes Test: (See Appendix F, page 306.) This was a test of how rigid and stereotyped or flexible and original a person's thinking was. It required the respondent to name uses other than the most usual one for six different common, everyday objects: "coffee," "paper clips," "matches," "cotton gauze," "string," and "books." Responses were classified and scored. The test as used in the sewing study was adapted from one developed by Guilford.

Controlled Word Association Test: This test was developed by Dr. Freedman to measure the respondent's relationship to her environment in terms of pleasure versus threat. He had used it experimentally in a number of studies to validate it before including it in the home sewing survey as an instrument of analysis. If a respondent found the environment threatening, the test further showed how she handled the consequent anxiety, whether it was by aggression, submission, etc. Several common consumer items or activities were listed. Under each appeared a number of words, some of which represented utility, others threat, and still others pleasure. For example, one of the items was "clothes." Among the words listed under the item were "wear," "spots," "warmth," "ruggedness," "parties," and "fashion." The respondent was told to underline those words which she would most likely think of in relation to the item. She could underline as many words as she wished, but was instructed to work quickly. The results were scored.

Human Figure Drawing Test: This was a standard clinical test based on the premise that everyone has a body image and that this is projected on paper in a figure drawing, revealing the individual's unconscious self-appraisal. The drawing, therefore, provided information on a number of personality characteristics such as the person's security with her own femininity, her ability to relate to other people, and her feelings of aggression and hostility.

The respondent was handed a blank sheet of paper and asked to draw a human being. Sex was not specified because it was significant whether a man or woman was chosen. After the picture had been completed, she was asked for another, this one to be of the sex opposite to that first illustrated. The interviewer then placed the drawing of the female figure in front of the respondent, asked her to imagine that the drawing was of a real live individual and to tell about her by filling out a drawing questionnaire (see Appendix G, page 307.)   The latter included questions such as "Is this a physically strong person?" "Is this person feminine looking?" and "Does this person look mature?"   The respondent could check one of five answers ranging from "extremely" to "not at all."

After the respondent had completed the questions about her drawing, she was given another sheet of paper containing 10 of the same questions.   This time she was to answer them as they applied to herself.   A comparison of the answers to the two questionnaires afforded a measure of how well satisfied the person was with herself.

The figure drawings were scored statistically and average scores were computed for each of the three groups: heavy sewers, light sewers, and nonsewers.   The statistical significance of the differences was calculated.   Qualitative analyses of the drawings also were made by Dr. Freedman who reviewed them in terms of the three groups to refine further those psychological dimensions on which the groups differed significantly.   Conferences between Dr. Freedman, Dr. Miles, Dr. Herzog, and others working on the study then took place concerning the relationships between sewing behavior, the depth interview material, and the personality test results.

Dr. Freedman explained that the clinical tests, such as the figure drawing, assume that all people have certain basic needs.   These needs, however, manifest themselves in various ways and it is important to establish the relationship between them and the product or activity in question.   Much can be learned by this process of how a person resolves her needs and why she behaves as she does.

The Planning Scale, the Unusual Purposes Test, and the Controlled Word Association Test were not clinical tests. They were developed outside the clinic, given to people representative of the community population, and validated against results of other tests similarly given. The figure drawing test, however, was developed in the clinic and was widely used for clinical purposes. Dr. Freedman explained that scores to tests administered in the clinic to emotionally disturbed people tended more to the extremes. In motivational studies, many respondents were not unduly disturbed emotionally, and the range of their personality test scores tended to be narrower. Significant differences between groups of people, such as sewers and nonsewers, frequently were found, however, and these could have important implications for marketing.

THE SAMPLE

Three hundred interviews were conducted with women in selected areas of the United States. One hundred were made with each principal subsample group of respondents: heavy sewers (women who made at least 10 dresses a year); light sewers (women who sewed from 1 to 10 dresses a year); and nonsewers (women who made no dresses even though they may have done simple mending and repairing). The groups were defined from information found in market studies.

Factors controlling sample size included the type of information sought, the use to which it was to be put, the number of groups of respondents being compared, the number of other groupings to be examined separately (age, income, etc.), the complexity of the attitudes under investigation, and the number of basic psychological variables involved. Past experience and pilot interviewing on this study indicated that 300 interviews probably would be ample for determining the important patterns of attitude, motivation, and sewing behavior. It became apparent that this was correct as the analysis proceeded and results stabilized. Had this not occurred, more interviews would have been added.

Motivational interviews for McCann-Erickson's studies

generally were made with crucial subgroups of the population which already had been identified by other market research. The analyses were aimed at differentiating among the groups. Although individual differences were noted within groups, the majority attitudes and motivations were of greatest importance since the purpose usually was to determine promotional strategy and advertising themes suitable for mass media. For this reason, the size of sample in motivation studies generally could be smaller than in many conventional market research surveys.

Interviewers were told how to apportion their interviews among heavy, light, and nonsewers and between rural and urban women. (See Appendix A, pages 293–294.) In addition, they were instructed to choose women between the ages of 20 and 40, most of whom should be housewives with children, and to get a scattering of different income and occupational groups. A check was maintained on sample composition by income, age, and number and age of children as well as by the completely controlled factors of amount of sewing activity, rural vs. urban, and geographical location.

Similar instructions governed the selection of teen-age respondents. The sample here was somewhat smaller than 100, interviewing being continued only long enough to determine whether teen-age attitudes toward sewing differed from those of adults.

INTERPRETATION OF DATA

Responses obtained in the depth interviews, including those to projective devices, were analyzed independently of the personality test results. The former were handled by Dr. Miles and her assistants and the latter by Dr. Freedman. They consulted with each other while making their analyses, thereby checking and aiding each other's thinking. Their findings were integrated into one final report.

Several senior motivation research assistants were assigned

to read the depth interview reports. Each interview was viewed as a whole to obtain an integrated picture of the respondent's behavior and reasoning. Working independently, the analysts took notes which later were discussed in conferences at which various categories of interview response and sewing behavior were developed. The interviews then were reread and coded for those categories for which both statistical and qualitative analyses were made to check on whether various hypotheses were useful in distinguishing among heavy, light, and nonsewers. Responses to each subject area on the depth interviewing schedule were analyzed in this manner. Verbatim quotations were selected for inclusion in the final report to illustrate how women typically talked about sewing.

REPORT OF FINDINGS

The final report of findings, completed in April 1955, consisted of 157 pages of material organized by the following topics:

Purpose of the Study
Changes in the Psychological Context of Sewing
Sewing Habits and Background
The Rewards of Home Sewing
Psychological Characteristics of Heavy Sewers Compared to
    Light Sewers and Nonsewers
Teen-Age Sewers and Nonsewers
Attitudes Toward Zippers
Summary of Results
Implications for Advertising and Promotion
Appendix (descriptions of research method and sample and
    copies of interviewing schedules and tests)

A summary of findings is presented in Appendix H, pages 308–319. The sections on sewing habits and background and personalities of heavy sewers as contrasted with those of light sewers and nonsewers are presented in greater detail than the others to reveal more of the character of the text of the report and to show how some of the research techniques contributed evidence on which findings were based.

One of the most important findings had to do with short-comings in sewing instruction as practiced by mothers in the home and teachers in schools. While many respondents enjoyed their sewing instruction, frustration resulting from mother-daughter and teacher-student relationships was found to be a common cause of rejection of sewing. A number of women stated that their mothers discouraged them by demanding too much of their earlier efforts. Criticism of sewing teachers also was frequent. Many women looked back on their earlier experiences with sewing with a kind of horror. They remembered their eagerness to finish the garment they were supposed to make and they recalled only long sessions of reprimand, correction, and bickering. Consequences of poor early teaching were seen in the fact that 60% of the nonsewers had tried to learn how to sew. Many of these women now regarded sewing as too difficult for them.

The study revealed important personality differences among heavy sewers and light and nonsewers. Sewing was regarded differently by these groups and served somewhat different purposes. Heavy sewers tended to be women who had accepted their mothers' domination, although resenting it, often unconsciously. Psychologically, they tended to be compulsive, rigid, planful, anxious, and unimaginative in their thinking. They could not permit themselves just to relax, they had to be doing something. They tended to feel threatened by people and things around them and, therefore, devoted their efforts to controlling their environment. Household chores, including sewing, offered outlets for the pent-up aggression felt against the environmental threats. Sewing was regarded in the context of housework and as a part of their duty as a good wife and mother rather than as a hobby or source of pleasure.

Light sewers, on the other hand, tended to be more imaginative, more able to relax and have fun. They saw their environment as a source of pleasure and stimulation and wanted to enjoy leisure time. They regarded sewing more as a hobby than housework and did it more for practical benefits to be derived from sewing rather than for the underlying psychological gratifications which were so important for heavy sewers.

The typical nonsewer considered sewing old-fashioned and saw it in the context of housework which she resented. To her, the home was a place in which to live, not work. She often had bitter memories of early experiences with sewing instruction. She tended to be unaware of some of the practical benefits of sewing.

While the main psychological satisfactions from sewing differed for the various groups, certain rewards were experienced by both heavy and light sewers. They included the pleasure of creating something, the feeling of accomplishment, and the feeling of having done one's duty and meriting praise. Major practical benefits included saving money, an improved standard of living, improved social status, and personalized clothing.

Zippers generally were welcomed with enthusiasm and their use had increased in recent years. They were found to have masculine associations, however, which tended to restrict use by women who felt insecure about their femininity as did many heavy sewers. Several practical factors restricting use also were revealed by the study.

IMPLICATIONS FOR ADVERTISING AND PROMOTION

The agency made a number of recommendations for advertising and promotion based on the motivational survey. They included the following points:

1. Advertising should be directed toward light sewers and nonsewers and emphasize the practical benefits of home

sewing which would appeal to heavy sewers as well. Psychological gratifications should not be used as primary appeals because different women get such different psychological values from sewing.

2. Home sewing, considered by many light sewers and non-sewers to be old-fashioned, should be modernized. It should be presented as a creative way of using time enjoyably and to practical advantage rather than as something which will make women better homemakers and housewives. While some women will sew because they regard sewing as a duty, others reject this idea and the drudgery it suggests.

3. Teaching methods should be improved so that instruction encourages rather than discourages sewing.

4. Convenient neighborhood sources of help on sewing problems should be provided to counteract important drawbacks and tensions. Such assistance would serve to ease the anxiety which accompanies the inability of many women to cope with sewing problems as they arise. Many inexperienced sewers become panic stricken as soon as they tackle a problem, and nonsewers exaggerate the difficulties of sewing. The result is to make sewing seem like trouble rather than fun. Readily available help would encourage women to continue to learn and expand their sewing production after formal instruction had been completed.

5. Several other suggestions were made as to what might be done by various firms in a coordinated promotional program. They included the following: sewing machine manufacturers might offer special training at various levels of competence; women's magazines might offer more help on common sewing problems (both mechanical and psychological); pattern companies and yard-goods manufacturers might offer sewing kits for the novice which would include pattern, pre-cut material, thread, and accessories; zipper companies might help in relating home sewing to the latest fashions; retail stores

might offer displays and assistance in order to promote home sewing of all types of items in a practical way.

MR. SALMON'S COMMENTS AND PLANS

Mr. Salmon regarded the motivational survey as helpful because it revealed some important misconceptions and pointed the way to increased home sewing. In talking about the study in May 1955, he mentioned the following as points which stood out in his mind:

> The home sewing industry had assumed that girls were first exposed to sewing primarily in school — 7th grade sewing classes, etc. The study showed that many heavy sewers first learned from their mothers at home; that school instruction often was inadequate. It also showed that many women don't sew because of adverse reactions to their mothers at the time instruction at home was attempted.
>
> Some executives in the (home sewing) industry regarded home sewing as a part of the "do-it-yourself" development. It isn't. It existed to a great extent before that movement started. The study showed that many sewers do not regard sewing as "fun."
>
> The broad attitude of teen-agers toward sewing often is not favorable to their doing much of it in the future, judging from the reactions revealed by our study.

Mr. Salmon believed that companies dependent on home sewing such as those selling patterns, sewing machines, textiles, and sewing notions should undertake a cooperative program of research and promotion directed toward encouraging home sewing. He favored the establishment of a Sewing Arts Council which would be similar in character to organizations set up to promote the welfare of the leather, cotton, and other industries. He thought that such a council should have an operating budget of $250,000 a year at the outset.

With this objective in mind, he had given a copy of the

report on the motivational survey to executives in the leading pattern, thread, and sewing machine companies. He planned to meet with them individually to discuss the study and possible industry promotional efforts. His immediate objective was to persuade them to contribute a total of $20,000 for two additional motivational surveys. One would explore in detail mother-daughter relationships to determine what might be done to help mothers and daughters enjoy working together on sewing. Perhaps a series of simple patterns for the beginner might be offered to guide instructional efforts of the mother, Mr. Salmon said, to illustrate a possible outcome of the research. The other study would seek to learn more about teen agers and sewing and how unfavorable attitudes might be changed. Results of the first study, based on a small teen-age sample, were indicative only, but they showed this to be an important subject for further investigation.

Mr. Salmon said that the study prompted his company to give more promotional emphasis to a sewing machine attachment called the "zipper foot" which facilitated the sewing of zippers into garments. The finding that most women held zippers in high esteem eased the concern of company executives that zippers generally had suffered from the frequent kidding they had received from entertainers and others and from the negative advertising approach of a few zipper companies which stressed the failure of some zippers to function properly while claiming trouble-free service from their own products.

Donahue Sales Corporation
Commentary

Findings

The study dealt with matters of basic importance to an understanding of sewing and the problems confronting promotional efforts. The findings in regard to shortcomings of school instruction were of direct relevance to the Talon Educational Service designed to provide classroom assistance. So was the information that the first contact with sewing for many girls, especially those who later became heavy sewers, was in the home rather than in school as had been assumed. This served to focus attention on instruction in the home and related difficulties in mother-daughter relationships, identified as a highly important cause of adverse reactions to sewing. Further research into this area was proposed on the basis of this study.

The finding that sewing served different functions for heavy sewers than for light sewers was of special interest because of the marked tendency in marketing to assume that all people who engage in a certain activity or buy a certain product do so for about the same principal reasons. That assumption was not made here. The results had important implications for the choice of promotional appeals. Appeals based on the principal satisfactions obtained by heavy sewers, for example, were seen as likely to repel light sewers and nonsewers. In this connection, the study showed that many women, especially heavy sewers, did not sew for "fun," and that home sewing was not part of the "do-it-yourself" movement in this sense as had been assumed.

The generally unfavorable attitudes of teen agers served to raise important questions about the future role of home sewing and pointed the way for further research.

The study is noteworthy because it represented an intensive investigation of home sewing, how women felt about it, and why they felt that way. Its findings appear to be a most useful basis for thinking about the proposed cooperative effort in the home sewing industry. Much of the value was due to the fact that consideration was given to such things as the effects of sewing instruction, mother-daughter relationships, and the possibility that sewing might have different meanings for different people. It is appropriate, then, to ask how such matters, which have received little attention in marketing research, came in for study here, and how the researchers were able to get information on them.

The Research Approach

Answers to these questions lie in the fact that the research was the work of psychologists. Their clinical orientation can be seen in various concepts underlying the study's hypotheses and research techniques.

One of the most significant features of the study is that it brought together three types of data: (1) information on sewing behavior (respondents were classified as heavy, light, and nonsewers); (2) attitudes toward sewing (how women regarded it as revealed in the detailed interviews and cartoon responses); and (3) the basic dispositions of the respondents (what kind of people they were as shown by results of the personality tests as well as by the other interview responses). Such an effort is most unusual in marketing research. There have been a number of studies of buying or consumption patterns which have given only limited attention to explaining the behavioral differences. There also have been studies of attitudes which were based on assumptions that certain attitudes led to certain behavior. There have been fewer attempts to check these assumptions and very few attempts indeed at combining behavioral, attitudinal, and personality data.

This approach used in the sewing study embodies the concept that a person's behavior and his attitudes reflect something more basic about what kind of a person he is. The relationship implied here was found to be present in the case of sewing. To illustrate this point, let us consider the women who were classified as heavy sewers. The interviews showed that they looked upon sewing as housework, a duty of a good housewife, not as a source of pleasure. What functions were served by these attitudes? The study pointed to the basic dispositions of the women — that they tended to feel threatened by their own feelings and their surroundings and therefore devoted themselves to controlling their feelings and their environment.   They tended to be compulsive, rigid, and anxious. For them, sewing served as a means of control and also as an outlet for pent-up aggressive or hostile feelings.

We might go one step further by asking how they came to be this way. The report furnished some evidence in what it said about the competitive aspect of the mother-daughter relationship of the typical heavy sewer. Because of feelings of insecurity and hostility, the mother tended to be unable to stand the competition represented by a growing daughter and unconsciously proceeded to frustrate the girl and keep her dependent rather than allow her to grow up. The heavy sewers were pictured as women who submitted to their mother's dominance (rebels often became nonsewers), but not without accumulating feelings of hostility and insecurity which represented a need for great self-control. As a result, she typically did not allow herself to relax but instead kept busy with her "duties." Sewing often was one of these as was housework generally.

The light sewers were found to represent somewhat the opposite pattern. They accepted and found pleasure in their environment and regarded sewing as a hobby, and engaged in it more for its practical rather than its psychological benefits.

The above example illustrates certain ways of thinking about personality development which have grown out of clinical studies. There is an assumption, supported by considerable clinical evidence, that people have certain basic needs and that one's personality is shaped by how these needs are handled, especially in the younger years of life. The latter depends to a large extent on the nature of one's relationships with his parents and others close to him. Clinical evidence has shown that instances of parents unconsciously dominating and frustrating their children, as found in the sewing study, are common.

The inclusion of personality tests made possible more complete and more confident explanations of sewing behavior by checking hypotheses developed in the course of the research. The tests were specially selected or devised for this purpose. Without them, the researchers would have had to rely on inferences about the underlying motivational patterns drawn from the attitude and behavior data. Knowledge as to what kind of a person holds a given attitude provides an improved basis for determining what promotional efforts designed to change the attitude would be up against and what appeals might be effective. In this case, for example, it appears unlikely that appeals based on the main psychological satisfactions obtained by the heavy sewers would be successful in getting light sewers or nonsewers to do more sewing.

McCann-Erickson reports considerable success in using the same approach described here to differentiate among users of various brands within a product category. Information is obtained on what brand the person uses, what image he has of each of several brands, and what kind of a person he is. Hence, there is a check as to what kind of a person holds what attitudes and whether all this actually is related to buying behavior. The agency has conducted many studies which have shown that certain brands, through the images consumers have of them, do attract certain kinds of people. This has been demonstrated in a number of product categories including cigarettes, gasoline, automobiles, sanitary napkins, dentrifices, and hair tonics. McCann-Erickson also reports finding brand loyalty to be the greatest where the psychological or personality reasons for use of the brand are the strongest.

This type of information is helpful in deciding what kind of an image a brand should attempt to build through its product, advertising, packaging, service, etc.; in estimating what people might be switched to a particular brand; and in determining how advertising appeals would have to be slanted in order to convert these prospects and at the same time hold present users.

Only brief comments will be made here on several other features which represent topics considered in later chapters. The first is on the use of the incomplete sentences, word association tests, and cartoons in connection with depth interviews to tap the emotional or less rational aspects of attitudes by calling for spontaneous or top-of-the-mind responses. The respondent had only to tell what she felt or thought when confronted with the material. She did not have to analyze or remember, and she could respond regardless of whether she consciously had given the matter any thought previously. The devices made it easier to get responses on things that people often find hard to talk about, and they could be used with all respondents regardless of age, education, or cultural background.

While the subject of interpreting data will be discussed elsewhere, we wish to point to two precautions taken in this study to make for accuracy. One was the use of several different interpreters and the other was the use of quantitative checks on the qualitative analysis of the data.

In order for this investigation of behavioral differences to be undertaken, it first was necessary to know about how many women did how much sewing so that definitions of heavy and light sewers could be formulated. This information was obtained from market surveys which had been conducted earlier in other connections.

Summary

We have noted that the research supplied new information on matters of major importance to home sewing, sometimes contradicting assumptions of executives in the industry. It made its contribution by applying psychological concepts and by using an approach which started with information on sewing behavior and then proceeded to explain behavioral differences in terms of attitudes and basic dispositions of the women. While factors other than those emphasized here no doubt influence the amount of sewing a woman does, it is significant that this study showed that heavy, light, and non-sewers tend to be different kinds of people. This study and similar ones conducted by McCann-Erickson provide evidence that personality characteristics can be an important factor influencing what a person does, including his selection of branded merchandise. Hence, brands, which have their own images or personalities in the public mind, tend to attract different kinds of people as customers. This idea implies concepts of the consumer and the product which have received little if any attention except for the relatively recent work of a few researchers who got into marketing research after obtaining training and experience in dynamic psychology and other social sciences.

Appendix A

INSTRUCTIONS TO INTERVIEWERS:
HOME SEWING SERVICE

Purpose of this Survey

The aim of this survey is to discover all the motivations and attitudes of the respondent toward home sewing, and also toward zippers. From this survey, we expect to be able to tell our client how to increase home sewing and how to increase the use of zippers by home sewers. If additional questions occur to you on any point that would throw further light on these problems, don't hesitate to ask them.

The questions on this schedule have been thought out very carefully. *Please don't leave anything out.* When you have finished with a certain "area" of questioning, look back over the questions on the schedule and make sure you have covered every point.

Whom to Interview

You are to interview women only. The adults are to be between the ages of 20 and 40, mainly housewives with children. The teen agers are to be between the ages of 15 and 19. As usual, please make every effort to get a scattering of different income and occupational groups. We do not want lots of "white collar" and professional people.

Interviewers are divided into two groups: those who will do 12 interviews and those who will do 5.

If you are supposed to do 12 interviews, please make them with the following women:

3 with urban (or suburban) women who are heavy sewers.
3 with urban (or suburban) women who are light sewers.
1 with an urban (or suburban) woman who is a nonsewer.
1 with a rural woman who is a light sewer.
1 with a rural woman who is a heavy sewer.
1 with a teen ager who is a heavy sewer.

1 with a teen ager who is a light sewer.

1 with a teen ager who is a nonsewer.

12 interviews total

(Similar instructions for those who were to do 5 interviews)

As to definitions of these topics: a heavy sewer is a woman who makes 10 or more garments in the course of the average year. A light sewer makes less than 10. A nonsewer is one who does only a little simple mending and repairing.

The schedule and tests

(The various schedules and tests described. A gift — a chromium cigarette lighter — was given to each adult respondent because the interview would be longer than usual.)

1. Start with the short questions for all respondents.

2. Next do the regular depth interview. . . . This is the usual type of schedule, to be typed up in the usual way . . . as if the respondent herself were talking to us, written so we don't have to refer back to the schedule, typed double spaced, answers typed in next to the proper "area," number in each case, etc. . . . Adult interviews should run around 4 or 5 pages. Don't go out of your way to get very long interviews, although I will pay a bonus if any interviews are particularly good and detailed.

The last question on each of the schedules involves reactions to a particular ad showing a woman struggling with a zipper. A copy of this ad is also enclosed.

3. Next show the respondent the 6 cartoons, one at a time. It doesn't matter what order you show them in. They are numbered so that when you type up the answers, we will know what cartoon the woman was talking about. . . .

The respondent is to look at each cartoon and then is merely to say what the person in the cartoon is thinking. When there are several people in a cartoon we are only interested in the thoughts of the person with the comic-strip balloon. . . .

As you show each cartoon, just say to the respondent, "What is this person thinking?" pointing to the person with the balloon. Copy exactly what the respondent says. Please try to keep the respondent on the track of home sewing. . . .

4. Next comes the three personality tests. Two of them take only a minute or two apiece, and the third takes about ten minutes. Actually, you have 4 personality tests enclosed, but you will administer only 3 of them to any particular respondent. Each personality test has its instructions attached right to it.

a. Planning Test — to be given to every respondent.

b. Unusual purposes test — to be given to every respondent.

c. Word underline test — to be given to only half of the respondents. Try to make it come out so that half the sewers and half the nonsewers take this test.

d. Figure drawing test — to be given to other half of respondents.

Appendix B

SHORT QUESTIONS FOR ALL RESPONDENTS

Please give me your immediate reactions to each of the following words or phrases. I want you to say everything that comes into your mind. Don't stop to think. (If respondent replies with only a few words, prompt her to continue, as we want several sentences.)

A woman who sews at home:

Making a dress:

A woman who never sews:

Zippers:

Buttons:

Hook and eyes:

Snaps:

Talon zippers:

Please visualize a dress that has an inconspicuous front closure. It could close with a long zipper, or with buttons, or with snaps, or with hooks and eyes.

Which closure would you prefer?

Why?

Why not the others?

Now choose one of these four front closures for the dress, in answer to each of the following questions:

	Zipper	Buttons	Snaps	Hooks
Which is the prettiest?	( )	( )	( )	( )
Which is the most "creative"?	( )	( )	( )	( )
Which is the most feminine?	( )	( )	( )	( )
Which is the easiest to make?	( )	( )	( )	( )
Which is the most durable?	( )	( )	( )	( )
Which looks most expensive?	( )	( )	( )	( )
Which is the most conventional?	( )	( )	( )	( )
Which is the most unusual?	( )	( )	( )	( )
Which is the most practical?	( )	( )	( )	( )

Appendix C

INTERVIEWING SCHEDULE FOR WOMEN WHO
DO HOME SEWING
(Whether Much or Little)

History of sewing

1. How did you get started sewing? How did you learn? Did your mother sew? Was she a skilled sewer? Did she influence your attitudes toward sewing? In what way? What or who else influenced you? Did you sew when you were a child? When did you get really interested in sewing? Why then? What is the best piece of clothing you ever made? What was the most difficult? The easiest? The one you're proudest of? Did you receive help on these pieces of clothing?

Social context of sewing

2. Do you have a regular sewing routine? Do you set aside a special day for sewing? Part of each day? Or whenever free? What would you do with your time if you didn't sew? What does your family usually do while you are sewing? Do you have friends who sew? Do many of them sew? Do you get together and sew as a group? Do other women come to you for advice or help? Do you go to others?

Sewing ability

3. Do you prefer to start a job from the beginning or would you prefer to mend and remake clothing? Do you usually use a sewing pattern? Where do you get your patterns? How close do you stick to a pattern? What do you enjoy most in making a garment: The basic construction? The finishing touches? Etc.? Before you start, can you tell how long it will take to finish? How do you judge? What is the hardest thing about sewing? (Probe) Is it fun anyway? What is the most fun? How do you evaluate your own sewing ability? Do you think sewing is hard or easy? Do you knit? Do you enjoy knitting? How does knitting compare to sewing? Crocheting? Embroidering? Do you like doing things with your hands?

Sewing gratifications

4. Why do you sew? Is it fun? Is it creative? Is it economical? Etc.? Which is more important: the enjoyment or the practical benefits? What exactly are the practical benefits? To what other jobs would you compare sewing? Who wears the clothes you sew? Yourself? Children? Who else? Do you prefer to sew everyday things or special (Sunday) clothes? Why? How do you feel about the clothes you sew? Are they better than store bought clothes? In what way? Are they cheaper? Better patterns? More unusual? Fit better? Better quality? More suitable? Etc.?

Sewing machines

5. Do you have a sewing machine? Is it a good one? Why did you get it? How does it rate among your possessions? Do you think it was a worthwhile investment? How much of your work is done on the machine? Would you undertake the same jobs if you didn't have it? Have your attitudes toward sewing changed since you got your machine? In what way? Have you improved in sewing? Has that changed your attitude toward sewing?

Reading about sewing

6. Where do you get ideas about sewing? (Friends, magazines, articles, family, etc.) What kind of ideas do you like to hear about? Do you read any special sewing magazines? Columns? Articles? Which ones do you like? Why? What kind of information do you get? What *could* they tell you that they don't? What might influence you to make you sew more than you do? What holds you back now from sewing more?

Zippers

7. What thoughts does the word zipper bring to mind? What are the advantages of zippers over other forms of closure? The disadvantages? Do you like to use them in home sewing? Why?

8. What are the disadvantages or drawbacks you have encountered in using zippers? Have you had problems finding the right color, size, or mesh you wanted? Have you had any difficulties sewing the zipper in? Are there problems connected with the

durability of zippers? Have zippers ever stuck? What did you do about it? How do you feel when a zipper gets stuck (angry at yourself, at the zipper, feel like throwing garment away, etc.)? What do you actually do when a zipper sticks?

9. How do you decide when to use zippers and when not to? Is the decision influenced by pattern directions? Do you use zippers only when called for in the pattern? How do you decide where on the garment to put zippers, what size, width, etc., to use?

10. On what items (clothes or other items) do you always use zippers? Why these particular items? Are there other items where you would never use a zipper? Which, and why? Does the decision to use a zipper depend on the type of material used, the wear the item will get, the end use, for whom it is being made, etc.? Are zippers considered purely utilitarian, or are they used for decoration? How do you feel about a dress with a zipper up the front? With buttons up the front?

11. Has your use of zippers changed any since you began sewing? Do you use zippers more or less frequently? For more varied items? Please give me a history of your use of zippers in home sewing. Why do you use zippers more or less now than you did before, and what influenced this change? Was it due to differences in styling, wider experience with zippers, wider choice of zippers, changes in pattern directions, different needs, increased amount of sewing, or what? Do you replace zippers on older garments?

12. In what ways could zippers be improved? What would ideal zippers be like? Do you have changes to suggest for packaging, styling, color, size, etc., of packaged zippers? Would these changes affect your use of the product? Would you be inclined to use zippers on more things than you do now? Which? Would you sew more than you do now? Is it important for the color of the zipper tape to match the color of the dress?

Other points

13. Can you generally buy ready-made dresses without too much alteration, or do you have trouble getting fitted? Discuss. Do you have difficulty finding dresses that "do something" for

your figure? How do you feel when you disrobe in a store dressing room to try on dresses? Do you mind if the saleslady comments on your figure? In general, would you say you are fairly
well satisfied with your figure? If you had to undress in a public
bath house with other women around, how would you feel?

14. (Show the respondent the "Stop Struggling" ad.) What is
your reaction to this advertisement? Discuss the whole question
of zippers getting stuck. Does this ad make you think the zipper
advertised is better than other zippers?

Appendix D

INTERVIEWING SCHEDULE FOR WOMEN WHO DO NOT SEW
(OR WHO DO MENDING AND REPAIRING)

Resistance to sewing

1. Have you ever done any sewing of any sort? How did you feel about it? Did you have any specific problems with it? What is your attitude toward sewing on buttons and other simple mending jobs? Do you have any special problems with the sewing jobs you undertake? Do these jobs ever present you with an interesting challenge? Or are they just additional chores? Do you ever enjoy them? To what other jobs would you compare sewing? Why haven't you done more sewing? What is the hardest thing about sewing?

2. Do you knit? Do you enjoy knitting? How does knitting compare to sewing? Why have you not done very much sewing? Do you visualize any difficulties with sewing? What kind? Have they deterred you from sewing? Did you ever try to learn? What happened? Would you like to take sewing lessons? What do you think is the hardest thing about sewing? Do you think you could ever enjoy sewing? Is there anything that might make you do more sewing? Do you enjoy crocheting? Embroidering? How do they compare to sewing? Do you like doing things with your hands?

Sewing influences

3. Did your mother sew? Was she a skilled sewer? Did she influence your attitudes toward sewing? In what way? What or who else influenced you? Did you sew when you were a child? How did you feel about sewing then? Do you have friends who sew? Are they good sewers? Have they influenced you? Did anyone ever teach you to sew?

Sewing gratifications

4. Why do you think women sew? Do they enjoy being creative, or is it to save money, or what? If you did much sewing,

do you think you would do it for the practical benefits?   In the long run, do you think women who sew at home save money? Why would *you* sew?

5. How do you feel about homemade garments?   **Are** they cheaper? Better? Different? Not as good? Etc.? How do they compare to store bought clothes? Are there any clothes you can't buy because of style or cut which you might like to make? Are there dresses you can't buy because of price that you might like to make?

Sewing machines

6. Do you have access to a sewing machine? Have you ever used one? Do you think you will ever buy one? If you got one as a gift, would it encourage you to learn to sew? Does a machine make sewing much easier? Do you think there is anything you can do on a machine that you can't do by hand? What problems do you think it would solve for you? Do you wish you could be a skilled sewer by magic, or don't you care? Do you want a sewing machine? Do you think it's hard to use?

Reading about sewing

7. Do you read any of the women's magazines? Which? (Mc-call's, Ladies' Home Journal, Woman's Home Companion, Good Housekeeping, etc.?) Do you ever read articles on sewing? Cooking? Would you like to read articles that give simple lessons in sewing? Why not?

Zippers

8. What does the word zipper bring to mind? What are the advantages of zippers over other forms of closure? The disadvantages? How do you think they would compare to buttons, snaps, etc., in home sewing? On what items (clothes or other items) do you like zippers? What does the decision depend upon? How do you feel about a dress with a zipper up the front? With buttons up the front? In what way could zippers be improved? What would the ideal zippers be like? Do you think the color of the zipper tape should match the color of the dress?

Other points

9. Can you generally buy ready-made dresses without too much alteration, or do you have trouble getting fitted? Discuss. Do you have difficulty finding dresses that "do something" for your figure? How do you feel when you disrobe in a store dressing room to try on dresses? Do you mind if the saleslady comments on your figure? In general, would you say you are fairly well satisfied with your figure? If you had to undress in a public bath house with other women around, how would you feel?

10. (Show the respondent the "Stop Struggling" ad.)   What is your reaction to this advertisement? Discuss the whole question of zippers getting stuck. Does this ad make you think the zipper advertised is better than other zippers?

Appendix E

PLANNING TEST

BELOW ARE SIX (6) STATEMENTS ON THE AMOUNT OF PLANNING YOU DO IN YOUR EVERYDAY LIFE. PUT AN "X" ANYWHERE ON THE LINE AT THE POINT WHICH YOU FEEL DESCRIBES YOU BEST. (YOU MAY PUT AN "X" BETWEEN THE DOTS INDICATING TWO STATEMENTS OR RIGHT AT THE DOT IF YOU AGREE FULLY WITH THE STATEMENT.)

• I plan everything down to the last detail.

• I plan things out in advance most of the time.

• I tend to plan things out more often than not.

• I just go ahead with things without making plans more often than not.

• I may make occasional plans but I usually let things take their own course.

• I just don't bother with making plans.

Appendix F

UNUSUAL PURPOSES TEST

INSTRUCTIONS: Below is a list of common objects. List the number of purposes for which these objects can be used other than its most usual purpose. For example, a *newspaper* is usually used for the purpose of reading; it can also be used for *lining shelves, lining garbage pails,* or *swatting flies.* Put down as many unusual purposes as you can think of for each of the following objects:

	Usual Purpose	*Unusual Purpose*
Coffee	Drinking	_____
		_____
Paper Clips	Attaching	_____
		_____
Matches	Lighting	_____
		_____
Cotton gauze	Bandages	_____
		_____
String	Tying	_____
		_____
Books	Reading	_____
		_____

Appendix G

DRAWING QUESTIONNAIRE

	Extremely 1	Very 2	Fairly 3	Not very 4	Not at all, the opposite 5
1. Is this a physically strong person?					
2. Is this a good-looking person?					
3. Is this a healthy person?					
4. (If male) Is this person masculine looking?					
5. (If female) Is this person feminine looking?					
6. Is this a bright person?					
7. Is this person well-built?					
8. Is this person proud of his/her body?					
9. Does this person look acceptable?					
10. Does this person look mature?					

Now a few more questions about this person:

11. How old is this person? _____

12. Is this person married or single? _____

13. What does this person do for a living? _____

14. How far did this person go in school? _____

15. Who were you thinking of as you drew this person? _____

16. Who were you thinking of as you answered the above questions? _____

Appendix H

A DIGEST OF SOME OF THE FINDINGS FROM "HOME SEWING, A MOTIVATIONAL SURVEY"

Changes in the Psychological Context of Sewing

1. Interview responses reflected a number of important changes which had taken place in the last decade or two to beneficially affect sewing's meaning, rewards, and motives. They include the effects of the war which forced an increase in home sewing, increased distribution of sewing machines, improved standard of living, greater availability of ready-made clothes (which makes sewing more a voluntary hobby and less a financial necessity), rapid changes in new fashions and styles, more leisure time, and the do-it-yourself trend.

Sewing Habits and Background

2. The importance of proper sewing instruction cannot be exaggerated. Sewing instruction at the wrong time and place and in the wrong manner can be a source of strong and continuing resistances to sewing. Those who accepted mother's domination made out fine. Those who did not found the situation a source of mother-daughter competition resulting in frustration and rejection of sewing. Other women (particularly light sewers) learned a few years later in school. Although there were many women who found their sewing classes enjoyable, others had important complaints. For a sizable proportion of the women who learned to sew in school, the experience fostered discouragement with sewing rather than satisfaction and a desire to continue.

Heavy sewers tended to become interested in sewing in early childhood, prodded by their mothers. Their interest in sewing was more apt to remain constant from childhood on. As adults their sewing output is double that of the average light sewer. Light sewers tended to become interested in sewing at a later age, often in connection with a school course. Their earliest interest generally occurred in their teens when they yearned for more clothes than their parents were willing to provide.

While at first glance it might seem that the best education to induce an interest in sewing should parallel that of the typical heavy sewer, a detailed examination of the two types of early sewing education (mother vs. school) shows that both have shortcomings and points the way to proper training methods which might stimulate greater interest in sewing in the future.

Learning from Mother

The first sewing activity of the embryo heavy sewer generally was in early childhood. . . . Some nonsewers also were first exposed to sewing early, and a number of them blame their lack of interest on their mothers to this day. The average child is interested in imitating her mother. She collects scraps from her mother's sewing and generally starts by making doll clothes. She may graduate to simple aprons and gifts such as pot holders and dish towels. She tries to "be like mother" because that is a symbol of "growing up." But many mothers fail to treat this early interest properly.

Some mothers cannot accept the fact that their daughters are growing up. Due to the mother's own feelings of insecurity and inadequacy, she is unable to cope with an "adult" daughter. She unconsciously frustrates the young girl. Whatever the precise motive in each individual case, the daughter perceives the situation as one of competition with her mother. Some children reject sewing as a direct result and maintain that rejection in varying degrees into adulthood. Others (particularly those who become heavy sewers) accept their mothers' domination.

Typical comments made by heavy sewers in the depth interviews:

> "My mother taught me how to sew. She was a wonderful sewer. I will never be as good as she was. I sew a lot myself, but I still go to mother for help when I have trouble with something."
>
> "My mother wasn't the best sewer in the world, but she was meticulous. She never let me finish a dress un-

less it was perfect. I hated it sometimes, but I have to admit that I owe my mother a lot for what she did for me."

Typical comments by light sewers and nonsewers:

"My mother used to sew. She sewed very well and she even gave lessons. She influenced me to not even try to sew, and I know if I had tried I'd soon have gotten discouraged and given it up because I never could have come anywhere near doing as good a job as she did."

"I haven't done more sewing because I just can't make anything right. Just everything about sewing was difficult for me. Some of the messes I used to make would make my mother so mad at me for ruining all the material. I never tried to learn again. The teachers in home economics in my freshman year of high school tried to teach me to sew, but it was unsuccessful."

"My mother never did help me very much in sewing. I could never sew to suit mother, so she would just take it away and finish it herself the way she liked things done. I couldn't ever really sew until I was away from home. Mother has a very definite negative influence."

"Yes, my mother is a very excellent sewer. She influenced me somewhat in the wrong direction. She is such a good sewer that she always finishes what I start. I rarely get a chance to show any initiative because when I start to cut a dress or even a simple item, she always comes to my 'rescue' and shows me how to save material."

Many women today still resent their mothers' behavior. They talk of their early sewing experiences with emotion and annoyance despite the many years that have passed.

Poor relationships between mother and daughter were illustrated by comments made about a cartoon which pictured a mother looking into a room at her teen-age daughter who was working at a sewing machine. Facial expressions in the cartoon were neutral. The respondent was asked to say what the mother was thinking. One-third of the respondents had the mother criticize the daughter for one thing or another. Examples of their responses follow:

"Here's another night's work for me."

"You are stitching back side to. The material should be waist down to the floor and not the bottom of the skirt to the floor."

"It is hopeless. . . . I wonder if she'll ever learn to sew. That posture sure shows inefficiency."

The consequences of poor early teaching can be illustrated by the fact that 60% of the nonsewers have tried to learn how to sew. Many of them now feel that sewing is too difficult for them. A number spontaneously stated that their mothers discouraged them by demanding too much of their earlier efforts.

Learning in School

Two-fifths of all the sewers interviewed said they became interested in sewing while in their teens. Light sewers were more prominent in this group. Another sizable group became interested after marriage or after the first child was born. Late interest is unfortunate because most women who learn after childhood never become heavy sewers. Women who were not exposed to sewing through their mothers generally encountered their first sewing experiences in late grammar school or high school. But sewing instruction in schools frequently fails to maintain and nurture the child's interest. Like instruction from mother, it may have a negative effect because of improper methods. When it is well done (and there were a number of respondents who praised their sewing teachers), it can have a strongly favorable influence on future sewing.

Criticism of sewing teachers was frequent in the depth interviews, although it was not as loaded with emotional overtones as the mother-daughter relationship. It is apparent that some teachers place stronger emphasis on the finished product than they do on teaching. Their "sewing conscience" forces them to demand more competence than their students can muster.

Many women look back on their learning experience with a

kind of horror. They remember their eagerness to finish the garment they were supposed to make, and they recall only long sessions of reprimand, correction, and bickering. They remember more ripping than sewing. These points are illustrated in the following quotes from depth interviews:

> "I tried to learn to sew in high school where I took a course in sewing. It was so hard for me. The teacher made me rip it so much, I decided never to sew again."
>
> "I don't like to sew. The teacher taught us how to do it, and if it wasn't right she made us rip it out and do it over until it was right. I got pretty disgusted with sewing. Everything had to be absolutely perfect, and yet we were just kids. She wanted us to be expert professionals."

3. It is essential to reach children early and to widen out-of-the-home teaching, promoting it to Girl Scouts, church groups, women's clubs, neighborhood groups, as well as in schools. Teaching methods should be reanalyzed and brought up to date. Perfection should not be expected of the novice. She should start on something simple that is quickly finished. The learner should be given confidence that she can meet problems as they arise. She should have some neighborhood center to which she can turn for help and guidance. Rewards for improvement should be apparent.

4. A number of typical characteristics of sewers were noted. For example, women are anxious to complete each item in the shortest possible time. This tends to make sewing a more tense and anxious job than it need be. The vast majority of sewers use patterns, but deviate from them for the personalized finishing touches. One-third use their discretion whether to use a zipper, regardless of what closure the pattern calls for. Women like to sew for themselves, with daughters second. They prefer to make everyday wear rather than "dress up" clothes.

The Rewards of Home Sewing

5. The satisfactions which women receive from sewing are twofold: practical and psychological. The major practical bene-

fits, as sewers themselves perceive them, are money-saving, money-stretching (getting more for same amount of money), an improved family standard of living (which includes home decorations as well as wardrobe), improved social status, and personalized clothing.

6. The main psychological satisfactions of sewing differ for the various groups. Among rewards experienced by both heavy and light sewers are the pleasures of creating something, the feeling of accomplishment when it is finished, the pride in "special touches" that personalize the item, and the feeling that they have done their duty and merit praise.

Drawbacks to Home Sewing

7. The very nature of sewing involves certain underlying difficulties which discourage some women from sewing. They include the tension and concentration machine sewing requires, the fact that present-day home sewing is generally an isolated job, the greater attraction of other leisure time pursuits which seem "less like work," the fear of failure, exaggeration of the complexities of sewing, and the fact that sewing is stigmatized as "housework."

8. Mechanical problems the women complained about included getting the proper fit, cutting without ruining or wasting the material, the final detail work (sleeves, collars, closures), following the pattern, and learning to make the best use of the sewing machine.

Psychological Characteristics of Heavy Sewers Compared to Light Sewers and Nonsewers

9. *Heavy sewers* typically were taught to sew at a very early age by their mothers. They generally accepted mother's domination and regarded sewing as a duty. As adults they are "professional housewives." They try to do more than their share. They cannot permit themselves to "just relax." They are less imaginative and more stereotyped in their thinking than light sewers. Psychologically, they tend to be compulsive, rigid, planful, anxious, and controlling of their environment. They are sewing in the

context of housework and voluntarily make it part of their duty as a good wife and mother.

The heavy sewer is devoted not only to sewing but to every "housewifely" chore. She feels that she must keep busy. Her relaxing lies in working which helps her to feel needed and useful. The following quotes illustrate the point:

> "I don't know what I would do if I didn't sew. I'd be lost like a painter without his oils or a carpenter without his tools. To me sewing is not only work, I can't do without something to sew. I guess if I didn't sew I could take up water coloring, but I'm too mercenary to take up a hobby that wouldn't bring in money."

> "I usually finish a dress if I start it early enough during the day. It's soothing for my nerves. I like to see things take shape and be useful."

The results of the psychological tests help explain why these women push themselves so hard. In response to the Planning Scale, heavy sewers characteristically said that they "plan things down to the last detail" or "plan things out in advance most of the time." They must plan their lives as they must organize their homes. They are not at ease unless they can control their environment.

The results of the Controlled Word Association Test explained their need to organize their surroundings. Heavy sewers tend to perceive their environment as potentially dangerous. They feel insecure and threatened by the people and things around them. At the same time they do not feel that they have the strength to fight back. Therefore, they devote their efforts to controlling their environment so that it cannot control them. They tend to control and dominate members of the family by organizing the household in such a way that there is a time and place for everything. Nothing is permitted to happen in the home which has not been prescribed and ordered in advance.

To the extent that the heavy sewer is unable to act aggressively toward the threats she feels in her environment, she tends to channelize these feelings into specific activities. Her regular household duties offer outlets for her pent-up aggression. She washes, cooks, irons, cleans. Her ceaseless household activities permit her to operate on physical things in an aggressive way. Sewing, too, is an aggressive outlet for her. Working with a heavy, fast-moving machine, she is creative with what underneath is an aggressive urge.

Heavy sewers tend to be unimaginative and stereotyped in their thinking. One would expect that because they are productive and creative with their sewing, their ideas would be original and imaginative. This is not the case. The psychological tests indicate that heavy sewers as a group tend to be rigid and compulsive in their daily living and in their thinking.

The heavy sewer's relationship to members of her family suffers as a result of her compulsive nature. She attempts to control them as she controls the rest of her environment. There is a tendency to resent these people who on the one hand create all the work she does and on the other hand are not controllable the way physical objects are. There is an element of martyrdom in the heavy sewer's makeup.

These attitudes are illustrated by responses to the cartoon which showed a wife sewing at her machine while the husband read the newspaper and two children romped on the floor. (Exhibit 2.) Facial expressions in the cartoon were neutral. Respondents were asked to say what the man was thinking. More heavy sewers gave him thoughts which were critical of the wife, a projection of the typical heavy sewer's own lack of self-acceptance and feelings of inadequacy. Some typical responses follow:

> "I wish she wouldn't sew while I'm trying to read."
> "When I'm home she should pay attention to me."
> "She should pay attention to the kids for a change. I suppose she wants me to put them to bed."
> "I wish she would stop clattering on that machine. But he doesn't have the nerve to say it because she is saving him money."

Heavy sewers are not confident of their own femininity. Only 25% of the heavy sewers said that the female figure they drew was very feminine. Over half of the light sewers and nonsewers thought their figures were feminine. Feminine feelings would

represent another source of anxiety to the heavy sewer. Therefore, she controls these feelings as she controls other aspects of
self and environment.

The heavy sewer's environment is not a source of pleasure in
the accepted sense of the word. She does not enjoy the simple
pleasures of reading, looking at TV, or just socializing. They
are too idle and unproductive. She enjoys washing, cooking,
cleaning, and sewing more, although she may complain about
them in order to garner praise.

10. *Light sewers* tend to become more interested in sewing outside of the parental home. They generally learn at a later age.
They do not consider the home and housework the "be-all and
end-all" of their existence. The environment is a source of pleasure and stimulation that they want leisure time to enjoy. Sewing to them is not housework but more of a hobby, and is done
more for the practical benefits than for underlying psychological
gratifications.

The light sewer is not compelled to regulate her surroundings
in order to feel safe. Her life is not compulsively oriented
around her duties and usefulness. Her way of life is not so set
and rigid. Her outlook is wider in scope. In contrast to the
heavy sewer, her inner security is such that she can experiment
and be original in her thinking. She is more imaginative, less
planful, more able to relax and have fun, more "outgoing," more
able to enjoy recreation and leisure.

The light sewer is more at ease with her own femininity than is
the heavy sewer. She is more at ease with other people. In responding to the cartoon which showed a woman sewing at her
machine while her husband read the newspaper (Exhibit 2), she
light sewer tended to put complimentary thoughts into the mind
of the husband:

> "I like to watch her sew. She really seems to enjoy
> herself."
> "What a good wife I have, she's saving me money."
> "I hope she isn't doing this because she thinks she has
> to. I want her to enjoy life."

Many light sewers learned to sew in their teens when they badly wanted clothes for themselves. Sewing was a means for getting new and exciting clothes at a cheap price. Light sewers do not place sewing in the context of housework. Because they personally benefit from their own sewing and because they are under no compulsion to sew, they feel that sewing is a hobby. They are more apt to compare sewing to wood-working, painting, ceramics, gardening, whereas heavy sewers are more apt to compare it to cooking, cleaning, ironing, and other household chores.

11. To the *nonsewer*, the home is a place to live, not work. The typical nonsewer dislikes housework and resents the work she has to do. She sees sewing in the context of housework, and considers it "too much like work." She exaggerates both the time needed to sew a useful item and the complexities of sewing. She is unaware of some of the important practical benefits of sewing. For example, she tends to think of sewing in terms of money-saving whereas sewers put equal emphasis on money stretching.

It is important to remember that the attitudes described characterize the "typical" nonsewer. Elsewhere in the report it was pointed out that two-thirds of the nonsewers said they would like to sew if they could learn by magic and one-third said they would like to take lessons. It is apparent that a good portion of non-sewers are "protesting too much" when they discuss their antipathy toward sewing. Because of unfortunate experiences with sewing when they were young and because they tend to avoid "work," they have perceived sewing in the wrong context. With greater awareness of the ease and speed of home sewing, and of the immediate and pleasurable personal benefits, some of their objections would disappear.

Teen-age Sewers and Nonsewers

12. The striking personality differences observed between adult light and heavy sewers are not apparent among teen agers. All teen-age sewers tend to resemble adult light sewers. They regard sewing as a hobby which has important practical benefits, mainly the ability to have more clothes than mother would buy. They

also enjoy the feeling of maturity and independence that sewing gives them.

13. Resistances to sewing on the part of teen-age nonsewers include the feeling that other things are more important; that sewing is just housework, old-fashioned and not for the modern woman; and that they have no need to make their own clothes because they have no figure problems to correct.

14. Teen agers show slightly different attitudes toward zippers than adults. They are less inclined to zipper use, less concerned with the convenience aspects of zippers, and more concerned with the feminine touch that fancy buttons can contribute.

Attitudes Toward Zippers

15. Women feel that zippers are a boon, the answer to their dreams of an almost perfect closure. Zippers are primarily viewed as practical, durable, and convenient. Buttons, on the other hand, are considered more expensive looking, prettier, more feminine, and more creative. Zippers have top-of-mind masculine associations. Women who are more assured of their femininity and who therefore do not have to fuss with frills to prove themselves to the world are more apt to be heavier users of zippers.

16. The advantages of zippers far outweigh the disadvantages. Major advantages mentioned: zippers provide a neat and invisible closure, they are easy to operate, they are easier to sew than buttonholes, they are durable, and they are a secure closure that cannot pop open.

17. Disadvantages of zippers were discussed academically whereas advantages were mentioned with enthusiasm. Disadvantages mentioned: zippers occasionally catch and stick, run off the track or break, are hard to sew in unless you have the knack, don't come in enough varieties of color, size, weight, and mesh.

18. Among factors restricting use of zippers are the position of the closure, whether the closure should be decorative and not just functional, the kind of material used, the pattern directions, and some preference for putting zippers in adult rather than children's clothing.

19. Sewers report that their zipper use has grown in recent years. As they have increased their skill as sewers, they have found additional uses for zippers, especially as they have been aware of improvement in the variety and construction of zippers.

20. The Talon "brand image" is highly favorable. Talon is seen as the most familiar and the biggest and, therefore, the best. But the image is a little vague. Only a minority of the respondents are able to attribute specific quality characteristics to the brand. Rather, they infer quality from bigness and from the general prestige of the name.

CHAPTER IX

Dieting Study

FORENOTE

This case describes research undertaken by Young & Rubicam, Inc., toward developing a basic understanding of overweight and dieting, including information on what women were overweight and why, what women would diet and why, and how dieting would affect the use of certain foods. It illustrates the systematic use of a group of specialists trained in psychology, anthropology, and sociology for identifying important dimensions of the subject and formulating hypotheses for testing. As for methodology, the study illustrates an indirect approach carried out by means of a structured questionnaire of direct questions.

YOUNG & RUBICAM, INC. — DIETING STUDY

A Descriptive Case

YOUNG & RUBICAM INC., New York, launched consumer research in 1955 to learn more about weight and dieting among women in the United States, a subject of increasing importance to the advertising agency and its clients. A basic understanding was wanted of the importance of overweight as a problem, what women were overweight and why, what women would diet and why, and how their dieting would affect the use of selected foods.

The problem was turned over to the Research Department's Special Projects Section which had been established in 1951 by Dr. Peter Langhoff, Vice President and Director of Research, to bring to the agency more of the thinking and research tools of psychology, sociology, and cultural anthropology. Dr. William Stevens, a cultural anthropologist and psychologist, headed the section. His staff included four persons with graduate training and professional experience in sociology, social psychology, clinical psychology, and experimental psychology.

It was decided that the first research effort on dieting would make use of the Young & Rubicam Consumer Poll, a continuing activity started in 1948. About five polls a year were conducted among samples of 1,250 families chosen to be representative of the United States. Several subjects were covered in a poll, each being assigned a section of the questionnaire.

The use of the poll confined the research method to a limited number of direct questions which could be answered quickly and which could be successfully administered by field interviewers with limited training. This precluded the use of depth questions to which the respondent would be encouraged to talk fully about a topic in his own way. It also made impossible the use of a number of psychological questions which were reserved for a later study.

The consumer poll, however, offered certain advantages. It was an economical way to obtain information from 1,250 families. Differences by social class, educational level, age, and geographical area, which were expected to be important in this case, could be measured quantitatively. Most of the people to whom the results of the study would be shown were accustomed to this type of survey; hence, the findings were more likely to be accepted than if strictly qualitative research were used. The study could be repeated in subsequent years with comparable samples so that trends could be noted and measured. Also, statistical analyses of results could be handled economically by machine.

Dr. Stevens frequently preferred to start investigation into an area with a qualitative study using unstructured interviews in which people were encouraged to talk at length.

Such exploratory studies helped to reveal important factors and patterns and provide a basis for developing hypotheses which could be tested in a succeeding phase of the research. In this case, however, it was believed that the members of the Special Projects Section staff, drawing upon their social science training and experience, knew what many of the important factors related to weight and dieting were, and that more could be accomplished in a first study by submitting certain hypotheses to a quantitative test.

The decision to undertake research was preceded by discussions by members of Dr. Stevens' staff about the subject and what might be involved in researching it. In this connection, Mr. Art Wilkins, a sociologist and member of the group, prepared a memorandum on some of the sociological and psychological aspects of weight and dieting. Some of his observations and tentative thoughts which indicated topics for research follow:

> The notion people have as to what is a satisfactory weight is a reflection of group norms and bears no strict relation to health considerations. In recent years, ideas as to what was "too fat" and "too thin" for women have varied with fashions in clothes and prevailing ideas of attractiveness.
>
> Weight norms in the United States today are more narrowly defined and more uniform in their application among different social and age and rural and urban groups than in the past. The development of mass media and mass production of "stylish" clothing have contributed to the greater uniformity of standards.
>
> "Attractiveness" has involved an increasing emphasis on physical standards, including weight. Women today are far more dependent on their own ability to "catch a man" than was true in the past when marriage choices were limited to a small number of neighbors of similar social position to whom they were "properly introduced."
>
> Today's standards of attractiveness, particularly in regard

to weight, are applied not only to young women but to married women almost without regard for age. Contributing to this change has been the development of mass communication media, a rising divorce rate (about one out of four marriages ends in divorce which means that married women have to compete with younger women to "hold their man"), and increased participation by women in economic activities outside the home.

Occupations today are more sedentary than formerly which means that a lower calorie intake is required to maintain a given weight. Dieting is not easy, however, because eating is not simply a response to a biological need for food. Eating itself is a gratification rich in meaning. It is an expression of self-love, acceptance of one's environment and of being accepted. These socio-psychological meanings are reflected in the widespread preference for eating with someone rather than alone and in the universal practice of making a "big feed" part of important social occasions.

Some people eat to compensate for feelings of loneliness and unhappiness while others express a sense of guilt by omitting from their diet some things they enjoy. If food is used to substitute for love and if loneliness and lovelessness are widespread in our society, this should prove to be of substantial importance in any explanation of concern about weight.

While persistent overeating is not rare, it probably is not characteristic of the great majority of persons. They probably overindulge occasionally but generally control their eating by "counting calories."

The way people classify a given food may determine whether they omit it in an effort to control weight. They might think in terms of "adult foods" and "children's foods" depending on whether weight or health considerations were primary. Cheese might be thought of as "a fat," "a protein," or "a milk product" with different consequences. Candy might be regarded as "fattening" or as a source of "quick energy." A person might even rationalize that "quick energy" makes him active, resulting in a loss of excess weight.

Discussions among research people and others in the agency lead to a decision to direct the first study toward the following questions:

1. What are some of the important facts concerning the weight of women in the United States? Are many overweight as measured against medical standards? How is weight distributed throughout the population? How do popular standards concerning ideal weight for women compare with medical standards?

2. What are some of the factors which influence weight? Do different groups have different weight standards which are effective in determining weight control? What are some of the psychological causes of overweight?

3. What are some of the basic characteristics of the dieting market? What are the characteristics of the women who are most interested in dieting? Which women are most interested in dietetic foods?

4. What is the effect of dieting on the consumption of selected foods and beverages?

5. What meanings are associated with the word "diet"?

THE QUESTIONNAIRE

A questionnaire, limited in length so that it could be included in the consumer poll, was developed. (See Appendix A, pages 335–339.) One of the main propositions it was designed to test was that standards of weight control vary by social status. The higher the social status, it was reasoned, the more strict the standards. An index of strictness was derived for each group by dividing the number of women who described themselves as overweight by the number who actually were overweight. The occupation of the husband and the education of the wife were used as indicators of social status. Cases of overweight were identified by comparing the weight given by a respondent with the standard weight for a woman of her height listed in the Metropolitan Life Insurance table of ideal weights. Women were classified as overweight, normal, and underweight on this basis.

As a check on the accuracy of the reported weights and heights, statistical distributions of the figures were compared with estimates made by the Metropolitan Life Insurance Company. They conformed closely, so it was concluded that the figures reported by respondents were reliable.

Another major hypothesis for which quantitative evidence was sought was that it is not the woman's actual weight that determines whether she will diet, but whether she thinks she is overweight. The first four questions asked for information for the above purposes. Questions 5 and 6 were directed to finding out how many people were dieting at the time of the interviews. Questions 7, 8, and 13 were used to learn about what constituted pressures on women to diet.

Question 9 represented an attempt to determine the vulnerability of selected foods and beverages to dieting. Women who were watching their weight were asked which of the listed items they would eat if they never had to watch their weight. Then they were asked which they would "eat freely," "cut down on," or "omit entirely" when they were watching their weight. The number of responses by these categories constituted a vulnerability scale. To aid in interpreting the results, a small sample of people (not included in the survey) was asked to rate the listed foods and beverages on "nourishment," "how fattening," and "enjoyment." Results showed that an item's dieting vulnerability was determined mainly by its standing on these three factors.

It was believed that variances in weight which were not explained on the basis of social class could be explained by psychological characteristics. It was not possible to test this hypothesis adequately in the first study, but a step in this direction was taken in questions 14 and 15. Question 14 was devised as an indicator of feelings of dependency and depression so that the relationship, if any, to overeating could be noted. Question 15 was to measure conscious anxiety.

The purpose of Question 16 was to determine whether "diet" had a sufficiently standard meaning among people generally so that it could be used effectively in advertising.

COMMENTS ON RESEARCH APPROACH

In commenting on the use of direct questions, Mr. Wilkins pointed out that respondents were not asked directly for a number of the important answers the study was designed to provide. They were not asked whether they had high standards for weight control, for example. Instead, questions were used to obtain information from which the desired answer could be inferred. Similarly, women's answers as to whether they thought they were overweight were not relied on to determine overweight conditions.

"We never assume that answers given to direct questions are correct answers," Mr. Wilkins explained. "We always interpret them. Inconsistencies in answers usually are explainable in terms of some basic consistency if we can but see it. Some direct questions will give you good answers, others won't. If a moral evaluation of the respondent is implied in the question, for instance, you can expect bias."

THE FINDINGS

A 54-page report of findings, including a description of research method and a number of statistical tables, was completed in June 1955. Half of the women were found to be overweight, 37% of them weighing almost 30% over medical standards. (See Appendix B, Table 1, page 340.) The Metropolitan Life Insurance Company had reported that men who were overweight to that extent had a mortality rate 42% higher than did men of normal weight.

The weight standards which most women applied to themselves were reasonably realistic, although there were significant differences related to socio-economic status and age. The standards were most lax among the more poorly educated, lower income, blue collar groups, and the most stringent among the highly educated, higher income, white collar groups. (See Appendix B, Table 2, pages 340–341.) Since the variation by income was smaller than the variation by education and occupation, the crucial factor appeared to be social status. For "upper-class" women, "keeping up with the Joneses" meant keeping their weight down.

The groups with the highest standards of weight control had the fewest overweight members, obesity being most common among blue collar and farm families of lower income and educational levels. Weight tended to increase with age. The desire to be attractive and the fear of ill health were responsible for the interest in weight control. Most overweight women were aware of their overweight condition although some of them made no serious attempt to reduce their weight.

Investigation of psychological factors, which were believed to hold the explanation for variances from the social group weight standards, was very limited. However, 48% of the women said that they were apt to nibble on food or eat more when they felt lonesome or had nothing much to do, this finding supporting clinical evidence that overeating is associated with feelings of dependency and depression.

Findings supported the hypothesis that it was the woman's evaluation of her weight rather than her actual weight which largely determined her attitude and behavior toward dieting. (See Appendix B, Tables 3 and 4, pages 341–342.) Fifty per cent of the women who believed themselves to be overweight said they were doing something to lose weight. The fatter women required more pressing reasons, such as a doctor's order, before they dieted, and were more likely to use medicines and drugs in trying to reduce.

A food's vulnerability to dieting appeared to depend on how it was regarded on three counts: how fattening it was, how healthful and nourishing, and how important it was in terms of enjoyment. Variations in the meaning of "diet" were found to be associated with geographical, rural-urban, age, and, to some extent, educational and occupational differences.

Eighty per cent of the women were seen as the "dieting market," although they were divided into four groups which varied in importance. They are listed below along with comments made in the report which went somewhat beyond the findings of the research in order to present a plausible picture of the groups.

Group 1. Women who consider themselves overweight and who are overweight according to medical standards (29% of the women). They are mainly middle-aged, lower-middle class women whose standards concerning weight are rather lax. Although the group includes most of the dieters in the population, it is apparent from their weight that they are not very successful dieters. It seems probable, then, that the group which is most likely to use dietetic foods is, paradoxically, the group which consumes a large amount of the rich, fattening foods. One might speculate that for these women dietetic foods are primarily a conscience balm which helps them relieve vague guilt feelings concerning self-indulgence.

Group 2. Women who consider themselves overweight, but who actually are nearly normal (12% of the women). They tend to be young, upper-middle class women who watch their weight and appearance carefully. They are successful dieters whose dieting efforts are less likely to be sporadic and half-hearted than is the case with Group 1. It is likely that these women use dietetic foods as a means of varying their diet rather than as an excuse for avoiding a diet.

Group 3. Women who are overweight, but who consider

themselves to be "about right" (8% of the women). They are mostly older, lower-class women who have no interest in dieting unless they have been ordered to diet by a doctor. It is possible that women in this group who are under a doctor's care diet rather stringently. Apparently the remainder do not give it a thought.

Group 4. Women who are normal in weight and so consider themselves (31% of the women). They are only marginally in the dieting market. Their eating habits are adjusted to their activity level and they do not have to give so much thought to what they eat. However, they are a younger group, and some of them will have a weight problem as they get older. On this assumption, it should be possible to interest some of them in guarding against obesity.

The remaining 20% of the women either believed themselves to be underweight or actually were underweight.

Plans for a Second Study

The first study raised a number of new questions with important implications for advertising and led to the planning of more elaborate research to be conducted independently of the Consumer Poll. Basically, the new study would seek to determine in greater detail the behavior patterns and attitudes toward food consumption of each of the four groups of women considered to be in the "dieting market."

The study would attempt to answer such questions as the following which were implied in the speculative comments made in the first report on the nature of each of the four groups:

1. Are the women who are overweight and know they are (Group 1) the ones who consume the largest amounts of fattening foods? Do they use dietetic foods? If so, do they serve them primarily as a balm to the conscience to help them relieve guilt feelings concerning self-indulgence?

2. Are the women whose weight is normal but who consider themselves to be overweight (Group 2) less apt to be sporadic and half-hearted in their dieting efforts than the women in Group 1? Do they use dietetic foods as a means of varying their diet rather than as an excuse for avoiding a diet?

3. What about the dieting behavior of the women who actually are overweight but who consider their weight to be about right (Group 3)?

4. Can the women who are normal in weight and so consider themselves be interested in guarding against overweight?

Answers to these questions would be used in determining what advertising approaches should be effective with each of the different groups of women. For example, Groups 1 and 3 might be more vulnerable to appeals based on "rewards." Prone to self-indulgence, they may be unlikely to give up between-meal snacks and rich desserts. If, however, the advertiser can suggest that there is a treat in store for them if they use Brand X cake frosting — a delicious, mouth-watering treat which also is nonfattening — perhaps they can be convinced of the desirability of the product. Women in Group 2, however, may be more readily influenced by advertising which focuses upon the actual dieting process. The "watch-your-middle" approach, coming directly to the point, could be more successful than a more roundabout approach which might cast doubt on the authenticity of the claims. Group 4 could be the most skeptical of nonfattening claims. A more "scientific" approach which would talk in terms of few calories together with results of actual taste tests may be the most effective with these women.

The new study would seek to determine which foods can successfully use a dietetic approach and which cannot. The following, for example, may be relatively unsusceptible to a dietetic approach: (1) foods regarded primarily as "treats" or "rewards"; (2) foods desired largely for their special flavor; and (3) foods so strongly associated with weight-producing elements that it is inconceivable to people that a truly nonfattening method of producing them could be found.

The study also would attempt to learn what images were associated with various words and phrases which have been used to describe nonfattening foods and beverages ("sugar-free," "dietetic," "water-packed," "low-calorie," "high protein," "nonfattening") and how these images varied according to product type.

Work on the questionnaire for the second study had not been completed in October 1955.

DIETING STUDY

Commentary

The dieting study, representing the first step in research planned on the subject, produced a number of interesting ideas with potentially important implications for both the selection of advertising media and the choice of appeals. Several were to be investigated further in a second study.

Of central importance was the picture developed of the dieting market, the latter consisting of several segments with somewhat different characteristics, including dieting motivation and behavior. For example, Group 1, which represented more than a third of the dieting market as defined, was made up mainly of middle-aged women of lower-middle social class who apparently were not very successful dieters. While they were seen as likely prospects for dietetic foods, the evidence was that they also ate much rich, fattening food. This suggested that for them dietetic foods were to a large extent a conscience balm and an excuse for avoiding a diet. On the other hand, Group 2 consisted largely of young, upper-middle class women who appeared to be reasonably successful dieters. It was considered likely that they used dietetic foods both to vary their diets and to aid them in keeping close watch on their weight.

These observations suggested that a "reward" appeal might be more effective for the first group while a more direct, watch-your-middle approach might be better for the second. Further research in this area was planned. An important question yet to be answered was how the groups compared on their use of dietetic foods.

Another important aspect of the survey was the method used to assess a food's vulnerability to dieting. The approach was to find out how the food was regarded on several counts by consumers, not "experts." The results suggested that foods vary in their ability to use a dietetic approach successfully, depending on the images people have of them, and the next study was designed to learn more about this subject.

More will be learned about the significance of this study's findings in the next phase of the research, but the results described here are both provocative and promising. In this connection, it is noteworthy that the study did not proceed by making the kind of assumptions so often made in marketing research. It did not, for example, assume that all overweight women are potential dieters, that dieting is primarily a health matter, or that all the women who buy dietetic foods do so primarily to lose weight. Neither did it assume that a food's vulnerability to dieting was dependent only upon whether it actually was fattening. The way in which the dieting market was defined did not rely on the conventional socio-economic factors. Instead, it grew out of the investigation of elements which seemed to be more directly related to dieting behavior. Emphasis was placed on finding out how people actually felt about their weight, dieting, and various foods.

The avoidance of some of the common pitfalls is directly related to the attention given in this case to the process of formulating a useful set of hypotheses for testing. The research approach was the product of the systematic use of specialists trained in the social sciences who functioned as a permanent and integral part of the research department. Their varied backgrounds, brought together in staff discussions, made possible a reasonably thorough review of the kind of behavior involved in dieting, including psychological and sociological aspects often overlooked in market research.

The ways of thinking of these specialists are reflected in the nature of the study which focused on the meanings of eating and dieting to people. The latter were viewed not only as individuals with nutritional and health needs, but as human beings influenced by the standards of the broad social groups to which they belonged and by their individual emotional needs as well. This is seen in some of the concepts used. One of them, developed in various studies of American communities, was that the population is stratified into social classes with somewhat different norms which influence behavior. This gave rise to the idea that standards of attractiveness and weight control vary by social status. The important influence of the concept that a person's behavior is a function of his self-image also can be noted. For example, it is seen in the hypothesis that it is not a woman's actual weight that determines her dieting, but whether she thinks she is overweight. The examination of psychological meanings of eating included noting clinical evidence that some people eat to compensate for feelings of loneliness and unhappiness. Such considerations led to the hypothesis that variances from social class weight standards could be explained by psychological factors. They also are related to the observation that many of the women who use dietetic foods also may consume large amounts of rich, fattening foods.

Another important feature of the research was the use of direct, restricted-answer questions for the purpose of testing the hypotheses. We should note, however, that the over-all approach was indirect in that the underlying hypotheses were not apparent to the respondent and that she was not asked whether she believed them to be correct. Instead, she was asked directly for responses from which it was assumed that correct conclusions about the hypotheses could be inferred. The questions were very specific, many forcing a choice among given alternative answers. The main purpose here was to test hypotheses, not look for more ideas. If the researchers proved to be incorrect in their assumption that they had developed useful hypotheses, a new search for relevant factors would be in order.

While the use of direct, restricted-response questions imposed certain limitations on what was done, it also offered advantages. Data collected in the interviews could be readily transferred to punched cards for quick and economical tabulation and statistical analysis by machine. Differences in response by various groupings of people of interest to the study could be expressed quantitatively and subjected to tests of statistical significance.

In summary, this case serves to emphasize that there are two phases of a research effort: the formulation of hypotheses and the testing of them. The skills and backgrounds of people trained in behavioral fields were brought to bear on both tasks. For the former, they explored the meanings of eating and dieting to people in terms of their social relationships and individual emotional and other needs. For the latter, they developed an indirect approach consisting of direct questions.

Appendix A

QUESTIONNAIRE FOR STUDY OF WEIGHT AND DIETING

EATING HABITS SECTION

Now I'd like to talk to you about a subject that we're all interested in — our eating habits and weight.

1. Most of us can be classified in one of three groups where weight is concerned — overweight, underweight, or just about right.

   At this time do you consider yourself to be:

   12

   Overweight ( )1   Underweight ( )2   About Right ( )3

2. Would you mind telling me about how much you weigh now? _____ lbs.

   13
   14
   15
   16

3. What would you consider to be the best weight for yourself? _____ lbs.

   17
   18

4. Could you tell me how tall you are in stocking feet?
   _____ ft. _____ in.   19____

5. Are you doing anything to try to lose or gain weight?

   20

   Yes ( )1   No ( )2

   a. Do you feel it is:

   Very important   ( )4
   Fairly important   ( )5
   Not at all important ( )6

   for you to lose or gain weight?

   b. Do you find it:

   Easy ( )8   Fairly Difficult ( )9   Very Difficult ( )o

   to lose or gain as much weight as you want to?

If Underweight (in Q. 1)   *Go to Q. 13*
If Overweight or About Right, Ask:

6. Do you ever make a serious effort to lose weight?

21

    Yes ( )x   *Ask Q. 7*   No ( )y   *Go to Q. 8*

7. Under what circumstances do you yourself make a serious effort to lose weight?   (*Show card X*)

When I notice that I've reached a certain weight.   24
   (specify) _____   22____   ( )1
                     _____ lbs.   23____
Usually in the spring, so that I'll look well in light
   clothes.   ( )2

When I feel heavy and uncomfortable.   ( )3

When the doctor recommends it for health reasons.   ( )4

When I notice my clothes are getting a little tight. ( )5

Other   (specify)_____

_____

8. Which of the following things do you do when you want to control your weight?   (*Show card XI*)

25

Exercise   ( )1   Do not try to control
Take medicine or drugs   ( )2   weight   ( )5
Massage or steam baths   ( )3
Watch what I eat   ( )4

     If Does NOT Watch What She Eats, *Go to Q. 13*

If Watches What She Eats
  (in Q. 8), Ask: Ask About Items Checked in Q. 9

9. Which of the following   a. When you are watching your
   foods and beverages would   weight, which of these do you
   you eat if you never had to   eat or drink freely, which do you
   watch your weight?   cut down on, which do you
                                    omit entirely:

	Would Eat	Eat Freely	Cut Down	Omit
	26			
Cake	( )1	29( )1	( )2	( )3
Mincemeat	( )2	( )4	( )5	( )6
Fruit pies	( )3	( )7	( )8	( )9
Coconut	( )4	30( )1	( )2	( )3
Puddings	( )5	( )4	( )5	( )6
Evaporated milk	( )6	( )7	( )8	( )9
Powdered milk	( )7	31( )1	( )2	( )3
Cocoa or chocolate	( )8	( )4	( )5	( )6
Regular milk	( )9	( )7	( )8	( )9
	27			
Beer	( )1	32( )1	( )2	( )3
Wine	( )2	( )4	( )5	( )6
Whiskey	( )3	( )7	( )8	( )9
Soup	( )4	33( )1	( )2	( )3
Tomato sauce	( )5	( )4	( )5	( )6
Spaghetti	( )6	( )7	( )8	( )9
Rice	( )7	34( )1	( )2	( )3
Cold breakfast cereal	( )8	( )4	( )5	( )6
Tea	( )9	( )7	( )8	( )9
	28			
Coffee	( )1	35( )1	( )2	( )3
Cola drinks	( )2	( )4	( )5	( )6
Salad dressing	( )3	( )7	( )8	( )9
Cheese	( )4	36( )1	( )2	( )3
Syrup	( )5	( )4	( )5	( )6
Salted nuts	( )6	( )7	( )8	( )9
Sugar	( )7	( )o	( )x	( )y

10. Will you please tell me any special nonfattening foods, food substitutes, and beverages which you sometimes use. We mean any that are commercially prepared or manufactured to be less fattening.

_____37

_____38

11. Can you name any of these special nonfattening foods and beverages which you do **not** use?

_____39

_____40

12. Please try to name **all** the regular foods you include in your menu mainly because they are less fattening:

_____41

_____42

_____

13. What do you think are the main reasons for people regulating how much and what they eat?

43

To lose weight	( )1	Some foods are particularly healthy	( )5
To gain weight	( )2	Pregnancy	( )6
To be attractive	( )3	Sick (special diet) ↘	( )7
Unhealthy to be fat	( )4	_____44 (specify sicknesses)	

14. When you feel somewhat lonesome or have nothing much to do are you apt to:

45

	Yes	*No*
Nibble on food or eat more	( )1	( )2
Smoke more cigarettes	( )4	( )5

15. When you feel generally nervous and unhappy, do you usually:

46

Eat More ( )0   Eat Less ( )x   Neither ( )y

16. What do you mean by the phrase, "He's on a diet," when you are talking to your friends? For instance:

a. If a person is trying to lose weight by carefully controlling what he eats and how much he eats, would you ordinarily say he is on a diet?

47

Yes ( )1   No ( )2   Don't know ( )3

b. Would you say he's on a diet if he is cutting down a little on sweets, starches, fatty meats, etc.?

Yes ( )5   No ( )6   Don't know ( )7

c. If a person never eats fats, starches, or sweets simply because he doesn't enjoy them, would you say he's on a diet?

48

Yes ( )1   No ( )2   Don't know ( )3

d. Now suppose the person you're speaking about has diabetes, and the doctor has given him a list of foods he should keep away from. Would you say that he is on a <u>diet</u> if he follows the doctor's orders?

Yes ( )5   No ( )6   Don't know ( )7

Appendix B

SELECTED TABLES FROM "A STUDY OF CONSUMER ATTITUDES AND BEHAVIOR CONCERNING WEIGHT AND DIETING"

1. *Per Cent of Women by Weight Categories*

Clearly overweight	37%
Clearly underweight	15
Normal	46
No report	2

(Normal includes women whose weight did not deviate from the medical ideal by more than 15%. It was estimated that 28% of the women in the "normal" group were overweight by about 10%.)

2. *Indices of Strictness of Weight Standards*

(Index derived by dividing number of women who described themselves as overweight by the number who were clearly overweight by medical standards.)

By Educational Level	Index
Grade school, incomplete	.76
Grade school	1.12
High school, incomplete	1.19
High school	1.35
College, incomplete	1.62
College	2.25

By Occupation of Husband	Index
Labor	.83
Farmer	1.00
Service	1.17
Operatives	1.27
Craft	1.24
Clerical, sales	1.30
Professional, manager	1.48

By Family Income	Index
Under $60 a week	.91
$60–$99	1.35
$100–$139	1.43
$140 and more	1.52

By Age	Index
65 and over	.75
55–64	.81
45–54	1.15
35–44	1.30
25–34	1.52
Under 25	1.55

3. *Importance and Difficulty of Dieting.* The women were asked how important it was to them to lose weight and how difficult they found it to lose as much as they wanted to. The percentage who gave various answers by category of respondent:

	Women Who Believed Themselves Overweight		Women Who Believed Their Weight Normal	
Importance of Losing Weight	Clearly Overwt. (100%)	Weight Normal (100%)	Clearly Overwt. (100%)	Weight Normal (100%)
Very important	53%	39%	23%	12%
Fairly important	31	45	11	17
Not at all important	16	16	66	71
Difficulty of Losing Weight				
Very difficult	61%	36%	20%	12%
Fairly difficult	23	36	24	20
Not at all difficult	16	28	56	68

4. *Effort to Reduce Weight.* The following statements, each of which appeared in a different place on the questionnaire, form a consistent series graded in terms of the degree of effort to reduce weight. The percentage of women by category of respondent who agreed with each statement:

Statement	*Women Who Believed Themselves Overweight*		*Women Who Believed Their Weight Normal*	
	Clearly Overwt. (100%)	*Weight Normal* (100%)	*Clearly Overwt.* (100%)	*Weight Normal* (100%)
I sometimes try to control my weight	84%	86%	45%	40%
I sometimes watch what I eat	75	76	38	33
I sometimes make a serious effort to lose weight	62	55	15	12
I am now doing something to lose weight	52	45	14	7

CHAPTER X

Jewel Tea Company Home Service Routes

FORENOTE

The case which follows deals with personal selling, a subject which has received very little research attention. Brief descriptions are presented of three studies conducted at different times by different researchers to learn how the sales effectiveness of the company's home route service might be improved. While all of them involved observations of route salesmen calling on customers, they represented somewhat different ways of thinking. As a result, there were differences in focus, in what was seen in the observations, and in the conclusions drawn as to what action should be taken.

The first investigation, made some time ago by a member of the company's own staff, was of the time-and-duty analysis variety. The second and third were concerned primarily with the nature of the routeman-customer relationship and how housewives felt about various features of the company's sales program. The second study was conducted by the Institute for Motivational Research, Inc., and the third, which came four years later, by Social Research, Inc. Both of these studies employed intensive detailed interviews in addition to the observations of sales calls and one also made use of two projective techniques — incomplete sentences and adaptations of the thematic apperception test.

JEWEL TEA COMPANY HOME SERVICE ROUTES

A Descriptive Case

IN A CONTINUING EFFORT to improve the sales effectiveness of its home service routes, the Jewel Tea Company of Barrington, Illinois, had for five years ending in 1953 employed the services of two research firms which specialized in the application of social science knowledge and techniques to marketing problems. Early in 1949 Dr. Ernest Dichter's Institute for Motivational Research, Inc., Croton, N. Y., completed "A Psychological Analysis of the Jewel Home Route Service." In 1953 Social Research, Inc., Chicago, headed by Dr. Burleigh Gardner, studied "The Jewel Routeman and His Customer."

Jewel employed 2,100 routemen who called regularly once every two weeks at the homes of one million customers in 42 states and the District of Columbia. They took orders for and delivered grocery products. Since 1951, when a Catalog Shopping Service was added, they also might take orders for any of 1,000 items of general merchandise which would be shipped directly to the customer. Routemen were paid a salary plus a commission on sales. They worked directly under 380 supervisors who in turn reported to 69 branch managers. In addition to the regular routemen, 350 advance salesmen specialized in obtaining new customers.

Premiums were offered to grocery customers. A housewife could receive a premium of her choice on the first call and pay for it later with "bonus credits" earned by purchases of Jewel brand grocery items. There was a $10 limit on the amount of premium credit which could be extended. Regular customers with established credit could charge purchases up to $75. Ten per cent of the amount of the bill was collected on delivery of the merchandise and the remainder by 10% payments each time the routeman called.

Sales per route customer, which had been increasing, showed signs of leveling off in the late 1940's. This led to the decision to have a study made by Dr. Dichter, who in early 1948 had completed a psychological analysis of the sales problems of Jewel's retail food stores (165 in the Chicago area).

THE 1932 STUDY

The last important investigation of routemen's activities had been conducted by Jewel's own research department in 1932. The object was to observe and measure what the more successful routemen did so that improved methods might be applied by the entire selling force. Accordingly, 15 men with the highest sales volumes and 4 of materially lower sales volumes were selected for study. The researcher, playing the role of silent observer, accompanied them on 353 calls.

Findings were in terms of how much time was spent at work, how it was used, and what steps were followed or omitted in the sales call. (See Appendix A, pages 363–365.) For example, the researcher found that too much selling time was devoted to items which accounted for a small portion of the sales volume. In addition, the salesmen were not following the prescribed five-point selling program. Many failed to present the order card at the specified time, show premiums, use suggested talking points for products, or ask for names of prospective new customers. Grocery items on which talking points were used were found to outsell others by a large margin. Recommendations included getting the men to work longer hours and devote more time to large volume items, developing further a standardized procedure to be followed in the sales call, and equipping and training the men for "automatic selling."

THE 1949 STUDY

The research by Dr. Dichter's organization in 1949 had as its broad objectives finding out how to sell more to present accounts and how to acquire new customers. The study included 200 depth interviews with customers, noncustomers, and ex-customers who lived in 20 towns in five states; observations of routemen making their calls; interviews with routemen and their families in their own homes; and talks with branch managers. In the depth interviews, people were encouraged to talk freely in a conversational manner. Formal direct questions seldom were used. Instead, the interviewer attempted by skillful probing to learn of what was important to the respondent and to investigate the emotional factors which often determined apparently rational behavior. The Jewel customers, for example, were encouraged to talk about their grocery buying habits, Jewel's products and service, and how they felt about buying from the routemen who came into their homes.

The report of findings and recommendations dealt primarily with the nature of the routeman-customer relationship, how housewives felt about receiving premiums and buying on credit, and factors which deterred people from becoming home service route customers. (See Appendix B, pages 366–369.)   Excerpts from a summary statement in the report appear below:

> We have attempted to answer the two major questions of how more customers can be acquired . . . and how present customers can be made more satisfied.
>
> As over-all answers, we have found that the personal pride and self-assurance of the customer are the most important factors. This psychological element is more important than the merchandise or the premium. The customer has to be flattered and entertained, made to feel good, and made to consider herself important.
>
> The route business differs from most other forms of business in that it involves a moral issue. The route salesman and everyone else concerned with the business must be well aware of this factor. Every time the salesman enters a home, moral problems of buying on time, or doing something foolish, extravagant, and possibly even sinful, come into play. The selling for Jewel thus has to be on a basis of reassurance. Moral resistance has to be combatted.
>
> Of prime importance is the total role played by the sales-

man in his relationship to the customer. The more the salesman can be pushed into the foreground by Jewel, and the more self-confidence he can be given, the better it will be for the business as a whole. Furthermore, in line with the two other points of making the housewife feel good about herself and assuaging her guilt feelings, it becomes clear that the role of the salesman far exceeds that of simply an agent. He is almost a psychologist-counselor and family friend.

All these factors together make the Jewel business unique. More than a food business, it is a way of dealing with people and understanding them. If it did not sound exaggerated, we might say that the food sold is almost incidental and secondary to the total operation, although, of course, the quality of merchandise and honesty of treatment are important aspects of what Jewel has to offer. But regardless of how excellent the merchandise might be, without the Jewel spirit it would be an empty shell.

THE 1953 STUDY — THE ROUTEMAN

Early in 1953 Mr. George L. Clements, who had become president of the company in 1950, decided that further research on route operations should be undertaken by an outside consulting firm. Social Research, Inc., which two years earlier had completed a study to guide the advertising policy of Jewel's retail food stores, was employed to do the work. There were two phases of the research. One concentrated on learning about the route customer and the other centered on the routeman himself.

The study of the routeman was directed to finding out what kind of a salesman he was, what he did, how he did it, how he dealt with customers and they with him, and what he thought about his job and his customers. To get this picture, one of three interviewers assigned to the project accompanied each of 19 routemen for a one-day period to conduct running interviews, make verbatim notes on what was said, and observe sales calls (a total of 600 calls were included in the study). The interviewers explained that they had been asked by management to make the study in order to try to improve things, that they were interested in anything the routemen might have to tell them, and that the interviews were confidential. A report was to be written on an over-all basis without quoting any one person. The 19 routemen were selected to represent two different branches of the sales organization; high, medium, and low producers; and newcomers and old-timers.

The study revealed three markedly different groups of routemen based on the way they organized and handled their work, their ability to cope with the demands of the company and the job, and their own needs and expectations. The groups: (1) the stable, satisfied man; (2) the ambitious man; and (3) the disorganized or unstable man.

The major source of satisfaction for the stable, satisfied routeman was comfortable, friendly relations with customers. He wanted to know the customer as a person and be so known by her. He did not like impersonal selling. He could not tolerate high-pressure selling, a finding which was interpreted to mean that a sales contest may result in anxiety for him. He saw his job as a permanent thing and coped comfortably with the pressures it imposed on him. He was a family man, a "solid citizen." He did not want close supervision that prescribed every move, but needed prescribed company routines and procedures for guidance, help, and protection.

The ambitious routeman differed in that he regarded his job as a step toward something better rather than an end in itself. While the stable, satisfied routeman might talk about moving up, at the same time he pointed out that the next step would be into supervisory work involving undesirable travel away from home. The ambitious man was willing to accept these difficulties. He was more detached, had less basic need for long, pleasant, friendly, interpersonal relationships. Hence, he found it easier to accept the fact that the work of a supervisor involved a large number of relatively impersonal and brief contacts with people. He established good relationships with his route customers, but for him this was less a personal necessity than a matter of good business practice. His primary satisfaction came from the accomplishment of tasks rather than from friendly relationships. The ambitious man was more likely to seek contact with his superiors so that he could learn and have his work evaluated and recognized.

The disorganized or unstable men were unable to organize or cope with their work. They were in almost a perpetual state of anxiety in their relationships with both customers and the company.

The stable, satisfied man was described as "ideal" in that he was most likely to accept the job of routeman as permanent and organize it effectively. The ambitious man was considered a better prospect for progressing to positions of leadership within the company, however. The report recommended personnel selection procedures which would distinguish between the types so that the disorganized, unstable men could be avoided and the number of ambitious men held within limits set by anticipated supervisory openings. If the ambitious men were not advanced within a reasonable period of time, they were likely to quit or become bitter toward the company.

The report pointed out that a new routeman had to face a number of problems at one time and made several recommendations relative to his orientation. A longer formal training program was suggested so that the routeman could concentrate on the important task of establishing satisfactory customer relationships without being under undue pressure to master job procedures at the same time. Provision for frequent contact with the supervisor was recommended for the first month when the new routeman would need guidance and reassurance. If he had to wait for answers to the many important questions likely to arise, he might quit rather than continue to try to function in the face of frustration and mounting tension.

THE 1953 STUDY — THE ROUTE CUSTOMER

The second phase of the research attempted to learn about the kind of people who bought from Jewel's route service and why they had become customers. Among the points investigated were their relation to the routeman, their grocery buying habits, their knowledge and concept of Jewel and its merchandise, and factors which limited their buying.

Information was obtained from the observations of route-men's sales calls described in the previous section and from long interviews with 152 customers selected from different routes in three geographical areas. They represented different age groups as follows: 30 years of age and under, 34 respondents; 31 to 45 years, 61; and 45 and over, 57. Most of the customers were of the "middle majority" social classes which comprised the mass market for most products. More specifically, the social class distribution was as follows: Upper Middle Class, 14 respondents; Lower Middle, 56; Upper Lower, 81; and Lower Lower, 1.[1]

In the interviews, which often lasted from two to three hours, the respondent was encouraged to talk freely. Interview guides indicated topics and suggested questions for use in starting and maintaining conversation. While all listed subjects were to be covered, the questions did not have to be asked in any set way. Instead, the interviewer was instructed to let the interview develop naturally and probe for full response.

Many questions were general so that the respondent would have ample freedom to bring in any ideas she considered important. More specific questions were used, particularly

[1] See Appendix I, Automobile Case, pages 254–255.

later, to check on certain points. Grocery buying in general was introduced as the first topic in an effort to find out how the Jewel route service fitted into the larger context of the respondent's food buying habits and whether an orderly approach to shopping was associated with use of the route service. (See Appendix C, pages 370–371.)

Route service buying behavior and attitudes were subjects of detailed investigation. Later questions were designed to find out how the housewife got started buying from the routeman, how much she knew about the premium and budget plans and how emotionally involved she was with them, and how much she systematized her buying. A series of questions (11 through 15) were designed to establish the nature of her relationship with the routeman and something about what kind of a routeman she responded to well. The respondent was provided with an opportunity to condemn a nonuser of route service (question 17), if she was so inclined, in order to learn something more about how important the service was to the respondent herself.

In addition to the usual questions, incomplete sentences were used to obtain reactions quickly to a number of aspects of route service buying. (See Appendix D, page 372.) As each sentence stem was read, the respondent was asked to complete it with the first thing that came to mind. Examples:

> When I order my groceries . . .
> The best thing about buying from Jewel . . .
> If only my routeman would . . .
> My husband thinks the Jewel man . . .
> Buying appliances from a catalogue . . .

Two pictures also were used. The first showed a routeman, a little girl, and a housewife in the latter's kitchen. (See Exhibit 1.) The respondent was asked to tell a story about what was going on in the picture, what led up to the situation, who the people were and what they are thinking, and what the outcome might be. This technique was used to obtain free response material which would reveal how the housewife structured her relationship with the routeman. Such points as whether she told a story with emotion and

EXHIBIT 1.

A Picture Technique Used to Study the Routeman-Housewife Relationship

friendliness and whether she had the woman tell the routeman exactly what she was going to buy were of interest.

The second picture about which the respondent was asked to tell a story showed a housewife and her husband apparently talking about the Jewel catalog which the husband held in his hands. (See Exhibit 2.) It was designed to learn something of the nature of the interaction between man and wife regarding the catalog such as whether they argued or agreed, talked enthusiastically or critically.

THE FINDINGS

The report of findings emphasized the customer-routeman relationship as the keystone to the housewife's buying. (See Appendix E, pages 373–380. The study showed it to be

EXHIBIT 2.
A Picture Technique Used to Study Reactions to Jewel's Catalog

gratifying to most customers, but marked with potential conflict and anxiety over which the housewife had to exercise self-control. This explained why she wanted, above all, a routeman who would allow her to maintain the position of control; why she was concerned about being "high pressured" even though she had not been subjected to such sales tactics by her routeman; and why she often set up defensive rituals for him to follow.

Ideally, the relationship should be of fairly low, positive emotional tone which would not arouse a great deal of anxiety. Inasmuch as the routeman was not only a company representative, but also a man the housewife saw in her home biweekly, she had to establish an emotionally meaningful relationship with him within the bounds of propriety and convention. This usually was not a question of what she might do if she did not exercise proper control, but, rather, it was a matter of what feelings and fantasies she might have. There was concern that the relationship might become too important, causing her to act more in accord with his interests rather than those of the family. One of the most common worries of the route customer was that she would be tempted by the system (its convenience, premiums, and the routeman) to buy more than she should. To guard against this, she often developed a "budget" by which she limited her purchasing more than she did for her other shopping.

For the housewife to please her husband and maintain her own self-respect, she had to perform her role as homemaker so as to avoid criticism over what was done in the home, especially in regard to social activities with men. While most customers said their husbands had no interest in the Jewel routeman, there were enough mentions of a husband's irritation at this "other man in the house" to indicate that this was not an uncommon source of friction.

The husband, as the nominal head of the family in our society, can call his wife to account and tell her what she can or can not do. The routeman, however, should have no such power. To be caught between two dominating and directing men would place the housewife in an immoral position, according to her code. On the other hand, if the routeman became her ally in trying to satisfy her husband, she would be more secure.

Many middle majority housewives are not personally assertive in meeting "outsiders." As route customers, they must depend heavily upon the routeman to allow them to direct (or feel that they are directing) the relationship. Their only defense, if he proved too dominant, was to withdraw completely.

Middle majority customers wanted a routeman who was friendly, congenial but "not too nice," submissive, and conforming to requests and routines. He should be sensitive to the amount of socializing desired by the customer, allow her to set the pace, and then follow it quickly and willingly. He should follow a regular schedule of visits. Failure to do so diminished the customer's feeling of control. Upper middle-class women had more detached, impersonal attitudes toward the routeman and tended to look upon him as they would upon a servant.

Home delivery and premiums were found to be main attractions of the Jewel route system. The former was convenient, saved time, and brought shopping into the home where most middle majority women felt more secure than they did while shopping in stores. Premiums were happily received as gifts most of the time, although there was a certain amount of suspicion of "getting something for nothing." Upper middle-class women emphasized convenience more than premiums as a reason for using the service. They tended to regard premiums as a "trick" to obligate them.

The typical route customer stayed at home a great deal because she had two or more children and a lot of housework to do without hired help. She also put a great deal of energy into establishing a routine. The customers who found trading with Jewel most gratifying were those who were able and willing to organize their shopping in detail.

Executive Comments on the Studies

Mr. George L. Clements, President, voiced satisfaction with both the 1949 and 1953 studies. He said that their main benefit was that they stimulated thinking of people within the company and that this was more important than immediate changes in policy. As an example of one direct effect, he pointed to "Jewel's Code for Customer Satisfaction," a statement of company policy formulated on the basis of the 1953 research. (See Appendix F, page 381.) Copies were distributed to all Jewel routemen and customers.

Mr. Clements observed that while the researchers could tell what they had found out, they could not always tell what should be done about it. He regarded some of their recommendations as impractical, this reflecting their limited knowledge of the operating pressures of the business.

Mr. Clements, whose previous experience had been largely in the retail store division, became president in 1950 and made the decision to have the 1953 study of route operations undertaken. He assumed active direction of route selling early in 1954 when the former general manager of that activity left the company. Mr. Clements had two route department executive assistants for route operations, both of whom had served in similar capacities with the former general manager.

Speaking of the reports based on the 1953 research, one of the assistants stated that they had been helpful. "For the most part, they reaffirmed what we already knew," he said. "They helped us sharpen our thinking. The findings had been presented to people in the organization so that they could take whatever action their responsibilities and their own thinking indicated. They also were presented to branch managers at a convention." He commented that many of the findings of the 1932 study, in which he had participated, were similar to those of the 1953 research.

The second route department assistant to the president expressed the view that both the 1949 and 1953 studies had been useful. He said that the 1949 report led to the following action:

> Inviting wives of route salesmen to attend with their husbands meetings conducted by top company officials from the home office.
>
> The inauguration of a plan whereby branch, district, and national "queens" were selected each year from the wives of routemen. Selection was made on the basis of the routemen's performance in sales, collections, and acquisitions of new customers.
>
> More emphasis on promoting the positive factors of buying from Jewel in order to offset negative feelings the research had shown to exist among housewives about buying on credit.
>
> The granting of more liberal budget terms and more emphasis to advertising of the budget plan.
>
> Making the collection of money the last point in the five-point selling program so that the housewife would not be feeling guilty about money she had spent in the past when it was time for her to re-order. The assistant said that the 1949 report "showed the need for sticking to the five-point selling program."

Speaking of the contributions of the 1953 study, the second assistant stated that it showed what help was needed from the company by the branch managers faced with problems like the selection of routemen. He mentioned that the 1953 branch managers' convention program had been based on the Social Research reports, the latter suggesting both the topics and the amount of time to be allotted to each. Among those discussed were the selection of routemen, obtaining better quality route customers, and problems in handling mail orders. The second assistant reported that the 1953 study also led to simplifying the selling program the routeman was supposed to follow so that he would not be required to do too much in the limited time available with each customer.

JEWEL TEA COMPANY HOME SERVICE ROUTES
Commentary

We shall note at the outset that while the studies described in the case differed, all three were regarded by certain key excutives as contributions to their thinking.

The objective of the first study was to find out what the better routemen were doing so that all routemen could be instructed to do it. In making his observations, the researcher thought in terms of the time spent and what the routeman did in terms of the mechanical aspects of the call. For example, the observer checked to see whether the order card was presented at the right time, whether premiums were shown, whether suggested talking points were used, and whether names of prospective customers were requested.

This approach relied heavily upon the assumption that successful salesmanship was a matter of spending a certain amount of time and following prescribed steps with all customers. The objective was to develop further a standard procedure so as to equip and train the men for what was termed "automatic selling."

The study was not designed to make a real attempt to learn whether following the set procedure actually did make for greater sales. The benchmark for evaluating routemen was what management thought a good routeman should do. This may or may not have been sound. On the one hand, a number of potentially useful observations appear to have been made. An example is the one that only 15% of the customers were asked for names of prospects and the routemen generally were afraid to make such requests. This raised a serious question relative to getting new business which warranted further attention.

On the other hand, management's preconceptions also represented a limitation. If effective salesmanship was not primarily a matter of spending so much time on the job and following a prescribed sequence of mechanical steps, the research approach taken by the first study was not likely to find this out. Mostly high-producing routemen were observed so that there was little opportunity to study the relative sales effectiveness of differences in routeman conduct. The fact that groceries were not named in 40% of the homes or the fact that the order card was not presented at the "right" time in 26% of the calls may or may not have been important in terms of making sales.

A different view of the selling process was taken in the other two studies. They saw salesmanship primarily in terms of establishing and maintaining a satisfactory routeman-customer relationship. They were interested in what made for satisfactions, their focus being on qualitative aspects. By means of detailed interviews as well as observations of sales calls, they attempted to learn how people felt about the routeman and what he did, the company's sales offers and procedures, and the like. While generalizations were made, the concept was not one of developing a set procedure to be followed with every customer.

By using such an approach, the 1949 study gave attention to such things as the housewife's need to feel important, her need to feel that she was an efficient shopper, her feeling of security that came from regular route service, her fear of installment buying and of the temptation to be extravagant, and the tendency for husbands to feel hostile toward routemen's calls. These considerations led to recommendations in regard to the routeman's conduct, ways of minimizing unfavorable connotations of installment buying, giving more attention to pleasing the husband, and helping to establish the routeman and his family as friendly and substantial members of the community.

The 1953 study was somewhat broader in scope. It attempted to learn what kind of a woman the route customer was, what she wanted from the relationship with the routeman and the service he represented, and what kind of a person made a good routeman in terms of the demands of the job. The latter information is important for the purposes of personnel selection. In this case, the analysis of currently employed routemen showed three different types of men in terms of their own needs and expectations and ability to cope with the demands of the company and the job. The type of man best suited to rising to more important positions within the company was not the one most likely to be the most satisfactory routeman, a finding which served to point up the desirability of clarifying selection policy.

The 1953 study also emphasized the key importance of the customer-routeman relationship as the 1949 study had done, and it went into considerable detail as to what the nature of the relationship should be. It also dealt with feelings of the housewife on various things such as buying on credit, the premium plan, and home delivery. Differences in attitudes by social class were noted on some of these points.

While the 1949 and 1953 studies were somewhat similar in approach and the factors to which consideration was given, there was a marked difference in their recommendations as to how the routeman should conduct himself in the sales call. The 1949 recommendation was that he should take a strong lead and plan each sales call so as to give the customer a good show. This grew out of the emphasis placed on the unconscious personal needs and desires of the individual woman to be flattered, entertained, made to feel important, "to be wooed by the salesman at every visit."

While the 1953 study did not disagree that these desires for stimulation were present, its findings were that the housewife could not allow herself to give in to these feelings by assuming a passive role. To do so would remove her too much from the business of buying and violate her concept of her role as a homemaker. The study saw the customer-routeman relationship as one marked with potential conflict and anxiety over which the housewife had to exercise self-control by maintaining the position of control, or at least apparent control, in the sales call. A relationship of fairly low but positive emotional tone which would not arouse a great deal of anxiety was recommended.

The contrasting recommendations appear to reflect differences in orientation of the researchers concerned. In the earlier study, the emphasis was on the personal desires of the individual, assuming that the individual would act to satisfy them. The second study put more emphasis on restraining social pressures represented by commonly accepted norms of conduct for a "good" homemaker, and, in this case, saw them as being controlling for most women.

The topic of conflicting recommendations by different researchers typically was raised at business and professional meetings a few years ago when motivation research started to receive a great deal of attention. In fact, a few cases of lack of agreement which had been noted were viewed with alarm by some. The implication usually was that if two researchers working on the same problem could not come up with the same recommendations, then research was bad and not to be trusted. This usually was intended as a criticism of motivation research by people who overlooked the fact that such differences are not uncommon in conventional marketing research as well.

In the Jewel Tea Company case, we have an example of conflicting recommendations on an important point. We do not view this with alarm, however, even though it constitutes a problem to be resolved. In the absence of complete knowledge of the nature of something, especially when it is as complex as human behavior, it is probable that different people with different backgrounds and viewpoints are likely to see somewhat different things in their observations and make somewhat different recommendations. This kind of thing happens regularly among social scientists, business executives, and marketing researchers. While such differences can, of course, result from careless thinking or research, they also are bound to occur when new ways of thinking are introduced and when new insights are gained. This would seem to constitute an argument for making use of all available knowledge and viewpoints in order to minimize chances that important considerations will be overlooked. It also points to the need for testing recommendations as a part of the effort to advance our state of knowledge as well as to resolve differences preliminary to formulating a course of business action.

In summary, we wish to emphasize that the studies described in this case represent research on selling and as such are significant because so little work has been done in this area. In the past, selling has been thought of largely in terms of the rational aspects of the sales offer — product features, service, price, and the like. While these are of obvious importance, they do not explain why a person elects to buy from one salesman rather than another when the usual rational factors are about the same, or why he even may choose one salesman rather than another who in the usual sense of the word makes him the better offer. The development of an understanding of salesmanship which will cover such questions would seem to depend upon detailed examinations of what goes on between the salesman and the customer, or, the nature of the personal relationship. The 1949 and 1953 studies for the Jewel Tea Company were steps in this direction.

Appendix A

A DIGEST OF "A STUDY OF SERVICEMEN'S ACTIVITIES"

(Study Conducted in March 1932 by V. T. Norton, Research Department)

Scope of Study — The thought behind the study was to measure methods used by the better servicemen and then apply them to improve the performance of the poorer men. Fifteen of the highest volume salesmen in the country were studied as were four salesmen of materially lower volumes. The researcher was a silent companion of these men as they made their routes.

Principal Findings and Recommendations

A. *How Salesmen Spend Time*
  1. Average time spent in presence of homemaker, 2.84 hours a day. Range: 1.98 to 3.99 hours.
  2. Average time at which the first home was called on was 8:11 A.M. Get men to start earlier — at 7:30 A.M.
  3. Men spent 7.26 hours a day not counting lunch time.
  4. Men are getting through too early in the afternoon — average quitting time, 3:54 P.M.
  5. The salesman spends 5.51 minutes in the presence of each active customer.
  6. The salesmen are not covering enough points of the five-point program.
B. *What Salesmen Do in the Home* (Observed Sales Action in 353 Homes)
  1. Only 26% of deliveries had order card presented at proper time (after delivery and collection). Recommendation: Must show salesman how to present a grocery order card.
  2. Groceries not even being named in 40% of homes. Recommendation: Give each man a list of five fastest moving items other than tea or coffee. Ask him to memorize them in order. Require him to name each item clearly and distinctly when suggesting an order.

3. Men often get turned down even before they start saying something about grocery items. Recommendation: We must teach them how to use the talking points they already know.

4. Men are weak in their technique in showing bargain goods.

5. Premiums were shown on only 35% of the deliveries. Recommendation: Use of special premium ordergraphs. Concentrate on showing one article at a time.

6. Men do not show premiums automatically. They select certain customers to show certain premiums. Recommendation: (a) equip salesmen for automatic selling and teach them to do it; (b) train men to tell customers a high point or two about premium picked; (c) fasten a sales aid to the premiums.

C. *New Customers by Servicemen*

1. Only 15% of customers were asked for names of prospects; of these, 18% gave names.

2. Salesmen seemed to hate to ask for prospects and used poor approaches: "You don't know any people I could get for customers, do you?" or "You don't know any friend I could call on, do you?" Recommendation: Get away from begging type of approach.

3. These things are fundamental in getting a prospect: (a) get customer to do part of the approach at the prospect's door; (b) servicemen should have more information about the prospect than just the name; (c) determine in advance what the prospect's main interest is and cater to it.

D. *Selling Groceries*

1. 51.6% of groceries on which talking points were given were sold. Only 12.8% of groceries on which talking points were not given were sold.

2. In presenting bargain sales, the men did not tell customers what the item would cost if it were to be sold at regular price. Recommendation: Teach them to do this.

3. The researcher recommended a small talking point manual designed so that it could fit into the salesman's pocket and so he could read it quickly.

    4. Packages should be studied by the servicemen for talking points.

    5. 30% of sales time for groceries was taken up by presenting "in and out" items which account for only 7% of the sales. This is a misapplication of sales effort and a waste.

E. *The Jewel News*

    1. Salesmen did not present the copies of the Jewel News well. Yet, when the Jewel News was opened by the salesman, noticeable interest was shown by the customer. Only one salesman out of 18 pointed out the features of the Jewel News. Recommendation: A standardized procedure for delivering a Jewel News. Train salesmen to use it.

(The remainder of the report consisted of notes on the selling practices of individual salesmen and pointed out weaknesses in what the salesmen said and how they said it.)

Appendix B

A PSYCHOLOGICAL ANALYSIS OF JEWEL
HOME ROUTE SERVICE

(Some of the principal findings and recommendations are summarized briefly here to illustrate the nature of the study and the final report.)

A. *Ego Benefits For The Buyer Are More Important Than The Merchandise*

The housewife who is sold on Jewel merchandise is more than a bargain hunter — she is very anxious to acquire increased self-prestige. She wants to be wooed by the salesman at every visit — a demand for perpetual re-selling. From our observations, whenever the salesman had confidence enough to make himself the center of the show for the few minutes he was in the home, he sold more. He and the customer had a good time. It is wrong for a Jewel routeman to kowtow and be servile. It is his job to give the customer what she really wants which is a good show.

A major benefit from using home route service is the feeling that "I am important." It comes from the salesman remembering the customer's family details, her special likes and dislikes.

Jewel customers like to feel they are using a more efficient and convenient method of shopping than their neighbors. They are proud of having traded with Jewel for many years and feel their loyalty should be rewarded. The housewife likes to feel that by using Jewel premium and budget plans she has worked out a smart financial maneuver whereby she can buy luxuries she could not otherwise afford.

There is a feeling of relief from being spared the indecision that would be involved in going out to a store to purchase. When a Jewel salesman shows the housewife a product, the housewife is confronted with an on-the-spot decision. She has no time to feel guilty or doubtful and in this way she psychologically is permitted to buy many things that longer consideration would forbid or at least make more difficult.

Housewives like the feeling of security they get from the regularity of the salesman's visits and his attempts to provide many of the products they need. This gives the housewife assurance that she will be taken care of and will be able to run her home well.

Among the recommendations made in connection with the above findings was one that the salesmen plan each sales call so that it became almost a stage show with a warming-up period, a climax, and a dramatic exit. The object was to give the customer a good show and to avoid the call's becoming a routine visit which was seen as "deadly." Suggestions were made relative to remembering and recognizing customer habits, special likes and dislikes, and years of patronage; providing assurance of the regularity of the service; and crediting the housewife rather than the premium and budget plans for shrewdness in the management of money.

B. *Buying From Jewel Involves A Moral Issue*

Each transaction involves deciding when buying on credit is morally permissible. Housewives fear installment buying and to them the housecard (record of purchases and payments) becomes a symbol of sin and indebtedness. Buying on credit involves a single immediate gratification which wears off a long time before full payment is made. Consequently, the attitude toward the company often becomes increasingly harsh and critical with each succeeding payment.

The housewife tends to consider articles bought not as necessary foodstuffs, but as money paid out for a premium. This leads to holding expenditures to a minimum.

Many husbands are hostile to the idea of routemen coming into the house. This makes the husband aware of his own lack of power, and the housecard record of purchases provides him an opportunity to check and criticize his wife's buying.

Ways of minimizing indications of installment buying and emphasizing savings realized through purchases were recommended. The report suggested that more attention be given to pleasing the husband by carrying special luxury merchandise for men, preparing pamphlets addressed to them, and by having the salesman call on them.

C. *The Salesman Is The Most Important Factor In Keeping The
     Housewife Buying From Route Service*

What kind of salesman is best?   Housewives say they don't like
high-pressure salesmen, but actually they resent routemen who
can't sell them on something.   The reason for this ambivalent attitude is that the housewife does not want to admit to herself
that she has been talked into buying, but she wants still less to
accept personal responsibility for having done something foolish.

Almost all routemen say they do not use high-pressure selling
and disapprove of it.   They are afraid of such tactics because
they give rise to anxiety over being unable to control repressed
aggressive feelings.   Also, the salesmen don't want to take responsibility for talking someone into something.   The defensive
attitude of the housewife against being lured into excessive purchases is sensed by the salesman and this increases his feelings of
guilt.   He tries to reassure both himself and the housewife that
he can be trusted and will do no harm.

Routemen are extremely reluctant to make "cold calls."   They
hate to have "the door slammed in their faces."   They prefer to
approach people only after some trust and confidence have been
built up through recommendation or acquaintanceship.   New
customers are distrustful at the start.

Many housewives like to help out the routeman.   They like to
feel they are important to him and that he must keep in their
good graces.

The routeman likes to think of himself as being a psychologist-
educator rather than as simply a salesman.   This reassures him
of his own worth.   Jewel provides him reassurance by offering
good products and having policies which back him up.   The
routeman likes to feel about his job as if he were running a business of his own.

The routeman's wife often keeps the books, takes care of the
stock, and otherwise participates in her husband's work.   She
feels she deserves credit for this and that her role is not properly
appreciated.

The report recommended that the routemen be helped to
understand the full psychological significance of the sales rela-

tionship, what high- and low-pressure selling mean to the customer, and how the methods can be combined successfully. High-pressure selling might be introduced indirectly through persuasive sales aids. Folders telling of the routeman, his family and their community activities, and a special gift independent of the premium plan were suggested as means of helping with new customers. Greater recognition of the role of the routeman's wife was advised, including monetary reward to give her a greater feeling of participation.

D. *Barriers To The Use Of Route Service*

Fear of temptation is a major obstacle. Having a routeman come to the door endangers the housewife's status as a smart buyer because he brings articles into the home, forceably engages her attention, and offers premiums. The new customer has to be won by methods which will assuage guilt feelings about getting into debt or being a lazy and inefficient housewife when buying from the route service.

Many consider route service more expensive, although this partially is a rationalization. It is not enough to convince the potential customer otherwise. She must be sold on the idea that trading with the route service is honorable and is done by many other people. Installment buying commonly is regarded as something for poor people and bad managers. It should be emphasized with new customers that trading with Jewel is on a cash basis and that the installment feature is only a voluntary measure for convenience.

Noncustomers expressed fear or dislike of "having a salesman come to the house." One reason is that they hate to turn him away or refuse to buy from him. Premiums frequently are regarded as a "trick," something that has to be paid for some way. Housewives complained of the nuisance of regular visits. Psychologically, the coming of a routeman every two weeks meant that the housewife's powers of resistance were going to be put to a test. Noncustomers frequently were vague about the coffee companies and did not know exactly what they did or whom they served.

Appendix C

INTERVIEW GUIDE

We are doing a study of housewives' grocery shopping habits.
We'd like to talk about the things you buy, the places you shop
at most frequently, and what grocery problems you have.

1. How do you usually plan your grocery buying? How often
   do you shop? Where? Do you make daily purchases? What
   are they? Do you buy groceries any other way?
2. (If not mentioned, does respondent ever buy from routemen?)
   Which routemen do you buy from? What items do you buy?
   How frequently? How do you like buying this way? (Probe
   for specific advantages, and disadvantages — price, quality,
   convenience, etc.)
3. What do you think of buying this way? How like? Any
   items like to buy which don't get now? (If respondent says
   canned goods, ask what else.)
4. When did you first begin using the Jewel routemen? How
   did it happen? (Get who, why, and what thought of idea.)
5. Let's talk about the bonus system and the premiums the
   routeman gives. How does it work? (Let respondent describe how the choice is made and how payments ef-
   fected.) . . . What do you think of this arrangement?
6. What premiums have you gotten? How did you decide upon
   those? (Talk it over with husband first?) What do you
   think of them? Any trouble with them?
7. Why do you think the company gives out "premiums"?
   How does the company benefit? What do you think about
   the policy of "trusting" the customer with the merchandise
   until it is paid out?
8. How about the budget system? How does it work? Ever
   used it? What get? How did it work out? What think of it
   in general?
9. What do you think about the Jewel catalogue? How compare with other catalogues? What kinds of items are advertised? Ever buy anything from the catalogue? How come to

do so? What think of the idea? What advantages and disadvantages?

10. Now let's talk about the system your routeman uses. What do you think about the customer's record chart? (Ask respondent where she keeps hers.) Do you always get a shopping list from your routeman? Use it? Do you budget in advance what you're going to spend on groceries? Buy things from the basket? (Get examples. Ask her to tell you about his last visit.)

11. How long have you had your present routeman? Did you know him socially before he became your routeman? How? (Families ever meet at gatherings, on street, etc.)

12. Is he first Jewel Tea man you've done business with? If not, what was the other like? How this one compare?

13. What kind of a person is your routeman? (Draw respondent out on this.)

14. What do you think about the way he does his job? Does he have any special techniques? Is he efficient, friendly, reliable or not? (Get examples.)

15. What do you think of him as a salesman? Really try to *sell* you or does he more or less just take your orders?

16. What does your husband think about your buying from the Jewel routeman? Did he ever object? Does he know him? Does he ever buy anything from the basket? From the catalogue? Ask you to buy things?

17. Do you know anyone who never buys from a routeman? Why doesn't she? What kind of a homemaker is she? How different from you?

The Image

Now that we've talked a good deal about Jewel, I'd like to sum up your ideas.

18. What's your general impression of Jewel Tea Company? What do you know about it? What kind of reputation does it have around here? How important would you say the company is to you compared to your routeman? How does it compare with the other grocery companies in town? With a company like Sears Roebuck? (Not in terms of size.)

Appendix D

INCOMPLETE SENTENCES

Now I have some incompleted sentences I would like you to complete for me. I'll read the first part and you finish it with the first thing that comes to your mind.

1. Waiting two weeks for an order _____
2. Door-to-door salesmen _____
3. The clothes in Jewel's catalogue _____
4. The hardest thing to order in advance _____
5. My husband thinks the Jewel man _____
6. Running out of soap _____
7. When I order my groceries _____
8. With my children, I need _____
9. The best coffee _____
10. It's hard to remember _____
11. Jewel Brand products _____
12. The best thing about buying from Jewel _____
13. When I am getting ready to have company _____
14. If only my routeman would _____
15. The bonus items _____
16. Buying appliances from a catalogue _____
17. I wish my routeman could _____
18. Around here, the catalogue _____

Appendix E

DIGEST OF PARTS OF REPORT: "THE JEWEL ROUTEMAN AND HIS CUSTOMER"

Two characteristics typically differentiate the Jewel route customer from other middle majority housewives:

1. She stays at home either because she likes to or because it is difficult for her to go out. Some women in this category are elderly, but most are mothers with two or more children and a lot of housework to do without hired help.
2. She puts a great deal of energy into establishing a routine and planning her shopping. Housewives who are able and willing to organize their shopping in detail find trading with Jewel more gratifying than those who are not.

Attitudes Toward the Jewel Route System

Delivery at home perhaps is the main attraction because it is convenient, saves time, and reduces the burden of outside shopping. It also serves a real emotional function. Inasmuch as middle majority housewives generally have considerable anxiety about the outside world and easily feel "put on the spot" when they shop in stores, they may well value a shopping system which brings products into their homes where they feel more at ease and more the master of things.

Most customers seem to understand the system of record keeping. Mastering it helps them demonstrate to themselves and their families that they are doing a good job of managing the home.

Premiums are a potent attraction but attitudes toward the premium system are mixed. While housewives like the idea of "getting something for nothing," they feel that no company really gives anything away and that premiums are just a way of getting one to buy more. They seem quite happy to regard the premium as a gift most of the time, however. Only when someone asks for an explanation of the system does the other attitude come into operation. The idea of receiving a premium first and paying for it through subsequent purchases is attractive. While this may be seen as "a way of keeping you buying," most customers have no real intention of stopping so this idea recedes into the background.

The premium system is distinctly less attractive to the upper middle class customer. She tends to regard premiums as a trick and disapproves of the installment buying feature of accepting an item which must be paid for later. She does not want to be obligated to the company. She emphasizes convenience much more than premiums as a reason for buying.

Jewel's route customers regard the prices as high. This is more an emotional than a rational response related to the housewife's feeling that she must be paying some place for home delivery and premiums. Prices, therefore, must somehow be higher than they are at the local store. This feeling probably does not seriously deter her from buying. She regards Jewel products as of very high quality, high enough to justify the "higher prices." This allows her to dismiss some other aspects of the system which make her uneasy.

One of the most common concerns of the route customer is that she will be tempted to buy more than she should. To guard against this, she often develops a "budget" to limit her purchasing. This means that she buys less than she might if she did not feel she had to control herself. To change this situation, she must be convinced that in buying more from Jewel, she would not be self-indulgent, but would be doing a better job as a housewife.

The customer wants the routeman to follow a regular schedule of visits. While the routemen do pretty well on regularity, deviations are one of the most frequent causes of complaint.

The Housewife's Relation to Her Jewel Routeman

The customer-routeman relationship is the keystone of the housewife's buying behavior. It determines whether positive attitudes toward the route system and the company get translated into purchases. The relationship is a delicate one in which many forces come into play to determine how two people get along together.

Generally, the customer is well satisfied with the routeman. He is regarded by middle majority women as important to them in her role of homemaker and the relationship is a friendly one. Upper middle class women have more detached, impersonal attitudes. By and large they think of the routeman as they would think of a servant. He should be honest, trustworthy, stay in his place, and cater to their needs.

While the relationship with the routeman is potentially gratifying, it also is potentially loaded with conflict and anxiety and requires self-control by the housewife and acquiesence to her by the routeman. Above all, the middle majority housewife wants a routeman who will allow her to maintain the position of control. For her, a good routeman is friendly, congenial, but "not too nice," submissive to her desires, and conforming to her requests and routines. He should be open and positive in his dealings, not taciturn, cool, or withdrawn. He should be sensitive to the amount of socializing desired by the customer, allow her to set the pace, and then follow it quickly and willingly. The housewife wants to be the center of the stage.

Since many middle majority housewives are not personally dominating or assertive in meeting "outsiders," they must depend quite heavily upon the routeman to allow them to direct (or feel that they are directing) the relationship. If he proves too assertive or demanding, her only defense is to withdraw completely.

Housewives were almost unanimous in mentioning their concern that the routeman not "high pressure" them. They also used other words along this line such as "being a pest," "not letting me decide," and "trying to sell me things I don't want." Very few accused their routeman of these things, but they seemed to be very aware of the possibility that their nice, quiet, submissive routeman might suddenly turn into an aggressive person.

Because the routeman is not only a representative of a company, but also a man she sees in her home biweekly, the housewife must establish an emotionally meaningful relationship with him without going beyond the bounds of propriety decreed by her highly moral middle majority world. It usually is not a question of what she might do if she did not exercise the proper control, but what feelings she might have about the routeman and what fantasies she might have about their relationship. Also, there is concern that if the relationship becomes too important to her, she may find herself acting more in accord with his desires and needs than with those of her family. Ideally, the customer-routeman relationship is one of fairly low, positive emotional tone. It should under no circumstances become intense (either in hostility or intimacy) because this arouses a great deal of anxiety.

Psychological techniques employed in this study revealed a persistent tendency by middle majority housewives to contrast their relationships to the routemen with those to their husbands. Our society formally defines the husband's role as one of over-all control and direction of the family. Thus, the housewife must worry about pleasing him. Avoiding his criticism over what is done in the home is no easy task, and the housewife may feel a good deal of tension in her role as homemaker because of the necessity of always considering how her husband might judge her social activities with men.

The housewife seeks a relationship with the routeman which is in many ways the reverse of her relationship to the husband. The husband can call her to account and tell her what she can or can not do, but the routeman should have no power in this regard. The housewife's fear of "high pressure" and worry about maintaining the position of control with the routeman is directly related to the husband's important status in the family.

If the housewife were to be caught between two dominating, directing men, she would be in an immoral position, according to her code. On the other hand, if the routeman becomes her ally in trying to satisfy or "get around" her husband and his demands, she is much more secure and can gain a great deal of satisfaction.

As a result of the concern the routeman generates, the housewife confronts him with a defensive ritual. Each customer evolves her own private etiquette to which the routeman is expected to conform. One housewife prefers that he wipe his feet very, very carefully before entering the kitchen, another that he put his basket on the chair rather than the table, another that he ring the bell in a certain way. There are special rules about when the routeman may come, where he stands, what he says, and what is done with the record chart. Often, each event must occur in a prescribed sequence. He may talk about certain things at certain times and he always must be soft spoken. After a housewife has dealt with a particular routeman for some time, if things go well, the ritual becomes routinized and she then can say, "We have an understanding, you know."

The Husband's Role in the Housewife-Jewel Relation

The housewife regards all shopping and homemaking functions as her province. The husband is entitled, from her point of view, only to judge the end result. She prefers that he stay out of the whole matter of shopping with Jewel, and, by and large, she seems successful in keeping him out.

Most customers said their husbands had never met the Jewel routeman and had no interest in him. There were enough mentions of a husband's irritation at this "other man in the house," however, to indicate that this is not an uncommon source of friction. While husbands seem somewhat touchy on the subject of a man entering the home regularly while they are away, there is little they can do about it except gripe about prices or some flagrant incident. Anything the routeman or company can do to communicate a sense of propriety would help cut off at the real source various husband complaints.

A fair number of husbands read the catalogue (general merchandise) and like the items shown. Some have received presents selected from the catalogue by their wives. The more active the husbands are in purchasing from the catalogue, the more positive they are likely to be in their attitudes toward the company.

Consumer Attitudes Toward the Jewel Tea Company

The housewives' image of the Jewel Tea Company can be outlined as follows:

> It is an old, established firm without being old-fashioned. The housewife feels that "they must be good because they lasted this long."
> It is a reliable firm — one that can be trusted to do

right by its customers and admit and rectify errors
quickly and willingly.

It puts out products of consistent good quality.

It is large, widely known, and respected. Its size is
evidence to the housewife that it must be a good company.

In spite of the favorable attitudes, the customers have only a
hazy conception of what the company is like aside from the above-
mentioned points which are general and somewhat vague. They
know little of its merchandising operations, testing laboratories,
and kitchens. By and large, the company is a distant, unfamiliar
operation.

The housewife's relation to the routeman is not closely tied in
with her attitudes toward the company. Emotionally, she con-
ceives of them as separate phenomena.

The company is seen as the guarantor of the excellence of both
its products and routemen. It serves the valuable function of
protecting the housewife against all the things she fears might go
wrong in her relation to the routeman. She expects the company
to provide a pleasing routeman and indulge her with premiums,
bonuses, and convenient deliveries.

As long as the company continues to fill the basic expectancies,
it can innovate with some impunity whereas the routeman, circumscribed by ritual and demands of the housewife, probably
cannot push new things too strongly without disturbing the delicate balance of his relationship with the customer and being
accused of "high-pressure" tactics.

Regional Differences

The pattern of attitudes, opinions, and behavior was quite consistent from one area to another (interviews were conducted in
three different areas). The few differences which did appear
seemed related more to differences in routemen than to regional
variations in customers.

Factors That Limit Buying From Jewel — A Summary

Factors which limit the customer's buying from Jewel are listed briefly on the basis of the analysis presented in the previous sections of the report:

Factors Related to the System of Route Shopping

1. The housewife has to be at home. Women who are active outside the home and who don't want to be tied down cannot be steady, active customers.
2. The housewife has to systematize her purchasing if she is to maximize her Jewel buying. Women who can't do this buy only a few items steadily and buy others in a more unorganized way at stores.
3. The routeman comes only once every two weeks. If the customer has difficulty systematizing or if she is impatient, she buys little. Housewives would prefer weekly visits.
4. Prices are believed to be high, although not out of line for the high quality merchandise.
5. There is suspicion of the premium system. This is found primarily among upper middle class customers, although some lower middle class women share it. If these people were persuaded that the premium system is a straightforward business proposition — neither a gift nor an enticement — they would feel more comfortable.

Factors Involved in the Relation to the Routeman

1. Turnover of routemen upsets the delicate adjustment the housewife has made and cuts down on her willingness to buy.
2. Deviation from the regular schedule by the routeman diminishes the customer's feeling of control over the relationship and her feeling of familiarity with it. It makes her anxious, then irritated.
3. Deflection by the routeman from a submissive, catering role. This challenges the housewife's position of mastery. She protects herself and punishes the routeman by withdrawing from full participation.

Factors in the Customer's Psychological Position

1. Central to all these factors limiting the customer's buying from Jewel is the fact that she must, for her own self-respect and security, retain unchallenged control of her relation to the Jewel route system. To do this she must:

   (a) be careful that she doesn't "overbuy" in her own eyes;
   (b) be careful that she not shift her loyalty from her husband and family to the Jewel man;
   (c) keep close watch on the self-indulgence she feels in the convenience of buying from Jewel and the personal gratification she gets in her relation to the routeman, and the receiving of premiums.

If she is to overcome these limitations to buying (which, in the most important respects are internal, rather than existing in the world outside her) she must be given experiences which decrease the potential guilt she may have about the temptations involved. She needs encouragement in the form of specific, rational reasons why she should buy from Jewel — why by so doing she is doing her job as a homemaker better, why by so doing she is spending her money wisely.

In general, the limitations to buying will be overcome when the rational elements involved in the situation which encourage buying are brought more prominently into her mental focus, while at the same time she still is able to retain both her position of control of the relationship and the personal and emotional gratification she gets from it.

Factors Involved in the Relation to the Company

1. The distance and vagueness of the company in the customer's eyes substract from the loyalty and trust which she might otherwise place in Jewel.

Appendix F

JEWEL'S CODE FOR CUSTOMER SATISFACTION

1. *To Call On You Regularly Every Two Weeks* — On the same day of the week — as nearly as possible at the same hour of the day.
2. *To Allow You To Shop Freely* — To make your own selections — To anticipate your needs and help you shop quickly, easily, with no red tape and no high pressure — you order only what you want.
3. *To Offer You Only High-Quality, Dependable Groceries, Household Supplies, And General Merchandise* — First class, fresh and clean. (Any goods not meeting our rigid specifications will be clearly identified and specially priced.)
4. *To Present All Merchandise Honestly* — No False claims — No deceptive descriptions — Honest packages — No concealed "carrying charges" on Budget purchases.
5. *To Offer You Full Value — By Sharing:*
   The savings from Jewel's large purchasing power in world markets.
   The money we would otherwise have to spend in national advertising.
   The benefits of efficient operation.
6. *To Cheerfully Advance To You As Your Premium, Useful, Valuable Items (general merchandise) Of Your Own Choice, Which You Receive As Your "Bonus for Trading"* . . . (This is Jewel's way of advertising.)
7. *To Leave With You (on your house card) An Accurate and Easy-to-Understand Record Of* — Your purchases and payments — Balance due on your premium — Balance due on your Budget Account.
8. *To Refund Your Money and Cheerfully, Without Argument, Take Back* — Any purchase that is not completely satisfactory to you.
9. *To Display An Interesting Variety of Merchandise For Your*

Selection — A full basket of useful items — Well-illustrated catalogs — Easy-to-order from Sales Flyers.

10. *To Serve You In A Friendly, Courteous, Helpful Manner At All Times* — *With Sincere Respect For You* — *Your Family* — *Your Home* — The Jewel Tea Co., Inc. promises that Jewel people everywhere will live up to this Code for Customer Satisfaction.

PART III

The Meaning of Motivation Research for Marketing Knowledge and Administration

CHAPTER XI

Toward Conceptual Schemes of Consumer Behavior

IN PART I of this book, we examined the state of thinking about the consumer, concluding that progress has been hobbled by restricted backgrounds and, consequently, by circumscribed ways of thinking and by limited methods of research. We observed that marketing research itself has been concerned mostly with techniques and amassing data rather than with evolving ideas as to what research should research. While there were reasons for this in terms of the needs of the times, it still represented a serious barrier because the most difficult part of gaining a greater understanding of consumer behavior is that of learning what the right questions are to ask.

With this in mind, we took a look at some recent work referred to as motivation research, examples of which appear in Part II. They illustrate applications to marketing problems of various ways of thinking about people and about research which stem for the most part from several of the behavioral sciences. They were commented upon both in Chapter IV and in commentaries on the cases. It is not our purpose to go into more detail here. But what broader observations can we make about the selected studies and the development they represent?

In the first place, it is apparent that that part of the scientific approach which we may call idea getting or hypothesis formulation now is coming in for new emphasis and more systematic attention. And the manner in which this is happening seems to presage a new era of conceptual development in marketing. It involves behavioral specialists who are contributing to this result in two important ways which often go hand in hand. One is by consultation which represents a direct application of their concepts, knowledge, and judgments whether research is involved or not. The other is through their investigative approaches to obtain an improved flow of data from people which, in the hands of skilled interpreters, will be revealing about the nature of what is being investigated. Hence, there is a much greater use of research in a creative role — research designed to aid directly in the creative thought process by which ideas are brought into consciousness. In other words, research is being undertaken specifically to help give rise to the ideas which later may be the subject of research in the evaluative sense.

The effect of many of these efforts has been to develop the psychological and social aspects in addition to the material and economic. While marketing in the past has recognized the importance of emotional factors, it has had no systematic way of thinking about which ones may be present in a given situation and of determining how and why they are important. The case for making greater use of the behavioral fields rests on the recognition that buying and consumption are human acts serving human purposes about which marketing has known too little. The assumption is that they can be better understood if we know more about what people are like and what kinds of lives they lead. This is where behavioral theories, concepts, and methods enter the picture.

Some researchers have thought primarily in terms of individual psychological factors while others have been more concerned with cultural and social influences. A number of different techniques have been employed. This is to be expected. Behavioral specialists differ in training, experience, and thinking. No one has a complete background in any one of the behavioral fields, much less in all of them. Recognizing this, several organizations have taken care to bring together on their staffs people of somewhat different view-

points. Another reason for differences is that the fields themselves are in a young stage of development even though important advances have been made. Thinking and research
within them continue on an expanding scale. While current behavioral studies in marketing can represent important
forward steps, it is probable, of course, that they will prove
to be very incomplete developments compared with what will
come in the future.

A major feature of much of the work is the conscious recognition that such things as products and brands have meanings for people; that they are, in fact, symbols. Once this is
seen, it opens the way for the study of symbolic communication. In many of the motivation studies, the behavioral
specialists have attempted to develop pictures of these meanings by investigating the feelings from which meaning comes.
No single attempt is complete, of course, but it may contribute to our understanding. It is through a number of such
efforts that marketing can build broader and more useful
concepts of the consumer, product, brand, the buying process, and the like.

CONCEPT OF A CONSUMER-PRODUCT RELATIONSHIP

Various of these concepts may, in turn, give rise to larger
concepts or conceptual schemes which are more or less systematized plans for looking at things. Many of the studies,
for example, imply an over-all concept of a relationship between the consumer and the product (or the brand, the salesman, etc.). Let us consider this matter further in reference
to the consumer-product relationship. The latter has several
facets including the psychological, social, cultural, economic,
and material. This broad concept serves as a reminder that
a product may fill several functions at once. The term, "relationship," implies that the consumer has expectations of a
product in terms of his own needs; that he has feelings about
it. These feelings may be very strong for some products

and brands and weak for others because of differences in the character of the needs to be met and the varying abilities of the products or brands to meet them.

In order to explore the nature of the consumer-product relationship, it may be useful to keep in mind a number of things such as these:

> That the consumer is a human being with certain basic needs and a certain concept of himself as a person; that he may or may not be conscious of these things.
>
> That he was reared in a culture which dictated to a large extent how these needs were to be handled.
>
> That he has (and aspires to) a certain social status and belongs to various social groups, informal and, perhaps, formal, by which he needs to be accepted.
>
> That he has limited financial resources for acquiring products and services.
>
> That his buying takes place in a certain situation which in itself influences what he does. We refer here to the time of day he shops, the proximity of stores to his home, the brands carried by the stores of his choice, the availability of parking space, the exposure of goods through displays and shelf position, and the like.

The above constitute categories of factors of possible importance to his buying behavior and represent a broad framework for thinking. The latter can serve to give a sense of direction to research by pointing up considerations and suggesting that a number of related factors may be working together in determining buying action.

For illustrative purposes, let us elaborate such a framework as an aid to thinking about the question of why people use a given brand of coffee. Without the benefit of exploratory research, we shall list everything we can readily think of as possibly being a part of the explanation. We shall do this in terms of satisfactions a person may get from buying or drinking coffee, any of which may be associated with a particular brand and influence brand selection. Here they are:

Satisfaction from Coffee's Generic Qualities: There is sensual pleasure in drinking coffee, derived from its taste, strength, aroma, warmth, color, clarity, and feel in the mouth. A person may drink it for its effects of relaxation or of stimulation. It can help bolster one's self-control and serve as a means of temporary escape from the usual demands of work and living. Its stimulating effect might help one to overcome inertia, to wake up in the morning.

Satisfaction from Participation in Social Activity: Coffee is a symbol of sociability. This is apparent at coffee breaks and at social events ranging from neighborhood visits to formal dinners. Because of the cultural role of coffee, the drinking of it may be accompanied by a sense of belonging to a larger group.

Satisfaction of Other Personal Needs: The drinking of coffee or of a particular brand of coffee may help a person meet psychological needs related to his self-image. For example, if he is particularly concerned about exhibiting masculine characteristics as they are defined in our culture, he may drink coffee instead of tea or he may tend to choose a brand which is seen as more of a symbol of masculinity than others. He may be influenced by implications of social status and choose a brand because it connotes prestige, fine taste, connoisseurship, or because it has other meanings regarded more as appropriate for the social status of the user. If his need for a feeling of security is especially great, he may tend to choose a well-known brand made by a large, substantial company. If he is eager to appear as modern and up to date in accepting new things, he may choose a brand that fits into this picture rather than one which is associated by most people with good, old-fashioned cooking. A need for a feeling of power may make him more inclined to use a strong brand. The need to feel mature and competent may play some part in his drinking coffee (a symbol of maturity) rather than milk or tea and choosing one brand rather than another because of maturity differences in brand images. A person may elect to drink no coffee, drink caffein-free coffee, or limit his consumption of regular coffee because he feels that drinking coffee is harmful and, therefore, wrong or immoral. There is considerable evidence that one of the reasons women have resisted accepting instant coffee is that it connotes laziness and violates their concept of being a good housewife. The desire to be identified with or accepted by certain people may lead to the use of a brand used by them.

Satisfaction from Pleasing or Displeasing Members of the Family Group: The housewife may cater to the brand preferences of one or more members of her family if she wishes to please them. It also is possible, of course, that she may deliberately ignore them as a means of expressing hostility.

Satisfaction from Complimenting and Gaining Approval of Guests: The desire for this satisfaction may work to the benefit of the more popular or more distinctive brands or types of coffee. It has to do with the brand or type of coffee being widely recognized as a symbol of fine taste, friendliness, good hospitality, and the like.

Satisfaction from the Act of Purchase Itself: The housewife may have a strong need to be regarded as a good homemaker in the sense of being a good purchasing agent. Hence she may be particularly attracted by considerations of price, quality, and more cups per pound. Her brand choice also may be a function of the fact that she likes to trade at a particular store. This means that her purchase will be made from the brands it carries and that she may be favorably disposed to buying the retailer's private brand or some other brand which he promotes. Her satisfaction from trading at the store may come from its reputation, pleasant relationships with the sales people, its use of trading stamps, or from various convenience considerations such as the store's location, parking facilities, check cashing service, and charge accounts.

Satisfaction from Other Factors: Satisfaction may be gained from the meanings a particular kind of package has for a person because of the material of which it is made, its shape, size, and color. The shopper may prefer to select goods from particular shelf locations or displays of merchandise. There are no doubt other sources of satisfaction.

IMPLICATIONS OF THE RELATIONSHIP CONCEPT

The above points were listed for illustrative purposes. They represent possible dimensions. It is a matter for research to determine whether they actually are operative in a given situation, and, if they are, how much influence they exert on the buying decision. More would be known about this, of course, had the list of factors been developed with the aid of exploratory detailed interviews interpreted by competent specialists in human behavior.

Now, let us consider further the importance of a conceptual scheme. After all, has not marketing in the past been concerned with many of the things mentioned in our illustration? The answer is "yes." But this is only a part of the story. While many of the individual items certainly are not strangers, whether they actually came up for attention in a given situation has been too much a matter of chance. It has been all too usual for marketers, limited as they necessarily are by their backgrounds of training and experience, to guess about what things might be relevant, one or several factors being pretty much pulled out of the air in the absence of a well-rounded understanding of how they may be related to the total picture of meanings.

A concept such as the consumer-product relationship, then, provides a more systematic way of thinking. It can suggest factors for investigation and, perhaps, call attention to the need for the services of specialists to deal with some of them. Once items of possible importance are identified, an improved basis exists for deciding which ones should be studied. At least the decision can be made with a greater awareness that there are other factors as well.

Perhaps we should point out here that any of the satisfactions cited in the consumer-coffee relationship as sketched above, even though they relate to qualities of coffee in general or to the act of purchase, might be associated by the

consumer with a particular brand and be part of its image.
While coffee itself is a symbol of sociability, for example,
some brands may be considered to be stronger on this count
than others. With this in mind, the relationship approach
suggests a number of questions for research: What images
do people have of the various brands? How strong are they?
What differences exist among brands? How important are
these images in influencing sales? What images seem to attract what kinds of people? What constitutes a desirable
image for a given brand of coffee? What factors seem to make
for brand loyalty?

THEORY OF CONSUMER BEHAVIOR

Let us turn for a moment to that complex subject and
long-range goal — a theory of consumer behavior. In our
opinion, it is from many detailed explorations of the various
relationships with which marketing is concerned that a
meaningful, over-all theory of consumer behavior is most
likely to be developed. These studies would attempt to add
to understanding of consumer behavior by viewing it in relation to the total picture of human behavior of which it is
a part. They are likely to be most fruitful if use is made of
the relevant viewpoints and research techniques of all behavioral fields.

A broad framework for a beginning can be developed by
integrating key concepts and knowledge from several fields —
particularly dynamic psychology, anthropology, sociology,
and marketing. The starting point, according to our current thinking, should be the basic needs of the individual.
In this connection, we would draw heavily upon what the
psychoanalysts have learned. There is a long and challenging road from basic needs to a specific act. An adequate
explanation of consumer behavior will be developed only
when the psychological aspects are treated together with the

cultural, interpersonal, situational, economic, and material which determine how man's needs finally are handled.

It should be apparent that by a theory of consumer behavior, we have in mind no single statement or formula. We are very skeptical of attempts to oversimplify behavior by lumping it into one or several broad categories of one dimension or by applying across the board the ideas of just one school of thought. An adequate conceptual scheme must encourage the recognition and explanation of differences among people, products, brands, and situations.

IMPORTANCE OF CONCEPTUAL DEVELOPMENT

The need for more meaningful concepts and conceptual schemes of the consumer and the things with which marketing deals was developed in earlier chapters. They are of vital importance because strategy is built upon assumptions which grow out of them. Research which serves to challenge old concepts and build new ones, then, tends to force rethinking of basic policy. This was illustrated in the case examples in Part II. The findings of the study of the meanings of automobile insurance and what people want from an insurance company not only suggested a major change in advertising approach, but also related to service and the training and conduct of agents and claim adjusters. The study on what coffee means to people served as a focal point for new efforts in advertising, merchandising, and trade relations. The investigation of the meanings of automobiles, undertaken for the purpose of improving advertising content, appeared to have implications for product design and selling. The research into a food company's home route system embodied a new way of looking at selling, and the results related to the entire sales effort including the selection and training of routemen and the handling of premium and installment buying plans.

Developing better concepts and conceptual schemes is important to marketing because progress consists of the evolution of new mental images of what things are or should be; more meaningful ways of looking at things. The change from the concept that "the world is flat" to the concept that "the world is round," for example, opened new horizons. Perhaps this is more dramatic than any conceptual change we can expect in marketing. Perhaps not.

CHAPTER XII

Some Observations Relating to Research Techniques

ASSOCIATED with the behavioral science concepts in motivation research have been techniques especially suitable for the study of buying behavior. The two, of course, necessarily are interrelated. Techniques rest on assumptions as to what people are like and consequent judgments as to what constitute appropriate means of obtaining data from them. In addition, their value in use depends directly upon the quality of the conceptual thinking and skill of their user.

In this chapter we shall examine the characteristics of the more commonly used techniques which relate to their ability to obtain valid data. Our objective is to provide useful information for the marketing executive who wishes to take whatever steps he can to improve his chances of getting sound research in the first place, and who later must decide whether to accept the results as a basis for action. Drawing on this background, the problems of appraising research findings will be considered further in the chapter that follows.

FUNCTIONS OF RESEARCH

So that our discussion may be as meaningful as possible, it will be based upon actual applications, drawn largely from our selected cases in which the techniques were described and illustrated. Techniques are question-asking devices employed in the process of inquiry which is research. Inquiries, however, can be made for different reasons. At the outset, then, it is well to identify the principal research functions for which a technique's appropriateness must be judged.

In Chapter III we noted the two essential elements of the

scientific approach (which marketing research represents) to be (a) getting ideas and (b) testing them. Here, then, are the major research functions. The first is essentially creative, the second evaluative. Both are involved in many researches, often concurrently. There may be great variation in emphasis, however, both among studies and among their parts or stages. This can be seen in the questions which appear below. They represent a more detailed description of purposes for which data may be gathered. They may be regarded either as separate activities or as constituents of an integrated research program:

What Is Going On? (The Control Function) Information may be gathered to keep management informed so that control may be exercised over business operations. Estimates of sales, share of market, and sales potential are examples. They may be useful in directing and appraising the over-all sales effort and in signaling the existence of special problems. The figures reflect what is happening, but do not in themselves explain it.

How Do You Account for It? (Hypothesis Formulation) This is the idea-getting or hypothesis-formulating function which may be served by research undertaken specifically to aid in the creative process by which ideas are brought into consciousness. It is receiving more and more attention as interest mounts in seeking better explanations of consumer behavior. It may consist of any of a number of steps designed to reveal more about the nature of people, things, and relationships.

Is the Explanation Valid? (Hypothesis Testing) The objective here is to check on the soundness and importance of ideas and tentative explanations by measuring the prevalence and/or strength of a factor, a condition, or a reaction to given stimuli. This may be done by using a greater number and variety of tests and by increasing the number of cases studied or both.

What, Then, Should Be Done? (Prescription for Action) This step involves reasoning from the evidence obtained (above) on the nature of the motivation, behavior, or situation with which one must deal in order to determine what course or alternative courses of action appear to be appropriate.

What Results Can Be Expected? (Prediction) **Predictions** as to the nature and/or strength of response to a proposed course of action may be made solely on the basis of the understanding of a situation gained from the results of the preceding steps. For additional evidence, however, various tests may be employed to note reactions to stimuli believed to resemble actuality. They may take the form of specially designed survey questions, product tests, advertising copy tests, market tests, and the like. The prediction may be that a given product or promotional offering will meet with a favorable or unfavorable response or that one alternative will outperform another. The predictions may or may not be expressed in numbers. The precision of the estimate may vary with the need for accuracy as well as the margins of error normally associated with the tests employed.

How Successful Was the Action, Once Taken? (Evaluation of Performance) This step consists of attempting to find out whether the action achieved its purpose. It may include an examination of sales figures or the use of tests to measure such things as advertising readership and changes in knowledge, impressions, and attitudes.

The suitability of a given question-asking device will depend importantly upon the relative emphasis to be placed on the creative and the evaluative functions (which often overlap) and the kind of data desired from people. Relevant to these considerations are the following two ways in which techniques can vary:

> They can vary as to the degree of freedom allowed the respondent in what he says and how he says it. On the one hand, the response may be restricted to a choice between alternative answers like "yes" and "no." At the other extreme, the question may not be specific. The respondent may be allowed to say whatever comes into his mind in his own words which are recorded in full.

They can vary in the extent to which their purpose is apparent or disguised. If the purpose is apparent, the respondent presumably is aware of the meaning of his response; if it is disguised, he presumably is not.

A question's ability to produce meaningful data also depends upon how well the interviewer and the interpreter perform their roles. As we shall see, the different techniques vary in the demands they make of these people. With this background, we now shall consider the following techniques in turn: direct questions used in formal questionnaires, the qualitative or "depth" interview, the group interview, and projective techniques.

DIRECT QUESTIONS

Let us first consider the direct questions upon which marketing research has relied so heavily. They can serve as a useful reference point against which to view other techniques. A direct question, in our use of the term, is one which asks for specified information in a relatively straightforward manner. While many such questions are employed in the course of qualitative or depth interviewing, our attention here will be confined to those appearing in formal questionnaires. Even with this restriction, however, we note that direct questions appeared in most of the studies described in our case examples.

The conventional market surveys described in the State Farm Mutual and the Pan-American Coffee Bureau cases relied entirely on direct questions, as did the Dieting Study. The motivational study for the Coffee Bureau started with informal depth interviews and worked toward a structured questionnaire which included many direct questions. This is a rather common pattern which is being used more and more. The automobile study is a somewhat similar example. It started with unstructured interviews which led to developing more focused interview guides, projective devices, and a number of attitude and opinion questions which were direct in character. The Donahue Sales Corporation study used only a few direct questions relating to women's preferences for various forms of closure for dresses.

The direct questions in these studies differed in kind and form. For example, those in the State Farm Mutual and the Coffee Bureau market surveys were not disguised as to purpose and most of them restricted the interviewee's response. They took several forms, including the following:

Yes — No Question
Do you ever serve iced coffee?   (Yes or No)

Multiple Choice
What does your husband think of the coffee served in your home?

Generally very good	_____	Generally poor	_____
Generally good	_____	Sometimes good,	
Generally fair	_____	Sometimes poor	_____
		Don't know	_____

Comments: _____

Ranking
Here are some of the things about auto insurance companies that some people feel are important. Now can you tell me which one of these is most important to you personally? And of these left, which one is most important? (Proceed until all items have been ranked)

_____ Quick settling of claims
_____ Low cost of insurance
_____ Good service from local agent
_____ Well-known company
_____ Claim adjusters in all parts of U.S.
_____ Fair treatment by company
_____ Installment plan for payment
_____ Other (explain)

Request for Specific Fact
Which member of the family drives this car most?

Others with Greater Freedom of Response

Here are some nondisguised questions which allow the respondent more freedom in his answering:

What reasons were more important to you in choosing the company you did? Any others?

Which closure (of several types mentioned) would you prefer? Why? Why not others?

How do you judge a good cup of coffee?

The questions used in the Dieting Study were largely of the restricted response type, but their purpose was not necessarily apparent. The questionnaire represented an indirect approach for checking certain hypotheses which were unknown to the respondent. For example, she was not asked directly how strict her standards for weight control were or what her social status was. But she was asked for answers from which the desired information could be inferred and used to check the hypothesis that standards of weight control vary by social status. The following question will serve as a further example:

When you feel generally nervous and unhappy, do you usually eat more?_____ Eat less?_____ Neither _____

The immediate purpose, of course, was to obtain the requested information. The respondent would not know the meaning of her response, however, which had to do with checking on clinical evidence that overeating and overweight are associated with feelings of dependency and depression.

Obtaining Data

A most important characteristic of direct questions, relating to their ability to gather the desired quantity and type of data, is that they restrict response, most of them to a marked extent. If the questioner knows what he wants and can get it in reply to a specific question, this is an advantage. If not (as often is the case in the early stages) , it is a limitation.

Restriction of response may take place in different ways. The very process of asking a series of direct questions may have an inhibiting effect by evoking a defensive reaction against interrogation. The respondent may hold back because of a feeling that there are "right" answers and that he will be judged, at least silently, by the interviewer on the basis of his response. The specificity of the question itself limits the scope of the reply. As the preceding examples illustrate, some questions force a choice among answers supplied by the questionnaire. In these cases, there is the danger of putting the researcher's words in the respondent's mouth, and preventing the expression and recording of ideas and feelings which might be important to him. If the question implies that the respondent should have had conscious reasons for what he did, he may give some whether he actually had them or not. This is particularly likely to happen if he is presented with a check-list of items. The temptation to make at least a few checks may well be strong. Any reason omitted from such a list is likely to be ignored or at least slighted. Ranking questions can lead to distortions for another reason as well. People may be unable to rank listed reasons because they are not accustomed to thinking in terms of ranking or because the items are not meaningful in the abstract.

It is difficult to allow for much freedom of response in a formal questionnaire. While there may appear to be considerable latitude in the open "why" question, this often proves illusory in practice. If the question comes up rather abruptly, the respondent has little time to think in answering. The interviewer often is able to do but little probing to help draw out the respondent's ideas or clarify his meaning. Vague and stereotyped responses are likely to be the result. As greater provision is made for flexibility in this regard, the approach moves from that of a formal questionnaire to that of an informal, depth interview.

In addition to the considerations of the wording and form

of the question, valid results also depend upon the respondent's understanding what is wanted and being both able and willing to give it. These conditions are fulfilled in a number of research situations. Many facts and feelings can be verbalized fairly readily. The direct question should work satisfactorily in tapping clearly formulated ideas and explanations which do not conflict with the respondent's ideas of how he should think or act. It should be useful, for example, for learning about user reactions to major product features, especially the practical ones. If something major is wrong with the product, a direct question is likely to discover the fact.

Inability and unwillingness of people to give complete and accurate information about their buying behavior, however, are major obstacles facing the user of direct questions. A number of the difficulties were noted in earlier chapters and in the commentaries on the State Farm Mutual and the Pan-American Coffee Bureau cases. We shall attempt to summarize them here.

People may be unable to answer simply because they do not know. They cannot tell you directly about factors of which they are not conscious, and there is growing evidence that much buying motivation is unconscious. The existence of unconscious influences has been demonstrated often in tests which first ask people which of several items they prefer and later allow them to select one to keep. It is not uncommon to find that the item actually selected is not the one for which preference was openly expressed. In addition, many persons seldom do much conscious thinking about why they do what they do and, therefore, may be unable to readily produce much in the way of an explanation on the spur of the moment. They may be unable to recall immediately reasons of which they once were aware, and they may lack the necessary words or concepts to express themselves.

In regard to unwillingness, the respondent is likely to

avoid discussing anything of great emotional consequence with a strange person (the interviewer), especially in response to an abrupt question. There are cultural taboos against expressing emotions. A person is not likely to give answers which tend to reflect upon himself because they are socially unacceptable or because they do not seem to make sense logically. Distortion also may result from efforts to please and impress the interviewer by giving answers the respondent thinks the interviewer wants to hear or by giving false answers which he thinks will make him appear in a favorable light.

The limitation of unwillingness to answer frequently can be circumvented by devising direct questions which together comprise an indirect approach such as was represented in the Dieting Study. Here the interviewee was asked for information which she could and presumably did supply while being unaware of the real meaning of her response in terms of the hypotheses being tested. Devising disguised questions requires uncommon skill and ingenuity, however, and, most important, it presumes that you know what it is you want to ask about.

Handling the Data

The formal questionnaire offers important administrative and cost benefits. Restricted-response questions can be answered quickly which cuts down on the interview time required. In addition, the questions can be administered fairly easily in the field by the average survey interviewer. While there is a danger that he may inadvertently influence what is said, misunderstand it, or fail to record it correctly, these dangers probably are at a minimum with direct questions.

Responses can be coded easily; in fact, many can be precoded. Inasmuch as the assumption usually is made that the answers mean what they say, no major interpretive step is necessary prior to coding. The responses can be tabulated readily and analyzed statistically by machine. These are major advantages in terms of savings in time and cost. Qualitative interviewing and interpretation take much longer and require more highly skilled personnel.

Another feature of a formal questionnaire which often is regarded as an advantage over the informal qualitative interview is that all respondents are asked the same questions in the same way. Hence, the assumption of standardized stimuli can be made in viewing the resulting measurements.

Interpretive problems, however, may be present with open "why" questions due to meager or vague answers and to varying interpretations of the question by respondent. For example, some people, in responding to a "why" question about a purchase, may answer in terms of product attributes; others in terms of the use to which the product is to be put; still others may speak of influences which reminded them of their need or directed them to a particular store or brand. If the purpose is to note what kinds of answers are given, then this is not a problem. If the objective, however, is to assess the relative importance of different considerations, then there is a question of comparability of totals because of differences in initial interpretations of the question.

Concluding Remarks

There has been a tendency among marketing researchers to give the direct question an unchallenged position of assumed validity. This is understandable in view of its administrative advantages and the assumption commonly, if wrongly, made that buying behavior is governed largely by conscious and rational thought.

There are a number of reasons why the direct question may not work when it comes to finding out how and why people buy. The difficulties involved have led a good number of researchers to conclude that direct questions seldom are useful in the area of motivation.   Whether this is so would seem to depend upon the main purpose of the questioning, the nature of the subject under investigation, and whether disguised or nondisguised questions are used.   If the circumstances are such that meaningful data can be obtained by direct questions, important administrative and financial advantages can be realized.   The latter relate principally to the gathering of facts you already have decided that you want and to the testing of hypotheses.   Inasmuch as the direct question does not permit a free, full flow of data from the respondent, it has limited value in the exploratory or idea-getting stage of research.

QUALITATIVE OR DEPTH INTERVIEWS

One of the more striking trends in marketing research has been the growing use of open, informal interviews in order to minimize some of the problems of gathering data discussed in connection with direct questions.   Probably the most popular words for what we are talking about are "depth interview" and "qualitative interview." [1]   While they will be employed interchangeably in this book, this will be done with full recognition that neither has a standardized, specific meaning.   Both are relative terms which have been used to refer to such a variety of work that it would be well in practice to ask anyone using either to explain exactly what he means.

In the motivational sense, the concept of depth refers to the psychological level of the material.   An interview is deep, then, to the extent that it uncovers basic predispositions — unconscious feelings, needs, conflicts, fears, and the like. Many marketing investigations claiming a motivational label

[1] Interviews of this general type also have been referred to as detailed, informal, intensive, conversational, and nondirective.   See "Questionnaire Preparation and Interviewer Technique," a report by a subcommittee of the Marketing Research Techniques Committee of the American Marketing Association, *Journal of Marketing*, Vol. XIV, No. 3, October 1949, pp. 399–433.

have not been very deep in this way. In many cases, "depth" has been used more to indicate an intensive exploration regardless of the extent to which an effort has been made to find out what kind of a person behaves in a certain way or holds certain attitudes.

In this section, our interest is in conversational interviews which seek free, flowing responses which are recorded as nearly verbatim as possible for later interpretation by specialists in the study of human behavior. This, of course, allows for considerable variation in psychological depth. Generally, for these interviews there is no set list of questions which must be asked in a prescribed way. The interviewee is encouraged to talk at length in the subject area of interest. The emphasis is on letting the respondent lead the way in order to find out what is important to him and why, and to allow opportunity for unanticipated responses to be made. The objective is a detailed study of each respondent rather than a series of short answers to questions prepared in advance.

The term "depth interview" has been so much in vogue recently that it frequently has been used to refer to work which does not fit into the rather broad description just presented. There are marked differences among researchers in their understanding of the concept and in their skill in obtaining and interpreting qualitative data. Some so-called depth interviews have consisted of little more than a series of relatively open response direct questions for which short answers were recorded which represented the interviewer's version of what was said rather than a word-for-word account. Statistical tabulations of the literal responses have been attempted by persons lacking in ability to discern many of the meanings in the interview reports. The result in these cases, of course, has been a limited contribution to the understanding of the nature of the subject under investigation.

Our remarks will relate to interviews of the general description given earlier. For illustrative purposes, we shall draw upon the depth interviews described in the selected cases in Part II which represent work of experienced people with behavioral science training.

Obtaining Data

Our examples illustrate the growing practice of varying the qualitative interviews within an individual study as the nature of the research task changes. The early interviews usually are the most open or nondirective as to response because at this stage the least is known about what dimensions of the subject should be explored. For the first interviews in the Pan-American Coffee Bureau motivational study, for example, the interviewers were told that "it would be most helpful . . . if you could just get people talking freely on all their feelings about coffee for an hour or so." They were instructed to "encourage maximum spontaneity and feel free to probe any area that seems likely to be significant." While a brief interview guide was supplied, the topics listed on it were to be explored "only after the fullest possible rambling free association is exhausted."

As more is learned about what should be investigated, interview guides usually are prepared to focus the conversation to a greater extent. This is illustrated in the Coffee Bureau, Automobile, Donahue, and Jewel studies. The guides frequently started with very broad questions and became more specific to make sure that each interview would provide data needed for checking certain hypotheses.

A major advantage of the qualitative interview, properly conducted, is that it provides favorable circumstances for the respondent to recall and talk. There probably is a greater opportunity for good rapport to be established, and the informal, conversational tone can do much to alleviate inhibitions and embarrassment surrounding product use. The process of following one's own thoughts can bring out information which would otherwise be neglected or regarded as unimportant. It can produce a wealth of detailed material on personal frames of reference and feelings. The verbatim records of responses provide evidence on the significance of what is said not only through the content, but the way in which it is said and the apparent omissions. The qualitative interview, then, is especially useful for exploratory purposes. Its advantages for identifying considerations and suggesting hypotheses mean that this technique is strong where the formal questionnaire is weak.

In order to dispel any confusion which may exist on this point, we shall emphasize that the depth interviews characteristic of motivation research are not psychiatric interviews in a clinical sense. Their object is not therapeutic nor is it to get a detailed personality profile of individual respondents. Instead, they seek to identify important motivational patterns characteristic of the product or activity being studied. Personality data may come from the interview itself, the respondents revealing something about what they are like as people by what they say and how they say it. In addition, various projective devices frequently are used in order to test hypotheses involving personality dimensions believed to be important to the subject of study. The Donahue case provides a marked example of this in that it included several personality tests relating to hypotheses about characteristics of heavy sewers, light sewers, and nonsewers.

Interviewing

Effective use of depth interviews assumes that people will talk freely and honestly and that the free association principle will be given a chance to operate. To a large extent, satisfactory response depends upon the interviewer's skill in establishing a productive relationship with the respondent and in probing to help him express himself fully.

The ability to develop rapport quickly is a function of

the interviewer's personality, training, and experience. It also depends upon such characteristics as apparent social class, race, and age. A well-dressed interviewer of the upper middle social class, for example, probably would be viewed with suspicion by a houewife of the upper lower social class. Similarly, a white person may be ineffective in interviewing a Negro and vice versa. These considerations are important in determining whether the atmosphere will be conducive to free expression. The experience of several firms which have done a great amount of qualitative interviewing has been that obtaining the cooperation of respondents is not a serious problem if the factors just mentioned are favorable. On the contrary, many housewives seem to enjoy the rare experience of someone being interested enough in how they think and feel to listen to them at length.

The actual interviewing itself, of course, calls for a relatively high degree of skill. There is a greater chance for interviewer bias than with a formal questionnaire because of the freedom allowed. It is essential that the interviewer be able to get more than superficial responses by drawing out the respondent's thoughts and feelings. He also must be able to record the proceedings substantially verbatim.

The above demands mean that interviewer selection, training, and supervision are of special importance. While the usual survey field interviewers cannot be assumed to be competent qualitative interviewers, it does not follow that the latter must be trained social scientists. The interviewer's task usually is to obtain data, not interpret it. While he should have an understanding of the interviewing process, interviewing skill is something that can be developed without a great deal of academic knowledge. Many of the research firms doing this kind of work rely primarily upon housewives who are particularly good in getting other people to talk.

Qualitative interviewing and the interpretation of the data both are time consuming and require the services of more highly trained personnel than are necessary for surveys using questionnaires of direct questions. Therefore, the cost per interview is considerably higher. This often represents a compelling reason for moving from informal to more formal approaches as the research progresses.

Inasmuch as the conclusions drawn from qualitative research depend upon what meanings are seen in the data, interpretation is the crucial step. It is for this function more than any other that a need exists for people well trained in human behavior and skilled in working with qualitative data. Meanings apparent to an experienced worker can be missed entirely by one lacking in background. Because of its importance, we shall explore the nature of the interpretive process in some detail.

Interpretation When Formal Questionnaire Is Used

Let us begin our examination by considering further this question: when, and to what extent, does interpretation enter the picture when direct questions are used? In order for survey responses to be tabulated, some judgment must be made as to their meaning. Appropriate categories of meanings must be identified so that the responses can be counted. Once this has been done, statistical analysis may proceed to determine whether differences in response exist between groupings of respondents, and, if they do, to try to explain them by cross-tabulations with other data.

The categorization of responses may be relatively simple. For example, take the question, "Do you own an automobile? Yes_____, No_____." Here only two alternative answers are provided and the categories they represent can be coded in advance. In this case, there appears to be little risk involved in the researcher's assumption that he knew what the possible answers were and what they meant.

These same assumptions may have been made in preparing this question:

Here are some of the things about auto insurance companies that some people feel are important. Now can you tell me which one of these is most important to you personally? And of these left, which one is the most important? (Proceed until all items have been ranked.)

_____ Quick settlement of claims

_____ Fair treatment by company

_____ Well-known company

_____ Low cost of insurance

_____ Good service from local agent

_____ Claim adjusters in all parts of U.S.

_____ Installment plan for payments

It is less certain here that all the important categories of possible answers actually were represented by the alternatives. The likelihood that they were depends to a large extent on how much was known about this from exploratory research and other sources. There also is less certainty as to just what meaning the listed alternatives had for each respondent. Some were more specific than others. In any event, standard meanings were assumed and, therefore, the categories of meaning were determined in advance of the field work rather than afterward.

With open response questions, the respondents supply their own answers in their own words. Someone must examine them to determine their meaning, identify the appropriate categories of answers, and code them accordingly. This is qualitative interpretation, normally on a small scale. Usually, the assumption is made that the responses to direct questions mean what they say they mean so that the job of the interpreter or editor is that of classifying them on this basis. Answers to this type of question often are short and vague which, of course, complicates the job of the interpreter who has little to go on to determine meaning. The use of broad and less meaningful categories often is a result.

Interpreting Qualitative Data

The preceding discussion has pointed out that categories of answers to direct questions, especially for those which restrict response, may be established on the basis of assumed meanings in advance of the field interviewing. Doing so becomes less possible, however, as greater freedom is allowed the respondent in choosing what he wants to say and how he wants to say it. As interviews become more informal and detailed, the post-interview interpretive work which must be done becomes greater in amount and more challenging. Once it has been completed, however, categories may be established for coding, and tabulation and statistical analysis may be undertaken if this is deemed appropriate.

In discerning meanings, the interpreter may go to a large extent on literal interpretations of statements about product features or habits of purchase and use. All the depth interviews described in the case examples sought information of this sort. They also often used it in connection with more intensive explorations of the meanings of products and activities. The studies were interested in attitudes and feelings, some of which could be reported on directly by the respondent, but some of which could not. The burden on the interpreter, of course, increases with the importance of unconscious material and the necessity of inferring meanings.

In order to identify motivational patterns successfully from clues contained in what may be a sizable quantity of data, the interpreter must know something about people, their needs, and their behaviors. He must be able to detect rationalizations and projections of feelings and recognize and interpret symbolic communication by which people often express themselves without realizing it.

The interpretation of qualitative data involves clinical concepts which often are unfamiliar to researchers whose training has been largely in survey work and statistical analysis. The motivational studies described in earlier chapters attempted to learn of the underlying meaning of acts of behavior, including interview responses. Everything a person did or said, including the way in which he said it, was regarded as a clue to the meaning the product or activity in question had for him. The problem was to interpret it.

At the same time, however, it was believed that the significance of any single act or statement could not be fully appreciated without viewing it in terms of the whole motivational pattern to which it belonged. The meaning of the whole was regarded as something more than just the sum of its parts. Acts or statements which appear to be different in a literal sense may be reflecting the same needs and feelings. For purposes of analysis, they are regarded as symptoms of the real meaning. Allowance must be made for the possibility that the same activity may have different meanings for different participants.

Efforts to develop complete pictures of the functions of products and activities were noted in the selected cases. The home sewing study, for example, explored in detail the respondent's sewing history, the social context of which sewing was a part, the respondent's sewing ability, habits, gratifications, and some of her personality characteristics. All of these were directed to finding out how she felt about sewing and what needs it served. The results showed that its meanings were somewhat different for heavy sewers, light sewers, and nonsewers.

The emphasis on looking at the whole motivational picture has not been characteristic of market surveys in the past. Instead, the tendency has been to reason or guess that some factors might be related to buying behavior and to deal with them one at a time pretty much as isolated entities rather than possibly interrelated influences. The importance of a factor has been gauged primarily in terms of the number of mentions received in response to direct questions rather than in terms of how it fitted into an over-all motivational pattern serving human needs.

We may agree to the desirability of developing a complete motivational picture and subscribe to the concepts relative to determining meanings. It still is appropriate, however, to inquire as to how this process is to be carried out. A criticism commonly made of qualitative interviews is that there is no standard method of arriving at inferences comparable to the customary use of literal interpretations of answers to formal questions. Our discussion already has indicated that, regardless of the technique used, any attempt to quantify data requires the exercise of judgment in order to make what at least are tentative assumptions as to their meaning. The decision may be to use literal interpretations. This is a blanket judgment which, of course, offers advantages because it practically establishes the meaning of all responses without examining them individually. Whether this is a virtue, however, depends upon whether the answers are sufficiently accurate and complete to serve the research purpose. Earlier, we noted that direct questions may or may not be adequate, depending upon the circumstances. If they are not, then it is necessary to use other approaches like qualitative interviews which make it possible to bring to bear the services of specialists trained to draw inferences.

While no prescription exists for inferring meanings, this should not be an unfamiliar process because it is something everyone does to some extent every day, some of us being more successful at it than others. We learn what people are like by observing how they act and by making inferences. We may infer what is going on in a business situation from what we consider to be clues or pieces of evidence which suggest the meaning of the whole situation. Yet, we are unable to tell someone else exactly what steps were followed and how we came to infer the particular meanings we did.

Much the same situation exists when it comes to the interpretation of qualitative data in marketing research. Experienced interpreters cannot describe in detail just how they draw their inferences, and, so far as we know, there has been no step-by-step study of these interpreters at work. In fact, there have been very few such investigations in any field. One such study, however, has been described by Charles McArthur.[2] It sought to learn more about the clinical process by which psychologists diagnose personality. Several distinguished guest scientists were invited by the Study of Adult Development, Department of Hygiene, Harvard University, to discuss clinical case material which included tests, interviews, questionnaires, and school records for the individual in question who was a college student at the time the data were collected. Each visiting scientist was asked to order the facts in a given case in any manner he wished, then predict the behavior of the subject individual during the first 10 years following his college graduation. The true history of those 10 years was known to the members of the staff who sat in on the conference.

There were both hits and misses in the predictions made. The visitors, whether successful or unsuccessful in making predictions, were asked how they arrived at their formulations and none, especially the most successful ones, could give a satisfactory answer. Observations of the process were made by others in the course of the study, however, and reported on by McArthur.

One was that the successful predictions did not depend upon the merit of any single psychological theory employed or on the results of any one piece of evidence in the case data. Equally valid predictions were made by a Freudian, a social psychologist, and a nondirective counselor. McArthur observed that this came as no surprise because "most clinicians are becoming aware that the point at which one enters the

[2] Charles McArthur, "Analyzing the Clinical Process," *Journal of Counseling Psychology*, Vol. 1, No. 4, 1954, pp. 203–208.

data has no bearing on the accuracy of the conclusion one reaches." [3]

What all the predictors seemed to do was to build a clinical construct or a conceptualization of the man in the record. McArthur observed that it was from the construct as a whole and not from any single datum that the good predictions were made. He reported that the least successful predictors were applying systematically rules derived from previous cases or from existing psychological theory. McArthur's conclusion was that "the preferable approach seems to be far more inductive than deductive. Indeed, it seems to be necessary that for any individual case the very categories in which the facts are to be cast must arise inductively from the data." [4]

The process of interpreting qualitative data, then, appears to be that of construct-making, and, as McArthur noted, this seems to be done best when the interpreter makes use of an eclectic approach, seeking with an open mind the interpretation of any piece of evidence that would fit with all the other data.

Construct-making seems to describe the activity in which interpreters of qualitative marketing data engage, too, the principal difference being that the construct has to do with the nature of relationships such as those existing between products and people rather than the personality structure of an individual. The large amount and variety of information and expressions contained in verbatim interview reports can provide many clues needed for identifying motivational patterns. The reports also represent a means of bringing a great quantity of detailed data together at a central place so that efficient use can be made of the services of well-qualified interpreters.

It has been the experience of research groups which have

[3] Ibid., p. 204.
[4] Ibid., p. 205.

done a great deal of qualitative interviewing that relatively few intensive interviews are needed for identifying most of the factors important to the behavior under study. Figures cited range from a dozen to 100, with those on the lower end of the range being the more usual. The number will vary somewhat depending upon the nature of the problem, the extent to which homogeneity exists within the relevant population, and how much is known in advance about probable variations so that respondents can be selected accordingly.

In talking with persons engaged in interpretive work and watching them in action, we have been impressed with something McArthur noted in his study — the absence of a rigid application of any single theory or any set of rules derived from past experience. The interpreters, of course, were helped by their knowledge of theories and related research results which contributed to their understanding of human behavior. But it appeared to be this understanding plus a developed skill — indeed, the product of their total backgrounds of training and experience — which they brought to the data.

These observations indicate that the more the interpreter knows about people and the more experience he has in working with data, the better able he should be to see possible meanings and build fruitful constructs. This amounts to a strong argument for an individual interpreter to have training and experience in as many of the behavioral fields as possible and for research groups to have various social science fields represented on their staffs.

In view of the nature of the process, drawing inferences from data is, to a large extent, an art. No detailed prescription exists for doing it. No doubt there are a variety of ways in which data can be approached successfully. There always is a danger, of course, that inaccurate or at least incomplete interpretations will be made. Mistakes can result from ignorance, lack of skill, or bias. Probably everyone is inclined to give special attention to that which tends to confirm what he already believes, so there is a temptation to read into data something that is not there. This can happen without the interpreter's being aware of it. At the same time, however, the specialist's theories and understanding of behavior make it possible for him to see meanings in the data which would escape notice by the less well qualified.

Incomplete interpretations can be expected simply because no one person or group of persons has anything resembling a complete understanding of behavior. There have been a number of viewpoints in the behavioral sciences. All interpreters, of course, do not have the same backgrounds nor do they necessarily think alike. We should expect to find some disagreement among them, or at least variations in what they see in data and what they choose to emphasize, just as we expect differences of opinion in other walks of life. In making this point, however, we do not want to overemphasize it because our observations have not shown disagreement to be a major problem in motivation research. Contradictory conclusions have been relatively few in the several instances reported to us in which more than one research firm worked on substantially the same assignment.

Several means of minimizing the dangers described above were illustrated in the case examples. One way is to have the planning of the research and major interpretive decisions reviewed in staff meetings, especially when the staff members have varied backgrounds. Another is to have more than one interpreter work with the data so that they may serve as a check on one another.

It also is possible to run rough quantitative checks on the interpretation of qualitative data. Quantification may serve no real purpose with the highly unstructured exploratory interviews usually undertaken at the outset of a study. As the interview guides become more focused, however, it becomes both more feasible and more useful to count responses by broad categories of meaning. The results can serve to focus attention on points which might otherwise be neglected and contribute to an understanding of their importance.

Quantification of Data

Successful measurement of the prevalence or strength of something depends upon obtaining useful evidence on these dimensions and then categorizing it so that it can be counted. The measurement advantages of qualitative interviews relate primarily to the first point. Quantification itself becomes increasingly difficult as the interpretive task becomes more challenging and time consuming. This problem is formidable with very open depth interviews which produce a great volume of complex data. It diminishes as the interview approach becomes more focused, and is at a minimum with highly structured questions.

The value of qualitative interviews for measurement, then, depends upon the nature of the task. If the objective is to ascertain the prevalence of given patterns of motivational factors, for example, a simple, structured approach may or may not be adequate. It may be possible to devise a series of direct questions such as were used in the Dieting Study. On the other hand, qualitative interviews themselves may represent an advantageous way of collecting the amount and kind of data needed for identifying the patterns and categorizing the interviews accordingly.

The use of an open approach, in which no formal stimuli are presented in the same manner to all respondents, raises the question of comparability of interviews for purposes of statistical analysis. The result usually is a lack of uniformity in coverage of the different aspects of the subject. If too few reactions are obtained in certain question areas to provide satisfactory tests of hypotheses, this is a critical limitation. Otherwise, it may not be. The use of a standard set of specific stimuli, of course, facilitates the handling of data.

Whether it otherwise is an advantage, however, depends upon the relative merits of specific vs. ambiguous stimuli for the purposes of obtaining meaningful responses to be quantified.

Earlier, we recognized that if a question is too specific, it may produce invalid responses because of its nature or simply because of the fact that it was asked. Direct questions with suggested alternative answers, for example, may lead to an overstatement of the importance of the factors represented by the alternatives. The opposite approach is to allow the respondent to choose what he wants to say within a topical area and how he wishes to say it. The results can be revealing, in many cases being directly indicative of the significance of various factors to him. On the other hand, the importance of certain things may be understated because of the absence of aided recall. We know too little about the question of whether a specific or a more ambiguous stimulus is best for testing different kinds of hypotheses. We need to learn more about which will produce the more valid results and when it will do so. When doubt exists, it may be well to avoid relying on only one kind of approach.

Variations in coverage and quality of interviews, of course, also can reflect differences in interviewer conduct, willingness of respondents to cooperate, and their ability to express themselves — factors which may be of greater potential influence in informal interviews.

In Summary

The very open depth interview and the highly formal questionnaire offer a sharp contrast in characteristics. The former permits the gathering of a variety of data in volume which may permit the researcher to learn a lot from people, but interpreting it is time consuming, costly, and often challenging. It may be difficult, even impossible, to realize the advantages of statistical analysis. The situation is pretty much the reverse with the highly structured questionnaire. It confronts all respondents with the same questions and affords marked advantages in ease of field administration, processing, and statistical analysis of data. On the negative side, it is necessary to assume that the questions shoot at the right targets in a way that will not prejudice the response and that the meanings of what often turn out to be brief responses are clear.

We have tended to talk in terms of extremes for explanatory purposes. It is not necessary, however, to choose between the structured and the unstructured means. They can be combined in the same research effort, although much remains to be learned about how to do this to best advantage. In addition, there are various question-asking devices in between the extremes. Our case examples illustrate combinations of techniques and the growing practice of conducting consumer research in stages, one logically leading to the next and serving to make it more effective. The studies characteristically started with exploratory qualitative interviews to identify the dimensions of the subject under investigation. Once this information was obtained, the interview guides became more complete to make sure that certain aspects would come up for attention. The guides contained the hypotheses to be tested, often in an indirect manner. With greater focusing, more comparable data are obtained in a more orderly way in the different interviews and quantification of the results is facilitated. While the individual responses must be interpreted, determination of meaning must be made at some stage of the research and there are advantages to doing this in the context of the interview on the basis of what the respondent actually says in his own words.

In addition to qualitative interviews and direct questions, motivational studies frequently make use of various projective questions which will be discussed later in this chapter.

THE GROUP INTERVIEW

This technique, which was illustrated and described in the State Farm Mutual Automobile Insurance Company case, is qualitative interviewing on a group basis. Briefly, it consists of bringing together a small number of people for a discussion led in a nondirective manner in a relaxed, informal, and permissive atmosphere. The assumption is that these conditions are conducive to honest and free expression. The few researchers who have made extensive use of the group interview in marketing have found this to be true for a good many topics.

Mention was made in the State Farm Mutual case of the cumulative or snowballing effect which leads to a broadening of thinking and stimulates the flow of ideas as the group members accept and often enjoy their responsibility as participants. It is by talking, especially when reactions of others are taken into account, that many people develop their thinking and become aware of their feelings. George Horsley Smith, who has conducted many group interviews for several advertising agencies in New York, has found that the group situation can serve to break down inhibitions. He reports getting highly personalized group discussions for such products as laxatives, cold tablets, deodorants, weight reducers, and sanitary napkins.[5]

Whether these benefits actually will be realized depends heavily upon the interviewer. His role includes setting a favorable tone, getting things off to a good start, and seeing that all participants get into the act. His behavior can have a pronounced effect upon the group. Therefore, he should understand the interviewing process and be sensitive to what is going on so that he may act appropriately. He must be skillful in nondirective and projective questioning in order

---

[5] George Horsley Smith, *Motivation Research in Advertising and Marketing,* (New York: McGraw-Hill Book Company, Inc., 1954), p. 61.

to draw out the ideas and feelings of the participants. He also may have to tactfully but effectively prevent a participant from dominating the discussion and unduly coloring the proceedings. While these requirements are high, the interviewing of several people at once makes it more feasible to use a well-qualified social scientist as the interviewer — a major advantage.

Analysis of the data presents the same problems discussed in the previous section. It is time consuming and it requires the services of experienced and highly trained people if the potential value of the data is to be realized. Tape recordings, which preserve the tonal qualities and the timing of what is said as well as the verbatim content, are available for detailed study. Researchers who have worked with groups report that the presence of a recording microphone seems to be quickly forgotten and has little if any dampening effect upon discussion. The use of more than one interpreter offers the same advantages described in connection with individual qualitative interviews.

While the group interview offers many of the advantages of qualitative interviewing on an individual basis, it does not permit going as deep psychologically. Intensive exploration of any one person's feelings would require devoting too much time to him with a loss of the desired group spontaneity. Quantification of data is especially difficult. Except on a very rough basis, it usually is not practicable because of the nature of the discussions and the limited number of group interviews undertaken for a given study.

The selection of respondents has been a problem because of refusals to participate in discussions proposed by a stranger and involving strangers as discussants. Interviews sometimes have been conducted among established social groups. It has been particularly difficult to get the cooperation from certain population segments like the suburbanites and the lower social classes. Aside from this limitation, there is the possibility that people who agree to participate may be different psychologically from those who refuse. While these points raise the question of representativeness of sample, they do not negate the value of group interviews for exploratory purposes.

Concluding Remarks

The group interview offers a relatively quick and inexpensive means of tapping a great deal of useful material which would fall within the bounds of conventional acceptability. It proved useful, for example, in the State Farm Mutual case for finding out what automobile insurance meant to people and how they went about choosing a company, a topic for which intensive probing of individuals was not essential. Considering its apparent advantages for exploratory research, the technique has been employed surprisingly little in marketing. Its use can be expected to increase as more attention is paid to the research function of developing hypotheses.

The chances are against the successful use of the group interview for learning of feelings about which there are strong cultural taboos. Its limitations for obtaining material of much psychological depth already have been mentioned. Smith has found the technique relatively ineffective for developing explanations of habitual behavior such as why people patronize a particular gasoline service station or why they drink their favorite brand of beer. He also reports that discussions of good and bad features of a well-known, standardized article such as men's shirts fail to get much beyond the usual familiar information. He concludes that if group interviewing is to be used in these areas, it needs to be supplemented by other techniques.[6]

PROJECTIVE TECHNIQUES

A variety of projective techniques have been adapted for use in consumer research as the examples in Part II illustrate.

[6] Ibid., pp. 66–67.

While they differ in form, they usually have two principal characteristics. One is that their specific purpose is not apparent. The respondent, then, cannot be aware, or at least fully aware, of the meaning of his answers. The other is ambiguity. The projective question contains no specific meaning. It can be interpreted in different ways. The object is to find out what meanings the respondent will read into it.

The underlying assumption is that in responding promptly, the interviewee will reveal something of himself — his thoughts, feelings, values, and needs. The main principle which is assumed to be at work is that of projection, or the unconscious imputation to others of characteristics of oneself. The respondent presumably does this as he describes persons or situations appearing in the projective device. Another principle may enter in here as well, namely, that of free association — one thought suggesting another and so on, the combined chain of thoughts being related in meaning and revealing about the respondent.

At the outset we should distinguish between two main objectives of projective devices as used in motivation research. The most common is to learn of the important ideas and feelings people have toward the product or situation under investigation. A second may be to learn something about the personality characteristics of the respondent. Both functions may be served at the same time, although many such questions are designed with only one purpose in mind.

Before further discussing characteristics, let us review the kinds of projective techniques most frequently employed in motivation research and the ways in which they have been used.

Examples

Here are a few examples, most of which are from the studies described in Part II. In each case, the technique was only one of several used in combination in the research approach of which it was a part.

Word Association

In the Donahue Sales Corporation home sewing study, the respondents were asked to give their immediate reactions (several sentences were desired) to words and phrases such as the following:

Zippers	Making a dress
Buttons	Talon zippers
Snaps	

In a study of motivations relating to soaps and chemical detergents sponsored by the *Chicago Tribune* and conducted by Social Research, Inc., the respondent was read words such as the following, one at a time, and asked to tell the interviewer the first word that came to mind for each:

Towels	Scrub	Babies
Sudsy	Soiled	Detergents
Homemaker	Family	Spick-and-span

Incomplete Sentences

Insurance of all kinds is . . .
Mutual auto insurance companies . . .
The Pan-American Coffee Bureau is . . .
A woman likes a car that . . .
People who drive convertibles . . .
A woman who sews at home . . .
A woman who never sews . . .
My husband thinks the Jewelman . . .
Jewel brand products . . .

Narrative Projection

"A friend of yours has just bought his first car. He asks you what he should do about getting insurance for it. What would you tell him?"

"Every year a man shopped around very carefully for the

least expensive auto insurance he could find. How much do you suppose he saved by this practice?"

"Suppose you are traveling in a foreign country and a friend of yours introduces you to a resident of that country who is a coffee-grower. In what country would you most likely be traveling? Now try to imagine what this coffee-grower would be like. If you don't know anything at all about _____ coffee-growers, just guess. Answer 'yes' or 'no' as quickly as you can." (Interviewer read off list of qualities).

Cartoons

A man shown listening to his wife who was saying: "Here's an ad that says you can save as much as 40% on your auto insurance. Do you think we ought to look into it when ours expires next month?" Respondent was asked what the man replied.

Faces of a father and son were shown. Respondent was told: "The boy asked dad for advice about getting a car. Imagine that you are the parent; what would you tell him?"

A woman was pictured working at a sewing machine. Respondent was asked what the woman was thinking as she worked.

Requests for Descriptions of Others

Various open questions used in qualitative interviewing are projective in character. Here is an example taken from the automobile study:

Think of a friend who is a very good driver. What kind of a person is he (she)?
Now think of the worst driver you know. Describe the kind of person he is; what he's like.

The purpose of the question is to obtain evidence of the respondent's attitudes toward driving and some of his related personal characteristics such as his values, whether he is aggressive, cautious, and the like.

Thematic Apperception Test Adaptations

In the automobile study, a drawing pictured the open highway as seen from the driver's seat of a moving automobile. Hands were shown on the steering wheel and the speedometer reading was between 60 and 70 miles per hour. Respondent was asked to put himself in the position of the driver and tell a story about what was going on.

In one of the Jewel Tea Company studies, a sketch showed a grocery route salesman, a little girl, and a housewife in the latter's kitchen. The respondent was asked to tell a story about what was going on, what led up to the situation, who the people were and what they were thinking, and what the outcome might be.

Personality Tests

The Donahue case contained four tests selected specifically to check on certain hypotheses about personality characteristics of women who were heavy sewers, light sewers, and non-sewers. For example, there was an "unusual purposes test" designed to test how flexible and original a person's thinking was. It asked the respondent to name uses other than the most usual one for six different common, everyday objects.

The same study also used the human figure drawing to learn of personality structure in terms of basic needs. In particular, this test called for a projection of the respondent's unconscious self-appraisal of herself through the medium of the drawing. This is one of the few comprehensive and standard clinical tests of personality patterns we have seen used in marketing studies.

Obtaining Data

The preceding illustrations show that all projective techniques pose questions, but that the latter may vary in number and complexity. Word associations, for example, call for only brief, top-of-the-mind responses. Sentence completions require a somewhat different mental set in that the person has to make a little more sense to answer. This is more true yet with the narrative and cartoon devices which usually raise more potential questions at one time by picturing a situation. Adaptations of the thematic apperception test put the interviewee considerably more on his own resources by asking him to tell a story about what is going on in the picture.

The freedom of response characteristic of most of the projectives makes them valuable in exploring for ideas. A major feature, of course, is that the devices often represent a means of penetrating the barrier of people's inability and initial unwillingness to talk about certain things. All the respondent has to do is to react by expressing whatever thoughts and feelings come to mind. This approach increases the chances of getting behind the usual rational defenses and uncovering feelings which otherwise might be deliberately withheld or unconsciously repressed. Hence, the respondent can divulge a great deal of unconscious as well as conscious material. He is more likely to express socially unacceptable attitudes and feelings if he can attribute them to someone else. A number of illustrations of these points appeared in the selected cases. The heavy sewer, for example, could not have told an interviewer that she had strong emotional needs for sewing because of her insecurity and inability to relax and enjoy her environment. But she could indirectly supply data from which this could be inferred by a psychologist. Similarly, housewives are not likely to explain their rejection of instant coffee on the basis that it symbolizes to them a lazy homemaker who is inconsiderate of those to whom she serves coffee. Yet, this is a finding that has come out strongly in several studies using projective questions.

Researchers who have used projective devices a great deal often regard them as more likely than direct questions to produce full and valid responses of conscious information about which the respondent has no reluctance. Several reasons are advanced as to why more satisfactory results may be obtained. The inhibiting effect of direct interrogation is avoided. By encouraging free association, the projectives, with the help of skillful probing, afford an opportunity to get more detailed information. Because of their ambiguity, there is less chance of bias from the question itself. Yet, by providing familiar stimuli, they can promote cooperation by making it easier for people to talk. Respondents often find the cartoons, pictures, and word games enjoyable. The indirect approach, accompanied by interview informality, also should reduce the likelihood of deliberate deception by the respondent.

Self-analysis or introspective articulateness is not required in answering. The respondent merely has to report his initial feelings and ideas. In view of this, projective devices may afford an improved means of approaching difficult topics and interviewing in all educational, cultural, and age groups. There is some evidence, however, that they are less satisfactory with the upper social classes where people tend to be more sophisticated, more knowledgeable about projective techniques, and less willing to play word association or story telling games with a strange interviewer.

The majority of the projective devices used in marketing research have been devised primarily for the purpose of learning of the prevailing patterns of knowledge, thought, and attitudes toward products, brands, or activities. As our discussion has already indicated, however, the techniques also are used to learn about the respondent's personality. This may be done by taking small samples of his behavior, in the form of his responses, and noting their content and feeling tone.

Let us illustrate this dual function by considering word associations. The latter frequently are used to guide the choice of company and brand names, and advertising words and slogans. Popular meanings of such things as "zippers," "making a dress," "detergents," and "family," for example, can be identified by analyzing the associations to these words made by different people.

Something can be learned about the personality characteristics of the individual respondent which are related to the product or activity being studied by examining the pattern of his word associations. For example, these responses of two women to words used in the *Chicago Tribune's* detergent study reflect sharp differences in attitudes:

Stimulus	*Mrs. M.*	*Mrs. C.*
washday	everyday	ironing
fresh	and sweet	clean
pure	air	soiled
scrub	don't — Ray (husband) does	clean
filth	this neighborhood	dirt
bubbles	bath	soap and water
family	squabbles	children
towels	dirty	wash

Here are some of the interpreter's comments about the above responses: "Mrs. M's associations suggest that she is more resigned to dirt, seeing it as somewhat inevitable, with little implication that she can or wants to do much about it. (Note associations: filth — 'this neighborhood,' towels — 'dirty,' washday — 'everyday.') It is her husband who must do the hard cleaning (scrub — 'don't; Ray does'). Nor does she seem to get pleasure from her family (family — 'squabbles'). Her most positive associations are sensible, self-oriented ones (pure — 'air,' fresh — 'and sweet,' bubbles — 'bath'). Mrs. C. sees dirt, too, but is energetic, factual minded, and less emotional. She is ready to actively combat dirt and her weapons are soap and water."

In the detergent study from which the above example was

taken, evidence on personal characteristics, including attitudes toward dirt, also was obtained from depth interviews and other projective questions as well as the word associations. It was on the basis of the total picture to which they contributed that conclusions were drawn.

For another illustration, let us consider a response consisting of what a housewife thinks a person pictured in a cartoon is saying or thinking. The character of her answer depends more on her make-up and attitudes than the situation portrayed because the latter is neutral in emotional tone. Any feelings in the answer necessarily come from the housewife herself. The character of the material which can be obtained is indicated by the two responses reproduced below. They were made to a cartoon used in the detergent study which showed a mother and daughter together. The respondent was asked to pretend that she was the mother telling the little girl how to wash her doll clothes, what to use, and how to go about it. Our sample responses reflect marked differences in attitudes toward both clothes and children.

> Well, Marilyn, your doll has some very lovely clothes. We mustn't use a strong soap when we wash them. Honey, I'm going to let you use some of this Ivory Snow. Your doll's clothes will come out nice and fresh and clean.

> Don't give my girl any ideas! She tried it once and had water all over the floor. Is that a washing machine? Looks like she's going to put the doll in it. I suppose you would tell her to take a little water and a little soap. Just wash them and rinse them and hang them up to dry.

The possibility of providing systematic means of measuring personality dimensions is a major potential advantage yet to be developed for marketing research. This function was illustrated in the Donahue case which included a tailor-made battery of tests for checking on motivational interpretations made from qualitative interviews.

Thus far, we have talked mostly about potential advantages. While a good deal of evidence exists that they have been realized in many instances, there is, of course, no guarantee that this will be so. There is the possibility that the respondent may not actually reveal his basic dispositions and attitudes. If the purpose of the question is not fully disguised, he may be unwilling to answer correctly for the same reasons he may withhold information in replying to a direct question. His responses may be in terms of transitory impulses rather than permanent dispositions, or he may be answering not for himself but for another person of whom he was reminded.

Much remains to be learned by experimentation as to when the projectives are most likely to work and when they are not; when they are most likely to be more effective than other techniques. This, of course, does not mean that they should not be used. All techniques have limitations and, as has already been indicated, the projectives offer the promise of tapping material which has eluded more direct approaches. In the presence of uncertainty, there is an advantage to using projective devices in combination with other means to provide internal checks on the data obtained. In this connection, it should be pointed out that the successful design of appropriate projective adaptations and the planning for their effective use as integrated parts of a research effort require a kind of specialized knowledge and skill which the usual marketing researcher has lacked.

Interviewing

Projective techniques often are used in combination with qualitative interviews which we already have discussed. Considered by themselves, however, many of those in common use do not pose unusual interviewing problems. Techniques like word association, sentence completion, and the cartoon can be administered by conventional survey interviewers of reasonable competence with a limited amount of extra instruction. This becomes less true as greater freedom of response and more probing is expected, as may be the case with adaptations of the thematic apperception test. Here, the requirements tend to become more those of the depth interview. It is especially important with projectives that the actual responses be recorded in the respondent's (not the interviewer's) own words.

Interpretation and Quantification of Data

Most of what already has been said on these topics earlier in the chapter applies at some point here as well because of the variations in the ways in which projective techniques are used, the techniques themselves, and the character of the responses they produce. The projective category includes highly structured tests like some of those in the Donahue case; brief response questions like word associations and sentence completion; fuller response devices like cartoons, projective questions in focused interviews, and T.A.T. adaptations; and, occasionally, more comprehensive tests of personality structure which may take various forms.

Many of the projectives can be useful in connection with both the creative and the evaluative functions of research, although some of the special tests are limited to the latter. The devices may be employed singly, several may be used together, and they may be combined with other approaches. For some purposes and with certain techniques, the literal responses can be immediately tabulated for statistical analysis; for others, qualitative examination for the inference of meanings is required; sometimes both are used. In view of these variations, personnel requirements for the handling of data range from statistical clerks to highly trained clinical psychologists. For many of the projectives commonly used in marketing research, the demands are similar to those made by focused qualitative interviews.

Most of the projective adaptations have several potential advantages for the testing of hypotheses. They offer a means of confronting all respondents with the same stimuli, yet there is flexibility as to the latter's ambiguity or specificity. Responses often can be quantified fairly readily. In the majority of cases, categories of meaning first must be determined by well-qualified personnel before coding and tabulating of the responses can proceed. This usually can be done from a sample of the data. Once it is, less highly skilled personnel can be instructed to carry out the detailed coding. The difficulty of the task, of course, varies with the length and complexity of the response.

Further Comments on Validity

The validity of projective techniques has been strongly attacked by certain marketing research people. In view of this, special attention now will be given to what they have said, the preceding discussion serving as a background. Their principal argument has been that the projective tests of the psychological clinic have not been proved as effective predictors of human behavior; therefore, adaptations of these approaches in marketing research are dangerous. In supporting this view, they have not talked in terms of actual marketing applications; instead, they have quoted from articles in psychological and other professional journals which have reported on unsuccessful attempts to predict behavior from results of a projective test of personality. For example, they have cited failures in the use of the Rorschach ink blot test for selecting successful trainee pilots; for predicting which clinical psychologists would graduate and pass their licensing tests; and for predicting which mental patients would continue to undergo treatment.

In regard to these criticisms, it is true that such attempts at prediction have met with mixed results. There has been considerable controversy over the predictive value of clinical vs. actuarial methods. Little empirical evidence exists, however, which sheds much light on the question. In reviewing this subject, Paul E. Meehl found that the literature contained almost no carefully executed studies of the clinical-actuarial issue.[7] He did find about 20 studies which afforded some comparison of methods, and in all but one of these the actuarial predictions were found to be either equal or superior to those made by clinicians.

The studies examined involved predictions of three sorts of things: success in school or in some kind of training program; recidivism; and recovery from a major psychosis. A number of limitations of these studies were noted for the purposes of comparing predictive methods. Meehl found that they did not tell much about the kind and amount of clinical study which was competing with the actuarial methods, that too little was known about the skill and qualifications of the clinicians, that individual clinicians usually were not evaluated separately, and that the clinicians usually did not have an opportunity to "formulate the personality" in detail. Nevertheless, clinical predictions did not show up well.

Now, how do the above observations relate to the validity of the projectives commonly used in marketing research? Their relevance is limited. The reason is that the criticisms which they supposedly support tend to be based on these tenuous assumptions: (1) that the "projectives" in marketing research are the comprehensive tests of personality like the Rorschach and others used in the psychological clinic; (2) that the immediate objective of their use is to predict behavior; and (3) that responses to projective devices are of no value if they do not permit predictions of behavior.

Actually, the comprehensive projective tests of personality, in their clinical versions, thus far have had very little use in

---

[7] Paul E. Meehl, *Clinical vs. Statistical Prediction* (Minneapolis: University of Minnesota Press, 1954).

marketing research. When they have been employed, they commonly have represented only one of several means used to test hypotheses. The projectives characteristic of motivation research have been special adaptations of the original tests, and many have not been very projective in the clinical sense of the word. They have been used for much less ambitious purposes than that of serving as a single basis for predicting behavior. Often, they have been designed to fish for ideas in exploratory studies, and to learn the extent of knowledge, the usual habits of thought, and the important attitudes and feelings about a given product or situation. The usual practice has been to combine a number of these adaptations with still other approaches and to draw conclusions after examining all the data obtained rather than to rely on that produced by a single question or technique.

In the context of the actual application, then, the relevant validity question is whether a given device will obtain the data for which it was designed, not whether this in itself is adequate for predicting behavior. To illustrate, let us consider the task of finding out whether people distinguish between mutual and stock automobile insurance companies, and, if so, what their attitudes toward mutual companies are. One of the questions used in the State Farm Mutual study was this incomplete sentence: "Mutual auto insurance companies. . . ." The practical consideration here is whether the sentence stem will serve the purpose as well or better than a direct question or some other technique.

To take another example, let us use one of the objectives in the Donahue study: to learn of women's attitudes toward various forms of closure for dresses. One of the approaches included asking women to give their immediate associations to the single words "zippers," "buttons," "snaps," etc. The validity question here, then, is whether this attempt will yield the desired results and whether it is likely to do so as well or better than an alternative means.

In the automobile study, one of the objectives was to learn what factors people take into account in buying a car. Use was made of a cartoon which pictured a father and son. The respondent was told to imagine that he was the parent and to say what he would tell the boy. Again, the research consideration is the relative effectiveness of the cartoon for producing the desired data.

Similar questions could be raised in regard to any of the devices illustrated in the various studies. Our purpose here is not to pretend to know the answers. Perhaps direct questions could have been devised which would represent an improvement over the means actually used, perhaps not. No doubt any of several different approaches could be useful for many problems. Our point is that we have no reason to believe that other means would produce more valid responses than the devices described. In fact, the researchers concerned cited advantages for their chosen approaches and reported satisfactory results.

When viewed in the light of actual cases, the validity question, while difficult enough, is not of the alarming proportions the critics have implied. In fact, it takes on much more the character of the problem which always has existed with the more conventional methods. Experimentation is needed. Tests are needed of the reliability and validity of projective methods, and they, in turn, should make possible new tests of more conventional approaches.

While we should like to be able to predict the behavior under study, prediction to this extent often is not a realistic criterion of validity in marketing research. The identification and individual measurement of the importance of the many influences at work is difficult, and it usually is necessary to settle for considerably less. In research on advertising effectiveness, for example, one of the most common measures has been readership, yet the relationship between readership scores and sales results in most cases is not known. Inability to predict sales on this basis, however, does not in itself reflect upon the validity of the scores as measures of readership or upon the techniques which produced them.

Similarly, psychological tests may produce sound data on attitudes or more basic personality dimensions which, by themselves, will not permit predictions of behavior simply because the latter is affected by other things as well. The problem, which was discussed at greater length in Chapter XI, is to develop an understanding of the several factors at work and their interrelationship so that the appropriate combination of them may be taken into account.

While further testing of the usefulness of projective techniques in marketing is desirable, a great deal already has been learned from experience. In the conduct of a given study, it is not difficult to determine whether a question is producing a full enough response, and to include alternative approaches which will permit internal checks on the data obtained. In addition, and in spite of the difficulties mentioned above, there have been checks against actual behavior.

Much of what has been learned has not been published, although there are a few exceptions. Dietz Leonhard has described some of his uses of projective techniques in which he noted advantages over direct questioning.[8] An early article on this subject was Mason Haire's description of his shopping list projective technique and accompanying pantry checks which showed both that women associated instant coffee with lazy and poor housewives and that the women who had these associations were not likely to buy the product.[9]

In regard to behavioral checks on data obtained by projective techniques, it is of interest to note the work of McCann-Erickson which was illustrated and described in the

[8] Dietz Leonhard, *Consumer Research with Projective Techniques* (Shenandoah, Ia.: Ajax Corporation, 1955).
[9] Mason Haire, "Projective Techniques in Marketing Research," *Journal of Marketing*, Vol. XIV, No. 5, April 1950, p. 649.

Donahue case and commentary. Given people behaving in certain ways, they have developed batteries of personality tests by which they have been able to distinguish between behavioral groups of consumers on the basis of personality dimensions in a number of studies.

CONCLUDING REMARKS

The discussion in this chapter has emphasized that there is no such thing as an inherently valid technique irrespective of the manner or situation of its use. Research can serve different functions, and techniques vary importantly in ways which affect their ability to obtain different kinds of data and the form in which they gather it. Whether their characteristics should be regarded as advantages or limitations depends upon their appropriateness for the task at hand.

Well-conducted and interpreted qualitative interviews represent a potentially rewarding source of ideas. They are highly desirable, if not essential, for most exploratory studies of buying behavior. The infrequent use of both informal interviews and projective techniques in the past has been associated with inattention to the hypothesis-formulating function and a neglect of emotional and unconscious factors. As the research objective becomes more that of providing quantitative measurements, there are advantages to using more structured means ranging from focused qualitative interviews through projective devices to direct questions. Regardless of what technique is employed, however, it is necessary that someone at some point exercise judgment to determine what the responses mean.

As the very open approaches tend to be strongest where those which restrict response are weakest, and vice versa, benefits can be realized from combining them in a research effort and from using other techniques of a more intermediate character as well. This practice was illustrated in our case examples. Direct questions and projective devices frequently were employed in combination with depth interviews in order to approach matters from different angles and to move to a more structured approach as the research progressed.

Our discussion necessarily has been based on our observations of research, theoretical analysis, and the reported experience and opinions of various researchers. Much remains to be learned by experiment about the relative merits of different approaches. It always has been difficult to establish the validity and completeness of data on how and why people buy. The growing use of qualitative interviews and adaptations of projective techniques offers the opportunity for further testing of both the newer and the more conventional methods. In view of the inevitable limitations of techniques, interviewers, and interpreters, checks on the accuracy of findings are desirable regardless of the research means employed. Various ways of obtaining evidence as to validity have been mentioned in this chapter and in the case examples. They will be summarized in the next chapter in which further attention will be given to judging research findings as a basis for business action.

CHAPTER XIII

Judging Research Findings

WHILE marketing is making increasing use of specialized knowledge and skills from the behavioral fields, it nevertheless is the business executive who ultimately must accept or reject the findings as a basis for action and decide whether the over-all research effort was worthwhile. It is the exercise of this responsibility to which we now turn our attention.

In considering the subject of appraisal, it may be helpful to keep in mind that most marketing decisions have been, and still are, made without the benefit of research and that they involve passing judgment on ideas of unsubstantiated validity. Dealing with uncertainty is pretty much the nature of the marketing executive's job. He is dependent upon somehow getting ideas and being able to recognize good ones whatever their source.

Viewed in this context, marketing research can be of value in two general ways. First, it can serve as a source of ideas which can stretch the executive's own thinking and prompt him to re-examine present policies and practices in a somewhat different light. Findings of proved validity are not necessary for this purpose. The ideas from research can at least be subjected to the same scrutiny as those from any other source. If the number of new and provocative ideas is increased, presumably there will be a net gain. Second, research can serve to remove some of the uncertainty which characterizes the decision-making process by testing ideas or proposed courses of action. The results of such tests frequently are quantitative measurements which may vary widely in their precision depending upon the needs of individual cases.

In assessing the value of a study, then, it may be viewed in terms of the extent to which it contributed to one or both of the broad objectives just described. For a more specific appraisal of the soundness of the findings and the likelihood that all important factors were identified for consideration, the following inquiries might be made:

Was the research conducted by a reputable firm well qualified to handle an assignment of this nature?

Were the objectives clearly identified and stated?

Was adequate attention given to exploratory work to identify the relevant dimensions of the behavior under study?

Were the techniques appropriate to the objectives and the circumstances of the research?

Were proper steps taken to assure competent interviewing and recording of responses?

Was the sample of respondents adequate for the purpose in composition and size?

Was the interpretation of the data competently handled by well-qualified personnel?

What other evidence is there that the conclusions drawn from the data and the resulting recommendations for action are sound?

The above points may warrant considerably different emphasis depending upon whether the creative or the evaluative research function is dominant or whether both are of about equal concern. Most studies necessarily serve both to some extent. At least some evaluation usually is involved in formulating potentially fruitful hypotheses, and meaningful measurements, of course, depend upon having good ideas about what should be measured. Normally, then, all of the above considerations will be of some relevance. The detailed nature of their examination, however, will differ with the character of the research approach.

Before going into the above points in detail, we should like to comment briefly that several check lists have been prepared for use in appraising conventional marketing surveys.[1] They have dealt primarily with procedure for quantitative studies, emphasizing that such things as the phrasing and sequence of questions, interviewing, sampling, and processing, interpretation, and presentation of data must be done with care. In this way they have provided valuable assistance. Generally, they have not concerned themselves with exploratory research and hypothesis formulation. Instead, they have tended to assume that the researcher understands the nature of the subject under investigation and knows what it is that he wishes to measure. They also usually have assumed that the question-asking techniques employed will produce accurate and meaningful responses. This amounts to assuming the validity of direct questions because the lists were prepared largely with them in mind. Words of caution about their use, however, were included in the Advertising Research Foundation's list which warned that responses to simple "why" and "why not" questions often are inaccurate, and that people might not be able to give valid answers to questions involving memory, certain kinds of knowledge, or predictions of behavior.

We now shall discuss the previously enumerated points of inquiry in greater detail, giving special attention to qualitative aspects which have been a prominent feature of motivation research. A number of these comments will be brief because they summarize what already has been covered in earlier chapters.

[1] Examples: Advertising Research Foundation, Inc., "Criteria for Marketing and Advertising Research" (New York, 1953) ; Association of National Advertisers, Inc., "A Check List for Evaluating Marketing Research Studies for Advertising Executives" (New York, 1950) ; Warren Cordell, "Six Ways to Appraise the Reliability and Usefulness of Marketing Research," *Printers' Ink,* July 1, 1949, pp. 36–38.

Qualifications of Researchers

This consideration deserves more emphasis than it has received. As the trend toward the greater use of specialists continues, differences among research groups become more marked. Some are considerably better equipped than others in training and experience for handling certain kinds of problems.

When the matter of qualifications has appeared in check lists for market surveys, it usually has referred to technical abilities to prepare formal questionnaires of direct questions, conduct and supervise field interviewing, design and execute a sample plan, and process and statistically analyze field data. Seldom has knowledge of human behavior or experience in dealing with marketing problems in a broad sense come in for special attention. This reflects the emphasis which in the past has been placed upon the mechanics rather than the getting of ideas for research. Both, of course, are important.

When the objective is to learn more about how and why people buy, the most challenging task, as we have noted earlier, often is that of identifying the dimensions which should be explored. It is here especially that background in the behavioral sciences is important. In this day and age, training in dynamic psychology and familiarity with the clinical ways of thinking are rapidly becoming musts. Earlier, we cited the advantages to having as staff members people with somewhat different backgrounds and points of view. Specialties which appear to be particularly appropriate for behavioral studies include clinical psychology, psychoanalysis, social and cultural anthropology, and sociology.

As the research mission becomes more that of quantitative measurement, the services of a competent statistician become important in connection with the problems of sampling and statistical analysis of data.

We also wish to emphasize the importance of being thoroughly familiar with the range of problems with which marketing executives are confronted and their decision-making point of view. Knowledge of what has happened in the market place over the years can be valuable background for the researcher, as can knowledge of what information might be available from company records and from the regular information-gathering services such as consumer panels and store audits. Unfortunately, it is not uncommon for research groups to be lacking in these respects. Many of the well-established researchers have kept themselves too occupied with the important but narrower matters of techniques and procedures to have acquired as much marketing knowledge and insight as we should like. Management often has contributed to this situation by keeping research personnel too far removed from the decision-making process. Many of the social scientists engaged in motivation research entered the field relatively recently with little marketing background. While a number of them now have become well-versed marketing-wise, this is something that takes several years of concentrated experience.

Generally speaking, the research firms known primarily for conventional marketing surveys have lacked desirable behavioral science knowledge and skill. At the same time, the groups known primarily for their qualitative work have tended to be weak on quantitative measurement and statistical analysis. A few firms of both categories, however, have made important moves toward removing their respective deficiencies.

Clarification of Research Objectives

Failure to clearly identify the objectives and specify just how they were to be met probably has led to more waste of research funds and disappointment of unrealistic expectations of executives than any single factor. In many cases, this has resulted because management did not know what it wanted from research in the first place, and research either did not or could not force a clarification.

Exploratory Research

The importance of that part of the scientific approach called idea-getting or hypothesis formulation has been emphasized repeatedly in this book. An appraisal of a study of consumer behavior might well include inquiry into what attention was given to this vital function. Such questions as these would seem to be appropriate: Who decided what direction the study should take and how was the decision reached as to what factors should be included? Was there a systematic attempt to learn of the nature of the behavior in question and the research problems it posed, or were "possible" factors more or less just pulled out of the air with little if any attempt to understand where they might fit into the consumer-product relationship? Were specialists consulted? If so, who were they? Was exploratory field work undertaken to make available concrete data relative to the subject in question? If so, who reviewed it and what were their qualifications? Specifically, what were the principal hypotheses which guided the research?

Research Techniques

This subject was discussed in detail in the last chapter. It will suffice here to say that while the choice of the means of asking questions is that of the research specialist, the business executive should expect a clear statement of what techniques were used and why. He then can make at least some judgments as to whether the choice was made with due regard for the objectives of the individual study, recognizing the differences in requirements of exploration and providing specified measurements; the character of the information sought and therefore the respondent's ability and willingness to give it; and the qualifications of the researchers to use the techniques effectively. The question-asking devices and their sequence should be carefully planned so as to avoid biasing the answers. Inquiry might be made as to whether internal checks were provided on important points. Within a single interview, for example, the same topic might be approached in more than one way, perhaps by using different techniques, to afford a test of internal consistency of response. Another check is provided by the growing practice of conducting research in successive stages marked by somewhat different approaches, each taking advantage of the earlier work.

Interviewing and Recording of Data

The important matters of selection, training, and supervision of field personnel take on added significance as the research approach increasingly depends on skillful, nondirective probing and verbatim recording of what is said. This kind of interviewing requires a somewhat different mental set and an understanding of the interview process which have not been characteristic of interviewers customarily used for surveys based on structured questionnaires. Recording of the responses in the respondent's own words rather than those of the interviewer is difficult for many people to learn to do. Skill at note taking is essential, as is the development of an ability to retain much of the proceedings in one's head so that, with the aid of brief notes on key points, they may be reproduced immediately upon the conclusion of the interview. In practice, much of what is said is lost unless a recording device or shorthand is used. This means that the interviewer must exercise some judgment as to what is important for him to be sure to record in full. As the interviews become more focused, these matters are less of a problem. The ability to establish rapport is particularly important in qualitative interviewing so that special care is needed in selecting interviewers who will be compatible with the kinds of people they are to interview. It is important that the work of the interviewers be watched closely. Comparing reports on different interviews made by the same person and reports of different interviewers are means of checking on interviewer bias and performance in general.

Sample Design and Size

Sampling has received a great deal of careful attention in marketing research and much has been written about it. Nevertheless, it still has been a focal point of controversy and confusion in public discussions of motivation research. A number of motivational studies, particularly the earlier ones, have been deficient in sampling and in the handling of statistical matters generally, so criticisms have not been without some justification. At the same time, however, much of the protest has reflected a failure to recognize that there is no absolute definition of a "good" sample either as to size or as to the method of selecting respondents. Instead, what is adequate must be determined by the purpose for which the sample is to be used. As we have noted earlier, research may serve different functions. Individual studies may vary widely as to objectives and the nature of the behavior under investigation, and, hence, in their sampling requirements.

As to the matter of size, there has been a marked tendency for researchers who have specialized in large surveys designed to produce fairly precise measurements to assume that all research should seek such measurements, and, therefore, that large samples of respondents randomly selected are inherently good. Actually, of course, they could be wasteful. Sample size also has tended to get more than its share of attention from business executives who frequently are not well-versed statistically but who seem to believe in large samples on general principles. We encountered one case, for example, in which a well-established marketing research firm recommended a sample of 800 persons as adequate to produce the accuracy needed in a given survey. A top executive, whose acceptance of the findings was of major importance, firmly asserted that this was not large enough. Bowing to the realities of the situation, the research firm went along with a suggested figure of 1,300, or 500 more than were regarded as necessary by experienced statisticians.

Sample size, then, must be determined on the basis of objectives, how much accuracy of measurement is desired, and how much money is available for the research. The same is true for the question of whether respondents should be selected at random, by a quota system, or by other methods. For many marketing questions, rough measurements are satisfactory and greater precision could make no difference in terms of what action might be taken on the basis of findings. Many motivational studies have been primarily exploratory, and it has been a common experience of research groups that relatively few depth interviews frequently will permit the identification of the important dimensions. As the function becomes more that of measurement, as it usually does in the later stages, larger samples and more formal methods of selecting respondents may be needed.

A feature of a number of motivational studies is that the researchers, on the basis of their knowledge of people and the cultural and social influences on behavior, are able to make assumptions that certain population groups are reasonably homogeneous in pertinent attitudes and behavior. They then proceed to test whether the assumption is correct. If it is, a relatively small sample will suffice. This approach is in contrast with that characteristic of many market surveys which have proceeded on the assumption, in the absence of information to the contrary, that differences exist among people classified by any of a number of the usual geographic, economic, and other factors. Larger samples are required for this purpose in order to provide for reasonably accurate checks on each of the several groupings. There may be reasons for obtaining these checks. On the other hand, the approach may be needlessly inefficient, being used as a matter of convention in the absence of thorough preliminary work directed toward learning what the significant groupings of the population might be for the behavior in question.

There is nothing sacred about any of the factors commonly used for classifying respondents. They are, or should be, used because someone has reason to believe they might be related to behavior — or because he does not know whether they are or not and is "just fishing." If more useful factors can be identified, so much the better, and this has been done in some of the motivation work. Greater use of psychological and social factors can be expected as more is learned about their behavioral influences.

A number of motivational studies have failed to distinguish between users and nonusers of the product or brand in question in selecting respondents when this might have proved rewarding.

In summary, our remarks have indicated that the principles of sampling are something independent of the techniques used to question respondents, and that they are generally applicable in marketing research. One of the most important principles, however, is that sample size and composition should be appropriate to the research objectives. For further information, we should like to refer the reader to some of the excellent references on this subject.[2]

Interpretation of Data

In the case of surveys based on formal questionnaires of direct questions, it is possible for the business executive or his research representative to inspect the tabulations of results,

[2] James H. Lorie and Harry V. Roberts, *Basic Methods of Marketing Research* (New York: McGraw-Hill Book Company, Inc., 1951), pp. 83–197; Harper W. Boyd, Jr., and Ralph Westfall, *Marketing Research: Text and Cases* (Homewood, Ill.: Richard D. Irwin, Inc., 1956), pp. 276–373; W. Allen Wallis and Harry V. Roberts, *Statistics: A New Approach* (Glencoe, Ill.: The Free Press, 1956), pp. 101–126, 483–492.

check them for their statistical significance as well as for what he believes to be their marketing importance, and determine for himself whether the data seemed to support the researchers' interpretations. Theoretically, it is possible for him to retrace the steps involved in processing and analyzing the field data. Complete records of what was done should be available so that spot checks could be made on the editing of the questionnaires and the coding and tabulation of responses. These comments, of course, assume that the literal meanings of the answers to direct questions are useful. This is an assumption that the executive may or may not be willing to make without seeking counsel, depending upon the individual case.

The kind of check which has just been described becomes impossible as greater use is made of free response data from which meanings are inferred. The executive can, of course, inspect any statistics based on the interpretations, but he cannot directly check the interpretive work itself which is the heart of the matter. In the first place, there usually is no detailed record of the many interpretive judgments which led to the final conclusion — the clues to meaning which were seen, how the patterns of meaning emerged, and why the interpreter read into the data the meanings he did. The difficulties involved here were noted in the last chapter. Even if such information was available, neither the business executive nor his marketing researcher is likely to be qualified to pass judgment on what was done. This is particularly true when there is a large amount of free response material, and when unconscious factors of much psychological depth are important. Qualitative interpretation is specialized work for which the executive employs experts upon whom he must rely heavily.

The executive can, however, inquire as to what steps were taken by the researchers to guard against incorrect and incomplete interpretations. Some of the possibilities, mentioned in the last chapter, include the use of more than one interpreter on the data; the use of rough counts on major groupings of respondents and categories of meaning established by the interpreter, the figures being regarded primarily as an aid in the interpretive process; a review of the major interpretive decisions at staff meetings by several experienced persons, preferably of somewhat different specialized backgrounds; and the use of more structured devices specifically designed to test hypotheses.

When quantitative measurements are important in the interpretation of data, their estimated margins of errors should be specified.

The Research Conclusions

Thus far, several kinds of evidence relating to the soundness of research findings have been discussed:

Evidence that the work was done by well-qualified and reputable people.

Evidence that adequate attention was given to the important exploratory stage in which ideas and hypotheses are developed.

Evidence that the research approach, including the techniques, was well suited to the purpose.

Evidence that sound procedures were followed to minimize the chances of things going wrong.

Evidence in the form of results to specially designed tests of interpretations. More will be said about testing shortly.

This brings us to the main conclusions to which all the interpretations of the data lead as to the nature of the behavior or situation which was studied. It is here that the business executive usually will concentrate his attention. He can go only so far in examining the points represented above. Even if the research is well conducted by competent people who have been careful to provide internal checks on the data, sound findings are not guaranteed. The work still must be that of human beings of considerably less than perfect ability and understanding, and within the complex field of human behavior these limitations can be substantial.

There is bound to be uncertainty of some magnitude, and it is the business executive who bears the responsibility for any action taken as the outgrowth of research. From an operating standpoint, then, the practical test of validity is whether the findings win his acceptance. While this, too, obviously has its drawbacks, one also can argue that it is for the best. Not only is the marketing executive in command, but it usually is he rather than the researcher who has the broadest background of repeated exposures to all the complexities of the total market scene. This chapter is concerned with how he may make his appraisal, and our immediate interest is in scrutiny of the conclusions themselves, granting, for the moment, that all the precautions referred to earlier have been taken.

We are interested especially in the broader findings such as those on motivational patterns and the nature of product-consumer relationships. While our immediate concern is with motivational studies, the problem is essentially the same as exists in appraising any idea or explanation, regardless of its source. In the final analysis, the executive decides something is right because he feels that it is; he elects to take certain action because he feels that the chances for favorable consequences are worth the risk. His feeling of confidence in research results may be the product of a number of influences. In addition to obtaining the evidence described above, he may consider the following points: [3]

His Feelings of Certainty. We are speaking here of what have been called "feelings of subjective certainty" based on

[3] In developing these points the author was aided in his thinking by the Social Science Research Council's criteria for validating a social theory and related comments by Donald Snygg and Arthur W. Combs, *Individual Behavior* (New York: Harper & Brothers Publishers, 1949), pp. 274–279.

what one believes he knows about the reality to which the research results relate. One may not be able to explain these feelings fully; indeed, he may not be completely aware of them until they are evoked by something such as a research report. Nevertheless, they have been the basis for making many judgments in business, and they may constitute an important, practical test of research findings. The underlying assumptions are that the feelings are the product of experience and that experience is a valuable means of learning. Feelings of certainty about an idea or explanation, then, may indicate a degree of agreement or consistency with other factors whose influence has been felt in the course of experience.

This criterion should be particularly important in the case of studies dealing with the essential nature of a business and its products such as the investigations described in the selected cases. In talking with executives, we frequently heard declarations of feelings of certainty, indicating that it is probably the most important single criterion used in appraisal. For example, one executive described the findings of the psychological study conducted for the State Farm Mutual Automobile Insurance Company as "an extension and broadening of our thinking," and declared that "they seemed so right in terms of what we knew about our business." An executive of another company commented that a motivational research report "expressed many things more clearly and with greater depth than I had conceived of them. Many of these things were my opinions before, but now I have confirmation."

Feelings of certainty can constitute important evidence of validity, but they, in themselves, are not proof. They must be handled with care because experience can be a poor teacher as well as a good one; that is one reason why more research into consumer behavior is needed. The potential value of this test would appear to be related directly to the open-mindedness, curiosity, perception, and insight of the executive who uses it.

How Others Feel About the Findings. If others, especially those who are regarded as experts, accept the findings, there may be a greater presumption of validity. This is especially true if they reached the same conclusions independently. We know of several cases in which social scientists and marketing researchers have been employed as outside consultants to review research reports. There also have been several instances of hiring more than one research firm to work independently on the same problem. This test, like the others, can be helpful but it does not constitute proof. If the people serving as reviewers of the findings happen to share the same but erroneous ways of thinking, their opinions do not represent a check. There may be danger as well as comfort in company. In fact, one could argue that social agreement is very unlikely to be realized in the case of any really new ideas of consequence because of the problems of resistance to change, and the use of old frames of reference which are inadequate for appraising new concepts. After all, many of the great insights in various fields were rejected when they first made their appearance. It is quite possible for hasty and mistaken judgments to be made in marketing, too. On the other hand, many marketing studies, because of their nature, are not likely to produce radically new ideas. They are more likely to represent an extension of someone's past thinking.

Observational Tests of Findings. There are several observational tests the executive can make. One is that of internal consistency. Earlier we mentioned checking responses made in a single interview for this quality. Here we refer to using the same kind of test on the various conclusions drawn from all the data. The assumption is that every interpretation should contribute to a dynamic whole which is consistent within itself. If the interpretations are found to represent conflicting points of view, they are suspect.

The findings also can be reviewed to determine whether they seem to be in conformity with all known facts. Conformity may constitute evidence of validity. A danger, however, is that what are regarded as "facts" may actually be erroneous interpretations made from a faulty frame of reference.

Another test consists of subjecting an idea or explanation to "mental manipulation" to see whether it meets the requirements of the case at hand. This is a process followed by a diagnostician who makes an interpretation and then determines whether it fits the problem. If it does not, he discards it and tries something else.

Prediction of Behavior. This often has been regarded as the most important single test because the goal of research is understanding which will provide a basis for successful prediction. For example, we should like to be able to say that people will choose a given insurance company over others if it offers certain things; that people will drink more coffee if they are introduced to varieties of flavor and if steps are taken to counter unfavorable connotations; that improved sewing instruction will lead to more women doing more sewing in the home; that a certain kind of grocery routeman-customer relationship will lead to increased sales.

Studies such as those we have examined provide reasons to believe that people will behave in certain ways under stated conditions, but direct evidence in the form of sales results from well-conducted experiments that such behavior has, in fact, taken place, is rare in marketing. This lack of evidence is due in part to the underdeveloped use of controlled experiments when conditions would make them feasible. But it also is due to the expense and difficulties involved. The problem of identifying and controlling the many variables which influence sales already has been noted. Unless the factors in question are of major consequence, it may be impossible to clearly demonstrate their sales effect. In many cases, important influences do not lead to immediate sales; it takes time for them to be felt. For reasons such as these, experimental sales tests would be difficult, if not impossible, to conduct on the conclusions of the studies described in the selected cases in Part II. The changing of coffee habits, for example, may require considerable time. Similarly, it probably is impossible to show in behavioral tests conducted under actual conditions the relative effects of different kinds of sewing instruction on the amount of sewing women will do as adult homemakers years later.

Because of the problems described above, experiments often must be conducted under other than the actual conditions of the market place, and they must settle for results in terms other than the final behavior of interest. In other words, the test must be of a prediction about something which presumably is related to the final behavioral goal. Readership tests of advertisements were given as an example in the last chapter. A prediction may be made that an ad using a certain appeal will get a higher readership score than a similar ad using an alternative appeal. In this connection, a recent study by Franklin B. Evans of the appeals and readership ratings of advertisements for beer and detergents is of interest.[4] He concluded that the findings of motivational studies conducted in these product areas by Social Research, Inc., for the *Chicago Tribune,* seemed to be predictive of the readership the advertisements received. While readership, of course, is not sales, it can be measured and it may have to do. Its value depends on the validity of the assumption that a readership score is indicative of an ad's sales power.

Various other advertising copy tests also have been used

[4] Franklin B. Evans, "Motivation Research and Advertising Readership," *The Journal of Business of the University of Chicago,* Vol. XXX, No. 2, April 1957.

on findings of motivational studies. They involve testing for certain consumer reactions identified in advance and assumed to be favorable to the advertising's sales effectiveness. In the motivational study for the Pan American Coffee Bureau, a taste test was conducted to determine whether people would be more likely to drink stronger coffee if it were offered in the form of variety.

Survey questionnaires may make use of the principle of experimental design to test hypotheses.[5] Questions may be prepared which present stimuli under conditions believed to be sufficiently realistic to warrant the assumption that the verbal responses they elicit are indicative of the behavior which could be expected under actual conditions.

While prediction can be a useful test, it does not constitute positive proof. For example, a correlation may be found between two variables in the absence of a causal relationship. It may be possible to predict on the basis of past experience, then, without understanding why the result occurred. Under these conditions, of course, prediction is not an adequate test of a rationalized explanation.

Recommendations for Action

Most of what has just been said about conclusions can apply here as well. Recommendations are given special mention, however, to emphasize that they represent an additional step in which judgment is exercised. This can be an important distinction. The conduct of inquiry and the drawing of conclusions from the evidence obtained are in the area of the researcher's special competence and responsibility. Determining what action should be taken on the basis of this information, however, often is not.

[5] Two articles in which this subject is discussed: Samuel A. Stouffer, "Some Observations on Study Design," *The American Journal of Sociology*, Vol. LV, No. 4, January 1950, pp. 355–361; Alfred Politz, "Science and Truth in Marketing Research," *Harvard Business Review*, Vol. 35, No. 1, January–February 1957, pp. 117–126.

The failure of business executives to recognize this difference has led to researchers frequently being subjected to strong pressure to go much further in making recommendations than they felt they should. The problem contributed to the decision of one research director to issue two separate reports in many cases. One would present the findings themselves. The other would include expressions of related ideas and opinions which went beyond the data gathered in the study. The former bore the researchers' authoritative stamp; the latter did not.

A good many researchers, because of their training and experience in marketing or in human behavior, may well be in a position to express opinions of great value as to what action should be taken. Several of the behavioral scientists engaged in motivation research have made important contributions in this way. Their qualifications for so doing, however, are not identical to their qualifications for conducting a given study and reporting on the data, and they should be evaluated separately.

Concluding Remarks

The value of research to the marketing executive depends upon the extent to which it contributes important ideas or evaluations or both. When it comes to deciding whether findings should be accepted, he must, in the final analysis, go on how he feels about them just as he must in passing on ideas from other sources. If the conclusions are a product of research, however, his feelings often can reflect a review of a significantly greater amount of evidence as to validity.

The findings of many motivational studies have dealt with the nature of a business or its product. Inasmuch as these are matters of major interest to the executive, he usually is able to ask good questions of the researcher. While knowledge of behavioral science concepts would be helpful, it is not essential. The researcher has an explanatory burden to assume, and some of the more experienced of them have developed excellent communicative skill.

As a practical matter, if the research appears to have been well conducted and the findings tie in with existing thinking, even if they stretch it, there usually is little question raised about validity. A useful operating rule under these conditions is to accept the findings. Further tests can be made if greater assurance is desired because of the importance of the contemplated action.

In the case of explanations of behavior which include material of psychological depth, the acceptance issue may not be so clear cut. It is possible, however, to use several kinds of evidence which, in combination, may provide reasonable substantiation. If the executive is not satisfied with the findings and the supporting explanations, further checking is a next logical step. This may include consulting with outside specialists and the undertaking of further research designed to test the findings in question. Absolute certainty, of course, is not a requisite, nor is it possible in the absence of knowledge of absolute truth. Much of today's "knowledge" will be disproved later or at least be shown as incomplete. This is the process of progress. The business executive can do no more than act on the best understanding attainable at the time.

The results of some motivational studies, because of their nature, may represent a marked departure from past and current business thinking. History shows that rejection of new ideas in any field is not unusual whether they are right or not. It is important, then, to be aware of this danger and to take care to guarantee such findings a hearing as well as careful scrutiny.

CHAPTER XIV

Some Administrative Problems Related to the Use of Social Scientists in Marketing Research

ADMINISTRATIVE difficulties always have plagued efforts to employ research effectively as an aid in the making of decisions. As might be expected, the introduction and greater use of social scientists in marketing research have meant an increase in both the number and the complexity of these problems.

In order for research findings to be used effectively, someone must have a study made in the first place; someone has to see that the research is appropriate to the problem situation; someone must understand the findings and think about their implications; and someone must translate the results of the research and subsequent deliberations into action. It is such things as these that we have in mind when we speak of administrative problems, and they will claim our attention in this chapter. While our special interest is in the use of social science research in marketing, it will be apparent that many of the factors involved have broader application.

Our information on administrative problems was obtained from interviewing both researchers and executives of client companies and, in several instances, of observing meetings of the two parties at which research plans or results were discussed. We attempted to identify the kinds of problems which arise and determine what management might do about them. On the basis of the observed extent to which research findings received consideration and led to action, it was apparent that some firms were able to realize much more of the potential value of their studies than were others.

We can scarcely overemphasize the importance of this topic. In considering the nature and significance of the motivation research development, we necessarily have been concerned in the preceding chapters with concepts and approaches which may lead to more fruitful investigations. It may well be, however, that the greatest barrier today to the successful use of research in marketing consists of the related and unsolved administrative problems rather than conceptual or technical limitations of the research itself. We have been impressed repeatedly with the observation that in spite of the forward strides of the past 20 years, continuous and systematic use of research as an integral part of marketing decision-making is a rarity. Too little research is done and much of that apparently is deliberately ignored or for other reasons fails to become a part of executive thinking. Company file cabinets are well stocked with reports which never really had a chance to see the light of day.

In regard to motivation research, administrative troubles are particularly likely to accompany first attempts at use. While a number of early experiences have met with apparent success, conditions favorable to this result usually are not present. It often takes a while for the social scientist and the businessman to learn to understand one another. In fact, social scientists and their research have met with considerable emotional resistance from both business executives and marketing researchers because they represent different ways of thinking and doing things. In other words, some of the reasons why their services may be of value also are reasons why their services may encounter opposition. Their research frequently has served to challenge assumptions underlying basic operating policies dear to the hearts of certain executives, and it also has had the effect of bringing to light failures to formulate marketing and advertising strategy clearly. We shall elaborate on these points shortly.

SOME BACKGROUND INFORMATION

Before describing the problem areas in detail, we shall make a few relevant, general observations. The most important one is that motivation research has been the subject of heated controversy in research circles. To a large extent, this has taken the form of the old resisting the new, and the significance of many of the criticisms lies more in their emotional quality than in their substantive content. The troubled waters have quieted some now. We believe that the emotion-letting is on its way out and that a desirable integrating trend is under way. We have no wish to interfere with the latter by any unnecessary examination of soiled linen. At the same time, however, it is important for the business executive to know that people can have very strong feelings on this subject and to understand something about why this is so. These feelings no doubt will continue for some time to give rise to resistance to attempts to use social science research in marketing.

The emotionally charged atmosphere was much in evidence in the summer of 1954 when we interviewed a number of marketing research leaders preliminary to deciding to go ahead with the study on which this book is based. Subsequently, we attended a number of meetings of research groups featured by hostile questioning of speakers identified with motivation research. In 1955 the heads of several established firms which specialized in quantitative surveys launched a vigorous and bitter public attack against motivation researchers and their techniques. This went so far that *Printers' Ink* magazine noted in a September issue that "discussions of motivation research have reached full-fledged feud basis," and that "observers are concerned that such feuds will scare advertisers away from m.r." [1] In October of the same year *Advertising Age* commented editorially that "some of our research experts are too inclined to shoot off their faces

[1] *Printers' Ink,* Vol. 252, No. 12, September 23, 1955, p. 18.

in entirely unscientific blasts at their fellow researchers." [2]
The turmoil abated in 1956 to such an extent that in its
yearly review issue, *Advertising Age* was able to say: "It was
a relatively quiet year in research, free from vituperative has-
sles over motivation research. . . ." [3]

We think it better at this stage of events to avoid any detailed recounting of what happened. Our purpose here is to
go only far enough to establish that a number of research
people, including some of the recognized leaders in the field,
became highly emotional. It is this fact and an understanding of it that are relevant to a discussion of administrative
problems designed to be of help to the business executive
who wishes to employ researchers effectively in the future.

We should point out that not all marketing researchers
were participants in the controversy. While many shared to
some extent the feelings expressed so strongly by a few spokesmen, others were quietly learning more about the subject.
At least two large advertising agencies which were among the
first to bring social science trained people into their research
departments had by this time made excellent progress in solving related administrative problems and were quietly going
about their business which included using the services of
these people more than ever. The demand from business
for motivation research continued to increase, and more organizations — advertising agencies, research firms, and even
a few manufacturers — added some people with social science
training to their research staffs. In a survey in 1954 of its
Jury of Marketing Opinion made up of several hundred
business executives, *Printers' Ink* found that there were many
more nonusers than users of motivation research, but that
most of the users liked it and reported that the research had
led to changes in advertising copy, product, and package design, and basic marketing strategy.[4]

[2] *Advertising Age,* Vol. 26, No. 40, October 3, 1955.

[3] *Advertising Age,* Vol. 27, No. 53, December 31, 1956, p. 4.

[4] *Printers' Ink,* Vol. 248, No. 13, September 24, 1954.

WHY THE HEATED CRITICISMS?

In any relatively new field, there are bound to be examples of technically deficient work, even, perhaps, some of questionable integrity. There also are likely to be proponents who make extravagant claims to attract attention to their wares. The motivation research development has been no exception, and the critics have been quick to point to examples of weakness.

As important as these points may be, they do not in themselves explain the character of the critical outburst and the marked tendency toward wholesale condemnation. Inferior workmanship and malpractice have been present in the young field of marketing research before and have been critically noted without high emotional involvement. It is necessary to look beyond the literal substance of the criticisms of motivation research to understand their emotional intensity. We shall mention several things which we consider relevant. Each can give rise to feelings which may make for administrative troubles.

Perhaps we first should observe that the leadership in making marketing applications of the concepts and methods of dynamic psychology and social anthropology has come primarily from a few social scientists who became interested in marketing rather than from established marketing researchers who became interested in the social sciences. The studies described in five of our selected cases, for example, were made by people who had been brought into a few advertising agencies or who had joined two independent research firms which became important factors on the marketing research scene only since World War II by specializing in work of this kind.

It is not unusual for established practitioners to give newcomers something less than a cordial reception, especially if the latter pose a competitive threat and take over the spotlight of popular attention. This the motivation researchers did. Suddenly, it was they who were in great demand as speakers before marketing groups rather than the sampling experts and the pollsters who had dominated the research scene in the past.

Another important factor which made for some intense feelings was that more often than not the initiative in calling for the services of the social science researchers was taken by top management rather than by their marketing research people. The latter often found themselves pretty much sitting on the sidelines. Typically, marketing researchers have been primarily technicians with backgrounds in statistics, economics, and business. Few have had training in the behavioral disciplines which figured most prominently in motivation research. To make matters worse, many of these people had tried for years with only limited success to get their managements to take a greater interest in research. Suddenly, this happened, but not because of their efforts. The interest turned out to be in research of a kind that most of the marketing researchers did not know how to do. In fact, in the earlier years of the motivation research development, they were at a loss to answer their management's questions about it.

The reaction of the marketing researchers in this situaton, naturally enough, often was hostility. Many quickly became critics, often without having any firsthand knowledge of what they were criticizing. In the course of our field interviewing we discussed this situation with a psychologist who served as a consultant to survey firms. "After all," he commented, "if something new comes along in my field and people start asking me about it, I can do one of two things. I can take the time and trouble to bring myself up to date on it or I can fight it." In this case, many chose to fight at first, although a trend toward acceptance set in a little later as more was learned about the new development.

Another sore point with marketing researchers has been the implication that they were merely "nose counters" and that only motivation research, meaning that done by the newcomers with their social science concepts and techniques, could really find out why consumers behaved as they did. Actually, of course, much information of value in this area has been furnished by researchers using various techniques other than depth interviews and projective devices. On the other hand, it also is true that their ways of thinking and methods carried with them limitations which gave rise to the need and opportunity for those with training in the behavioral disciplines to make additional progress.

Conflict in Ways of Thinking

A matter of fundamental importance is that conventional marketing researchers and motivation researchers typically represent contrary ways of thinking. Proceeding with a number of opposing assumptions, they consequently look at the world differently. Until this is understood, there are bound to be clashes.

Various of the differences have been discussed in earlier chapters. They have to do with assumptions about such things as the nature of human behavior, what constitutes research and scientific method, what the best ways are to get information from people which will help explain their buying behavior, and what are meaningful data. Some of the principal points of contrast appear below in the indented paragraphs, each of which opens with a statement of position which tends to be true of marketing researchers whose training and experience have been largely in survey techniques and statistical analysis. The viewpoint then is compared briefly with that typical of clinically oriented persons trained in the behavioral sciences, particularly dynamic psychology and cultural and social anthropology.

Research means measurement. Good research, then, is primarily a matter of carefully following certain procedures. They see scientific method in terms of testing hypotheses and omit from serious and systematic attention the matter of getting ideas to be tested. The latter has been of major interest to motivation researchers who emphasize inquiry into what things mean to people. They generally have been much less interested in quantification.

Most people are motivated principally by logical and rational factors. Many marketing researchers have been unable to understand the motivation researcher's concern with how people feel about things, often unconsciously.

The preferred way of getting information from people which will help explain their buying behavior is to ask them specific questions directly which facilitate quantification of results. They regard the less direct approaches and the use of more ambiguous stimuli, characteristic of motivation research, as "unscientific."

Literal interpretations of responses are preferable because they make it possible for the figures "to speak for themselves." The clinically oriented person, on the other hand, is very skeptical about taking responses at face value. He emphasizes ascertaining of meanings by inference.

The statistically oriented researcher prefers to deal with factors one at a time and tends to have little patience with a clinician's efforts to develop patterns of factors which work in combination to influence action. To the former, the size and relationships of statistical totals determine whether the data are meaningful. The clinician emphasizes viewing data in the context of the whole of which they are a part in order to determine their meaning and importance.

The fact that important differences in orientation exist usually is not recognized, much less understood, when two schools of thought first come into contact with each other. Until it is, strong emotional reactions are very likely indeed.

Members of the established school tend to hear the newcomers as saying, in effect, that the former have been wrong in the "knowledge" which constituted their qualifications to do consumer research. They naturally fear and resent what they interpret to be the implication that their services have been made obsolete. Among the marketing researchers whom we have heard voice grave concern about this was a research director who had been with the same large corporation for 25 years. Speaking privately and at length, he reflected a note of desperation as he built up to the declaration: "After all, this is my life. At this stage, (conventional) research is all I can do."

It has been our observation that abstract discussions of techniques, typical of research meetings, had the effect of fanning aroused fears because it was difficult for a person of one orientation to understand what a person of another was talking about. There is much less chance for misunderstanding when the discussion is focused on a specific research problem. Under these conditions, the participants are more likely to be able to illustrate what they mean. They are more likely to recognize the contributions that can be made by each school of thought and to appreciate that an integrated effort often can make for better research.

Implications

The above considerations suggest that many of today's marketing research directors may be unlikely to take the initiative in investigating how their companies might benefit from using the services of people trained in the behavioral sciences. In fact, they may resist efforts along this line. Several illustrative examples are presented below.

Company A. This large manufacturing company became an early user of motivation research because one of its top executives personally was interested in the social sciences.

He had done considerable reading in psychology and anthropology and frequently discussed these subjects with a good friend who was a prominent social scientist. This led to his decision to hire an outside firm of people trained in the social sciences to make a motivational study on a product which presented difficult marketing problems. Satisfied with the result, he had other such studies conducted on several products for which he was responsible. Some were made by the same research firm, some by another one. The research led to product improvements and changes in advertising policy. The executive liked the research as is indicated by these comments:

> To a large extent, motivation research has confirmed what we suspected or thought we knew all along. But we didn't know for sure, so this was an important function. But it also has told us things we didn't know before. These are things we had tried to find out by direct questioning in a good many instances, but direct questions didn't work.

The head of marketing research had been with the company for 20 years. His orientation is reflected by the fact that when hiring personnel for his department he preferred young statisticians who had some academic training in business administration. An interview two years after the company's first motivational study found him very cool to motivation research. He voiced most of the technical questions which had been raised repeatedly in the past several years by research people at their meetings. He talked about sampling and what he considered to be the questionable validity of techniques drawn from other fields. He regarded motivation research as a technique. "It is only one tool and it will be recognized as such just as was probability sampling," he commented. "It's just one technique to be used, among others." He indicated no awareness of or interest in social science concepts and the possibility that they might be of some value in marketing research. Also at no time did he speak in terms of perplexing marketing problems or indicate that he was seeking new research approaches to solve them. He spoke almost entirely in terms of technical matters. In these respects, he represented a direct contrast to the top executive previously mentioned. While the marketing research head was careful to avoid direct expression of opposition to the research for which the top executive had contracted, it was plain that he represented at least passive resistance. "I've been studying this thing (motivation research) for several years, evaluating it, to see when we should use it," he said. This was two years after the top executive had taken action which resulted in the first study. The contacts between the company and the outside research firms usually were handled by the top executive himself or by his assistants, not by marketing research people.

Company B. Following are excerpts from an interview with a former marketing research director who had recently been moved to another position with the same company.

My reaction to motivation research is negative, I'm afraid. I'm in sympathy with the objectives, but I read these m.r. reports and I'm not convinced. Maybe their findings are right, maybe they are not. There is no proof. It's just the judgment or opinion of the researcher. . . . The motivation research people should call themselves consultants and admit they give judgments or opinions. They are useful in this way by stimulating new ideas. But what they do is not research — it is not scientific. . . .

I'm writing a report now based on a study I made and for which I interviewed people. I am convinced that what I say is right. But people will have to take my word for it. I can't prove it. . . .

I should tell you that I am a mathematician by training. . . . I like things to be scientific and proved.

The company for which this man worked had used the services of two outside research firms which specialized in motivation research, and it was beginning to conduct some of this kind of work within its own research department. This move had the active support of the president as well as the director of research.

Company C. The company's principal product was falling behind its leading competitors in share of market. The president questioned the effectiveness of the current advertising approach and, without telling his advertising agency, hired an outside research firm to conduct a motivational study. Several months after it had been presented to both the client and the agency, the president reported agency opposition to it. "So far nothing at all has been changed," he said.

Research spokesmen for the agency had been publicly critical of motivation research. The agency had not followed a few of its competitors which several years earlier had added to their staffs people trained in social sciences. In fact, Company C's study appeared to be the agency's first experience with this kind of research. We subsequently interviewed agency personnel connected with the Company C account and obtained the reactions described below.

Account Executive. "First of all, our attitude is that these (motivation research) studies must be taken with a grain of salt." He later said that the study in question had led to some changes which he enumerated. He concluded by saying that "the study has been helpful in confirming ideas we had all along and in helping sell them to the client."

Research Director. He began by speaking abstractly but critically of motivation research, then commented: "People sometimes say I'm against motivation research, but I'm not." His subsequent remarks on the subject, however, were mostly criticisms. Among them were the following:

The techniques are not validated for market research purposes. [A research assistant later commented privately that this also applied to conventional techniques.]

[A verbal attack on a person identified with motivation research.] He's an idea man but not an honest researcher.

Motivation research is not motivation research anyway — it doesn't get down very deep into causes.

Motivation research results often are not usable. They leave you with the question: "What do you do about it?"

Motivation research is biased because of the orientation of the researchers, and this affects both the planning of the research and the interpretation.

His conversation indicated that the type of research problems with which he was most concerned were such things as whether the headline should appear above or below the illustration; whether long or short copy should be used; whether research results are quantified "so they mean something — so you can tell what to do on the basis of them"; and whether a representative sample is used. In regard to Company C's study, he conceded that it was useful in stimulating creative ideas. He made it plain that he resented the fact that the client had not consulted him in regard to the decision to have the research done.

Research Assistant. "I differ from Mr. X [research director] in that I think motivation research is here to stay and can be very useful. The older research people can't see motivation research — they aren't used to thinking in those terms. Motivation research should be integrated into the existing research." The assistant had some social science training; the research director had none.

Copy Writer No. 1. On the whole he was enthusiastic about the study which "opened up many new avenues for creative thinking and experimentation." He detailed a number of points which he had found helpful to his thinking. Most of them related to advertising strategy, but one finding had given him an idea for a change in the product itself. He championed some of the findings within the agency, but encountered opposition from members of the account group to a proposal to change the advertising theme. He spoke of the problem of different people making different interpretations of what the research meant in terms of what should be done in the advertising. In this connection, he called for more information and clarification of certain points from the research firm. Speaking more generally, he called motivation research a "big advantage." "In the past," he said, "copy people would put on their hats, go out and talk with people. But there is only limited time available to do this kind of thing now. Motivation research does the same thing more comprehensively and with trained people interpreting the data. But I also would like to read the actual interview reports." As a result of his experience with Company's C's study, he asked the research department to undertake similar research for other accounts.

Copy Writer No. 2. "It was a real eye opener," she said of the research report. She referred particularly to being able to learn what women actually said and felt, how they reacted to different types within the subject product category. She voiced considerable concern over the problem of interpreting the findings in terms of advertising copy, but regarded them as a stimulating and valuable source of ideas. "My boss, as a result of this study, became sold on motivation research and called for more of it. As a result, the agency is trying studies copying the motivation research firm's techniques. A young psychologist has been doing depth interviews and branching out from there. The agency now is hiring another psychologist, so there have been additions to the research department."

Several months later (or about seven months after the research report had been presented), the president of Company C decided to change advertising agencies. One of his expressed reasons was dissatisfaction with the attitude the agency described above had taken toward the motivation study and its failure to make effective use of it.

Concluding Comments

The danger of resistance from conventional researchers should diminish as time passes. The growing interest in and use of motivation research represents a counter influence. It increases the chances that education will take place which will allay fears, and that research directors will decide to go along with the trend to avoid possible disfavor of their bosses. While the above discussion has centered on research people, it should be recognized that many business executives share to some extent the orientation of the conventional marketing researcher and therefore represent similar potential administrative problems.

ADMINISTRATIVE FACTORS UNFAVORABLE TO EFFECTIVE USE OF THE SOCIAL SCIENCES IN MARKETING RESEARCH

Below we have attempted to summarize what we have observed to be the principal reasons why companies fail to obtain the potential value from social science research in marketing. They relate to the matters of initiation, guidance, and implementation of studies and their findings.

Background Limitations of Marketing Researchers

We already have discussed why some marketing research people have resisted motivation research. Even if resistance is absent, however, they may be unable to suggest potentially useful applications of the social sciences simply because they do not know what they are. Social science training among today's marketing researchers (indeed, marketers generally) is a rarity because business has emphasized other qualifications. Most of these people, through no fault of their own, probably have never seen a motivational study at firsthand. While many have tried to learn something in this area, this is difficult to accomplish under the time pressures of daily operations, especially for one who starts with no knowledge of the concepts and methods.

The Gap Between Research and Decision-Making

Probably the most important single barrier to an optimum use of research in marketing is the great distance that commonly separates research from the on-going process of meeting policy and operating problems. Marketing research usually is not regularly represented in the important decision-making circles by an influential spokesman. By the latter, we mean a high-level executive who can mix easily with other executives and who is well acquainted with both marketing problems and the various specialized resources, including those of the social sciences, which might be utilized for their solution.

While progress has been made, marketing research generally continues to suffer from low status as is indicated by its usual place on the organization chart and, more importantly, by the apparent nature of the personal relationships existing between research directors and major line executives. This situation reflects an unenlightened attitude of top management toward the research function. For this reason, as well as others, marketing research seldom has attracted, or at least held, the imaginative, creative, persuasive man who gets a kick out of devising new ways of tackling problems and meeting the great challenge of getting research findings into the thinking of key personnel. Instead, marketing research directors tend to be technicians who operate sort of a job shop. They work on whatever is brought to them, provided the tasks can be handled by the tools they have on hand. In these circumstances, it is common to find no one thinking broadly about what research ought to be doing.

Several large companies have recognized this problem in recent years and have instituted organizational changes which have included putting a problem-oriented executive in charge of the research activity. We have been impressed with the observation that many of the apparently more effective uses of social science research in marketing have occurred where the gap between top management and research was bridged or at least narrowed.

Mistrust of Purpose of Research

It is common for the very people management is counting on to make use of the findings to resist research because they are suspicious of its purpose. Two of the reasons are apparent in the following comments made by an executive in an independent research firm:

> In the majority of cases, we are hired because the clier' has a problem. Something is wrong. Therefore, our hiring often is viewed by some as an effort by top management to show that what its executives or its advertising agency have been doing is wrong. As a result, these people are defensive. Or, they may fear we will attempt to tell them specifically how to do their jobs. We are seen as a threat to their security. This has been true with executives within client companies, and both account executives and copy people within advertising agencies. But perhaps it is most marked with research managers.

We have observed a number of examples of the above fears. They may cause people to go to extremes to discredit the research so they have an excuse to ignore it or to work out ways by which the study showed that they had been right all along. Needless to say, when people defensively devote themselves to either of these tasks, little learning is likely to take place as a result of the findings.

Generally, top level executives appear to be growing more favorably disposed to the use of research in the conduct of their businesses. There are many who are not, however, and there is a difference to agreeing that research in the abstract is a good thing and doing something about using it. Here are examples of resistance:

Company D. This family-controlled concern had been very successful in the food field for many years without using marketing research of any kind prior to 1950 when, with expansion plans in mind, it hired a marketing research director. Among other things, the latter's influence led to the undertaking of a major motivational study. After three years in his job, he commented as follows:

> Our vice presidents all have come up from the ranks, starting out as salesmen who drove trucks around to grocery stores. Their reactions to research is that it is fine if it confirms what they have thought all along. Otherwise, they ignore it. We have to work even harder to get our advertising agency to accept the motivation research findings than we do our own management people. Our director of advertising became sold on them, but so far the agency people have taken the attitude that they know advertising and don't need research even though some of the findings show that they have gone ahead on wrong assumptions.

Company E. This corporation has been a relatively heavy user of motivation research for which it employed an outside firm. We are interested here in the feelings of one senior executive who frequently took a strong stand against the motivation researcher's recommendations. "I'm afraid that marketing executives will use motivation research as a crutch instead of taking initiative in coming up with creative ideas," he said. "The executive must be his own psychologist." He cited several businesses which began and grew because one man had an idea and put it to work. " The executive must take command — it's his responsibility," he declared. "No one researcher can have a comprehensive picture of motivations. They'll only have parts of it and there is danger in this. It is the executive who must get ideas and decide which to use. He should draw from all of his experience, the Nielsen figures, what advertising agency people say, and product tests, but he's the general in charge." After all, he asked: "Who should you rely on most in deciding what will appeal to consumers — a consulting psychologist or one who has learned from many years of experience with Company E? Shouldn't we know why people buy our product and how to sell it?" Later on, he acknowledged with a smile: "I've been accused of thinking that good research is research that supports what I thought all along."

We noted somewhat similar reactions from some writers of advertising copy who resist encroachment into their creative domains. Generally, however, we found that those who had used motivation research were favorably disposed to it. Among them were some who admitted to opposition before their first experience which was more or less forced on them by clients. The copy people usually insist on doing their own creative thinking on the basis of the research findings, however, and are quick to resent any suggestion that a researcher is trying to tell them how to write copy.

Another cause of mistrust is the feeling that someone is having the research done just to prove that he was right in his ideas which, perhaps, members of his organization resisted. This appeared to be one important factor in this example:

Company F. A motivational study ordered by the president had little apparent effect on the thinking or action of those responsible for the activities with which the research was concerned. After voicing negative feelings against the use of outside research, a key operating executive made these comments, among others, relative to the study in question: "Sometimes people have an idea they want to sell — but haven't been able to put across. So they hire an outside researcher who can sell it easier. Maybe Mr. X [the president] had something like this in mind when he hired Y [the researcher] . . . at least he did have an idea he wanted to get across. Why, right now I have some ideas I know are right from work we've done — but I know that right now I could not sell them. If an outside researcher came up with these ideas, maybe he could sell them. . . . There has always been some question as to how much the researcher came up with what management wanted to him to say."

Meddling in Research Details by the Unqualified

We refer here to interference which makes it impossible for qualified researchers to use the research approach which would be the most appropriate for the circumstances. This can happen without the offender's realizing it. Business executives sometimes make too big a display of what little they know, or think they know, as to what constitutes good research. In so doing, it becomes apparent to the researcher that any study which fails to conform to the executive's preconceptions faces an uphill fight to gain acceptance.

Earlier in the book, we cited an example of an executive whose chief criterion of good research was that of a large sample. His influence led to making several hundred more interviews for a study than actually were needed. While this represented unnecessary expense, it did not mean a less desirable research plan which apparently came about in the following case:

Company G. Executives in this large manufacturing company wondered whether they should improve the quality of their principal product in certain respects and took the question to an independent research organization with which the company had a continuing business relationship. In discussing the research plans, the chief marketing executive of Company G insisted that the sample of respondents be representative of his marketing area in terms of several population characteristics. The research was designed accordingly. When the final report was submitted, the client was impressed with how closely the sample matched the population from which it was drawn on the previously designated criteria. He enthusiastically praised the research. The head of the research group, however, had recommended a different approach to permit intensive, qualitative explorations of certain factors. "When the client insisted on the sample's being representative in the usual respects — which were not important to the main objective — this meant that money had to be spent for the sample instead of other things. . . . He thought the study was great. If we had insisted on doing the kind of research we should have done, we probably would have lost the account."

Inadequate Advance Thinking and Planning

Failure of business executives to clarify research objectives and to give the researchers enough time to do their work are common causes of disappointment and forced sacrifices of research quality.

A marketing research director of a manufacturing company described his first use of a psychological research firm as disappointing. One of the main reasons he gave was his own lack of participation in the thinking and planning. The study, as it turned out, had not been set up to generate the right kind of information. Profiting from this experience, his second try led to a successful result. In this case, thinking was carried to a point where the research firm was given two major and clearly stated questions to answer, and he maintained a closer working relationship with the researchers.

A motivation research director in an advertising agency reported that one of his major problems was the tendency of account executives to think abstractly in these terms: "I want some research on this. Will you tell me how many interviews would be needed and how much it would cost?" The director said he now was replying to them: "We no longer deal on that basis. Let's first talk about what the problem is and then consider what, if anything, should be done."

A complaint we heard frequently from researchers was that business executives fail to appreciate that good qualitative research requires time and cannot be rushed. The researcher quoted above spoke on this subject as follows: "Ideally, we would like to do a microcosm of a big job on a few people, then do a little bigger one, etc., working from a very open toward a little more structured approach. This allows you to develop your thinking and correct yourself as you go. But our people too often want results on an emergency basis. They spend the money available for research all at once — so you just have to do the best you can. If you have to rush your thinking which gives you your hypotheses, you can lose an awful lot."

Resistance to the "Ologies"

Since World War II there has been a great upsurge of public interest in human behavior and the fields which specialize in its study. More people know something about them than ever before. In business, many companies have made some use of the services of social scientists, particularly psychologists, who have aided in the working out of problems in personnel selection, placement, training, and morale. More recently, marketing has turned to behavioral specialists for help in learning more about consumer behavior.

In spite of the above, however, most business executives today have had little opportunity for direct contact with such fields as psychology, sociology, and anthropology, not to mention psychiatry, and, what is more, many are predisposed to view them apprehensively. Even if they took a social science course or two in school, their academic training probably was pre-World War II and before psychology textbooks belatedly got around to recognizing the works of Freud and the more recent clinicians. Psychology courses then seemed to be concerned not so much with everyday problems of human thought and action as with such things as white rats, the details of the human eye, and, to some extent, the bizarre and pathetic actions of insane asylum inmates. Unacquainted with later developments in psychology, businessmen may well fail to see how psychologists could be of much help in dealing with the practical problems of business.

It is not surprising, then, that unfriendly feelings may be evoked by first contact with motivation research reports. Mr. Morrill's remarks relative to the pschological study for the State Farm Mutual Automobile Insurance Company (see Chapter V) reflect a moderate attitude. "To be frank with you," he said, "I was lukewarm about doing the psychological study. Some of the psychological stuff . . . seemed like nonsense to me."

Another important reason why social science ideas may encounter opposition is that they seem to challenge important assumptions which have become a part of the businessman. Our culture has placed high value on logic, reason, and control over and even denial of feelings, and many executives subscribe to the attendant "economic man" concept of behavior. They are uncomfortable when they first come into contact with concepts dealing with people's feelings and social influences. The concept of social class occasionally runs into opposition because it appears to violate the commonly held belief that our country represents a classless society. This figured prominently in one executive's rejection of a research report even though he indicated in other ways that he was very conscious of differences in social status among people in his community.

There seems to be a widespread feeling that "most of what psychologists say is just a matter of opinion anyway," and, many would add, "my opinion is just as good as theirs." This is associated with a lack of knowledge as to just what social scientists do. Several executives have suggested that the chances for favorable consideration of research would be improved if social science researchers in marketing would take some of the mystery out of their activities by preparing a presentation on themselves and their methods.

Poor Communication

Well-intentioned attempts at an interchange of thoughts between social scientists and businessmen may be unsuccessful for reasons other than those already mentioned. The two groups tend to have their own languages as well as concepts. Failure to make allowances for these differences has led to major difficulties, even abandonment of attempts to establish satisfactory working relationships. A good many social scientists innocently have used unfamiliar "jargon" which not only was unintelligible to the uninitiated, but which quickly brought to the surface latent hostile feelings.

Several factors appear to be relevant to the difficulty experienced in both oral and written expression by competent social science researchers. Their primary interest usually is in inquiry and analysis, not in relating to other people in order to influence thought and increase understanding. As a result, they have tended to talk at advanced and technical levels, oblivious to the feelings of their listener who does not even pretend to know the first thing about research. The researcher often has failed to recognize the necessity for first getting acquainted with the businessman's problems and way of thinking so that new ideas can be presented meaningfully in terms of the latter's frame of reference. Social scientists, as well as the more familiar statisticians, also have incurred disfavor by what businessmen have regarded as nonbusiness-like appearance and conduct and a damaging lack of tact. In short, a good many researchers are not interested in contact work. They do not like it and they lack the skills needed to do it well. These factors probably are important among the reasons why they became researchers in the first place.

In emphasizing the importance of the communications problem, we wish to avoid leaving the erroneous impressions that it is peculiar to people from the social sciences and that all researchers are ineffective spokesmen. On the positive side, we should point out that several of the social scientists now prominent in marketing research have pooled apparent natural talent and experience to achieve very enviable reputations as effective communicators.

Resistance to Formulating and Re-Examining Basic Strategy

Motivational studies of the nature of product-consumer relationships inevitably deal with matters fundamental to over-all marketing strategy. The findings require a great deal of reflective thought if their value is to be realized, but this may not be forthcoming for several reasons. Perhaps the appropriate executives lack the necessary time or ability. If basic policy was never clearly defined in the first place, there may be resistance to anything that would bring this fact to light. If strategy has been defined, executives may be cool to re-examining assumptions they made some time back because they fear they might find out they have been wrong.

The regular use of social science research helped two advertising agencies to recognize that failure of account and creative people to formulate clearly and to apply basic strategy consistently constituted an important internal problem. One of the agencies made certain organizational changes in an effort to correct this situation and the other was considering a somewhat similar move. A research executive in one of the agencies reported that a major reason motivational studies had met with some resistance was that "it forced thinking in terms of strategy — thinking which too often has not been done. The account and creative personnel," he said, "tend to spend their time on details without facing up to developing an over-all plan to guide their work."

An account supervisor in a third advertising agency which had been using social science research for nearly two years had this to say: "The research often has been more useful in laying ghosts to rest than in telling us what new things to do. It keeps you from making mistakes. It is so easy in this business for erroneous ideas to start and grow without being challenged. Thinking tends to be in stereotypes: 'The consumer thinks this' or 'the dealer won't go for this,' etc." The challenging of ideas by research, however, was not always welcomed. In this same agency we encountered an example of resentment to a motivational study by a creative head. The research suggested the abandonment of an advertising approach built around a well-known symbol which he had originated more than 20 years ago and in which he obviously took a great deal of pride. The study showed the approach to have become inadvisable because of social changes. While the brand had been a leader for a long time, its sales had fallen off in the last decade.

Company H. An executive commented as follows on the difficulties this manufacturing company experienced in getting its people to use research findings: "The motivational reports can be very helpful if you have the personnel who can understand them. This requires people who can think reflectively about the meaning of the findings and the implications for action. Many of our men who should have used the reports lacked the necessary ability and background to do this, and all of them were too preoccupied with operating problems." Later, we talked with one of the principal operating executives concerned, and he opened his remarks by this declaration: "The first thing I want to say is that what we don't need is more researches. I have a whole drawer full of studies. It's a problem to interpret them — to find out what they mean and what should be done as a result. After all, we've got a business to run, too!"

Mistaken Expectations of Research

Criticisms of motivational studies indicate that many businessmen tend to assume that all research should "tell us exactly what we should do," "tell us only things new to us," and "contain figures." These assumptions appear to stem in part, at least, from the fact that most marketing research has been designed to measure the effectiveness of some action or to test already formulated alternatives in order to prescribe which one should be used.

While social science research often performs these functions, it also frequently has been employed for a less familiar primary purpose — that of diagnosis. This has to do with idea-getting or hypothesis-formulating. Information on the nature of something and the important variables involved is the kind that is needed for thinking about strategy and possible courses of action. But this thinking still remains to be done if it were not the purpose of the research to go that far. In such cases, the findings naturally fall short of specific prescriptions for action. If the purpose has been to develop a picture of all the principal factors or meanings of a product, the findings undoubtedly will include many things business executives know or think they know, as well as new information. If qualitative analysis was used, as has been customary in exploratory studies, the reports may consist of verbal descriptions and contain few if any figures.

Some executives have learned to distinguish between the different functions research may perform, and to see the value of qualitative studies in stimulating thought and pointing the direction for further inquiry. To others, however, the creative role for research is strange. Their preconceptions as to the nature of research have made for mistaken expectations and consequent administrative difficulties. Some illustrative examples follow.

Company I. The president of this growing manufacturing company praised a study which tested consumer reactions to several symbols. "A valuable study — addressed to a specific problem," he said. "We could take action on the results." He contrasted it with a broad investigation which had been made by the same research firm of motivating factors in the use of the kind of product he manufactured and their impact on brand selection. "This study was worthless — too general," he declared. "It told us things we already knew or things we could do nothing about anyway." The results of both studies were expressed quantitatively.

There appeared to be little doubt that the study he liked represented a valuable kind of research. As for the one he rejected, it dealt with such things as these: the types of users in terms of both the amount of use and various personal characteristics; motivational influences with special attention to several personality factors and psychological benefits from use; what people considered to be the qualities of a good product of this type; the times, occasions, and duration of the use of the product; and buying habits.

The study appeared to contain data relevant to marketing and advertising strategy. It did not, however, give results in terms of definite prescriptions of action — that apparently was not its purpose. The president did not appreciate this fact and either he did not know how to use this kind of research or he was not given to mulling over data of this type.

Instead, he dealt in terms of specifics and assumed that he knew the nature of his business well enough to identify what specific things should be tested.

Company J. A major motivational study failed to receive serious consideration from many of the company executives. One executive, who liked the study, commented on the initial reception as follows: "Our operating people wanted simple answers and suggestions for direct action. This report didn't give them. Also, a number of the findings were things everyone already knew or thought they knew. They didn't expect that. This made them less inclined to consider the report seriously." A year or so later, the executive we have quoted was in a position to get others to think about the report by holding a series of informal discussions of matters with which the research had been concerned.

Company K. When the sales of this manufacturer's principal product in the drug field showed signs of leveling off, an outside research firm was employed to do a motivational study. The action was taken on the recommendation of the research director who reported directly to the president and who participated regularly in top management meetings. The report of qualitative findings was favorably received by the research director and the medical people in the company, but rejected by a few top executives and the advertising personnel. "They felt it was too general," the research director said. "They objected to the fact that it didn't give specific recommendations as to what to do."

Some time later the study actually was put to use on the initiative of the research director. A consultant was hired to go over the report, help interpret its meanings and implications, and meet with advertising people from both the company and the agency to discuss the findings and help them think about advertising applications. Several follow-up meetings were held, attended by copy writers and the research director. As a result of this experience, plus subsequent events, the company had used half a dozen motivational studies on its products by five years later. Top management's reaction to the most recent study was described by the research director as "very favorable — you could have heard a pin drop attention was so great in the first presentation meeting." Profiting from earlier experiences, improved techniques of presenting findings now were being used, and the research firm was engaged to do the study, make definite strategy recommendations, and meet with advertising people at a later date to help them work out problems of application.

Company M. Several years ago this company employed a few people trained in the social sciences to comprise a research group to serve a number of product departments. The unit's director spoke of some of his difficulties: "In the beginning, we did a lot of high-quality qualitative research. We still do a good amount. But we learned of some practical problems. Sometimes when research is ordered, you know the executive already has made up his mind. If you are a big name, you can get by with telling him he's wrong on the basis of unstructured interviews analyzed qualitatively. But in our case, it's harder. We can come up with a beautiful qualitative job and they'll raise all sorts of objections so that they can disregard the research. So we have turned more to structured approaches which permit quantification of results. There are a number of things you can't get by a direct approach, but they seldom argue with figures even if the data are meaningless."

Valued Preconceptions

Research findings may run into strong opposition or be ignored because they challenge beliefs important to their holders. This problem was present in several of the illustrations already presented, including the Company M example above, and it had decisive consequences in the situations described below.

Company N. A social science research firm was employed to study the morale of this company's retail store managers, their concept of their role, and their relationships to their superiors and employees. Company management had taken pride in the belief that their store managers were aggressive, creative, and experimentally minded. The research, however, found that their role did not require these qualities to any degree; that the managers were a product of what they had been brought up to be — good operating men who could function effectively under the company's current system of tight controls and strong direction from the top. The report went on to point out that should the system be changed to stress development of aggressive merchants, many of the current managers would be hard pressed to produce. The study was not well received. One top executive reported: "They [top management] found the report hard to take. They read it and proceeded to ignore it. The effects of this report influenced [unfavorably] their reactions to later research done by the same firm."

Company O. Surveys had shown the percentage of people who expressed a preference for this large manufacturer's brand was considerably in excess of its share of market. Top management, upon the recommendation of the research director, employed an outside research firm of psychologists to find out why this gap existed and what could be done about it. Some of the findings and recommendations turned out to be contrary to strong beliefs held by the executive responsible for the sales of the product. He reacted violently against the research, criticizing it ruthlessly on many counts. His reaction can be moderately summarized by "I don't believe it — based on my experience!" The report was shelved.

Failure to Provide for Translating Findings into Action

"These reports have to get into your thinking to do any good. There has to be follow-through." So declared the chief executive of a corporation which has used a good deal of motivational research. His remarks help emphasize what already has been indicated at a number of earlier points; namely, that a major problem area is that of going from the findings to business action.

Because of their nature, motivational research reports often require considerable study and thought. Much research money has gone down the drain because no provision was made for consideration of findings beyond that which could be given in one presentation meeting or in one reading of the report. Part of the problem, then, has been failure to make formal time and procedural arrangements for the follow-through. Another part has been failure to understand how to use research in the creative process; failure to visualize steps that must be taken if a more effective program of action is to result from an improved understanding of a situation. This difficulty would seem to account to some extent for many remarks we heard to the effect that "we have a lot to learn about how to make use of the findings."

ADMINISTRATIVE FACTORS FAVORABLE TO EFFECTIVE USE OF THE SOCIAL SCIENCES IN MARKETING RESEARCH

The creation of a salutary climate depends not only upon avoiding negative influences, but upon introducing positive ones as well. In this section, anticipated by the preceding one, we shall attempt to summarize conditions which seem to be conducive to the making of helpful marketing research applications of the social sciences and the constructive consideration and implementation of the results.

Willingness to Identify and Re-Examine Basic Assumptions

Research should stand for judicious inquiry directed toward improved understanding. Its beneficial use in business, then, depends upon open-mindedness and desire to view objectively what one is doing and to scrutinize the underlying assumptions.

A willingness to undergo self-examination can come about in at least two ways. Perhaps the most common is through fear of loss. This has been the initiating force behind much marketing research. Many motivational studies, particularly those in the earlier years of the motivation research development, were made because something was wrong. Sales were disappointing, a competitor was gaining ground, or, for some other reason, the future appeared threatening.

Willingness of a more durable sort may be the natural product of the character of a company's management and working atmosphere. Desirable characteristics would appear to be a mutual interest in recognizing and solving problems and provision for regular consideration and joint discussions of policy and operating questions. The latter would be undertaken with the full expectation that today's basic assumptions will be modified as part of an on-going process which includes continuous efforts to improve on them. If executives share this concept, they are more likely to use research in the first place and to think and do something about the findings. Defensive resistance is less likely to be a barrier. Something of this kind was indicated in these comments of a manufacturing company executive:

> There was no real resistance to our motivation research, probably because of the informal, group way of operating. The product people and the research people are in frequent contact with one another — they all are in on the thinking and they know the problems. They had this background when motivation research entered the picture.

The environment described above also probably is more likely to include people who can and will entertain new ideas. In this connection, we asked a social scientist who had worked several years with many executives in a large company what kind of a person was most likely to become interested in social science research and use it effectively. His reply follows:

> One who is not defensive, who doesn't have to maintain tight control over things, who is willing to listen to new thinking. One who is willing to trust others some rather than do everything himself.

Favorable Attitude Toward Research

We refer here to looking upon research as a help rather than as a personal threat; something to be used regularly as an integral part of decision-making rather than as a desperate, emergency measure. Whether it actually will be regarded favorably will depend to a large extent on how it has been used in the past and whether it has top management's active support. If the boss is interested in research, his subordinates are more likely to be interested in it, too. The fact that the president of the State Farm Mutual Automobile Insurance Company (see Chapter V) personally participated in a series of discussion meetings on research findings appeared to be an important reason why the latter became a part of the thinking of key executives and why they exerted an influence on several aspects of the company's operations.

Experience in Regular Use of Research in Marketing Decision-Making

A number of first experiences with social science research appear to have been reasonably successful, administratively speaking. Some of these have been in companies which had no marketing research department and very little previous contact with marketing research of any kind. So experience is not required if other favorable factors are present, particularly an absence of strong internal resistance. On the other hand, we also have observed that experience can contribute a great deal. It is essential if an optimum use of research in marketing is to be attained.

There is much to be learned as to when research should be undertaken, what kind should be employed, who should do it, and what makes for an effective management-researcher working relationship. Through experience, the user of research becomes more aware of the variables which influence sales of his product and he learns which ones can be investigated and controlled with profit. He also learns how to define attainable research objectives clearly and how to plan and schedule studies in order to obtain work of high quality. One of the more important benefits of experience, particularly with motivational studies, is the recognition that research can be used for creative as well as evaluative and predictive purposes. With a greater understanding of the different functions, it is more likely that appropriate investigations will be undertaken at the proper time and less likely that there will be mistaken expectations of the findings.

A High-Level Research Spokesman with Administrative Skill

For reasons mentioned earlier, conditions for successful use of social science research (or research of any kind) are improved if that activity has a capable spokesman who moves with ease in the circles where important marketing decisions are made; who is both liked and respected by his colleagues. Ideally, he should be well enough versed in the behavioral fields so that he knows how they can be utilized in marketing and so that he can talk about the principal concepts and methods in language the businessman can understand. Lacking this background, he still can be very helpful in a liaison capacity.

Conditions are more favorable if the research director is

primarily problem-oriented and views his role as that of aiding executives in their thinking by encouraging the use of appropriate research at the right time. He should know both marketing and research problems. The research head should be well acquainted with the growing number of specialities which can be employed beneficially, but he need not be highly trained in any one of them. Of major importance is a high degree of administrative skill. In most organizations, research still has a long way to go to win complete acceptance, and, by its very nature, it involves suggesting new ideas and evaluating old ones. Inasmuch as both of these activities frequently incur opposition, an understanding of the nature of resistance to change and how to deal with it is very valuable equipment.

Favorable Attitude Toward Social Science

If people have a genuine interest in learning more about the nature of human behavior, they are more likely to be receptive to relevant new concepts, to experiment with new research approaches and to give the results full consideration. The use of social science research by several companies which now are relatively advanced in this respect can be traced to the personal interest of an executive which led him to become acquainted with one or more of the behavioral fields.

An advertising agency got its early start in the use of motivational studies because of the influence of one top executive. "In research, I had the feeling that we were missing something," he said to us several years later. "There were too many things we could not explain. I became interested in theology, influenced by a priest. Theologians seemed to be about the only people who were interested in the meaning of man. Later, I read a few books in anthropology such as the Yankee City Series and *Deep South*. They made sense. I first learned of firm X through an article in the trade press and I asked its director to visit us." This contact led to a decision by several agency executives to take Thematic Ap-perception Tests of personality, the results of which they discussed together. They also had the outside firm of social scientists analyze a network radio program which had never received very high ratings. This led to gradual changes with beneficial results. The agency also had members of the outside firm come in for a series of lectures and discussions with agency personnel. Executives who were particularly interested held a number of informal evening meetings at which reports of subsequent research done by the outside firm were discussed by themselves and their wives.

The use of social science research by another advertising agency came about because a top executive in a client com-pany had a strong personal interest in studying human be-havior. At his instigation the agency employed an outside firm to conduct a motivational study on one of the client's products. This experience led to the agency's retaining the same firm on a one-year trial basis to conduct research, meet with agency personnel in a series of informal discussions, and consult on special problems. The trial proved success-ful and the arrangement was continued.

Some of the social scientists who have become permanent members of marketing research departments have done much to create favorable attitudes toward their services by getting acquainted in their organizations and by conducting them-selves so that they are regarded as friendly as well as able human beings. "We found out these psychologists were pretty nice people," an advertising agency vice president commented. "Why, we even started going to lunch with them!"

Effective Liaison with Research Firm

We are speaking here with particular reference to the use of independent firms staffed principally by people trained in the behavioral fields. It has been our observation that the maintenance of a fairly close working relationship can make a tremendous difference in value received. This is due to the greater sharing of information and ideas which is likely to result, the closer checks provided on research planning and thinking, and the greater attention given to meeting a communications problem which must be solved if the research findings are to be well understood by those who are in a position to use them.

An important first step is thorough discussion of the marketing problems and clarification of the research objectives. Best results are more likely if this is done by the line executives to whom the report will be submitted and the research people who will direct the study and present the findings. Experience has led some research firms to adopt the practice of making periodic progress reports followed by full discussions of their work and tentative findings with client executives. This procedure serves as a check on the direction of the research and reduces the chance of later misunderstanding.

It is essential that the client representative assigned liaison responsibility be an effective communicator. He should be well acquainted with his company's problems and the thinking of its executives and, preferably, should have background in the social sciences and in research. A few firms have benefited by employing social science trained people as consultants to assist with the liaison function. A number of large companies would appear to have much to gain from employing one or more such persons on a full-time basis.

There is much to be said for establishing a continuing relationship with an independent research firm. Such a contact would allow the two parties to get acquainted with each other's problems and ways of thinking. The result should be improved research planning and more effective presentations of results.

Effective Presentation of Findings

If research is to play its important role in helping people develop their thinking about their work, it is essential that this major communicative step be taken successfully. The presentation should be planned to dispel fears that may be present and to make findings understandable and meaningful in terms of the listeners' problems, ways of thinking and language. Interest must be aroused and thought stimulated. Achieving these objectives takes a high degree of skill by the person making the presentation.

A matter-of-fact monologue by the researcher or the distribution of a written report usually is not adequate. Much research has met a premature death because the presentation amounted to no more than this. Ample opportunity should be provided for free discussion of the findings and their implications. It is here that an able leader can do much to encourage people to re-examine their assumptions and to assist them in efforts to get acquainted with new ideas. Ample time should be allowed. A series of several meetings may be necessary to cover the material and to provide optimum time for discussion. This arrangement also can encourage and capitalize on thinking between sessions.

Provision for Translating Findings into Action

The presentation discussed above is only the first step in the process of making use of findings which bear on important policy and operating questions. What remains to be done is of major consequence. Failure to visualize what it entails and to provide for its execution has made this a major problem area.

If the research is of good quality, there is new information which should make for greater understanding and an improved basis for making plans. Going from this foundation to specific action is a creative process. This is true whenever a program is to be thoughtfully developed. The use of research does not change that. It can and should help. If maximum value is to be realized from findings with strategic and tactical implications, attention usually must be given to the following steps:

Clarification of present strategy and identification of underlying assumptions so it is known from where one starts in his thinking.

Re-examination of the currently held assumptions in the light of the new research evidence and identification of important unanswered questions that arise from this step.

Consideration of and, if it appears advisable, the undertaking of research designed to answer these questions and to explore further certain areas pointed up as important by the initial study.

Revision of basic assumptions and re-formulation of strategy as appears to be appropriate in view of the above deliberations.

Identification of possible courses of action which appear to be appropriate to the re-defined situation and broad objectives.

Tests of these alternatives. This step may involve the use of research to arrive at a more definite prescription for action.

Ideally, there should be another step — that of checking on the effects of the action taken which will involve the use of research in its evaluative function.

In order for these things to be accomplished, management must recognize their importance, determine who should do what, and make the necessary time and procedural arrangements for the work to get done.

The above steps provide for the use of research in its several functions. The first, which has been a major one for motivational studies, is that of aiding in the creative process by introducing new ideas and providing information which adds to understanding of the situation for which strategy must be developed. Data may be gathered on the meanings a product has for people, the various influences on buying behavior, the nature of salesman-customer relationships, and the like. A second function is that of testing in order to prescribe specific actions appropriate to the situation, and a third is that of attempting to measure the effectiveness of the action once it has been taken.

Research in no way reduces the need for creativeness by business executives or advertising copywriters. In fact, its advantageous employment is dependent upon ability to think creatively. Research should help these people use their talents to better advantage by giving them more information to go on and reducing the necessity of their proceeding on false premises.

Our discussion so far has not given sufficient emphasis to the thought and skill required in interpreting findings to determine what they mean in terms of broad objectives and ways of accomplishing them. While research may clearly indicate what should be done, often it does not. Even if principal motivations in the purchase and use of a product are identified, the question remains as to the best way of appealing to them. A direct approach to psychological and social motivations may be inadvisable. There is a danger here that people without the background and skill for dealing with matters of this kind may leap to mistaken conclusions. This problem caused one advertising agency copy head to comment: "Giving some clients deep research is like giving a baby a pistol. They don't know what to do with it and you never know what is going to happen."

There is much to be gained from the growing practice of employing social science researchers not only to do the research but to work with client personnel in developing applications of the results.

CHAPTER XV

Concluding Remarks — With an Eye to the Future

In our examination of the work popularly referred to as motivation research, we found a number of systematic efforts to make use of the behavioral fields, especially dynamic psychology. Together, they constitute a movement, now young, which promises important conceptual growth and therefore appears destined to be a major landmark in the history of marketing.

The main points on which this viewpoint is based already have been presented, some of them being summarized in Chapter XI. Before exploring implications for the future, we wish to underscore the importance of the development. Significant change, such as it represents, usually does not come in the form of an immediate, complete switch from one extreme to another; hence, it may escape appropriate notice. To a large extent, we have been talking about trends in emphasis. Nevertheless, they are of major proportions and there has been rapid movement within a relatively short span of time. Here are some of the changes:

Marketing's Purpose. Inquiry directed toward identifying and understanding consumer wants is gaining more recognition as a function of first importance. This might seem to be only natural in view of marketing's over-all purpose. A contrary attitude, however, has enjoyed considerable popularity in the past. It is that marketing research does not exist to find out what the consumer wants; that consumers really do not know what they want; and that the marketer's purpose should be to make them want what he wants them to want. To our mind, this is an unfortunately narrow way of thinking which puts the emphasis in the wrong place. The starting point must be consumer wants, not manufacturer wants, if our economic system is to attain its potential effectiveness and efficiency in serving people. The prospective success of selling efforts is directly related to the presence of want-satisfying qualities for the customer. If a product or service lacks these, it is doomed. The task of learning about consumer wants, of course, has been a very challenging one, but it is on this front that motivation research is making headway.

Research Functions. The getting of good ideas to guide research, and, subsequently, the planning of products and marketing programs, now is receiving more systematic attention. The growing recognition that research may serve both creative and evaluative objectives in a number of ways should lead to an expansion of its use in marketing decision-making. (Research functions were discussed in some detail in Chapter XII.) In the past there has been a marked tendency to assume that the getting of good ideas was easy. Hence, many have equated research with testing by certain conventional techniques rather than regarding it in the broader sense as a process of inquiry directed to increasing understanding.

Consumer Behavior. A most important trend is that toward viewing buying and consumption in the context of total human behavior of which they are a part. More attention is being given to the view that all behavior is purposeful, comprising an integrated whole in terms of its meanings to the behaver. Greater recognition now is being given to the idea that motivation is multiple; that it is rare indeed if any one act serves only one need. This has led to more intensive studies to discern motivational patterns. Psychological needs and cultural and interpersonal influences are receiving systematic study as determinants of buying behavior as well as the economic, material, and situational factors. The existence of unconscious mental processes has been recognized and marketing research now is going beyond what people say they think and feel in order to explain their behavior.

All of this represents a marked departure from past attempts to deal with buying and consumption as separate entities primarily of an economic and utilitarian nature, or to distinguish between rational and emotional influences on buying.

Research Approaches. In an effort to identify important variables and arrive at fruitful hypotheses, research approaches are being used which provide for a much freer flow of information and feelings from the consumer. The people themselves are being increasingly regarded as an important source of ideas. In order to learn more about behavioral factors of which the respondent may not be fully aware, indirect techniques have been developed which make use of the principles of free association and projection. In the past, research efforts have relied heavily upon formal questionnaires which allowed little freedom of response and which often were prepared without the aid of either exploratory studies or a well-developed understanding of the nature of human behavior.

RESISTANCE VIEWED IN PERSPECTIVE

In addition to noting trends, it may be helpful in our attempt to gauge the importance of the motivation research development to view reactions to it in greater perspective. As has been pointed out earlier, the introduction of new concepts and methods in marketing research has met with considerable resistance, yet their use has continued to grow. It is of interest to note that this observation can be made in other fields of study as well, including most of the social sciences, which encountered many of the same ways of thinking at earlier dates.[1]

Let us illustrate our point by centering our attention on psychoanalysis. While various disciplines have contributed ideas which marketing has found to be radical and has been slow to accept, psychoanalysis is of major importance. Its influence has been both direct through psychoanalytically trained people and indirect through the various behavioral fields which themselves have been heavily influenced by psychoanalysis.

Originating with Freud, psychoanalysis refers to a theory and a body of knowledge of personality structure and development and to a method of research. Hence, it has influenced the study of behavior, including motivation research, in a number of ways. A fundamental hypothesis of psychoanalytic theory, for example, is that in the human mind nothing happens by chance; that each psychic event is determined by those which have preceded it and none can be dismissed as meaningless or accidental. Another basic premise is that unconscious mental processes are of very great frequency and significance in normal mental functioning.[2] Clinicians report abundant confirmation of both of these hypotheses. The principle of free association and the mechanisms of projection and rationalization which are of particular relevance to methods of investigation were discovered by Freud. Various psychoanalysts in more recent years have developed the concepts of multiple motivation and basic needs of man, and some have emphasized the cultural and social influences on behavior. The clinician, of course, has

[1] Calvin S. Hall and Gardner Lindzey, "Psychoanalytic Theory and Its Application in the Social Sciences," in Gardner Lindzey (editor), *Handbook of Social Psychology* (Cambridge, Mass.: Addison-Wesley Publishing Company, Inc., 1954), Vol. I, pp. 143–145, 170–175.

[2] Charles Brenner, *An Elementary Textbook of Psychoanalysis* (Garden City, New York: Doubleday Anchor Books, Doubleday and Company, Inc., 1957), pp. 1–15.

stressed intensive study of individual cases and the interpretation of observations in the context of the whole.

The brief sketch just presented should be sufficient to indicate the breadth and nature of the psychoanalytic influence. The ideas mentioned are of basic importance in much motivation research. Now, let us examine further the kind of reception which characteristically has greeted such ways of thinking, starting with psychology itself. While Freud today is recognized as having been an outstanding figure in this field, the psychologists of his era regarded his work as outside the bounds of their discipline. They were interested in different things and used different methods. To them, thought was conscious and they studied behavior of normal human beings under controlled laboratory conditions where motivational factors could be minimized. Freud introduced the startling idea that thought and consciousness were not synonymous, that much mental activity was unconscious. As a doctor, he became interested in this subject by studying emotionally disturbed patients (although psychoanalysis is a theory of behavior, normal as well as abnormal). His methods were not those of the laboratory psychologist. Instead of trying to control or limit motivational determinants, he sought to establish conditions in which they could operate at their maximum.

It was not until very recent times that the antipathy of conventional psychologists began to wane. Universities, for example, generally refused to recognize psychoanalysis until the 1930's. Resistance declined as psychologists and psychoanalysts developed mutual interests and got acquainted with one another. This was hastened by World War II when a number of them were thrown together in working relationships. It was about this time that the discipline of clinical psychology, which bears a heavy psychoanalytic imprint and which has been prominent in motivation research, came into being. It has had a substantial growth, has now been accepted in most universities, and has facilitated an interchange of thought between psychologists and psychiatrists. While opposition still is present, psychoanalysis today is a subject of major interest to psychologists.

Turning to another of the social sciences, we note that psychoanalysis has had a marked impact upon cultural anthropology and that this has come about despite the fact that "the early attitude of anthropologists toward psychoanalysis was one of firm hostility." [3] The development was characterized by vigorous early efforts to disprove psychoanalytic ideas, a growing interest in psychoanalysis as a means of explaining puzzling data, a shift in field work tactics to produce data more pertinent to psychoanalytic propositions, examples of fruitful collaboration of anthropologists and psychoanalysts, efforts by anthropologists to train themselves in psychoanalytic methods and interpretations, and the conduct of anthropological field work by some psychoanalysts.[4] As to the present relationship between the two fields, Clyde Kluckhohn has written that ". . . American anthropology, for good or for ill, has seemed to find only in psychoanalysis the bases for a workable social psychology." [5]

In sociology there was a long period of rejection of psychoanalysis before the latter started to have an impact which can be seen in the more recent writings. Talcott Parsons drew heavily upon psychoanalytic concepts in an attempt to develop an interdisciplinary theory of behavior.[6] The writings of David Riesman also are an important example of Freud's influence upon sociological thought.[7] A pattern of resistance

[3] Calvin S. Hall and Gardner Lindzey, op. cit., p. 170.

[4] Ibid., p. 171.

[5] Clyde Kluckhohn, "The Influence of Psychiatry on Anthropology in America during the Past One Hundred Years," in J. K. Hall, G. Zilboorg, and H. A. Bunder (editors), *One Hundred Years of American Psychiatry* (New York: Columbia University Press, 1944), pp. 588–617.

[6] Talcott Parsons and E. A. Shils (editors), *Toward a General Theory of Action* (Cambridge: Harvard University Press, 1951).

[7] David Riesman, *The Lonely Crowd: A Study of Changing American Character* (New Haven: Yale University Press, 1950).

followed by later interest in psychoanalysis also can be noted in the field of social psychology.

In summary, we briefly have examined reactions in other fields to new thinking, particularly that of psychoanalysis, in order to better understand what has been happening more recently in marketing research. To a large extent, marketing, with the motivation research development, has felt the impact of psychoanalytic theory for the first time. It has reacted just as most of the social sciences had done earlier — with hostility — and for some of the same reasons. To the social sciences, psychoanalytic theory and practice represented radically different ideas and methods which stemmed from the thinking of outsiders — doctors. In the case of marketing, motivation research, heavily influenced by psychoanalytic thought, represented strange concepts and methods brought into the marketing scene by outsiders — behavioral scientists. The social sciences have found much of value in the new ways of thinking and initial hostility has been followed by integration. Marketing seems to be following the same pattern.

Some Thoughts About the Future

Marketing will continue to make greater use of the behavioral sciences because an improved understanding of buying and consumption depends upon finding out more about all the functions they serve — the psychological, social, material, and economic. In order to do this, the activities must be viewed in their relationship to total behavior using the promising theories and knowledge which the behavioral disciplines have developed. While the potential to be realized cannot be fully appreciated now, initial efforts in this direction have been encouraging. We now shall describe some of the developments which we expect to accompany the future expansion of this kind of work.

Integration in Research

Integration will become an increasingly important theme in marketing research with important moves to bring together personnel of varied backgrounds and skills, concepts of behavior, and methods and functions of research. Spurring the movement will be the further coming into its own of the hypothesis-formulating part of the scientific approach.

The few groups which thus far have specialized in social science research can be expected to move further in the direction of including a greater variety of specialties and experience in their organizations. We have in mind not only the social sciences but marketing and statistics as well. If the firms which have specialized in quantitative surveys are to retain their positions of prominence, they must give hypothesis formulation considerably more attention. This will mean important additions of social science trained personnel. No longer will it be possible for an organization whose purpose it is to help marketers learn how and why people buy to successfully ignore today's thinking and knowledge of the nature of human behavior. To do so makes no more sense than does the omission of the services of a competent statistician from the planning and conduct of important projects of measurement and statistical analysis. With a greater integration of the clinical and statistical ways of thinking, research units will be better prepared to move effectively through all the stages of research from the getting of ideas to the testing of alternative courses of action.

Research Departments

As more emphasis is placed on knowledge of human behavior, an understanding of the social sciences will become an important requirement for marketing researchers. Indicative of the future is the position taken by the director of research of a large advertising agency which has a dozen men who function as research heads for various accounts. He now is insisting that they develop a sufficient understanding of social science ways of thinking and research methods to enable them to make appropriate use of the behavioral specialists in the department and to communicate about this work effectively with account executives, creative personnel, and client representatives. In hiring young men for the future, he prefers undergraduate specialization in the social sciences plus graduate work in business administration.

Large advertising agencies are well situated to have their own specialists and conduct much of their own social science research. Manufacturing companies will employ more behavioral specialists, too, although they also will make greater use of outside research firms in order to benefit from the varied experiences and backgrounds of a group of well-qualified people. In order to do this to best advantage, however, the companies must have someone who knows when and how to make appropriate use of the outside resources and to provide effective liaison.

We expect that the future will see more and more firms rethinking the role research should play in marketing decision-making and insisting on the qualifications for a director of marketing research outlined in the preceding chapter. The days are numbered when a research unit of any size can be headed by a relatively narrow technical specialist lacking in administrative skill and background in the behavioral fields and in major marketing problems.

Education for Marketing

Early in the book, we stated that marketing's basic reason for being is the satisfaction of those human wants which can be satisfied through goods and services. To this end, it is concerned with designing products which will be as satisfying as possible to people, making them conveniently available to people, communicating about them effectively to people, and maintaining satisfactory relationships with customers. In line with its over-all purpose, greater emphasis now is being placed on understanding consumers as people — what they want in products, services, and relationships with business firms and sales representatives and why they want it.

In the light of these observations, let us ask what kind of education is desirable for marketing. This question is important not only to academic institutions, but also to business which looks to the schools for manpower and which is becoming increasingly interested in developmental programs for its own personnel. Among other things, courses dealing with the nature of man and how he lives would seem to be very much to the point. Unfortunately, however, the conventional business school curriculum today provides virtually no training of this kind. It consists largely of functional courses in such areas as accounting, finance, production, and marketing. An exception exists in the form of some human relations courses which deal with concepts and ways of observing and listening to people in order to better understand their motivation and behavior.

In regard to marketing, if the course is taught from one of the conventional textbooks, it gives little consideration to the nature of human wants beyond a recognition that, whatever they may be, they are of prime importance. A better situation exists if the course is devoted to discussions of actual marketing problems presented to the student in case form. In the handling of a case, the student at least must think specifically about a given situation and usually he cannot go very far without attempting to identify relevant consumer buying motives and habits. This is a beneficial exercise which can cause the student to become aware of his own assumptions about what people are like and how they will behave and to re-examine them.

A limitation of this procedure is that thinking is not likely to go beyond the conceptual and experiential boundaries represented by the discussion participants, the instructor, and the case material itself. There is a real question as to how far students should be encouraged to go in speculating about consumer motives and habits, particularly in unfamiliar product areas. The result can be a great deal of loose thinking and over-generalizing about such abstractions as "the consumer" and "the dealer." The most sensible thing to do in an actual business situation might well be to identify carefully the knowns and the unknowns and, in regard to the latter, seek opinions of outside specialists or have research undertaken.

In existing academic circumstances, probably the most desirable educational background for marketing is this: (a) an undergraduate liberal arts program with specialization in the behavioral fields; and (b) graduate training in business administration under the case method of instruction (at least, for the marketing courses). For such a program to be fully effective, however, the marketing instructors should be familiar with the behavioral fields as well as marketing and the case discussion process. This, of course, is a rare combination by today's standards. One of the objects of marketing case discussions might well be that of giving the student practice in determining whether marketing research should be used in the process of making the necessary decisions. If research is proposed, it would be necessary to specify at what point it should be used, what its specific purpose should be, what kind of research is appropriate, who should conduct it, and what is to be done with the findings once they are available.

While the program described above may be desirable, it does not help the student who takes no graduate work; nor does it benefit one who has had little undergraduate background in the social sciences but who, nevertheless, enters a graduate school of business to develop a special interest in marketing. In both cases, the answer might well be a combination social science-business program, the mix to be determined by the variety and quality of the offerings available. Graduate schools of business might also do well to consider changes in curriculum and pedagogy. Our work has suggested two ideas along this line.

Addition of a Course in Behavioral Science Concepts and Methods: Introductory in character, this course would be designed to provide a badly needed communicative bridge between the behavioral sciences and business. Its function, of course, would not be to prepare specialists, but to serve the interests of students who are to become business administrators. There might be at least three principal objectives:

To describe briefly the scope of interest of each of such specialties as psychoanalysis, clinical psychology, laboratory psychology, cultural and social anthropology, sociology, and semantics.

To familiarize the student with the principal concepts and methods of study of each field.

To promote an understanding of the collective activity of behavioral science as a continuing process of developing conceptual schemes and methods.

The course, then, would serve to answer such questions as these: What is a social anthropologist? What does he do? How does he do it? What are his principal ways of thinking? How have these developed and changed over the years? What relationship has there been between anthropology and the other social sciences?

The reasoning behind the first two objectives should be apparent. In this day and age, when the behavioral fields are growing so in importance, it is highly undesirable that words such as anthropology and psychoanalysis should conjure up many ill-founded images and fears. That the terms often do have this effect not only represents a lack of desirable understanding, but an emotional block against acquiring it by venturing into such "strange" areas. As to the second objective, there is the important possibility of useful applications in business of the concepts and methods of other disciplines. These may or may not be direct. Any course which stresses ways of thinking about people, however, is bound to be broadening with important benefits in intellectual development. This type of background also should enable a businessman to work more comfortably and effectively with behavioral specialists.

The third point represents an intent to give the student a "feel" for the behavioral disciplines which will help him recognize important developments when they are under way, identify opportunities for timely and worthwhile applications in business, and appraise the attendant risks and the potential benefits. An important part of this perspective is an understanding of science as a continuing process, a recognition that certainty frequently turns out to be illusion, and an appreciation that conceptual innovations usually are given unfriendly receptions.

Training in Conceptual Thinking for Marketing. There is an important need for improved training for fostering the continuing evolution of better concepts upon which progress depends. This might be provided through courses which would encourage participation in the activities which contribute to the process of conceptual development as described early in Chapter III. The over-all purpose would be to help the student to become aware of his own concepts; to reexamine them, employing suitable tests; to become aware of other relevant concepts, particularly in the behavioral fields; and to use this background for creative thought to bring into being improved ways of looking at the people and the things with which marketing deals.

One way of implementing such a program would be to

work from such basic questions as these: What is a product? What is a brand? What is a consumer? What is selling? They represent things for which marketing needs improved understanding in terms of their meanings to people. The answers, of course, must be developed by detailed consideration of specific examples. To illustrate our point, an early class session might be devoted to discussing the question: "What is coffee?" The students would be encouraged not only to verbalize their images of coffee, but to think about how they came into being. Later, they would be asked what they would like to do in order to develop a meaningful concept of the product if they were starting from scratch, all preconceptions being brushed aside. Once their suggestions had been obtained, they would be assigned the task of carrying them out.

Imaginations and creative talent should be given a real opportunity. Activities in which the students might engage include intensive observation of people purchasing or using the product; qualitative interviewing; small-scale tests or experiments; reviewing research conducted by others; reading any literature containing information on uses of the product and furnishing a basis for inferring its symbolic meanings, past or present, in this culture or in another.

As for teaching materials, to a large extent the students would generate their own. In addition, they might be exposed to depth interviews conducted by experts; selected readings in the behavioral fields; and, perhaps, specially prepared cases on creative problems relating to product innovation and development. After the students had identified important questions of special interest and advanced in their own thinking about them, specialists from the social sciences or from business might be invited to meet with the class for discussions.

In handling the question on selling, students could be assigned to accompany salesmen as silent observers who would make complete notes of what took place, including nearly verbatim transcripts of salesman-customer conversations. Tape recordings and even motion-pictures of salesmen at work might be used. These would be analyzed later for insight into the nature of selling.

Learning must take place from the images which already exist in the student's mind. A most important feature of the training is that of encouraging students to get their own ideas about what they should do, having them do these things, and allowing one experience to suggest the next step and so on. Firsthand observation of people as buyers and consumers would play an important part. It can be a beneficial way of stimulating thinking if the student is aware of what he is doing. He must become a competent observer, become sensitized to people and things about him.

The main goal is the development of individual capacities, not the collection of data or the learning of any pre-determined "facts." The common academic practice of having students memorize "the answers" obtained from instructors or textbooks is the enemy of creative thought and directly opposite to what we have in mind. We should be most disappointed if, as the result of training in conceptual thinking, the students had done nothing more than become acquainted with other people's concepts or had reached conceptual agreement among themselves. If an idea wins unanimity, it probably is not very new, and the purpose should be to stimulate a continuing process of conceptual development and the flow of new ideas in marketing.

Research Activities

In this section, we shall comment on research which can be expected to receive more attention in the future in both business and academic ranks.

There will be a marked increase in work to identify personality, cultural, and social factors which may be used to differentiate among consumers as to their behavior, and to learn of the types of activities and products for which they seem to be important. Among other things, meeting these objectives will require much more developmental and experimental work with personality tests. Once identified, the factors can be taken into account in planning research approaches and in selecting samples of respondents.

We look forward to the day when information on personality and social characteristics of consumer panel members is available in addition to that now supplied on geographical location, income, age, and the like. The combination of all these data plus the purchase records of the panel families would open the door to a whole new series of investigations. An initial step in this direction already has been taken by the *Chicago Tribune* which has been working to stratify its consumer panel by social class and learn more about the influence of the social class variable. Results so far have shown it to be highly important for some product categories and much less so for others.

Several research areas which appear to offer great potential rewards are described below.

Interdisciplinary Exploration of Buying and Consumption. Much might be gained from an interdisciplinary, comprehensive study of a small number of families undertaken to get more intimately acquainted with the nature of consumer behavior by viewing it in the context of total behavior. Conducted over a rather substantial period of time, its goal would be to produce fruitful hypotheses needed for the development of improved understanding and theory. For this task, use should be made of some of the newer ways of thinking, methods, and information from several fields — notably psychoanalytic psychiatry, clinical psychology, social and cultural anthropology, sociology, and marketing.

A record would be maintained of purchases made by the

families and an effort would be made to develop a full picture of the consumer-product relationship for a number of items singled out for special attention. These might range in apparent character from a staple like sugar to the automobile which presumably has very important personal meanings. An effort would be made to learn how and when people got started using brands for which they have a marked preference. Extensive personal information would be accumulated on the participating families with special attention being given to their cultural setting, social participation, and personality characteristics. Information would be obtained on their images of various brands, and their purchases would be checked to see whether they tended toward certain kinds of images. Efforts would be made to trace interpersonal and other influences on purchases made during the period of the study. In brief, the project would be a concentrated attempt to learn more about what various products and brands mean to people in the light of information on the kind of human beings they are and the kind of lives they lead.

The research approach would include any techniques deemed appropriate by the specialists in charge. In all probability, use would be made of observations by trained personnel, qualitative interviewing, projective and other tests to obtain personality and brand information, and sociometry to trace interpersonal influences.

A project of the general character we have in mind was undertaken in another connection in 1946 and 1947 at the Harvard Psychological Clinic by a group of social psychologists, clinical psychologists, and an anthropologist.[8] This was an exploratory study to learn more about the nature of opinion. The group felt that while a great advance had been made in the theory and practice of measurement of attitudes

[8] M. Brewster Smith, Jerome S. Bruner, and Robert W. White, *Opinions and Personality* (New York: John Wiley and Sons, Inc., 1956).

and opinions, very little had been done to develop a theory of attitudes themselves. Therefore, they set out to gain a clearer conception of what attitudes are and what aspects are worth measuring. Opinions were viewed as an inseparable part of the personality. Their relationships to other aspects of a person's life were investigated to learn what functions were served by the holding of an opinion. A limited area of opinion was selected for intensive study in 15 two-hour sessions with each of 10 mature men. Twenty-eight different research procedures, including a number of qualitative interviews and tests, were used in the process.

We have cited this example for several reasons. It is an interdisciplinary, clinical attempt to develop needed hypotheses and theory. The approach of exploring opinions as a part of personality was rewarding. The subject and findings also are of interest to marketing because of the role opinions presumably play in consumer buying. The function of an opinion was found to be a resultant or compromise among reality demands, social demands, and inner psychological demands. "The three are inseparable." [9] The individuals studied differed, however, in the extent to which the three sorts of determinants predominated in the bases for their opinions. Consideration of all these factors was found to be necessary for a full explanation of changes in attitudes. The investigators concluded that "it is only when we recognize the embeddedness of opinions in the functioning of personality that we begin to understand the significance of an opinion and the conditions for its change." [10]

We believe that it is from intensive studies which treat personality, social, and reality factors together as comprising a whole that insights are most likely to be gained which will lead to fruitful hypotheses about many of marketing's problems. Here are several examples of questions for which answers are needed:

[9] Ibid., p. 275.
[10] Ibid., p. 279.

This situation exists in certain product areas, coffee being one. Brand A and Brand B are both well-known, regularly sell at the same price, and people are unable to distinguish between them in taste tests. Brand A is dominant in Market X where repeated, aggressive promotional efforts by Brand B, a national leader but a minor factor in Market X, have failed to make much headway. The reverse situation exists in Market Y where Brand B is the leader and Brand A has a minor position. How did the brands achieve their positions and why have the market leaders been relatively immune to assault?

What factors are profitable for exploration as a creative aid to a designer who faces the question of determining what a product should be?

What does fashion mean to people? Psychologically, what is the nature of the process involved in changing fashions? Is it not possible to do a better job of predicting these changes?

Why have people enthusiastically accepted two-tone cars, more colors in various products including major household appliances, the do-it-yourself movement, station wagons?

What is the nature of resistance to product innovations and what is the process involved in their gaining acceptance?

Do people consciously make buying decisions? If so, how? Why are a good many people careless purchasers in the usual sense of the word?

How does advertising work, when it does? That is, what is the nature of the process in the consumer's mind?

Why do many lower income families buy the higher priced brands when good quality is available at lower prices? Why have low prices been self-defeating in certain instances?

Product Innovation and Development. This is a major marketing research frontier on which there has been relatively little work. In the future, we can expect to see much more attention devoted to investigating the nature of the creative process of product innovation and development, and exploring how it might be aided by the application of behavioral science concepts and methods. The goal, of course, is that of getting better answers to the very important question: "What should a product be?"

Inasmuch as there has been an increasing amount of testing of alternative product ideas, we should emphasize that we are concerned here with the additional use of research to help bring product ideas into being in the first place. The neglect of this area may appear surprising in view of the expanding creative use of research in advertising. In part, it reflects the disposition of many marketing researchers to confine their research activities to testing.

Experience with behavioral science approaches, however, points to the prospect of important advances in the efficiency and effectiveness of use of valuable creative talent through contributing to the creative man's understanding of people, their wants, and what products mean to them. Information such as might be obtained from a project like that described in the preceding section would, of course, be relevant. An example of research undertaken for a specified product is a motivational study of the satisfactions sought by the mother who buys baby food and the criteria she uses for differentiating among brands (it showed that she takes nutrition for granted). The results prompted several product changes which were followed by a substantial increase in sales. The intriguing possibility of using research as a creative aid in product design and styling was commented on earlier in connection with the automobile case.

Salesmanship. The field of salesmanship still remains to be studied and taught on a sound human relations foundation. If successful selling is in large part dependent upon the salesman's establishing and maintaining a personal relationship which the customer finds satisfying, we need to know much more about what this activity entails. Much could be learned by detailed analysis of verbatim notes on actual sales calls, supplemented by information on characteristics of the people involved and the conditions under which they work. Such data are needed on different kinds of salesmen in terms of personalities and selling tasks. We should expect to find that many so-called principles of selling actually are ill-conceived, that there is no such thing as a formula of conduct suitable for universal application, but that different action is appropriate to different personalities and different situations. The research should serve to identify the variables and illuminate the nature of the selling process. By studying data of this kind, a salesman should become better able to identify the important factors in a given instance and decide what to do about them.

Sales Management. There is a great need for intensive studies of various aspects of administering selling organizations. While considerable use has been made of the behavioral sciences in selecting personnel, this is much less true for the other management functions. Typically, information is available on details of plans for such activities as training salesmen and controlling and evaluating their efforts, but much remains to be learned about how well they work. For example, excellent data have been collected on the mechanics and management logics of various compensation schemes, but very few intensive studies have been made of the effects they actually have on salesmen. Some of the new horizons of thought about management of sales personnel which await further development were made apparent in George F. F. Lombard's six-month study of 20 salesgirls who sold children's clothes in a large department store. Using an integrated social science approach, he tested existing concepts and explored more useful ways of thinking about the motivation and behavior of sales personnel, compensation plans, what constitutes skill in selling, and the problems of evaluating performance and improving sales service.[11]   In the concluding chapter of his book, he presented a thoughtful and comprehensive view of a program of training for more skillful behavior which has important philosophical as well as practical implications for business administration.

Use of Marketing Research.   In Chapter XIV we pointed out that administrative problems relating to the use of marketing research constitute a very important problem area. There is a need, therefore, for further clinical explorations to learn more about what factors can make for effective use of research as an integral part of the decision-making process. The behavioral scientists should be able to make an important contribution because to a large extent this is a matter of interpersonal relationships.

In Conclusion

An era of greatly expanded cooperative efforts by behavioral scientists and marketers lies ahead.   With it will come the development of improved concepts for marketing; more effective research approaches; an expansion in the use of research, especially in a creative role; changes in the make-up of research groups; and changes in the character of the schooling considered appropriate for the prospective marketer.

There are many problems to be met in the course of seeking more useful information about people and in learning to apply it to advantage once it has been obtained.   So we should not expect too much too soon.   On the other hand, some of the early efforts appear most promising and explorations of new territory can be rewarding indeed, especially when they are guided by conceptual advances regarding what is being explored.

[11] George F. F. Lombard, *Behavior in a Selling Group* (Boston: Harvard University, Division of Research, Graduate School of Business Administration, 1955).

The great promise of these developments, of course, is improved knowledge of human wants which will make possible better products and better marketing plans. Deficiencies in such knowledge mean waste — waste of economic resources and waste in unrealized potential consumer satisfaction. This waste can be seen in ineffectual sales efforts and in the putting on the market of goods which fail to sell because of unsuspected inferior want-satisfying qualities. Greater understanding, however, should make possible products, services, and sales programs which will enable the consumer to get more of what he wants for less money.